The Rise of Right-Populism

Bligh Grant · Tod Moore
Tony Lynch
Editors

The Rise of Right-Populism

Pauline Hanson's One Nation and Australian Politics

 Springer

Editors
Bligh Grant
Institute for Public Policy
  and Governance
University of Technology Sydney
Ultimo, NSW, Australia

Tony Lynch
School of Humanities,
  Arts and Social Sciences
University of New England
Armidale, NSW, Australia

Tod Moore
Newcastle Business School
University of Newcastle Australia
Newcastle, NSW, Australia

ISBN 978-981-13-2669-1   ISBN 978-981-13-2670-7   (eBook)
https://doi.org/10.1007/978-981-13-2670-7

Library of Congress Control Number: 2018955923

This Springer imprint is published by the registered company Springer Nature Singapore Pte Ltd.
The registered company address is: 152 Beach Road, #21-01/04 Gateway East, Singapore 189721,
Singapore

Contents

Contributors

Simon Burgess University of New England Business School, University of New England, Armidale, NSW, Australia

Jo Coghlan School of Humanities, Arts and Social Sciences, University of New England, Armidale, NSW, Australia

Raphaella Kathryn Crosby College of Arts, Society and Education (CASE), James Cook University, Douglas, QLD, Australia

Belinda J. Flannery School of Psychology and Behavioural Sciences, University of New England, Armidale, NSW, Australia

Bligh Grant Institute for Public Policy and Governance, University of Technology Sydney, Broadway, Sydney, NSW, Australia

Jim Jose Newcastle Business School, University of Newcastle, Newcastle, NSW, Australia

Gang-Jun Liu Geo-Spatial Sciences, School of Science, Royal Melbourne Institute of Technology (RMIT), Melbourne, VIC, Australia

Tony Lynch School of Humanities, Arts and Social Sciences, University of New England, Armidale, NSW, Australia

Graham Maddox School of Humanities, Arts and Social Sciences, University of New England, Armidale, NSW, Australia

Tod Moore Newcastle Business School, University of Newcastle, Newcastle, NSW, Australia

Ben Reid Geo-Spatial Sciences, School of Science, Royal Melbourne Institute of Technology (RMIT), Melbourne, VIC, Australia

Alan Scott School of Humanities, Arts and Social Sciences, University of New England, Armidale, NSW, Australia

Susan E. Watt School of Psychology and Behavioural Sciences, University of New England, Armidale, NSW, Australia

List of Figures

List of Tables

Chapter 1
Introduction

Bligh Grant

Abstract If viewed merely in term of Australia's electoral politics, Pauline Hanson and her Party are of minimal interest compared with the main political parties and are prone to dysfunction at the parliamentary level. However, if we choose to look at their impact upon Australian politics more generally and society *writ large*, they have unquestionably played a salient role since 1996. Noting that Hanson has now enjoyed two iterations of electoral success in Australia's federation, the first in the 1990s and the second from 2016, the literature generated from the first iteration is reviewed. The issue of racism, particularly toward Australia's Indigenous population, and more pointedly the hostility directed toward a state that was perceived as favoring Indigenous Australians are discussed, alongside the policy themes of immigration, engagement with Asia, economic policy, and the broader impact that Hanson was having on Australia's polity. The emergent literature on populism, in particular in Australia, is also examined. The discussions contained in this book are then described, organized into the four themes of IDEATION, ELECTION, POLICY AND POLITICS, and COMPARISON. Circling back to the concept of populism and the nature of Australian politics, we argue that populism generally, and right-populism in particular, will continue to have an impact upon Australian politics, understood as an electoral phenomenon and more generally.

Keywords Australian politics · Indigenous reconciliation · Pauline Hanson
Populism · Racism · Social class

B. Grant (✉)
Institute for Public Policy and Governance, University of Technology Sydney, 123, Broadway, Sydney, NSW, Australia
e-mail: Bligh.Grant@uts.edu.au

© Springer Nature Singapore Pte Ltd. 2019
B. Grant et al. (eds.), *The Rise of Right-Populism*,
https://doi.org/10.1007/978-981-13-2670-7_1

1

1.1 Introduction

On 14 June 2018, following the resignation of Senator Brian Burston from Pauline Hanson's One Nation Party (PHONP), Antony Green, election analyst for the Australian Broadcasting Corporation (ABC), decided that that it would be timely to provide a summary of the fate of all One Nation Party elected representatives in Australia's federation to that date. Noting that the Party "burst on the Australian political scene with a spectacular debut at the 1998 Queensland [State] election", wherein it polled 22.7% and gained 11 of 89 seats in Queensland's unicameral parliament (see Newman 1998), Green (2018) asserted that this "was the strongest debut by a political party in the century since the Country Party emerged after the First World War". Green (2018) also noted that on that day in June 2018 PHONP had six elected representatives in parliaments across the country—two in the Senate (Pauline Hanson herself and Peter Georgiou); three in Western Australia's Legislative Council (Robin Scott, Charles Smith, and Colin Ticknell) and one in Queensland's Legislative Assembly (Stephen Andrew).

However, the ever-vigilant Green (2018) also observed that the Party has failed to capitalize on its electoral breakthrough in 1998, suggesting that this failure has been "overwhelmingly due to internal disputes that have resulted in the departure of most of the party's elected members". Of the other parliamentarians elected as members of PHONP (which, notably, does not include Pauline Hanson's election the House of Representatives in 1996), 19 had "resigned from the party in their first term", "two had been disqualified from sitting in the Senate", and a third senator resigned from PHONP before then being disqualified from that office. Moreover, only two parliamentarians had lasted a full term before being ousted at the next election and "only one … had ever been re-elected for the party" (Green 2018). In essence, Antony Green was suggesting that in terms of Australia's electoral politics, PHONP is of minor importance. Indeed, we suspect (although we could, of course, be wrong) that he was not only providing a concise overview of the Party's electoral fortunes *and* dysfunctionality, he was also urging us to keep Pauline Hanson and her Party in perspective.

In fact, if we were to tell the story of Pauline Hanson and her Party merely in terms of electoral politics, strictly conceived, this might be a very concise book indeed. However, such an account would ignore the impact that PHONP has had upon Australian politics *writ large*. From this perspective, politics is conceived as more than the institutional arrangements for democratic election and decision-making. On the contrary: it also includes political *ideation*, which we can define as not merely the goals and aspirations of the polity and those it comprises, but especially the normative (i.e., ethical and moral) parameters that frame and comprise its conjecture and refutation—its *discourse*—and the policies that (however haphazardly) result from this. It would also ignore the impact that PHONP *and* Pauline Hanson herself have both had on Australian society *writ large*, which can be defined as those parts of our lives that can be set against the specifically political areas of our activity (and yes, the defining lines are slippery indeed). Moreover, as Anthony Green would no doubt remind us, telling the story of PHONP merely in terms of its electoral fortunes would place to one side the way that the politics of that Party and its people echo—or indeed otherwise—those in other polities, similar and dissimilar, across the globe. In this book, we have elected to label this general phenomenon "right-populism".

In this introduction to the examination of these issues, in Sect. 1.2 we briefly revisit the outpouring of interest in Pauline Hanson that resulted from her initial electoral success in 1996. Section 1.3 provides an overview of the individual chapters of this book, organized around four themes: IDEATION, ELECTION, POLITICS AND POLICY, and COMPARISON. In Sect. 1.4 we make some overarching observations.

1.2   All That You Can't Leave Behind

It is an understatement to say that the initial reaction to Pauline Hanson—that is., prior to the formation of PHONP—was centered on the issue of racism toward Indigenous Australians, and focused not exclusively upon her, but importantly upon the (then) Prime Minister, John Howard. This reaction concentrated upon two events. The first was Hanson's maiden speech in the House of Representatives and the initial reluctance of John Howard to condemn her, or even comment upon it.[1] The second was of far greater importance, namely the Howard Government's developing stance on the High Court's *(Wik)* decision as preceded by the Court's previous decision in *Mabo v Commonwealth (No 2)* (for an exposition at that time, see Bohill 1997). In fact, the first book to be published about Hanson was *The resurgence of racism: Howard, Hanson and the race debate* (Gray and Winter 1997). The book comprised the proceedings of a conference entitled 'Is racism un-Australian?' held in February of that year and it is overwhelmingly concerned with racism.

In it, Reynolds (1997) exhumed the racism plainly on display in Queensland public life in the 1880s to remind readers that racism, "developmentalism", and "egalitarian-ism" have been constant themes in Australian politics. He also stated (p. 38) that "the High Court has dropped Australia at a corner, an important corner, the corner is called the Wik case". Ricklefs (1997) investigated the anti-Asian controversies of 1994–95, 1988–89 and 1996–97, noting the importance of anti-Asian sentiment and policy for both sides of Australian politics historically and the controversy surrounding it in the Coalition at that time. Mickler (1997) discussed anti-Indigenous sentiment as an element of Perth's talkback radio; Markus (1997) discussed populism and Howard's anti-politically correct stance (included in the villains here (p. 82) were "republicans

---

[1]Brett (1997, p. 8) noted that: "In an address to the Queensland Liberal Party just twelve days after Hanson's maiden speech, Howard did not mention her speech. Instead, he chose to welcome the freer, more open climate of debate—lifting 'the pall of censorship on certain issues'. 'People', he said, 'can now talk about certain things without fear of being branded as a bigot or a racist'". Brett (1997, p. 8) also noted that on 8 October 1996, in response to (then) Opposition Leader Kim Beazley in the House of Representatives, Howard made a statement in support of "Australia's non-discriminatory immigration policy, and to racial equality and tolerance". It was 8 May 1997 that Howard spoke strongly against the claims in Hanson's maiden speech (see Ricklefs 1997, p. 57).

of Irish Catholic descent in the image of Paul Keating"). Read (1997) investigated what "non-British" Australians thought about Indigenous land rights, concluding (p. 95) that "similar opinions derived from profoundly different starting points" and that the (then) Reconciliation Council should work harder to engage these people. From her discussions with the Aboriginal people of the Victoria River District, Deborah Bird Rose (1997) concluded (p. 97) that they believed that "Whitefellas were in a state of epistemological crisis", and reminded us of how explicitly racist—sociobiologically—Australian government policy had been in the past. In her contribution, Curthoys (1997, p. 118) argued that "Australian political culture" makes it difficult for non-Indigenous Australians to see themselves as beneficiaries of oppression and that any recovery of an anti-racist tradition in Australia ought not to engage in a type of "good versus evil" reductionism. In their contributions Hollinsworth (1997) and McKee (1997) problematized the *concept* of race; Jakubowicz (1997) reflected on the long-standing research project "Making Multicultural Australia". All of these essays were principally concerned with racism and primarily in relation to Anglo-Celtic Australia and Australia's Indigenous people.

However, in that volume the links between (a problematized) racism on the one hand and political economy, in particular social class, on the other hand were clearly being drawn. In her contribution, Brett (1997) addressed the question of why a resurgence in the politics of grievance and resentment had taken the form of a racist politics. For her, the answer was two-fold. First, the liberalism of Australia's settler capitalism will always have a profound problem when it comes to Indigenous claims to land—Brett (p. 21) observed that John Howard was far more appreciative of the contribution made to Australia by people from Asia that he was about Indigenous politics. Second, she argued that with the continuing internationalization of Australia's economy, the idea of the "nation-state" in Australia had by that time fundamentally shifted from one that was grounded in the concept of "nation", understood in an organic (if constructed) sense, to one where both the concept and the mechanics of "state" assume over-riding importance in the "nation-state" equation. This distinctly pro-centrist (and as such pro-Labor Party) and at precisely the same time anti-liberal shift were what rubbed so keenly against what might be termed John Howard's "Liberal Party liberalism", combined with the fact that this same ideology, as articulated by former Prime Minister Sir Robert Menzies (1939–41 and 1949–66), had profound roots in the valorization of the petit-bourgeoisie who were, at that time, anxious in the face of a restructuring Australian economy and fertile ground for a politics of resentment (see also Tony Lynch in Chap. 3 of this volume).

As such, racism, specifically sentiment against a state that could be portrayed as being pro-Indigenous (when in fact it was faced with making policy, particularly on a question of land ownership, as directed by its High Court), was pointed to as *the* reason for support for Hanson. However, class, and in particular social class as an embedded and path-dependent phenomenon in Australia's political economics, was coming to the fore, alongside a broader discussion of Australian culture.

The second edited collection *Pauline Hanson, One Nation and Australian Politics*, which appeared later that year (Grant 1997), reflected the impact that Hanson was having across a range of policy areas; one of the principal themes was policy co-option, to varying degrees, from Hanson to the Conservative Government. The issue of the Australian Government's relationship with Indigenous people was present in an examination of the implications, alongside an account, of the justice of the Mabo and Wik decisions (Bohill 1997). Present also was an account of the impact that Hanson's virulent anti-Asian rhetoric was having in that region (von Strokirch and Low-O'Sullivan 1997). These discussions were joined by others examining the immigration debate at that time (Atchinson 1997); an examination of political correctness (Lynch and Reavell 1997); gender in politics (Ellison and Deutchman 1997); and Hanson and the (then) next federal election (Hughes 1997). There were also chapters examining the issues of identity (Phillips 1997) and the importance of symbolism in politics, the latter of which engaged principally with the rhetoric of John Howard (Archer 1997).

Subsequent books—in particular Manne et al. (1998) and Leach et al. (2000)—followed a similar division of labor across the aforementioned policy areas, with (arguably) a heightened emphasis upon Hanson's effect on the political system (party politics, leadership, and policy) and an analysis that viewed her and her Party as a consequence of the systemic problems of the Australian political system, particularly in terms of disenfranchisement (see, for example, Kelly 1998; McGuinness 1998). Nevertheless, and following from Brett (1997), within these discussions there always was a recognition that the phenomena of Hanson and her Party ought to be discussed in terms of the fundamental restructuring of Australia's economy and of social class (see, for example, Brett 1998; Dow 2000; Moore 1997). Other contributions (Kingston 1999; Pasquarelli 1998) were more journalistic in nature, while still others chose the issue of race as the central concern (see Markus 2001).

Yet there can be no doubt that populism—of both the left and right types—was in many ways a "novelty concept" only beginning to be fully explored in the Australian academic literature at that time (see, for example, Stokes 2000; Wells 1997; for important exceptions, see, for example, Brugger and Jaensch 1985; Goodman 1988; Mullins 1986). This writing was akin with Brett's (1997) analysis, in that clear lines were being drawn between populism as a political phenomenon on the one hand and its basis in social class on the other. However, populism was at that point certainly was not afforded a place alongside the canon of literature concerned with political ideologies—liberalism and socialism, for example. Nor, arguably, was it considered to be germane to an understanding of political campaigning or of Australia's political history (see, for example, Maddox 2004). Rather, for many it was a new-found form of high-handed derision. That this has now radically changed is borne out in the production of this volume, which is representative of a burgeoning literature internationally (see, for example, Gherghina et al. 2013; Judis 2016; Lukacs 2005; Mudde and Kaltwasser 2017). This contemporary literature draws, to a greater or lesser extent, on its antecedents (see, for example, Ionescu and Gellner 1969) and forms an underlying narrative to this present book. We return to this in Sect. 1.4.

1.3   Outline of Book

What Broinowski (2017) has labeled as "the rise, fall and rise again of Pauline Hanson" has afforded several of the contributors to Grant (1997) the opportunity of revisiting Australian politics through the lens of Pauline Hanson and her Party after some two decades. This is probably a unique scenario in Australian political writing; nevertheless, like most (but not all) examples of "getting the band back together", this project has taken on several new members, most—but by no means all—of whom now work at the University of New England in Armidale, located in northern NSW.

Part I of the book is themed IDEATION and comprises three chapters. In Chap. 2, Graham Maddox examines the rhetoric of One Nation, in particular the aim "to protect our sovereignty and democracy" and the claim that Australia is a "Christian country"—themes with which the author has some familiarity (see, for example, Maddox 1996, 2004). He commences with the observation that equality is a central tenant of democracy; however, in the hands of One Nation it receives an "exclusive twist": first, in turning a blind eye to our obligations under international law (particularly in relation to refugees); second by the quarantining of "Australian culture" from the recognition that Indigenous Australians have lived in here for over 60,000 years and ought to be recognized for this, alongside the observation that, as invaders and settlers, the agents of the British crown and its dominions very nearly visited genocide upon these peoples. In excavating democracy as it was initially practiced, Maddox does not take issue with the fact that in Athenian form it was initially confined to citizens. However, he is also at pains to point out that it was progressively inclusive and that in the current context what actually constitutes "Australian values" is in fact highly contested—and rightly so. Indeed, it is the closing off of empathy toward others epitomized in One Nation's privileging of "Australian values" which for Maddox is decidedly anti-democratic.

In discussing Hanson's repeated claim that Australia is a "Christian country" Maddox observes that both historically and contemporaneously many devout Christians have made distinguished contributions to Australia's democracy and society. However, he also argues that Hanson's application of the label "Christian country" to Australia is a type of "cultural Christianity" and one associated with nationalism; that it lacks the inclusivity definitive of both Christian and successful secular societies; and that, while Hanson (rhetorically at least) recognizes the separation of church and state, her labeling of Australia as "Christian" functions to exclude others—particularly Muslims—where in fact a secular state can govern for all religions. Maddox finds the anti-Muslim rhetoric of One Nation (e.g., the "infiltration of Islam and its totalitarian ideology") disturbing; so too the extension of this xenophobia to Muslims who have become Australian citizens.

Chapter 2 also addresses the issue of whether or not a defense of democracy—the development of a "militant democracy"—is warranted in situations where it is threatened by anti-democratic and ultra-nationalist political parties, in the mode advocated by Loewenstein (1937a) in his observations about the inability of the Weimar Republic to cruel the rise of Nazism in Germany in the 1930s. Maddox argues firmly against this, juxtaposing Loewenstein's (1937b) recommendation of "authoritarian democracy"—which would entail sanctioning rule by an elite coalition)—with an approach grounded in tolerance and recognizing that the repression of differing views undermines democratic ideals. Nevertheless, Maddox does argue that there is a role for parliaments (and, by implication, other institutions of state) formally censuring and punishing acts that openly transgress the underlying principle of toleration, pointing to Hanson's wearing the burqa in the Senate in 2017 as such an occasion that warranted more censure than it received. The author is also attuned to the relationship between political parties like One Nation on the one hand and those of the "so-called" Center-Right on the other, underscoring their similar stance on (for instance) Section 18c of the *Racial Discrimination Act*, and emphasizing the difference between free speech on the one hand and offense, injury, and insult on the other. He also notes the profound irony in One Nation's espousing "Australian values" on the one hand while simultaneously drawing inspiration and rhetoric from right-populist political parties in polities far distant and with differing democratic traditions.

It is in Chap. 3 that the revisiting of the general tenor of Grant (1997) and the associated literature is at its most direct. In his contribution, Tony Lynch argues that at that time, many saw PHONP as a brief aberration in Australian politics: a manifestation of US-style populism and one that would quickly flicker and die. For Lynch, the reasons why many thought this at that time are now clearer. First, it was assumed that Australia's robust, class-based parliamentary democracy would, in essence, "deal" with Hanson and that stasis would return. According to Lynch, this assumption was wrong: Australia's democracy was, even at that time, significantly undermined by the neo-liberal consensus. The second mistake was assuming that Hanson's perspectives on public policy wouldn't be co-opted by the Center-Right parties—or if they were, it wouldn't be for long until (again) stasis returned. Yet this faith was, and continues to be, proven to be radically misplaced across many policy areas, particularly in relation to those who have been progressively excluded from the neo-liberal consensus. And while we might be tempted to think of those that are radically disenfranchised—refugees, Indigenous people—it also applies to the economically disenfranchised—and not merely the unemployed, also the downwardly mobile, those that are falling, or fear falling, from the neo-liberal consensus. On this account, *class conflict*, which is unacceptable to the neo-liberal consensus, is replaced by *status anxiety*, which isn't merely a consequence of neo-liberalism but comprises an essential element of its logic and operations.

Lynch also argues that while right-populism, understood as status anxiety, is a consequence of the neo-liberal consensus and feeds back to reinforce its operations at an existential level, left-populism is necessarily marginalized in conditions of neo-liberalism. The explanation here is initially structural: the left elite, cut free from its traditional anchoring in unions and thus economic class, are also free to dispense with (or at least historicize) this class-based politics. Yet it is also status-driven: members of the left enjoy the freedom and parlaying in the elite world and (in particular) the possibility of *upward* mobility. Yet they also recognize that left-populism (for instance, Occupy Wall Street), grounded as it is in a thorough critique of the neo-liberal consensus, has to be denigrated in order for their aspirations to remain intact.

For Lynch, the politics of status also explains why "the easy claim of racism isn't quite right" when applied to PHONP. Rather, what is often seen as naked racism (an othering based upon difference—see, in particular, Marr 2017) is more accurately understood as "a moralized, status-centered downward blaming"; and notwithstanding the fact that naked racism can still be present (notice the role that government assistance, understood as racialized, can play in this status anxiety, rearticulating back into the neo-liberal consensus). Lynch then moves to distinguish between "billionaire populism" *a la* Donald Trump, which reinforces the consensus and the possibility of upward mobility, from the "bottom-up right-populism" of One Nation. It is in the latter that we find the especially Australian antecedents of Hanson's populism, understood as the class-denying (and status-reaffirming) politics of "home" in the rhetoric of Sir Robert Menzies. It is this ideology of "home"—which skates across varying occupational groups ("skilled artisans, professional men and women, farmers, and so on") and within which home is "freedom"—that explains the appeal, and synergy, of "bottom-up right populism" to elements of the contemporary Liberal Party, exemplified not only in policy co-option but also in the stream of former Liberal personnel so drawn to the ideology that they make a professional commitment to Pauline Hanson and her Party (John Pasquarelli, David Oldfield, and James Ashby, for instance).

Yet Lynch argues that this ideology of "home" does not sit comfortably with the neo-liberal agenda. On the contrary: however much the Center-Right might exhume Menzies (this was undoubtedly the case under John Howard and, arguably, Kevin Rudd, with his incessant mantra of "working families"), "in the end neo-liberalism is no respecter of the politics of home". With the ALP historically excluded on the basis that organized labor—unions—have always taken precedence over the family (so too for the elite left), Hanson can claim the purest form of this ideational rhetoric as hers—and attract a constituency accordingly. Like Maddox in Chap. 2, Lynch disagrees with the idea that "bottom-up right populism" is intrinsically fascistic. Yet he does not deny the possibility of it becoming so, particularly if left-populism were to gain significant electoral traction wherein it would be advantageous for neo-liberal elites to sponsor, and seek to escalate, Hanson's style of populism. For Lynch, the situation would be even more concerning if the neo-liberal elite consensus were to accelerate to a situation of oligarchy, where we would witness not merely the hollowing out of state capacity, but the possibility of conceiving of such authority, and where a charismatic "billionaire populist" would galvanize "bottom-up" populist sentiment.

Breaking with what, in political studies, is the more traditional analysis of rhetoric, policy and history offered in Chaps. 2 and 3, in Chap. 4 Belinda J. Flannery and Susan E. Watt empirically test for what they label as "Right-wing Protective Popular Nationalism" (RWPPN). Derived primarily from Gale's (2004, 2005) theoretical work on popular nationalism in contemporary Australia, the authors work up the concept of RWPPN (see also Broinowski 2017; Gray and Winter 1997; Leach et al. 2000; Markus 2001; Wear 2008; Wells 1997) and develop a ten-part scale—in essence, a series of propositions to test for sentiment for RWPPN—eliciting responses from 675 adult citizens, with the study also taking into account a range of (self-reported) demographic and socio-economic variables, including political orientation.

In testing for RWPPN the authors find three distinct clusters within the population which they label as "inclusive" (49%), "guarded" (30%), and "exclusive" (21%). The demographic and socio-economic variables that align with both the "exclusive" and "guarded" clusters broadly align with similar recent studies (see, in particular, Marr 2017). However, notably the authors' analysis is of a larger sample than simply electoral data. As such, it indicates that there may be broader support for the sentiments underlying the "guarded" and "protective" clusters than has been indicated in asking questions only of those that have voted for One Nation (see, in particular, Marr 2017).

Part II of the book, themed ELECTION, examines the outcome of the 2013 and 2016 federal elections, particularly in relation to One Nation and with the broad history of Australia's electoral politics informing the discussion. In Chap. 5, Ben Reid and Gang-Jung Liu examine the 2016 federal election from the perspective of electoral geography. The authors trace through the history of this discipline, arguing, in essence, it foregrounds "place" in examining how and why people vote. This emphasis on place by no means implies that other variables—social class, ethnicity, economic base—are not taken into account (indeed far from it) but it does mean that place has to be understood as not merely geography or location (see Malpas 1999), and that forms the framing of the analysis.

The authors observe that the idea of a "heartlands cleavage" has been strongly associated with right-populist politics in a range of electoral settings globally, from the low-income states in the US "red-versus-blue" analysis, to support for *Liga Nord* in Northern Italy, to similar support for right-populism in rural cantons in Switzerland as well as in Australia, especially in Queensland. Reid and Liu note that One Nation has always been what we will describe as a *non-metropolitan* phenomenon when viewed through electoral data (see, for instance, Grant and Sorensen 2001); moreover, when viewed through finer grained analysis has also been understood as a *peri-urban* phenomenon (Davis and Stimpson 1998). The authors seek greater precision in this mode, offering what they label as "a systematic qualitative analysis" which is both spatial and visual, utilizing methods of exploratory spatial analysis (ESDA), electoral geography, and geographic information systems (GIS).

The methodology is four-fold. First, they examine polling booth-level data for first-preference votes for One Nation for the Senate across the country. Second, they generate a heat-map of this vote (see Fig. 5.1), with this map revealing that ONP received its strongest support in Queensland. Third, the analysis adds socio-spatial data sets to create "Mesh Blocks" of 30–60 households, inclusive of variables such as age, employment status, and type of industry (agriculture, mining, services, for example) and housing status (owned, rented) and social class (from professionals to blue collar). As well, location data for a range of facilities (schools, hospitals, for example) is taken into account, as well as travel distances to and from these facilities. The fourth step utilizes a grouping analysis, which finds three main categories of voting regions in Queensland, before further delineating two, more finely calibrated categories derived from zone-specific location quotients (LQs), which were measured against the state average across a range of variables.

Reid and Liu present their findings in a series of maps and figures. Alongside producing a spatial distribution of the ONP vote in Australia and a detailed portrait of it in Queensland, they also develop a five-part "typology of zones by voter type" for the state, consisting of an "Agricultural Heartland", and a "Mining Heartland", alongside a "Medium-Level Support for One Nation" zone, a "Low One Nation Voting (Urban Zone)" and an "Indigenous Zone". The concept of a "heartland", as it has recently been discussed in the electoral geography literature in relation to right-populism globally, is borne out and analyzed with an impressive level of detail and with some *prima facie* surprising results—for instance, the high One Nation vote in 2016 is almost as significant a phenomenon of the "mining" as "agriculture" heartland. The authors are also careful to place their analysis in the context of long-researched patterns of voting examining the urban-rural divide in Australia (see, for instance, Botterill and Cockfield 2009).

In Chap. 6, Raphaella Kathryn Crosby notes that while Pauline Hanson is globally recognized as the quintessential populist leader, little is known about what people are actually voting for. In interrogating this question, the author distinguishes between three types of populism: the "personality candidate"; "populist campaigning"; and populism understood as a political ideology—that is, as it is overwhelmingly discussed in the rest of this volume (and notwithstanding the fact that the latter type usually incorporates some understanding of the first two).

Examining the "personality" or "celebrity" candidate, Crosby notes that previous psephological work in Australia (Mackerras 1974, 1976) has examined the effect of candidates' "personal vote" and found that this has been higher in Tasmania and Queensland, with Victoria registering the lowest personal vote variation. We are reminded of how salient a phenomenon are personality candidates, as representatives of political parties, in contemporary Australian electoral politics, with Crosby asserting that in many cases the candidate's name "might be the only piece of *information* that a voter associates with a political party". Crosby argues that this type of personality politics has been heightened by the Section 44 constitutional crisis, and provides a meticulous account of this, within which PHONP senators have featured.

Examining the political communication approach, or populist campaigning, Crosby argues that, conceived as such, populism is a "communication frame" designed to align a candidate with "the people" and to speak in their name. As such, it is a political style that, yes, is often characterized by simplistic solutions to complex problems; yet it is by no means limited to populist politicians as an electoral strategy—mass appeal and "ordinariness" can be sought out by anyone. Further, within the literature (see Grabe and Bucy 2011) the populist campaigner (Crosby mentions Bill Clinton as a paradigmatic example) is juxtaposed against both the "ideal candidate" and the "sure loser" types. To these three the author adds the "maverick" type, noting that all have been demonstrably masculine historically and that if a particular politician falls foul of their declared framing their credibility is undermined.

Examining populism as a political ideology, Crosby notes its contested nature, but nevertheless applies three tests to a range of artifacts from Australia's political parties in the period 2013–2016 in order to test for populism. The first tests rhetorical content for specific phrases, namely "the people", "the elite", and "the general will". The second examines political strategies for evidence of "the other" as a mechanism to unite "the people". The third searches for unambiguous anti-establishment or anti-elite narratives. On these measures, no less than 13 political parties qualified as "populist", nine of which are registered to this day. These organizations include the Australia First Party, the Citizens' Electoral Council, Katter's Australian Party, the Christian conservative party Rise Up Australia, and Socialist Alliance; alongside the (then) Nick Xenophon Team and the Palmer United Party (for the full list, see Table 6.2). While PHONP does pass all three tests, Crosby notes the general lack of consistency in its messaging, particularly over time and depending upon what artifacts—from parliamentary speeches to Facebook posts—are examined.

Turning to the question of the level of electoral support for populism in Australia generally, Crosby notes that electoral success can be defined either in terms of "electoral breakthrough" (where a party wins enough votes to enter parliament) or "electoral persistence" (where a party forms a stable element of a political system). Moreover, the author notes that a diminution—or indeed a complete collapse—of support for one populist party (say, Hanson's) does not necessarily signal the same for that ideology, or indeed that type of politics. Nevertheless, defined as such, populist political parties accounted for the entire cross bench in the Australian Senate at the 2013 and 2016 elections. Moreover, in terms of populist political ideology, electoral support for *all* populist parties increased by only 1.34% from the 2013 to the 2016 elections; yet the two are not comparable as the latter was a double-dissolution. Measured by these criteria also, *right populism* actually diminished by 0.87% across the two elections.

These results—unexpected when set against the putative rise of right-populism globally—ought not to detract from the fact that at both the 2013 and 2016 elections, the two parties that experienced significant gains, the Nick Xenophon Team (NXT) and PHON, combined personality populism and populist ideology as measured by Crosby. The author concludes by noting that "Pauline Hanson is certainly a brand; a known quantity with extraordinary name recognition". However, the rhetoric of the Party on the one hand (protectionist, nationalist) and the rhetoric of Hanson on the other hand are mismatched and, in any case, both are over-ridden by infighting and dysfunction—the point made by Antony Green (2018). Moreover, Crosby argues that Hanson herself is more "maverick" than populist in a political campaigning sense, and that given the dysfunction in the Party, support for the far-right in the Australian electorate may well coalesce behind Cori Bernardi's Australian Conservatives as a more stable option in future contests.

Part III of this book is themed POLITICS AND POLICY, and in Chap. 7 Simon Burgess discusses One Nation and Indigenous reconciliation. Burgess is well acquainted with the history of relations between Indigenous and non-Indigenous Australians, and his reflections draw upon a rich array of historical, ethnographic, philosophical, and sociological literature.

Some of the criticisms that he levels against Hanson relate to her impoverished sense of what it is to be Australian. In his words, it "seems not to involve any sustained critical reflection. Her love is blind, complacent, and unduly self-satisfied". She likes to wrap herself in the Australian flag, but "such jingoistic silliness remains embarrassing to most of us". Burgess also finds fault with Hanson's divisive and alienating approach to leadership. As he explains, her failure to engage thoughtfully with Indigenous, Asian, and Islamic community leaders is hardly conducive to the kind of national unity that she would like Australia to have.

Burgess brings some heterodox thinking to the challenges of reconciliation. When it comes to the question of racism, one basic point that he stresses is that the allegation should never be made without overwhelming evidence. We often hear the concern that thoughtless, baseless, or doubtful allegations of racism constitute a form of moral posturing or "virtue signaling". While Burgess certainly shares that concern, he also makes the point that such posturing is counter-productive: "The attempt to bludgeon conspiracy theorists, xenophobes, and Islamophobes with blunt accusations of racism is not likely to teach them anything, and is bound to make them feel even more contemptuous and resentful than they already do". Furthermore, he argues that when we throw around accusations of racism thoughtlessly, we are effectively treating them as if they were of little moral gravity, and so ultimately their moral gravity is precisely what they will lose. The careful articulation of such sobering thoughts is one of Burgess's strengths, and he does not present them as mere idle speculation; the kind of disturbing possibility that he describes is precisely what Steve Bannon—Donald Trump's former chief strategist—has been actively encouraging. As Burgess reminds us, Bannon recently delivered a speech to the party congress of France's National Front in which he slowly, confidently, and emphatically advised them as follows: "Let them call you racist … Wear it as a badge of honor. Because every day, we get stronger and they get weaker". As the audiovisual recording reveals, everything he said was warmly received.

With his background in moral philosophy, Burgess recognizes that the art of effective moral critique is a subtle one, and it does not readily lend itself to simple rules or speech codes. In a discussion of political correctness that is challenging, broad-ranging, and incisive, he draws upon sociological work on ethnic jokes and ethnic humor to reveal the positive role that political *incorrectness* can play in processes of social integration and the development of inter-ethnic friendships. It is clear that Burgess knows how distasteful and pernicious some truly racist jokes are. But as he explains, "even when confronted with such forms of racism, it is not clear that political correctness offers anything worthwhile". Citing evidence related to reform programs for racially motivated offenders, for example, he alerts us to the finding that "didactic moralizing about the evils of racism" is not an approach that works.

While Burgess accepts that political correctness is largely well motivated, he provides a critique of it. In short, he argues that it has been *intellectually corrupting, psychologically enfeebling*, and *socially divisive*. Rather than settle for political correctness, he suggests that we need to make greater use of certain familiar virtues, norms, and practices so as to engage with one another in ways of suitable depth and warmth. Some of the virtues, norms, and practices that he has in mind are simply those of good humor, a generosity of spirit, patience, politeness, principled thinking, and a "fair go". Of course all of these are bound to be valuable as Indigenous and non-Indigenous Australians continue to muddle towards a form of reconciliation. But what is most interesting is the idea that many of these virtues and the like are genuine features of Australian culture, and are arguably well recognized as such. That being so, perhaps Burgess's view is entirely realistic.

In Chap. 8 Jim Jose investigates the intriguing question of Pauline Hanson and the question of gender. Noting that previous work has focused upon the role of Hanson's sexuality as an element of her and her Party's electoral success (see, for instance, Ellison and Deutchman 1997), Jose argues that Hanson and her Party nevertheless "man up" by playing the gender card. By this he means that, in terms of policy rhetoric in particular, PHON has consistently demonstrated a support for men in (for example) its criticisms of the family law courts and the perceived injustices visited upon non-custodial (male) parents in particular—and that this rhetoric has remained substantively unchanged despite significant reforms to the *Family Law Act* in 2006 under the prime ministership of John Howard to "embed" the presumption of shared parental responsibility into the family law court framework.

Yet Jose is fully appreciative that the issues of Hanson and gender and sexuality are much more complex than this. On the one hand, while there is a negation—deliberately or otherwise—of gender in Hanson's appeal to "ordinariness" and to be "outside politics", on the other at almost precisely the same time this is contradicted by Hanson's own sexuality, in particular her dismissal of feminism in favor of equality, in her pronouncements about gender ("I call myself a lady because I like to be treated like a lady"). For Jose, Hanson is as much anti-feminist as she is anti-politician, yet both positions jar against the fact that she is both a professional politician *and* an independent woman ("I don't belong to anyone"). The author agrees with Johnson (2015) that observers need to develop a more nuanced account of "playing the gender card", reminding us that it is both legitimate and laudable to raise concerns about sexism in public life. Moreover, he suggests that in playing the gender card *in the ways she does*, Hanson is not seeking an "unfair disadvantage"; rather, hers is a negotiation of a masculinist Australian politics—a negotiation not confined to Hanson alone.

Chapter 9 by Jo Coghlan takes its cue from Marr's (2017) essay, as well as from the author's long-standing interest in Hanson (see Coghlan 1999). Coghlan asks whether the "re-branded Hanson" is a Party of policy or a Party of protest. In line with our assertion in this Introduction that a discussion of Hanson reveals as much about Australian politics as it does about her and her Party, and in line with several of the contributions to this book, Coghlan argues that it is significant that PHON has now enjoyed electoral success at two critical "junctures"—first in 1996 and second in 2016—and that populism generally has risen to fill "cracks in the consensus representatives and voters". The author advances three central claims. First, Hanson and populists generally have taken votes from the major political parties within a variety of electorates across the Australian federation. Second, she investigates to what extent Australia will "tolerate" populists. Third, comparing Hanson in 1996 and 2016, she argues that the ideological position of PHON, grounded in populism, has "hardened" over time, particularly on the issue of race and especially in relation to people of Muslim faith. Moreover, Coghlan asserts that PHONP can be qualitatively distinguished from other populist political parties (Jackie Lambie, Donald Trump) by a lack of interest in reform and by the iconoclastic nature of its arguments.

Excavating the historical junctures in more detail, the author underscores the break that the prime ministerships of John Howard (1996–2007) represented when set against his predecessor Paul Keating's agendas of Indigenous reconciliation, engagement with Asia, and the issue of an Australian Republic, noting also the policy co-option from Hanson to the Howard governments. For the author, the election of Hanson to the seat of Oxley in 1996 has to recognized as a watershed moment in Australian politics, as it entailed not merely a rejection of Labor by that electorate, but also a rejection of the Liberal Party *and* the (then) main alternatives, the Australian Democrats and the Greens. For Coghlan, the populism of PHON was exemplified in Hanson's speech in the House of Representatives in 1996, and the impact that Hanson had in the 1998 Queensland election cannot be underestimated. The author also cautions against ignoring the vote for Hanson and her Party between 1996 and 2016 (for instance, 10% in the 2001 Senate elections for Queensland) and argues that her time out of parliament—any parliament—does much to explain the hardening of PHON across a range of issues such as unions, the banks, the media (not confined to the ABC), foreign ownership, and the anti-Muslim rhetoric. For Coghlan, it is in the midst of these sentiments that we find the nostalgia for a mythical past, which—perhaps ironically—wins its appeal through Hanson's claim to (anti-elite) authenticity, exemplified in her quavering voice. The author concludes that ultimately PHON is a protest movement, not a Party of policy; nevertheless, to dismiss the reasons for its popularity is "irresponsible", as too is to overstate its importance. We would offer that perhaps herein resides a great irony in Australian politics.

Part IV of the book is themed COMPARISON. In Chap. 10, rather than refer to PHON and other parties of this type as "new-right populism", Tod Moore labels them "conservative backlashers". He does this principally to locate them within the traditional left-right political spectrum and, as such, discuss them as class-political phenomena rather than sheeting them off into the convenient category of "populists". Moore's premise is that it is a worthy exercise to compare both historical junctures of backlash politics across two similar, but at the same time very different, polities, namely the US and Australia. Against the backdrop of neo-liberalism in both places, defined by the triumph of financial capitalism, concurrent with infrastructure decay, a moralized under- and unemployed, a ruthlessly exploited class of working poor, and an assortment of "sectoral losers", Moore notes that, from a historical materialist perspective at least, the task is to explain why, and in a self-harming way, conservative backlashers are attracted to that side of politics rather than the political left. He reminds us that in both lacuna much of what Pauline Hanson has had to say has championed "economic nationalism" over "economic rationalism" (see, in particular, Moore 1997). Further, for the author this element of PHON is particularly important as it furnishes us with a means to explain a broadening of its support beyond the "extreme right fringe" of the electorate.

Turning his attention to backlashes in the US in the 1990s and drawing specifically on the work of Thomas Frank (2006, 2012, 2016), Moore highlights the role of religion in galvanizing anti-Democrat support against (for example) same-sex marriage and abortion, wherein cultural issues supplant material ones and where the traditional political party of labor is complicit in the neo-liberal consensus. Post 2008, the policy consensus was reinforced (with, for example, President Obama bailing out Wall Street). Moore distinguishes this iteration of backlash politics in the US as "hard times conservativism" that is more representative of small business *and* more libertarian, albeit finding a counterpoint in left-populist presidential candidate Bernie Sanders.

Examining the phenomenon in Australia, Moore argues that in Hanson and others we have experienced a similar phenomenon of "blue-collar self-harming backlashers". He also provides a succinct account of previous iterations of this form of politics in this country, from the Kyabram Movement in Victoria in 1902 through to the valorization of soldier settlers post-WWI and the anti-elite, anti-Semitic, and economically simplistic movements of this type during the Great Depression. While noting that post-WWII there has always been a "lunar right" in Australian politics, which usually accounts for around 2% of electoral support, support for PHONP cannot come merely from these people.

Comparing experiences across both polities, the author underscores that the US and Australia are grounded in "settler society dynamics"; yet there are profound differences. First, the religiosity of the US has been far more subdued in Australia, and while it most certainly shaped politics in profound ways it has not had the impact on the party-political divide when it comes to seeking explanations for backlashes. Second, the US political system is more right-leaning and, as such, the conservative backlash has had a major impact not merely upon mainstream party politics (for example, in the sense of policy co-option) but *within* them. Third, the libertarian element of the backlash has been far more muted in Australia; moreover, while (for example) Hanson and Trump are notionally protectionist, in both cases their bark may well prove bigger than their bite.

In turning to explain the similarities, Moore notes that it is significant that both polities experienced backlashes at approximately the same time, suggesting that the reasons are structural rather than to be found in (for example) electoral anomalies. In explaining the hiatus between the two periods in the two countries, Moore notes the global political economics post-9/11, the financial upswing from that time (albeit as a prelude to the 2008 crash), and the invasion of Iraq in 2003 as all contributing to conditions that kept backlashes at bay. Australia also had particular circumstances. These included the Howard Governments' absorption of the non-fringe right through policy co-option (border protection, pushing back Indigenous reconciliation, for example); generally favorable economic circumstances due to the burgeoning mining boom (particularly in the resource-rich "heartland" states of Queensland and Western Australia, and to a lesser extent NSW), and the possibility (not reality) of an alternative to neo-liberalism signaled in the election of Labor Prime Minister Kevin Rudd in 2007. Moore is critical of those who point to race in seeking an explanation for conservative backlash, noting not merely the paradox, but the tragedy and farce of backlashers' engendering support for a raft of neo-liberal policies. He also points to the role of "influential political scientists" in maintaining the status quo, instead of them actively prosecuting the case for a return to a type of democratic socialism *a la* Sanders and Corbyn.

Continuing the comparative focus of Part IV, in Chap. 11 by Alan Scott considers populism in Europe, again in its two recent historical iterations: in the 1980s/1990s in Austria, and contemporarily with an examination of Brexit Britain. Scott argues that this comparison is important, as we have a fair amount of evidence to suggest that Hanson and One Nation "are part of a wider international development" of a rise in populism. Moreover, when we look to Europe, far-right parties that have enjoyed significant electoral success in many countries, including France, the Netherlands, Greece, Hungry, Sweden, Austria, Finland, Denmark, Poland, and, most recently, Germany and Italy.

Noting the debate about the nature of populism—seen as a derogatory label for the both left and right (D'Eramo 2013), as a polemical term (Streeck 2017a, b), a discursive formation (Laclau 2005), or indeed as a political style (Moffitt and Tormey 2013)—the author initially settles on what he describes as a "minimalist" working definition, one that recognizes an appeal to the will of "the people" set against that of an "elite", and wherein the definition of "the people" is a matter of debate. Scott nevertheless pluralizes his working definition into various *repertoires* of populism that "shift and are open to innovation". He argues that alongside (broadly) structural (if not materialist) reasons for its contemporary salience, we ought to recognize that right-populist parties are globally networked (particularly in Europe, where—ironically—the networking is facilitated by the European Parliament, to which said populist parties are opposed); that these parties look to each other for political strategies and policy ideas; that new social media have "facilitated and accelerated this exchange of ideas"; and that, despite its diverse repertoires, populism does have stable components which are generally replicable across different polities.

Examining the case of Austria in the 1980s/1990s, Scott underscores the importance of understanding the depth of civil society organizations in that country (unions, chambers of commerce, strong political party affiliations, etc.) and the way that they are formally accommodated by the state. This produces a "consociational" or "neo-corporatist" political paradigm, in essence a "negotiated democracy". Scott highlights Papadopoulos's (2005) thesis that these types of political systems provide fertile ground for populism due to the high degree of formal consensus at the elite level; as such they come to "lack input legitimation" and are characterized by cartel-like behavior at an elite level (or what in Chap. 3 Tony Lynch labels "oligopoly" politics) and, as such, are prone to citizens' disillusionment in the state. Detailing the history of the electoral success the FPÖ under the leadership of Jörg Haider from 1986, inclusive of its coalition with the more moderate ÖVP in 2000, Scott provides a list of ideal features of this repertoire of populism, including the personalization of politics and candidate-centered campaigning, where the idea of allegiance to the leader is key. Also the ideas of provocation and scandal as continuous elements of politics—for example, "dog-whistling" (see Chap. 8 by Jim Jose); the non-metropolitan "heartland" concept (discussed in Chap. 5 by Ben Reid and Gan Jung-Liu); the valorization of plebiscites and other instruments of "direct democracy" as a more legitimate form of decision-making than (for example) that undertaken by parliaments; and a "neo-nationalism" which is (arbitrarily) defined against economic liberalism and deployed not as a coherent ideology, but in opportunistic and emotivist ways.

Turning his attention to the second iteration of right-populism, specifically Britain where the issues of sovereignty, borders, and Brexit have seen a "refinement" of the repertoire, Scott notes that British democracy—like Australia's—is formally more adversarial than negotiated. However, the policy consensus from Margaret Thatcher's infamous TINA (i.e., "There is No Alternative") pronouncement has witnessed the increasing abandonment of class politics and the creation of those "left-behind".

Scott argues that in Britain much academic and media discussion is framed in terms of "the left-behind", those who are said (or believe themselves) to benefit least from the opportunities offered by EU membership; who have lower levels of education; who are older and tend to live in non-metropolitan—or (perhaps more accurately) *non-cosmopolitan* areas. These are also the people who have suffered most from post-GFC austerity measures. At least in England and Wales, it is this group that has provided the core Leaver vote. In answering the question "Who were the left-behind left behind by?" (at the risk of over-simplification) his answer is "New Labour". New Labour continued to implement much of the neo-liberal and New Public Management reform agendas; and like Tony Lynch in Chap. 3 and following Wolfgang Streeck (2017a, b), the author points to the importance of the shift from class to status in explaining the divisions in the UK which were heightened from 2004 wherein ten countries (eight from the former Soviet bloc) joined the EU and Britain experienced an unanticipated inflow of immigration, followed by the impact of the GFC. For Scott, it is within the "leave" campaign that the parallels with Austria in the 1990s become clear: the personalization of politics in Nigel Farage, Boris Johnson, and Michael Gove (all pedigree members of the British upper class); provocation; the neo-nationalism and calling a referendum as a means to decide not just *a* policy decision, but one that would have longstanding and dramatic implications. Politically, for the "left-behind", the instrumental rationality of the "remain" campaign, cut very little ice compared with the value rationality (or emotivism) of the "leave" campaign—to the shock of many.

Reflecting upon the implications of the rise of right populism in Europe, the author argues that the recent Austrian election in October 2017, wherein the FPÖ gained 26% and the (more centrist, but nevertheless aligned) ÖVP gained 31.5%, raises the possibility of "the emergence of a bloc of states in Eastern and Central Europe" that will pull against German and French attempts at further integration. For Britain, the current situation is "much more dramatic": the hard-Brexit model, which at its most extreme envisages "a kind of North Sea Singapore" will deliver to those "left-behind" exactly what they *didn't* want.

It is with this point of irony, which, as noted by Tony Lynch in his conclusion to Chap. 3 is also a point of tragedy, that we move to make some broader observations.

1.4 Observations

A specter is haunting the world—populism. (Ghiţă Ionescu and Ernest Gellner 1969, p. 1)

The first of these observations is about the nature of populism itself and the related questions of whether there is an Australian populism of both the left and right—and/or politically centered types. We have already seen that populism is a contested and indeed polemical term (see also Delsol 2013). Nevertheless, beyond it being used as a term of derision, it is tempting—as Alan Scott does in his contribution to this book—to commence with a "minimalist" definition that initially makes a distinction between "the people" and "an elite", then bifurcates into left and right types, as determined by who is included as bona fide members of "the people", and notwithstanding the fact that we have the case of Menzies' "forgotten class" as discussed by Tony Lunch in Chap. 3. From here we can then examine (as it were) variations on a theme, albeit variations that are inter-related in interesting ways, honing our definition according to context—as indeed Scott does admirably when discussing the Brexit vote, utilizing the categories of class, education, age, and geography. Deploying the concept of populism like this is useful, as is the way that Raphaella Kathryn Crosby disaggregates the term as being defined by a "celebrity candidate", as a particular approach to political campaigning and then as an ideology. Again it is indeed admirable that her contribution examines all three and tests for populism as an ideology in the context of the two most recent Australian federal elections.

However, and notwithstanding the cautionary note by Isaiah Berlin et al. (1968, p. 6) that we ought not to suffer from a "Cinderella complex" when it comes to populism—wandering about with (as it were) the "populist shoe", looking for a perfect "populist foot" on which to place that shoe—there might be something ultimately unsatisfying about endorsing a pluralist, if not solipsistic, approach to the term. Moreover, behind the varying definitions discussed above there are deeper questions of ontology and epistemics at play, as suggested by Laclau's (2005) discussion of the term as a type of discursive formation, that is, as a particular way of approaching politics, and the ramifications of this, which link to earlier discussions of ideology per se (see, for example, Plamenatz 1970). Our goal here is not to resolve these issues of definition; yet it would be remiss not to flag them.

Additionally, it would be remiss not to underscore—however briefly, yet precisely because we inhabit an atmosphere of *pervasive modernity*—that populism has been frequently discussed as an historical and place-based phenomenon (and notwithstanding the fact that some of these places are very large indeed). Consider, for example, the volume edited by Ionescu and Gellner (1969) arising from a conference about populism held at the London School of Economics and Political Science in 1967 (and in which the editors infamously paraphrased the opening line of Marx and Engles' *The Communist Manifesto* cited at the beginning of this section). In that volume alone, Hofstadter (1969) discussed US populism in the later 19th century, arguing that it was grounded in "entrepreneurial radicalism" (agrarian and otherwise) and a Jeffersonian resistance to the emergence of financial capital and reflected in (seemingly contradictory) economic policy. Hennessy (1969, p. 30) discussed what he referred to as the "trans-class populism" of Latin America grounded, *inter alia*, in conspiracy theories about neo-colonialism that contributed to the detriment of that region and, in several states, served as a precursor to military-dominated regimes of both the left and right. Walicki (1969) investigated "Russian populism", which he argued was most accurately defined by Marxists of the late 19th and early 20th centuries and was inspired, at least in part, by early translations of *Capital Volume I* in 1872 and which (p. 78) bore a "grudge against political liberals". Ionescu himself (1969) examined populism in Eastern Europe, divided as it was between Russian Orthodox (Romanians, Bulgars, Serbs) and Catholic (Hungary, Poland) populations and comprising both fascist and communist populisms. For his part, Saul (1969) considered populism in "Africa". While surely this generalization would be proscribed in contemporary accounts, Saul (pp. 122–123) nevertheless drew a distinction between populism as the "will of the people" on the one hand and "as a response generated whenever capitalism has penetrated into traditionalistic peasant society" on the other, arguing that vacuums in leadership and aspirations for solidarity at these times engendered the rise of populist movements. Indeed, in the journal article arising from the conference (Berlin et al. 1968, pp. 152–155) he even discussed "Asian" populisms (again, the generalization grates).

Where, then, does this leave us in discussing Australian populism? It is clear that Australia has examples of left and right populism, both historically and contemporaneously. Historically, we can choose to examine the iterations that Tod Moore presents in Chap. 11 (see also Hume 1994; Love 1984). In the current context, we can examine what Kissane (2013) described as "rednecks" and/or "watermelons" (i.e., "green" political leanings on the outside, hard-left political leanings on the inside). And of course it is no mistake that both "redneck" and "watermelon" are derogatory labels—or at least they are designed that way. Yet the discussion in our book provides ample evidence that populism generally in Australia and right-populism in particular has complex underpinnings in social class, in particular downward mobility and the threat thereof, and the existential threat to the ideology of "home"—see, for example, Chap. 3 by Tony Lynch and Chap. 10 by Tod Moore. Our discussion also suggests that populism in Australia has strong underpinnings in place, in particular (but not exclusively) in what Stokes (2000, p. 33) labeled "Queensland proclivities" and particular patterns of political economics (see Chap. 5 by Ben Reid and Gang-Jung Liu) and electoral circumstance and gender (discussed in Chaps. 6 and 9 respectively).

As social scientists of a particular type we may be drawn to look for explanation in structure—and notwithstanding that a psychoanalytic strain of academic writing on populism has of late been gathering steam (see, for example, Short 2017—a strain that we will place to one side in this context). However, there are two important features of Australian populism, and in particular right-populism, that are worth underscoring as we think they will be enduring. First, as was emphasized in Grant (1997) *writ large*, populism can be understood in being grounded in what MacIntyre (1981) labeled "emotivism". In the literature on Hanson this has often been expressed as the politics of "gut-feeling" (see Wells 1997, p. 18). While the politics of emotivism and the politics of gut feeling are similar, the former is more accurate; MacIntyre's

(1981) thesis provides an *explanation* for why this type of politics is more, rather than less, legitimate in conditions of late modernity—namely because political discourse has been severed from thinking through the consequences of such expression. The importance of this observation and the danger that emotivism represents—not from Hanson in particular or anyone else who engages in populist political expression, but more generally—is difficult to underestimate. Emotivism—emotions as *ideology*—leads us away from the realization that democratic politics is, in essence, about compromise; moreover, it is a politics that requires a particular attitude to underscore its work. And it is no accident that it is this which Simon Burgess, in his discussion of Indigenous reconciliation in Chap. 7, chooses to emphasize. The second is that populist politics in Australia, indeed more generally, is iconoclastic. And while in Australia we might pride ourselves on being anti-elitist (if only to fool ourselves about our national character) it is perhaps not advisable that we take this attitude to the specifically political realm. It is on this point it would appear that politics in many comparable polities has "caught up" with Australia from the late 1990s, but at a scale that is truly concerning.

The second observation concerns Australian politics, reflecting upon how our understanding has changed from the first iteration of Hanson until now. Equipped as we now are with what is (arguably) a more nuanced understanding of populism—in particular as the "personality candidate" and as a style of political campaigning—it is evident that the populist mode of politics is a more salient feature of Australian politics than it then was, and that this shows no sign of abating. This is particularly the case when we consider the evidence presented in Chap. 6 of this book by Raphaella Kathryn Crosby. It also demonstrates a relatively commonplace point, namely the increase of new-right populist parties in the Australian electoral landscape (if not an overall increase in the total vote for them). It is easy to be dismissive of this change, to dismiss them as *mere* populists, or to label them—as Abbott (1998) did—as the "feral right". Yet this is counterproductive on a number of fronts. For one thing, it "others" not merely these politicians but the people who might support them and, as such, it is to engage in precisely the kind of emotivistic politics that we have cautioned against here. Nor is this merely a matter of being polite, or ethically consistent. On the contrary, an important element of support for right-populists is found in demonstrable evidence of this "othering", and so to engage in it is to add weight to their claims. Rather, we must seek the worth of their claims—for points of agreement—in either reaching a compromise or in ultimately disagreeing with them. Nor ought we engage in what might be labeled "Hanson reductionism", by which we mean turning instinctively to look at PHONP when thinking of right-populism in this polity. There are now plenty of other fish in the sea, which raises the possibility that Australia might encounter a more, rather than a less, competent person of this type.

This may appear unlikely. However, what is likely to continue is both the ideational and policy synergies from right-populist political parties on the one hand and some elements of the "Center-right" on the other. Nor is it merely a matter of blatant "policy co-option" on (for example) asylum-seeker policy or immigration or Indigenous issues. Rather, the Durkheimian concept of *anomic strain* is worthy of consideration here. One of the enduring tropes of Australian culture is the uncle who has too much to drink at Christmas lunch. While he as a stereotype is derided (and rightly so) it is not often pointed out that this person performs a valuable function for the rest of the people at that lunch every year, in that *their* consumption of alcohol is relative to *his* and as such the median is stretched. Arguably, since Hanson-Howard in the late 1990s right-populism in Australian politics—both within and outside the "Center-right"—has performed precisely this function, one from which the Labor Party has not been immune. It remains to be seen if *left*-populism can perform the same function for that side of politics in this country (see McKnight 2018). Some of the contributors to this book don't see much chance of this occurring any time soon (see, for example, Tony Lunch in Chap. 3). Others are less pessimistic (see Tod Moore in Chap. 10).

Finally, we as editors speak for all the contributors to this book in emphasizing that all of us bear no malice to Pauline Hanson or any of her supporters. In fact quite the opposite. You should be congratulated for your engagement with Australian politics. Moreover, it is no accident that the majority of us have spent the majority of our lives in non-metropolitan Australia (albeit in the university town of Armidale, NSW, but elsewhere as well). Indeed, many of the issues that animate you so much—of regional economies; of social cohesion; of opportunities for our youth; of Indigenous reconciliation—are very much visible in Armidale as they are in other regional centers, characterized less by the palpable socio-economic divisions that characterize Australia's sprawling cities. We offer this book to you in the spirit of democratic politics.

References

Abbott, T. (1998). The feral right. In R. Manne, T. Abbott, J. Brett, R. Brunton, M. Frazer, et al. (Eds.), *Two Nations: The causes and effects of the rise of the One Nation Party in Australia* (pp. 10–19). Melbourne: Bookman Press.

Archer, J. (1997). Howard, Hanson, and the importance of symbolic politics. In B. Grant (Ed.), *Pauline Hanson, One Nation and Australian politics* (pp. 88–100). Armidale: U.N.E. Press.

Atchinson, J. (1997). The sad state of the immigration debate. In B. Grant (Ed.), *Pauline Hanson, One Nation and Australian politics* (pp. 101–113). Armidale: U.N.E. Press.

Berlin, I., Alcock, J., Andreski, S. L., Brandt, C., Calvertt, P., Clive, N., et al. (1968). To define populism. *Government and Opposition, 3*(2), 137–180.

Bohill, R. (1997). For the record: Pauline Hanson, equality and Native Title. In B. Grant (Ed.), *Pauline Hanson, One Nation and Australian politics* (pp. 63–87). Armidale: U.N.E. Press.

Botterill, L. E. C., & Cockfield, G. (Eds.) (2009). *The National Party: Prospects for the great survivors*. Crows Nest, N.S.W: Allen & Unwin.

Brett, J. (1997). John Howard, Pauline Hanson and the politics of grievance. In G. Gray & C. Winter (Eds.), *The resurgence of racism: Howard, Hanson and the racism debate* (pp. 7–28). Clayton [Victoria]: Monash Publications in History in association with the Australian Institute of Aboriginal and Torres Strait Islander Studies and the Humanities Research Centre of the Australian National University.

Brett, J. (1998). Representing the unrepresented: One Nation and the formation of the Labor Party. In R. Manne, T. Abbott, J. Brett, R. Brunton, M. Frazer, et al. (Eds.), *Two Nations: The causes and effects of the rise of the One Nation Party in Australia* (pp. 26–37). Melbourne: Bookman Press.

Broinowski, A. (2017). *Please explain. The rise and fall and rise again of Pauline Hanson*. Melbourne: Penguin Random House.

Brugger, B., & Jaensch, D. (1985). *Australian politics*. Sydney: Allen & Unwin.

Coghlan, J. (1999). *Pauline Hanson and Paul Keating: A postmodern analysis*. Unpublished Honors thesis, University of Wollongong.

Curthoys, A. (1997). Entangled histories: Conflict and ambivalence in non-Aboriginal Australia. In G. Gray & C. Winter (Eds.), *The resurgence of racism: Howard, Hanson and the racism debate* (pp. 117–128). Clayton [Victoria]: Monash Publications in History in association with the Australian Institute of Aboriginal and Torres Strait Islander Studies and the Humanities Research Centre of the Australian National University.

D'Eramo, M. (2013). Populism and the new oligarchy. *New Left Review, 82,* 5–28.

Davis, R., & Stimson, R. (1998). Disillusionment and disenchantment at the fringe: Explaining the geography of the One Nation party in the Queensland election. *People and Place, 3,* 1–12.

Delsol, C. (2013). The "common idiot" of populism. In S. Gherhgina, S. Mişcoiu, & S. Soare (Eds.), *Contemporary populism: A controversial concept and its diverse forms* (pp. 31–52). Newcastle upon Tyne: Cambridge Scholars Publishing.

Dow, G. (2000). Beyond One Nation: Interventionist responses to economic liberalism. In M. Leach, G. Stokes, & I. Ward (Eds.), *The rise and fall of One Nation* (pp. 248–264). St Lucia (Queensland): University of Queensland Press.

Ellison, A., & Deutchman, I. (1997). Men only: Pauline Hanson and the far right. In B. Grant (Ed.), *Pauline Hanson: One Nation and Australian politics* (pp. 141–150). Armidale: University of New England Press.

Frank, T. (2006). *What's the matter with America? The resistible rise of the American right*. London: Vintage. [i.e. *What's the Matter With Kansas?*].

Frank, T. (2012). *Pity the billionaire—The hard-times swindle and the unlikely comeback of the right*. London: Harvill Secker.

Frank, T. (2016). *Listen, Liberal: Or, what ever happened to the party of the people?*. Melbourne: Scribe Publications.

Gale, P. (2004). The refugee crisis and fear: Populist politics and media discourse. *Journal of Sociology, 40*(4), 321–340.

Gale, P. (2005). *The politics of fear : Lighting the Wik*. Pearson Education.

Gherhgina, S., Mişcoiu, S., & Soare, S. (Eds.). (2013). *Contemporary populism: A controversial concept and its diverse forms*. Newcastle upon Tyne: Cambridge Scholars Publishing.

Goodman, D. (1988). Gold fields/golden fields: The language of agrarianism and the Victorian goldrush. *Australian Historical Studies, 23*(90), 19–41.

Grabe, M. E., & Bucy, E. P. (2011). Image bite analysis of political visuals: Understanding the visual framing process in election news. In E. P. Bucy & R. L. Holbert (Eds.), *Sourcebook for Political Communication Research: Methods, measures, and analytical techniques* (pp. 209–237). New York: Routledge.

Grant, B. (Ed.). (1997). *Pauline Hanson, One Nation and Australian politics*. Armidale: U.N.E. Press.

Grant, B., & Sorenson, T. (2000). Marginality, regionalism and the One Nation vote: Exploring regional socio-economic correlations. In M. Simms & J. Warhurst (Eds.), *Howard's agenda: The 1998 Australian election* (pp. 193–211). St Lucia: University of Queensland Press.

Gray, G., & Winter, C. (Eds.) (1997). *The resurgence of racism: Howard, Hanson and the racism debate.* Clayton [Victoria]: Monash Publications in History in association with the Australian Institute of Aboriginal and Torres Strait Islander Studies and the Humanities Research Centre of the Australian National University.

Green, A. (2018). Pauline Hanson's One Nation and the fate of its elected MPs. *Antony Green's election blog*, 14 June. http://www.abc.net.au/news/2018-06-14/pauline-hanson-one-nation-history-of-losing-elected-mps/9869814. Accessed July 7, 2018.

Hennessy, A. (1969). Latin America. In G. Ionescu & E. Gellner (Eds.), *Populism: Its meaning and national characteristics* (pp. 28–61). London: Macmillan.

Hofstadter, R. (1969). North America. In G. Ionescu & E. Gellner (Eds.), *Populism: Its meaning and national characteristics* (pp. 9–27). London: Macmillan.

Hollinsworth, D. (1997). The work of anti-racism. In G Gray & C. Winter (Eds.), *The resurgence of racism: Howard, Hanson and the racism debate* (pp. 129–138). Clayton [Victoria]: Monash Publications in History in association with the Australian Institute of Aboriginal and Torres Strait Islander Studies and the Humanities Research Centre of the Australian National University.

Hughes, D. (1997). Pauline Hanson, One Nation and the next federal election. In B. Grant (Ed.), *Pauline Hanson, One Nation and Australian politics* (pp. 129–140). Armidale: U.N.E. Press.

Hume, L. (1994). Foundations of populism and pluralism: Australian writings on populism and pluralism to 1860. In G. Stokes (Ed.), *Australian political ideas* (pp. 22–76). Sydney: University of New South Wales Press.

Ionescu, G. (1969). Eastern Europe. In G. Ionescu & E. Gellner (Eds.), *Populism: Its meaning and national characteristics* (pp. 97–122). London: Macmillan.

Ionescu, G., & Gellner, E. (Eds.). (1969). *Populism: Its meaning and national characteristiss.* London: Macmillan.

Jakubowicz, A. (1997). In pursuit of anabranches: Immigration, multiculturalism and a culturally diverse Australia. In G Gray & C. Winter (Eds.), *The resurgence of racism: Howard, Hanson and the racism debate* (pp. 149–160). Clayton [Victoria]: Monash Publications in History in association with the Australian Institute of Aboriginal and Torres Strait Islander Studies and the Humanities Research Centre of the Australian National University.

Johnson, C. (2015). Playing the gender card: The uses and abuses of gender in Australian politics. *Politics & Gender, 11*(2), 291–319.

Judis, J. B. (2016). *The populist explosion: How the great recession transformed American and European Politics*. New York: Columbia Global Reports.

Kelly, P. (1998). Hanson—Symptom of a deeper problem. In. Manne, T. Abbott, J. Brett, R. Brunton, M. Frazer, et al. (Eds.), *Two Nations: The causes and effects of the rise of the One Nation Party in Australia* (pp. 89–102). Melbourne: Bookman Press.

Kingston, M. (1999). *Off the rails: The Pauline Hanson trip*. Sydney: Allen & Unwin.

Kissane, D. (2013). Rednecks and watermelons. The rise and fall of populist parties in modern Australian politics. In S, Gherhgina, S. Mişcoiu, S. Soare (Eds.), *Contemporary populism: A controversial concept and its diverse forms* (pp. 234–257). Newcastle upon Tyne: Cambridge Scholars Publishing.

Laclau, E. (2005). *On populist reason*. London: Verso.

Leach, M., Stokes, G., & Ward, I. (Eds.). (2000). *The rise and fall of One Nation*. St Lucia (Queensland): University of Queensland Press.

Loewenstein, K. (1937a). Militant democracy and fundamental rights—Part 1. *American Political Science Review, 33*(3), 417–432.

Loewenstein, K. (1937b). Militant democracy and fundamental rights—Part 2. *American Political Science Review, 33*(4), 538–558.

Love, P. (1984). *Labour and the money power: Australian labour Populism 1890–1950.* Melbourne: Melbourne University Press.

Lukacs, J. (2005). *Democracy and populism: Fear and hatred*. New Haven and London: Yale University Press.

Lynch, T., & Reavell, R. (1997). Through the looking glass: Howard, Hanson and the politics of political correctness. In B. Grant (Ed.), *Pauline Hanson, One Nation and Australian politics* (pp. 29–49). Armidale: U.N.E. Press.

MacIntyre, A. (1981). *After virtue: A study in moral theory*. London: Duckworth.

Mackerras, M. (1974). *The role of the candidate in the electoral process in Australia*. Thesis (Ph.D.). Canberra: Australian National University.

Mackerras, M. (1976). *Incumbency as an electoral advantage: The influence of the sitting member on constituency voting patterns in Australian Federal and State elections, 1953–76*. Thesis (Ph.D.). Canberra: Australian National University.

Maddox, G. (1996). *Religion and the rise of democracy*. London and New York: Routledge.

Maddox, G. (2004). *Australian democracy in theory and practice* (4th ed.). Melbourne: Longman.

Malpas, J. (1999). *Place and experience. A philosophical topography*. Cambridge: Cambridge University Press.

Manne, R., Abbott, T., Brett, J., Brunton, R., Frazer, M., et al. (Eds.). (1998). *Two Nations: the causes and effects of the rise of the One Nation Party in Australia*. Melbourne: Bookman Press.

Markus, A. (1997). John Howard and the re-naturalization of bigotry. In G. Gray & C. Winter (Eds.), *The resurgence of racism: Howard, Hanson and the racism debate* (pp. 79–86). Clayton [Victoria]: Monash Publications in History in association with the Australian Institute of Aboriginal and Torres Strait Islander Studies and the Humanities Research Centre of the Australian National University.

Markus, A. (2001). *Race: John Howard and the remaking of Australia*. Sydney: Allen & Unwin.

Marr, D. (2017). The white queen: One Nation and the politics of race. *Quarterly Essay, 65,* 1–102.

McGuinness, P. P. (1998). The political elites' contribution to Hansonism. In R. Manne, T. Abbott, J. Brett, R. Brunton, M. Frazer, et al. (Eds.), *Two Nations: The causes and effects of the rise of the One Nation Party in Australia* (pp. 131–140). Melbourne: Bookman Press.

McKee, A. (1997). The "lack" of racism in contemporary Australia. In G. Gray, & C. Winter (Eds.), *The resurgence of racism: Howard, Hanson and the racism debate* (pp. 139–148). Clayton [Victoria]: Monash Publications in History in association with the Australian Institute of Aboriginal and Torres Strait Islander Studies and the Humanities Research Centre of the Australian National University.

McKnight, D. (2018). *Populism now! The case for progressive populism*. Sydney: NewSouth Books.

Mickler, S. (1997). The "Robespierre of the air: Talkback radio, globalization and Indigenous issues. In G. Gray & C. Winter (Eds.), *The resurgence of racism: Howard, Hanson and the racism debate* (pp. 63–78). Clayton [Victoria]: Monash Publications in History in association with the Australian Institute of Aboriginal and Torres Strait Islander Studies and the Humanities Research Centre of the Australian National University.

Moffitt, B., & Tormey, S. (2013). Rethinking populism: Politics, mediatisation and political style. *Political Studies, 62,* 381–397.

Moore, T. (1997). Economic rationalism and economic nationalism. In B. Grant (Ed.), *Pauline Hanson, One Nation and Australian politics* (pp. 50–62). Armidale: U.N.E. Press.

Mudde, C., & Kaltwasser, C. R. (2017). *Populism: A very short introduction*. Oxford: Oxford University Press.

Mullins, P. (1986). Queensland: Populist politics and development. In B. Head (Ed.), *The politics of development in Australia* (pp. 138–162). Sydney: Allen & Unwin.

Newman, G. (1998). 1998 Queensland election. Parliament of Australia Current Issues Brief 1998–99. https://www.aph.gov.au/About_Parliament/Parliamentary_Departments/Parliamentary_Library/Publications_Archive/CIB/cib9899/99CIB02. Accessed July 7, 2018.

Papadopolous, Y. (2005). Populism as the other side of consociational multi-level democracies. In D. Caramani & Y. Mény (Eds.), *Challenges to consensual politics: Democracy, identity, and populist protest in the alpine region* (pp. 71–81). Bruxelles: Peter Lang.

Pasquarelli, J. (1998). *The Pauline Hanson story... by the man who knows*. Sydney: New Holland.

Phillips, A. (1997). Travails in identity: An interpretation of Hanson's heat. In B. Grant (Ed.), *Pauline Hanson, One Nation and Australian politics* (pp. 151–166). Armidale: U.N.E. Press.

Plamenatz, J. (1970). *Ideology*. London: Macmillan.

Read, P. (1997). Pain, yes; racism, no: The response of non-British Australians to Indigenous land rights. In G. Gray & C. Winter (Eds.), *The resurgence of racism: Howard, Hanson and the racism debate* (pp. 87–96). Clayton [Victoria]: Monash Publications in History in association with the

Australian Institute of Aboriginal and Torres Strait Islander Studies and the Humanities Research Centre of the Australian National University.

Reynolds, H. (1997). Racism and other national discourses. In G. Gray & C. Winter C. (Eds.), *The resurgence of racism: Howard, Hanson and the racism debate* (pp. 29–38). Clayton [Victoria]: Monash Publications in History in association with the Australian Institute of Aboriginal and Torres Strait Islander Studies and the Humanities Research Centre of the Australian National University.

Ricklefs, M. C. (1997). The Asian immigration controversies of 1984–85, 1988–89 and 1996–97: A historical review. In G. Gray & C. Winter (Eds.), *The resurgence of racism: Howard, Hanson and the racism debate* (pp. 39–62). Clayton [Victoria]: Monash Publications in History in association with the Australian Institute of Aboriginal and Torres Strait Islander Studies and the Humanities Research Centre of the Australian National University.

Rose, D. B. (1997). Dark times and excluded bodies in the colonization of Australia. In G. Gray & C. Winter (Eds.), *The resurgence of racism: Howard, Hanson and the racism debate* (pp. 97–116). Clayton [Victoria]: Monash Publications in History in association with the Australian Institute of Aboriginal and Torres Strait Islander Studies and the Humanities Research Centre of the Australian National University.

Short, N. (2017). On the subject of far-right-wing politics. *Critical Sociology, 43*(4–5), 763–777.

Saul, J. (1969). Africa. In G. Ionescu & E. Gellner (Eds.), *Populism: Its meaning and national characteristics* (pp. 122–151). London: Macmillan.

Stokes, G. (2000). One Nation and Australian populism. In M. Leach, G. Stokes, & I. Ward (Eds.), *The rise and fall of One Nation* (pp. 23–41). St Lucia (Queensland): University of Queensland Press.

Streeck, W. (2017a). The return of the repressed. *New Left Review, 104,* 5–18.

Streeck, W. (2017b). Trump and trumpists. *Inference: International Review of Science, 3*(1). http://inference-review.com/article/trump-and-the-trumpists. Accessed April 28, 2018.

Von Strokirch, K., & Low-O'Sullivan, M. (1997). The Asian region: Does Hanson matter? In B. Grant (Ed.), *Pauline Hanson, One Nation and Australian politics* (pp. 114–128). Armidale: U.N.E. Press.

Walicki, A. (1969). Russia. In G. Ionescu & E. Gellner (Eds.), *Populism: Its meaning and national characteristics* (pp. 62–96). London: Macmillan.

Wear, R. (2008). Permanent populism: The Howard Government 1996–2007. *Australian Journal of Political Science, 43*(4), 617–634.

Wells, D. (1997). One Nation and the politics of populism. In B. Grant (Ed.), *Pauline Hanson One Nation and Australian politics* (pp. 18–28). Armidale: University Press of New England.

Part I
Ideation

Chapter 2
One Nation and Militant Democracy

Graham Maddox

Abstract The One Nation Party's unmistakable resemblances to historical "populist" parties have placed the defenders of democracy on alert. The party's official statement *Principles and Objectives* announces the name "Pauline Hanson's One Nation Party" and the ownership by the Leader unmistakably draws it into line with some notorious examples of "right wing" populism, where adoration of the leader became a cult. The statement promises "to speak for the voiceless and the powerless" against the established forces of the Australian party system, deliberately setting One Nation against the mainstream of Australian politics, while yet clamoring to influence it. This chapter asks whether activities of One Nation deserve the attention of a defensive democracy and seeks to examine in particular two of the claims of the "Principles": That One Nation aims "To protect our sovereignty and democracy", and that it repeatedly acclaims Australia as a "Christian country".

Keywords Australian politics · Christian country · Militant democracy
Pauline Hanson · One Nation

2.1 Introduction: Australian Democracy

Principle 2 of One Nation Party's official statement promises to protect "our democracy", which is evidently proffered as a "hurrah" word demanding automatic approval. Yet if one attempts to unpack what the principle involving sovereignty and democracy means to One Nation, one is at a loss to find any explanation. To follow some of the other stated principles, and especially many of the public announcements of the Leader, Pauline Hanson, it might appear that the Party is quite at odds with democracy. To be sure, the principles call for "equality" among Australians, an undoubtedly central tenet of democracy, yet there is an exclusive twist to this equality. *What We Stand For*, ignoring this country's international obligations, notes "Australian Val-

G. Maddox (✉)
School of Humanities, Arts and Social Sciences, University of New England, Armidale,
NSW 2350, Australia
e-mail: gmaddox@une.edu.au

© Springer Nature Singapore Pte Ltd. 2019
B. Grant et al. (eds.), *The Rise of Right-Populism*,
https://doi.org/10.1007/978-981-13-2670-7_2

ues", elaborating that "Australia is for Australians and under our constitution only Australians decide our laws and obligations, decide who will enter and live in our country, and decide how we ensure our nation's safety and economic security". These "values" are clearly exclusive and excluding. Leaving aside for the moment that One Nation has adopted a hostile stance towards Australian Muslims, it is clear that a certain disaffection also strikes out against Aboriginal peoples and asylum seekers. *Principle* 3 states that "One Nation opposes acknowledging Aboriginal and Torres Strait Islanders in the preamble to the Australian Constitution, as One Nation believes that *all Australians are owners and custodians of this land* and should work toward unification, not segregation, under the one law for all" (One Nation 2017, emphasis added). This statement is a calculated insult. Ms Hanson is not averse to keeping up the insults, while she denies being a "racist". She said that she was "disgusted" at the inclusion of a segment during the opening of the Commonwealth Games in January 2018 that was a tribute to Aboriginal culture. "They are not what Australia is about". She betrayed one of her many misconstructions of words, by claiming that she was "indigenous", being born in Australia. She was "sick and tired of being made to feel like a second-class citizen in my own country" (Bickers 2018). The insult was meant as a clear rejection of the common acknowledgement that Aboriginal peoples are, and have been for 60,000 years, the original owners and custodians of the land, and that European invasion has all but annihilated their identity and culture, often with brutal deprivation. That such antipathies may be shared with many ordinary Australians indicates the populist stand of the party, but scarcely accords with democratic solidarity or the "equality" otherwise proclaimed by One Nation.

Considering the question of populism and democracy, Fennema (2000 p. 29) seeks "a more substantial conception of democracy…[that] cannot, in a multicultural society, be based on popular consensus". Let us call this "strong democracy", rooted in history and philosophical reflections on that history. We need to observe here what democratic equality means in the long development of democracy. To take a working definition approach, the slogan of the French Revolution "liberty, equality and fraternity (let us say, solidarity or better, community)", supplemented by Abraham Lincoln's emphasis on the place of the people, equality is a grounded concept of democracy. It originated with the foundational democracy in ancient Greece, where equality of treatment was taken seriously. This statement has to take into account that the ancient Athenians looked internally to their own populace and did not regard dwellers of other communities as their equals. We also have to take into account that the Athenians owned slaves who did not enjoy "rights", although their general treatment as "fellow workers" was more benign than we might otherwise think. Moreover, Athenian women, who were carriers of Athenian citizenship, did not enjoy political "rights" in the same way as did the men. Yet even when these anomalies (to our modern way of thinking) are taken into account, no community before or since has paid as much attention to the value of the common person. Every Athenian *citizen* was invited, indeed compelled, to take part in the running of the state. If he was a citizen it made no difference whether he was abjectly poor or totally uneducated. The exclusion of women, slaves, and foreign residents from political participation makes a little more sense when we reflect that the Athenian citizen was conscripted into the armed forces, and a decision by the ruling assembly, in which all citizens were eligible to take part, could mean that they all had to go off to face the enemy at war on the same day as they took the vote.

The ancient Athenians took the scourge of poverty and inequality of wealth very seriously. Many of the highest aristocrats were devoted to the democratic constitution and contributed willingly to the communal treasury with their wealth. In one of the classic texts of the democracy, the aristocrat and devout democrat Pericles declared that the only shame in poverty was the neglect or refusal to fight against it (Thucydides 1968, p. 94). The first European communities in North America, having fled from oppression in the Old World, set up systems which, even if by an accident of history, closely resembled the Athenian method of government. In this case their citizenship depended on church membership wherein they were received as equals, since any person, uneducated, unskilled, poor, might still be a vessel of God's revelation to the community. In Massachusetts they were indeed compared with Athens but believed that they were far removed from the pagan Athenians by their common Christianity.

Thus far, none of this quite addresses Pauline Hanson's One Nation position. Indeed, the manifesto promises that "we care enough to speak for the voiceless and the powerless". Yet their *Principles* are happy enough to exclude Muslims from equal rights and to belittle the claims of Aboriginal peoples to recognition for their deprivations over the last 200 of the 60,000 years of continuous occupation of the lands as the oldest living culture in the world. Athens put its own people first, but in a few short steps its devotion to equality was extended to a worldwide "citizenry". A foreigner taking every advantage of the openness of Athenian society, Diogenes of Sinope, was allegedly the first to call himself "a citizen of the world" (although it just may have been Socrates who was first). As founder of the Cynic philosophers, Diogenes's followers evolved the Stoic philosophy that took the cosmopolitan idea of world citizenship literally, declaring that nature had endowed all people with souls that were of equal value around the world. The Christians, who in their first years were closely allied with the Stoics (and the Cynics [Downing 1992]), took all people created by God to be equally valuable in God's eyes. Setting aside the execrable wars against infidels and heathens led by people who did not understand the message they were supposed to be advancing, Christianity ideally held to a worldwide fellowship of humankind.

At this point, Hanson's repeated condemnation of foreigners began with Asians who 20 years ago "swamped" us; on her re-entry into the Senate in 2016 she had found a new stalking horse paddling in the marsh, for it was now Muslims who were "swamping" us, while Aboriginal peoples who have, according to her, no special claim for fair treatment by the government, make her stand profoundly against the spirit of democracy (as indeed are the positions of the Coalition and the Labor Party on asylum seekers who arrive by boat—on this score both the major parties are dog-whistling populists with no regard to the opprobrium history will heap upon them).

In her second maiden speech in the Senate, Hanson said: "In my first speech in 1996, I said we were in danger of being swamped by Asians. This was not said out of disrespect for Asians but meant as a slap in the face to both Liberal and

Labor governments to immigration targeting cultures purely for the vote …" (Butler 2016; Hanson 2016). Yet the disrespect was implicit in the statement. And she went on: "Now we are in danger of being swamped by Muslims who bear a culture and ideology that is incompatible with our own". The "incompatibility" was manifold:

> She criticised dedicated swimming pool times for Muslim women, halal certification ('a money-making racket') and shari'ah law; she also raised banning Muslim immigration, banning Australian companies from paying for halal certification, and stopping the construction of Muslim schools. She also spoke about welfare and unemployment… (Butler 2016; Hanson 2016)

In February 2018 Hanson introduced a private member's bill into the Senate to amend the *Migration Act 1958*. The intention was to increase the qualifying residency period for immigrants seeking Australian citizenship from one year to eight. During this period they should demonstrate behavior "in a manner consistent with the Australian values". They could also be observed as to whether they "want to go and fight for ISIS …" (Kainth and Schaller 2018). Again, she had Muslims in the crosshairs. In any case, "Australian values" are a highly contested topic, and one could assess some of the main "principles" of the One Nation Party as decidedly "un-Australian".

2.2 A Christian Country?

Pauline Hanson makes this claim repeatedly, but again, there is little indication that she understands the content of her words. Certainly, for the general public "Christian" is no longer a "hurrah" word with the force of "democracy". Indeed, many would dispute this as an accurate description of a multicultural society containing many religions besides the religions of "The Book": Christians, Jews, and Muslims. Undoubtedly, many Christians would claim at least a Christian heritage for Australia. The Encyclical of 1891 by Pope Leo XIII, *Rerum Novarum*, for example, had immeasurable influence on the growth of a fair society in Australia (as far as it has remained so), not least the introduction by H. B. Higgins of a "living wage", pitted explicitly against the "despotic" power of employers (Lake 2018, pp. 240–242; Sawer 2003, p. 59). Religious influences, both Catholic and Protestant, had profound influence on the formation of the main Australian political parties at the turn of the 20th century (Bollen 1972; Duncan 1991). From the start, when British settlers (invaders?) brought the Gospel to these shores, among the persons influential in setting up (European) Australia were many devout Christians, even if some of them sometimes acted in ways that were not true to their faith—among them colonial governors Richard Bourke, George Gipps, Lachlan Macquarie; the early prime ministers Andrew Fisher, Alfred Deakin, John Cook; and pioneers and leaders in various fields like Caroline Chisholm, Mary McKillop, Edith Cowan, John Dunmore Lang, William Spence, John Flynn, Vida Goldstein, Weary Dunlop, Douglas Nicholls, Neville Bonner, Betty Cuthbert, Peter Norman, Brian Booth, Nick Farr-Jones, David Pocock, and Israel Folau. Demonstrably much of their efforts for society were driven by faith. Examining the journals of the colonies' prominent explorers, Roland Boer discovers that so many—Sturt, Stuart, Mitchell, Eyre, Grey, Giles, Leichhardt—contextualized their exertions within the Bible narrative, confessing their dedication to unfolding new pastures for God's Word (and commercial benefit). For all that their universal reliance on Providence could be construed as an unconscious collaboration in "panopticism" (Boer 2001), they indicate that the origins of colonial Australia, far from the allegedly "post-Enlightenment" atheism favored by some journalists, were officially laid on foundations of a "Christian civilization".[1]

This excursus would no doubt be challenged by secularists, particularly journalists who use census statistics to show that church attendances and acknowledged Christian affiliations are falling, but such observations hardly bear on the historical basis of society-building. Since the unmasking of widespread sexual abuse among the clergy, they are right to say that the churches have lost much of their authority. Pauline Hanson's utterances give no hint that she is aware of any of this tradition. The passage is included here to demonstrate that her repeated declaration of Australia as a "Christian country" seems to be ignorant of the arguments on both sides of the question and, moreover, apart from wishing "to speak for the voiceless and the powerless", her policies bear little resemblance to some of the central tenets of Christianity. *Her use of the term is purely instrumental*. It is a type of "cultural" Christianity disconnected from the religion itself (Jenkins 2007, pp. 260–261). First, it is intended by association as a defense of a more-or-less fanatical nationalism often associated with right-wing populism. Second, by the juxtaposition of terms, it seems (correctly in my opinion) to associate Christianity with the foundations of secularism, without her following through the openness and inclusiveness that secularization implies. Third, it is used as a blunt weapon for beating Muslims. In her 2016 maiden Senate speech, Hanson announced: "Australia is predominantly a Christian country, but our government is secular. Our Constitution prevents governments from imposing religious rules and teachings. The separation of church and state has become an essential component of our way of life, and anything that threatens that separation threatens our freedom" (Hanson 2016).

The separation of church and state was certainly a Christian doctrine devised to avoid government interference in worship and the conduct of ecclesiastical affairs, and especially to prevent the "establishment" of any particular denomination as an officially imposed body associated in government. The establishment of the Church of England in Britain once imposed disabilities on many Roman Catholics and Dissenters that prevented them, for example, from any association with the great universities. Much of the early migration to the New World was intended to free people from such disabilities, and it is no surprise that the doctrine of separation was pioneered by the Charter of Rhode Island and eventually the Constitution of the United States (Hamburger 2004). The doctrine was designed to foster toleration but, curiously, Hanson rails against the "mantra" of tolerance: Her nationalistic declamation "is about belonging, respect and commitment to fight for Australia. This will never be traded or given up for the mantras of diversity or tolerance. Australia had a national

---

[1] Boer shows that much of the journalistic records were based on guidelines set by the Royal Society.

identity before Federation, and it had nothing to do with diversity and everything to do with belonging" (Hanson 2016). There is an echo of nostalgia here for the execrable White Australia policy, despite Hanson's protestations about welcoming foreigners who conform to "Australian values".

The undoubted target of those who allegedly do not conform to Australian values are the "swamping" Muslims. One Nation's *Principle* 21:

> To stop the teaching and infiltration of Islam and its totalitarian ideology, that opposes our democracy, way of life and laws. To ban the Burqa in public places, government buildings and schools. To make genital mutilation of young girls a criminal offence, carrying heavy sentences. To stop islamists (sic) and their families from receiving welfare benefits; we are a Christian country, only one marriage is recognised. Ban the building of any more Mosques.

There is some emotive language here: Islam is guilty of "infiltration" like a fifth column or a spy colony; Islam has apparently ceased to be a religion and is now an "ideology". To single out "islamists" as ineligible for welfare benefits, or to ban the building of mosques, is discriminatory in the extreme. In this "Christian" (but apparently intolerant) country only one marriage is recognized—that, at least, has changed radically. The "totalitarian ideology" opposes democracy, but this is a fundamentalist reading of the Qur'an (Maddox 2015). Just as few genuine Christians would take God's command to exterminate the Amalekites (1 Samuel 15: 18) as a serious recommendation for international policy today, few of the 1.6 billion Muslims in the world today would take literally conversion of infidels by the sword (Qur'an 9. 5, 29). As Kirk MacGregor (2017) shows, "A higher percentage of Muslim Americans reject killing civilians than any other group in America". Muslims have lived peacefully in democracies in many countries under benign interpretations of their own scriptures, while Muslim scholars have elaborated many ethical ideals conducive to democracy. Not least of democratic benefit was the preservation and publication of the writings of Aristotle by medieval Muslim scholars. The great Ibn Rushd (aka Averroes), indeed, followed Plato in advocating the absolute equal rights of women.

One Nation is particularly hostile to *Shari'ah* law. *Principle* 22: "To oppose Sharia Law ever being allowed in Australia. We are a *Christian* country with one law for all …". *Principle* 25: "One Nation supports the refugee program, but we must have a say in who comes in. We must be mindful of taking people that are *Christian*, and genuine refugees" (emphasis added). Yet nowadays, and often through history, many Muslims live happily in Christian or secular societies. There are signs of a friendliness towards democracy in North Africa, Iran, and Malaysia (Ghozzi 2002; Kane 2007; Rutherford 2006; Weiss 2004). Some recent Islamic leaders on the international stage—including Indonesia's ex-President Bambang Yudhoyono and Iran's ex-President Muhammad Khatami—were intent on advancing the cause of democracy. Law professor Abdullahi Ahmed An-Na'im believes that a secular state is necessary for the observance of *Shari'ah* law in personal life: Traditional Islam adopts a pluralist outlook, while the diversity of Muslim practice is evident on all sides (Sidahmed 2011).

Pauline Hanson's xenophobia extends to immigrants who have become Australian citizens, and her proposals, in effect aiming to disfranchise them, are an attack on our democracy. It is at the least a denial of Christian charity and humanity. It is argued here that the notion of human equality embraces all humanity worldwide, but the clear intent of One Nation *Principles* is to deem certain immigrant Australians as less than equal to the rest. The party has in effect established rules for "Australianness" through a myopic outlook that demands an intrusive probe into the thoughts and intentions of others as to their commitment to "Australian values". There are sinister echoes of McCarthyism in these tones.

2.3 Militant Democracy and One Nation

To the extent that these criticisms of One Nation's antidemocratic posture may be sustained, and to the extent that One Nation's ultra-nationalism resembles the right-wing activity of ultra-nationalist parties elsewhere, it is pertinent to ask whether a defense of democracy against it is warranted.

When democracy was undeniably under attack during the gathering mists of the Second World War, the German political scientist Karl Loewenstein, despairing of the inability of the Weimar Republic to defend itself from internecine attack, sought refuge in the United States. In 1937 he announced "militant democracy". The Nazi opponents of democracy had white-anted the republic from within and had taken over the German state by stealth. What exercised Loewenstein most was that the Nazis had come to power legally, and the democratic state was powerless to stop them. The legal processes of the state were its Trojan Horse, while its generic toleration had granted far too much leeway to the attackers. "It is the exaggerated formalism of the rule of law which under the enchantment of formal equality does not see fit to exclude from the game parties that deny the very existence of the rules" (Loewenstein 1937a, p. 424). To Loewenstein, Nazism moved with the irresistible force of populist "emotionalism". This entailed "high-pitched nationalist enthusiasm" and "permanent psychic coercion" (Loewenstein 1937a, p. 418).

Some defenses against attack were obvious and reasonable. It was perfectly fair for democracies to outlaw paramilitary parades on the part of anti-state political organizations, and the wearing of "indoctrinary haberdashery" or paramilitary uniforms. Loewenstein went much further, however, declaring that, to defeat the enemy within, the state should imitate its methods: "In politics, the defense is shaped according to the fighting methods of the assailant" (1937b, p. 642). He unashamedly advocated secret police to keep opposition groups under surveillance, and even the clandestine monitoring of communications. The obvious danger here is that a blanket interception of communications could scarcely exclude intrusion into the lawful discourse of innocent people. In the end he came down to adopting an "authoritarian democracy" (Loewenstein 1937b, p. 657)—surely a contradiction in terms. Loewenstein argued for the disfranchisement of fascist-leaning opposition groups, but Fennema (2000, p. 29) cogently argues against the "repression" of dissidents, since this itself undermines basic democratic ideals. In the end, Loewenstein's "authoritarian democracy" boiled down to rule by an elite coalition of "liberal-minded" leaders; but who would have the authority to choose and appoint such paragons of political virtue? It is pretty much the kind of elite government we have now, minus the liberal minds.

The question remains whether Australia needs a defense against such parties and groups as One Nation.

Recent events in the United States, to which Australia, according to the former prime minister, Malcolm Turnbull, is "joined at the hip", demonstrate the danger of anti-democratic elements as an enemy within. In August 2017 the neo-fascist demonstrations in Charlottesville, Virginia, on behalf of white men, and deliberately threatening to black people and alien residents, openly violated the democratic requirement of equality by seeking to deny "the other" a full place in society. The United States Government may feel internally secure in its multi-layered structures of power, but it has a responsibility, on behalf of all its people, to suppress such threatening "white supremacist" demonstrations. Observations on these phenomena may suffer from a "methodological whiteness" (Bhambra 2017). On Loewenstein's terms, all anti-system movements should be legally banned—in this case the Ku-Klux-Klan, historically responsible for so many innocent deaths, Identity Evropa, Proud Boys, Neo-Nazis, insolently chanting "blood and soil" (*Blut und Boden*), and other "white supremacists". There is no significant equivalent movement in Australia, but the One Nation Party should come under scrutiny for its often-expressed anti-social views. Pauline Hanson has repeatedly railed against welfare payments to Aboriginal peoples, justified by their ethnic origin. She has often spoken about them in obliquely racist terms, a position that amounts to "white supremacy", especially alongside her hope to exclude Asians and Muslims from Australia, and curtailing welfare for Aboriginal peoples. Since no violent demonstration is involved, there is no question of banning her party, especially when Australians value the proportional voting system for electing the Senate. Nevertheless, a strong democracy could consider a substantial system of suspension from Parliament when anti-democratic speech has been made public—serious suspension such as a week or a month. Her insolent and racist demonstration in 2017 of wearing a burqa in the Senate should have merited much more serious reproof than the scolding she received from the Leader of the Government in the Senate. It was contempt of Parliament at one level, but at another it associated her own voters, and the One Nation Party, with a gesture of directed insolence that shatters the democratic notion of toleration. At present, One Nation officially represents minority politics. Yet there are wider ramifications of the racist rhetoric in Australian politics, as Max Kaiser demonstrates:

> While it is fair to say that fascist groups such as the United Patriots Front and the True Blue Crew are quite marginal, the ideas expressed in this event description [a fascist rally in Melbourne, 25 June 2017] are certainly not. In fact, they express in crude terms ideas that are parroted daily in the Murdoch press and given representation in parliament by One Nation and politicians like Cory Bernardi and George Christensen. There is a discourse here that runs across a recognisable reactionary spectrum, from Blair Cottrell of the United Patriots Front to Chris Uhlmann *repeating alt-right talking points on cultural Marxist infiltration* [see Wilson 2016] to Malcolm Turnbull being unafraid of using veiled racist rhetoric on terrorism, refugees or citizenship tests to prop up his failing prime ministership. There was no better display of how integral a racist worldview is to large segments of Australia's ruling

class than the Bill Leak love-in occasioned by the cartoonist's death, while just recently the Institute for Public Affairs endorsed Avi Yemini's planned fascist Islamophobic rally in Sydney (Kaiser 2017; emphasis in original).

From the resemblance between much "mainstream" political rhetoric that is implicitly racist, Hanson might appear more centrist than she would like to be viewed. Pragmatism can trump "idealism"; at the 2017 Western Australia state elections Hanson made a preference deal, kept secret from some of her own candidates, with the Liberals (Probyn 2017). Candidates who resigned from the party to escape Hanson's "brutal dictatorship" reported inordinate financial demands made upon them, including at first a penalty requiring any candidate who left the party to pay a penance of $250,000 (a demand later withdrawn after complaint). A high-profile One Nation campaigner, Margaret Dodd, left the party over the Western Australia preference deal. "[Hanson] is a populist, she goes on things that will get her the attention that she wants, get her in that power position that she wants", she said. "It's about power for Pauline" (Meldrum-Hanna et al. 2017).

The fact that much of the so-called Centre-Right is prone to dog-whistling populism does not obscure the extremist position adopted by One Nation. In fact, Hanson is apparently more than willing to be guided by avowed populist extreme right parties in the United States and Europe. In the Netherlands, Geert Wilders provides Hanson with a template. As Nicholas Morieson points out, "Europeans appear to be reacting to their new Muslim neighbors by identifying Western culture as 'Judeo-Christian and Humanist', as Wilders, leader of the Dutch Party For Freedom, puts it" (Morieson 2016):

> The populist right has seized on this new identity. By arguing that Muslims threaten the West's Judeo-Christian and secular culture, it has propelled itself into positions of power in a number of countries, including Australia, France and the Netherlands (Morieson 2016).

Morieson (2017) draws upon Juergen Habermas's announcement of the return of religion to the public arena in Europe to explain why the political right draws on a Christian heritage to square off against Muslims (Habermas 2006). Wilders, the leader of the Netherlands Party for Freedom, the PVV (*Party vor vrijheid*), resorts to the Judaeo-Christian heritage of Europe, which he alleges is under threat from Islam. More broadly, the culture of Europe is said to be unified by Judaeo-Christian-Humanist ideals (Wilders 2015). The claim does not recall Europe's dark history in respect of Judaism, nor do conservative Christian anti-Semites often reflect that the Christian founder, Jesus Christ, was an ethnic, cultural, and religious Jew all his life. Speaking to a sympathetic American audience, whom he charged to maintain eternal vigilance, Wilders proclaimed: "My views, in a nutshell, are that Islam, rather than a religion, is predominantly a totalitarian ideology striving for world dominance. I believe that Islam and freedom are incompatible" (Wilders 2012). These words bear a striking resemblance to claims made by Hanson: "We're talk (sic) about a political ideology. They would say it is a religion. I know and they say it's religion of peace. We know that's not true either" (in Smethurst 2016). One view is that One Nation is under the spell of foreign right-wing ideologies: "Although ostensibly an Australian nationalist party, Pauline Hanson's One Nation is in large measure serving as a political portal for the introduction of American and European far-right positions, policies and rhetoric into the Australian political landscape" (Dorling 2017). One can scarcely disentangle the nationalist and xenophobic elements in the One Nation position, yet there is an irony in the fact that its "Australianness" is so far instructed by non-Australian rhetoric. On both counts, One Nation is gnawing at the foundations of Australian democracy.

In Chap. 3 of this volume, Tony Lynch explains how far One Nation resembles policies traditionally adopted by conservative forces in Australian politics during the White Australia era and since. The struggle to save democracy is uphill when populist elements are much in accord with ruling parties. Loewenstein's campaign, applied to Australia, could well include protecting democracy against the government. There has been much recent concern about hate speech in general, particularly over Section 18c of the Racial Discrimination Act, which was enacted in 1975 to prohibit vituperation motivated by "race, colour or national or ethnic origin". The section prohibits actions that are "reasonably likely, in all the circumstances, to offend, insult, humiliate or intimidate another person or a group of people". This wording has come under attack, mainly from conservative opinion, on the grounds that it restricts freedom of speech. The government's proposed amendment was to change the words "offend, insult, humiliate or intimidate" to the single word "harass". In March 2017 the amendments were defeated after fervid debate in the Senate. Free speech is of course a treasured attribute of democracy, but offense, insult, humiliation, or intimidation on the grounds of race, sex, or religion may imply the serious compromise of another's freedom and, in any case, it subverts a commitment to the equal worth and dignity of all people. Government action has exploited all these modes of speech, *including harassment*, against alien residents.

It is significant that the Australian Liberal-National Government sponsored the move to allow forms of hate speech. Erosion of the democratic ideal by governments in power is a patent threat. In the current Australian case, both major sides in the two-party system are complicit in the denigration of "the stranger at the gate". Both Labor and the Liberal-National Coalition have publicly implied that asylum seekers who have arrived at or near Australia by boat are illegal entrants, queue-jumpers, (illegitimate) economic migrants, potential terrorists, or even, in the case of the former Liberal Prime Minister John Howard, infanticides, and "we don't want people like that". It was also Howard's government that threatened to imprison *as a people-smuggler* the captain of the Norwegian vessel, the *Tampa*, who in abiding by international law, had sought to disembark rescued asylum seekers on Christmas Island (Brennan 2003; Marr and Wilkinson 2003, p. 33). It was more convenient for governments, especially Labor, to turn their fury on the "wicked" people smugglers and their "business model". There may have been some illegality or questionable ethics on the part of these "smugglers" (what price Oskar Schindler or Dietrich Bonhoeffer?), but the refugees themselves were in no respect illegals.

As a signatory to the Universal Declaration of Human Rights (indeed as a principal drafter of the Declaration and now, hypocritically, as a member of the UN Human Rights Council [Galloway 2017]), which ruled "Not only all people but also all races were equal in dignity and worth" (Fennema 2000, p. 4), Australia has an obligation to assist asylum seekers. The vile excuse used by politicians that they turn back the asylum-seeker boats to avoid drownings at sea is a hypocritical distraction from our own illegality. As if turning boats back, let alone casting away asylum seekers in rubber dinghies, removes their exposure to dangers at sea. It is true that many people did drown at sea, but it would undoubtedly have been much cheaper and more humane for Australia to organize a rescue force (as it once did for a single round-the-world sailor) and resettle the refugees in Australia, than to pursue them in predatory fashion and hold them indefinitely in damaging and dangerous concentration camps in Papua New Guinea and Nauru. A United Nations inspector, the French Judge Louis Joinet, declared that he knew of no "more gross abuse of human rights" than conditions in these camps (Manne 2004, p. 34). Conditions in the camps have grown worse in the subsequent 13 years of illegal detention. Australia's breaching of its international obligations to people held in offshore detention has been meticulously documented by Gleeson (2016, pp. 403–406). Appealing to the lowest instincts of decent people in the electorate, who, under strong democratic leadership, could well be persuaded to support measures of justice if they were not repeatedly told lies about asylum seekers, both alternative national governments in Australia stand squarely in the way of the defense of a "strong democracy". It is easier for leaders to stir up the emotion of hate rather than of love.

2.4 Conclusion

Drawing the focus on One Nation, it is tempting to conclude that it differentiates itself from the "mainstream" of politics by putting hate at the *center* of its platform and, on the terms adopted in this paper, its stand is distinctly anti-democratic. For reasons discussed, democracy may not be defended by outlawing parties or disenfranchising citizens. If One Nation were to adopt some of the more grotesque signs of populist parties, such as para-military displays, then the situation would be different. For all that, Hanson's leadership of large numbers of the nation's citizens into the halls of xenophobia undermines the basis of civil society, which depends on at least respect for other citizens, if not the actual bonds of friendship to which Aristotle adverted. The legislation against hate speech, still not watered down, should be applied rigorously to One Nation pronouncements that denigrate the status of any citizens or potential citizens. For arrant displays of xenophobia, such as Hanson's wearing of a Muslim burqa in the Senate, the Parliament should strengthen its own sanctions. To ban the senator from parliament for an extended time would not disenfranchise her supporters but would signal to them and to the nation that such assaults on parliament, and such blatant insults to certain Australian citizens, are also an attack on our democracy. Freedom of speech, freedom of assembly, freedom of religion are all privileges accorded by living in a democracy, but they are privileges to be neither spurned nor abused. In the end, the components of democracy should not be amplified into an excuse for undemocratic behavior. After all, it is the democracy itself that must be defended.

References

Bhamdra, G. K. (2017). Brexit, Trump, and "methodological whiteness": On the misrecognition of race and class. *British Journal of Sociology, 68*(1), S214–S232.

Bickers, C. (2018). Disgusting: Pauline Hanson blasts Commonwealth Games ceremony's focus on indigenous culture. *News.com.au*, 7 January. HANSON/Pauline%20Hanson%20blasts%20Commonwealth%20Games%20opening%20ceremony.html. Accessed June 8, 2018.

Boer, R. (2001). Explorer hermeneutics, or fat damper and sweetened tea. *Semeia, 88,* 71–95.

Bollen, J. D. (1972). *Protestantism and social reform in New South Wales, 1890–1910.* Carlton: University of Melbourne.

Brennan, F. (2003). *Tampering with Asylum. A universal humanitarian problem.* St Lucia: University of Queensland Press.

Butler, J. (2016). Pauline Hanson says Australia in danger of being swamped by Muslims. *Huffington Post*, 14 September. https://www.huffingtonpost.com.au/2016/09/14/pauline-hanson-says-australia-has-been-swamped-by-muslims_a_21471713/. Accessed June 9, 2018.

Dorling, P. (2017). The American far-right origins of Pauline Hanson's views on Islam. *Australia Institute*, 29 January. http://www.tai.org.au/content/american-far-right-origins-pauline-hanson%E2%80%99s-views-islam. Accessed June 9, 2018.

Downing, F. G. (1992). *Cynics and Christian origins.* Edinburgh: T. & T. Clark.

Duncan, B. (1991). *The church's social teaching. From* Rerum Novarum *to 1931.* North Blackburn: HarperCollins.

Fennema, M. (2000). Legal repression of extreme-right parties and racial discrimination. In R. Koopmans & P. Statham (Eds.), *Challenging immigration and ethnic relations politics* (pp. 1–35). Oxford: Oxford University Press.

Galloway, K. (2017). The empty platitudes of Australian human rights. *Eureka Street*, 24 October. https://www.eurekastreet.com.au/article.aspx?aeid=54201. Accessed June 9, 2018.

Ghozzi, K. (2002). The study of resilience and decay in ulema groups: Tunisia and Iran as an example. *Sociology of Religion, 63*(3), 317–335.

Gleeson, M. (2016). *Offshore. Behind the wire on Manus and Nauru.* Sydney: University of New South Wales Press.

Habermas, J. (2006). Religion in the public sphere. *European Journal of Philosophy, 4*(1), 1–25.

Hamburger, P. (2004). *Separation of church and state.* Boston: Harvard University Press.

Hanson, P. (2016). Transcript: Pauline Hanson's 2016 Maiden Speech to the Senate. *ABC News*, 15 September. http://www.abc.net.au/news/2016-09-15/pauline-hanson-maiden-speech-2016/7847136. Accessed June 9, 2018.

Jenkins, P. (2007). *God's continent.* Oxford: Oxford University Press.

Kainth, S., & Schaller, M. (2018). Pauline Hanson wants migrants to wait 8 years to become citizens. *SBS Radio*, 9 February. https://www.sbs.com.au/yourlanguage/punjabi/en/article/2018/02/09/pauline-hanson-wants-migrants-wait-8-years-become-citizens. Accessed June 8, 2018.

Kaiser, M. (2017). Six theses on fascism after Charlottesville. *Overland*, 18 August. https://overland.org.au/2017/08/six-theses-on-fascism-after-charlottesville/. Accessed June 9, 2018.

Kane, O. (2007). Moderate revivalists: Islamic inroads in sub-Saharan Africa. *Harvard International Review, 29*(2), 64–68.

Lake, M. (2018). *The Bible in Australia.* Sydney: NewSouth Publishing.

Loewenstein, K. (1937a). Militant democracy and fundamental rights—Part 1. *American Political Science Review, 33*(3), 417–432.

Loewenstein, K. (1937b). Militant democracy and fundamental rights—Part 2. *American Political Science Review, 33*(4), 538–558.

MacGregor, K. (2017). *Welcoming muslims. Understanding the differences between 98% of the world's Muslims, Islamists, and Jihadists.* https://www.youtube.com/watch?v=gRQN4lzeXMg. Accessed June 9, 2018.

Maddox, G. (2015). The prospects for democratic convergence: Islam and democracy. *Political Theology, 16*(4), 305–328.

Manne, R. (2004). The Howard years: A political interpretation. In R. Manne (Ed.), *The Howard years* (pp. 3–53). Melbourne: Black Inc.

Marr, D., & Wilkinson, M. (2003). *Dark victory*. Crows Nest: Allen & Unwin.

Meldrum-Hanna, C., Richards, D., & Drum, P. (2017). One Nation former candidates, party insiders, reveal Pauline Hanson's "brutal dictatorship". *ABC Four Corners*, 3 April. http://www.abc.net.a u/news/2017-04-03/one-nation-accused-of-brutal-dictatorship/8408978. Accessed June 9, 2018.

Morieson, N. (2016). By framing secular society as a Christian creation, Hanson's revival goes beyond simple racism. *The Conversation*, 8 December. https://theconversation.com/by-frami ng-secular-society-as-a-christian-creation-hansons-revival-goes-beyond-simple-racism-67707. Accessed June 9, 2019.

Morieson, N. (2017, September). *Religion and right-wing populism in the Netherlands*. Paper Presented to the Annual Conference, Australian Political Studies Association, Melbourne.

One Nation. (2017). *Principles and objectives*. Principles%20%26%20Objectives%20_%20Pauli ne%20Hanson's%20One%20Nation.html. Accessed June 9, 2018.

Probyn, A. (2017). Pauline Hanson responds to One Nation candidates' criticism of WA Liberal preference deal. *ABC 7.30*, 15 February. http://www.abc.net.au/news/2017-02-15/if-you-dont-li ke-it-dont-stand-pauline-hanson/8273600. Accessed June 9, 2018.

Rutherford, B. K. (2006). What do Egypt's Islamists want? Moderate Islam and the rise of Islamic constitutionalism. *Middle East Journal, 60*(4), 207–232.

Sawer, M. (2003). *The ethical state? Social liberalism in Australia*. Carlton: Melbourne University Press.

Sidahmed, A. S. (2011). Abdullahi Ahmed An-Na'Im, Islam and secular state: Negotiating the future of Shari'a. *Windsor Yearbook of Access to Justice, 29,* 249–251.

Smethurst, A. (2016). Pauline Hanson to push for ban on new mosques, royal commission into Islam. *Herald Sun*, July 4. http://www.news.com.au/national/federal-election/pauline-hanson-t o-push-for-ban-on-new-mosques-royal-commission-into-islam/news-story/1fde2f7903942cad6 387d93fc210d0dd. Accessed June 9, 2018.

Thucydides. (1968). *The history of The Peloponnesian War* (R. Crawley Trans.). London: Dent.

Weiss, M. L. (2004). The changing shape of Islamist politics in Malaysia. *Journal of East Asian Studies, 4*(1), 139–174.

Wilders, G. (2012). Speech at the Western Conservative Summit. Denver, 30 June. https://www.g eertwilders.nl/index.php/component/content/article/87-news/1795-speech-geert-wilders-at-the- western-conservative-summit-denver-30-june-2012. Accessed July 12, 2018.

Wilders, G. (2015). Speech, Bornholm, Denmark, June 13. *Geert Wilders Weblog*, June 13, 2015. https://www.geertwilders.nl/index.php/94-english/1937-speech-geert-wilders-bornholm-d enmark-june-13-2015 (as cited by Morieson 2017).

Wilson, J. (2016). Chris Uhlmann should mind his language on "Cultural Marxism". *The Guardian*, 22 February. https://www.theguardian.com/commentisfree/2016/feb/22/chris-uhlmann-should- mind-his-language-on-cultural-marxism. Accessed June 9, 2018.

Chapter 3
Pauline Hanson's One Nation: Right-Populism in a Neoliberal World

Tony Lynch

Abstract When Pauline Hanson's One Nation right-populism emerged as a political force in Australia many took it to be a radical threat to the health of political democracy. It was nothing of the sort. It was, rather, a symptomatic expression of the failure of that democracy as elites of the traditional labour and business parties embraced a shared policy orientation that undercut their ties to their traditional working-class and middle class bases. Hanson's right-populism emerged from the increasingly status anxious traditional Liberal Party base as it drew upon and reasserted the class-repressing, status elevating, middle class ideology of home that the founder of the party, Robert Menzies, had laid out in the 1940s. This ideology defined the status of the traditionally conservative middle classes as patriotic and self-reliant; frugal savers whose status demanded government refuse the entitlement claims of those perceived as the more feckless and less prudent in the community, and protect them from the philistine monetary aspirations of those Menzies derided as occupants of "great luxury hotels." Today, this conception founds a nostalgic populism of personal and nationalistic pride in being "at home", and having worked hard for that "home". Its broader politics are that of "border control" and a rigid control of access. Those "invited in" must share and respect the values of the household, and, domestically, of a powerful antipathy to government redistribution downwards that reflects a need to divide the deserving from the undeserving on the basis of the amount of pride one takes in one's home, its values, maintenance and cohesiveness.

Keywords Home · Neoliberalism · Populism · Racism · Status

T. Lynch (✉)
School of Humanities, Arts and Social Sciences, University of New England, Armidale, NSW 2351, Australia
e-mail: alynch@une.edu.au

© Springer Nature Singapore Pte Ltd. 2019
B. Grant et al. (eds.), *The Rise of Right-Populism*,
https://doi.org/10.1007/978-981-13-2670-7_3

3.1 Situating PHON in Australian Democracy

The essays in the predecessor volume to this book (*Pauline Hanson: One Nation & Australian Politics*, University of New England Press, 1997) were written in an environment that inclined some contributors, certainly myself, to see Pauline Hanson and the subsequent *Pauline Hanson's One Nation* (PHON) as a kind of unexpected irruption into Australian politics. While Hanson's political view had always had fringe expressions locally, typically with a strongly racist tinge, it was essentially a foreign, "anti-Australian", probably right-wing American-style "populism". In 1996 Hanson had won a controversial and crushing 1996 electoral victory as a dis-endorsed Liberal candidate for the federal House of Representatives in what previously had been the safest Labor (ALP) seat in Queensland. This was followed by the dramatic and secretive intervention of David Oldfield (at the time political adviser of Tony Abbott, federal Liberal member for Warringah) in turning the independent member, now famous or notorious for her maiden parliamentary speech, into leader of the eponymously named Pauline Hanson's One Nation. It seemed natural, therefore, to frame her political rise as a disruptive "Right Populist" challenge to the traditional Coalition/Labor two-party dichotomy, and so a challenge, indeed a danger, to the logic (at least, the decency and rationality) of liberal democracy itself. Certainly, this was the view I expressed at the time. I welcome the opportunity to reflect on this framing, for while PHON is certainly a style of right populism, the rest of that story now seems to me mistaken, and for a number of reasons.

The first mistake lay in thinking that Australia had, at the time, a well-functioning democracy. Such a democracy—where voting *means* something—requires that the choice be a real one: not merely one of branding, but of policy substance, with policies that valorize and express the interests and values of distinctive mass constituencies.

In Australia this was pretty much the truth, and certainly for the 40 or so years after the Second World War. We had an essentially two-party system, with the working-class unionist ALP, and the anti-Labor middle class, business friendly, Liberal Party, senior partner in a permanent Coalition with the rural conservative Country (later National) Party (see, for example, Maddox et al. 2002).

Things changed with the Hawke/Keating Labor Government's 13-year ascendancy between 1983 and 1996. This period, right from the start, saw the incoming ALP largely ditch its traditional working-class orientation. The ALP claimed that unexpectedly finding a budget "black hole" meant its traditional programs could not be funded. Alleviating this black hole meant immediately floating the Australian dollar, removing controls on foreign exchange and on Australian interest rates, and allowing foreign competition in banking. The ALP thus converged to the right on a set of "modernizing" business and market-friendly policies that saw the essential political task as one of returning more of the profit share to capital at the expense of labor. This strategy, inevitably and as a necessity, also reduced the political and bargaining power and reorganized the Labor movement both generally and within the party.

It marked a move—instigated from the Left—away from the politics of economic class to a "nationalistic" politics of universal "reform" in which all, capital and labor, were called upon to contribute their share as "entrepreneurial value creators" in Australia's fight to be competitive in a globalizing world.[1] For the ALP's federal Treasurer, Paul Keating, in 1986 there was no alternative to this class abandoning politics of "adjustment":

> If this Government cannot get the adjustment, get manufacturing going again, and keep moderate wage outcomes and a sensible economic policy, then Australia is basically done for. We will end up being a third rate economy... a banana republic.[2]

The second mistake emerged subsequently, when we observed (and against all the initial anti-Hanson rhetoric from the Coalition and Labor) the remarkable ease with which the John Howard's Coalition Government (11 March 1996 to 3 December 2007), after initially dis-endorsing Hanson, moved quickly on many of Hanson's core policies. These included abolishing the Aboriginal and Torres Strait Islander Commission (ATSIC), nullifying any post-Mabo possibilities for effective indigenous land ownership, hardening up immigration policies, in particular refugee admissions, impugning multiculturalism in the name of "Australian Values", attacking the authority of the UN when it came to matters of human rights and the environment, and showing continuous hostility to "greedy welfare cheats" (see Grant 1997). The ALP too, despite fading outbursts of disapproval in a series of class-blind "culture wars" for which it had no real stomach, tracked in the same direction. Indeed, as the Gillard ALP Government made clear on the litmus test of refugee and asylum policy, it was often resolutely unwilling to roll back such policy changes when it had the chance.[3]

This process of policy co-option, its ease, facility, and surprising bipartisanship, helped me to see that PHON was not some alien intrusion into an otherwise healthy two-party system. It was an organic outgrowth—if sometimes shrill and mildly disruptive—of an already unhealthy democracy.

What I, and many of my fellow authors in 1997, took to be a radical threat to the health of political democracy was, in fact, nothing of the sort. Rather, it was a symptomatic expression of the failure or collapse of that democracy. Party elites on

---

[1] Consider the ALP's elections slogans from 1983 until today. 1983: Bringing Australia Together. 1984: Put Australia First. 1987: Let's stick together. Let's see it through. 1990: Bob Hawke for Australia's Future. 1993: Australia Deserves Better. 1996: Leadership. 1998: A Safe and Secure Future for all Australians. 2001: A Secure Future for all Australians. 2004: Opportunity for all Australians. 2007: New Leadership. 2010: Together: Let's Move Australia Forward. 2013: A New Way. 2016: We'll Put People First. (See Young 2016).

[2] Speaking to John Laws on Radio 2 GB, May 14, 1986 (see Conley 2013).

[3] In typical fashion, Gillard later expressed her "regret" at these policies. Unsurprisingly this was a not a regret at their international law violating cruelty and sheer inhumanity, and so a repudiation of a PHON driven policy, rather a regret that "our government and our parliament was not better able to handle refugee and asylum seeker policy". She then added the absurd remark (for the entire policy area was driven by slogans: "Turn Back the Boats!", "Illegal immigrants!", "Border Protection!") "As the current government is already discovering, this is a policy area that defies the easy certainties of sloganeering" (Gillard, in Johnston 2013).

both sides embraced a shared policy orientation that focused on the interests of "the big end of town" and its aspiring "white shoes" aspirants. Such a focus tended to undercut these parties' ties to their traditional working-class and middle-class bases (their preference becoming, and increasingly so, for *donors*, not party members). Furthermore, this happened at a time when these bases were themselves shrinking, as neoliberal modernization saw much of the manufacturing industry off-shored and corporate monopolists gain an ever-larger market share at the expense of the small business sector.

This failure was but one instance of a more general democratic failure, as neoliberal policies and governance swept across the Anglo-American-European world. Parties of the right and left converged in an elite technocratic consensus that deregulated market capitalism could and should shape the logic and outcomes of everyday life, both individually and collectively.

It is out of this convergence between the traditional parties of the left and right that contemporary populisms emerge, and it was out of this convergence that it emerged in Australia with Pauline Hanson's One Nation.

3.2   Neoliberalism and Populism

On this view, PHON is not a uniquely Australian phenomenon, though, as we shall soon see, it has a distinctive Australian history. It is a manifestation—a right-populist manifestation—of a democratic politics that has, at the level of its policy elites, abandoned any interest in, or concern with, class interests and oppositions, for an "economic nationalism" of neoliberal reform. This nationalism is not the traditional "closed" employment-encouraging and income-protecting nationalism of tariffs and quotas and public ownership, but an "open", globalizing *laissez-faire* economic nationalism of open-border competition and transnational capital flows, labor arbitrage, deregulation, and privatization.

This political abandonment of class for a supposedly shared project of economic modernization is intrinsic to neoliberalism. Not only does it work to make the traditional expression of class interests merely the special pleading of sectional interests, it is essential to a politics that valorizes economic inequalities as the necessary "incentivization" for active, entrepreneurial, market players. Such inequalities, as the inevitable result of free-market competition as it ruthlessly sorts "winners" from "losers," are an essential component of the politics of neoliberalism. Thus, it is that Inequality, and so growing inequality, is not an economic, social, and political vice to be opposed and fought; if anything, it is a virtue to be encouraged and applauded. To think otherwise is "socialism". It is the "politics of envy". A failure to accept that, in the free market, "greed is good".

By excluding class, and so economic inequality, from the domain of legitimate democratic politics, neoliberalism radically constrains the possibilities for political expression, and so for the political expression of the destructive and disconcerting impacts of its policies.

It follows that what expression there is—or rather, what expression the neoliberal regime will tolerate—will tend to be expressed in terms of *status* rather than *class*, and express itself in terms *status anxiety* rather than *class conflict*.

3.3 Right-Populism and Left-Populism

It is because neoliberalism leaves room for the politics of status as it represses that of class that we see so much right-populism and so little left-populism today. Neoliberalism refuses class analysis for the categories of individualistic market moralizing (winners/losers, lifters/leaners, responsible/irresponsible, self-reliant/dependent, deserving/undeserving, etc.). Furthermore, the inequality-valorizing operations of a neoliberalizing economy tend of their nature to undermine any residual commitment of left party elites to meaningful notions of economic equality, and so to the politics and policies of social democratic redistribution.

This is because the project of neoliberal modernization allows party elites to operate with a new freedom of action not found in the traditional Keynesian macroeconomic policy framework. This is a freedom especially attractive to left elites. Traditionally servants of strongly unionized parties, they are now free to present themselves as fearless policy innovators in a generally bipartisan policy framework that allows them to move among a supportive business elite that welcome them (or so they imagine) as friends, allies even.[4] In this situation, left-populism poses a threat not simply to those on the right traditionally opposed to class analysis, but to the legitimacy, power, and leadership of the party elites on the nominal, and now thoroughly neoliberal, left.

As an assault and critique of neoliberalism's class-ejecting moralistic and inevitabilist rhetoric of virtuous—because market-caused and -driven—inequality, any nascent left-populism has enemies everywhere, and especially so on the "Left".

Thus the largest of these populisms, the Occupy Wall Street (OWS) movement, was rigorously, and often viciously, crushed in a mere two months (September–November 2011) in a nationally coordinated assault under the auspices of a supposedly progressive, working-class friendly Democrat, President Obama.

As so often the case with this spin master of "caring capitalism", his rhetoric was especially revealing an elegant example of class-conflict-denying, neoliberal (re)normalization:

> The most important thing we can do right now is those of us in leadership letting people know that we understand their struggles and we are on their side, and that we want to set up a system in which hard work, responsibility, doing what you're supposed to do, is rewarded. And that people who are irresponsible, who are reckless, who don't feel a sense of obligation

---

[4]For a typical celebratory expression of this conjunction, see the address by Paul Kelly (now Editor-at-Large of Rupert Murdoch's *The Australian* newspaper) to the Reserve Bank of Australia (Kelly 2000): "The politics of economic change in Australia in the 1980s and the 1990s."

to their communities and their companies and their workers that those folks aren't rewarded (Obama, in Halper 2011).[5]

Even the single real political success of left-populism thus far—the Corbyn Labour Opposition in the UK—was achieved in the face of party and policy elites that responded to it with all the horror and hysteria that used to be directed by the parties of capitalism at "Soviet Communism". Here is the ex-Labour UK Prime Minister and dedicated neo-liberalphile Tony Blair (a man who self-describes as "Labour through and through") in 2015 trying to sink Corbyn's run for the party leadership:

> Let me make my position clear—I wouldn't want to win from a traditional leftist platform. Even if I thought it was the route to victory, I wouldn't take it (Blair, in Sky News 2015).

Right-populism, on the other hand, poses no existential threat to the class-depoliticizing, inequality-fostering politics of neoliberalism, even if it does articulate a general hostility to the corrupt politics of "Big Money" or "Wall Street". This is because, lacking a class analysis, such opposition can't be expressed in structural terms, but only in moral terms of the kind Obama used in his neoliberal renormalization of OWS. That was a matter, in the name of leadership, of decrying corruption and "bad apples", a matter of insisting on "hard work, responsibility, doing what you're supposed to do", and of condemning "people who are irresponsible, who are reckless, who don't feel a sense of obligation".

It is just this class-denying, class-repressing, individually moralized politics that helps explain two things not always well understood: the "racism" of much, perhaps even all, right-populism, and the *prima facie* rather strange fact that many right-populism leaders are themselves of the neoliberal elite.

3.4   Right-Populism and Racism

Consider the question of racism. Many assume, as if obvious, that right-populism is always and fundamentally an expression of racism.[6] I think this often false, though this doesn't mean, ridiculously, that racist attitudes don't play a part, even a large part, in much right-populism. But the great fear that animates right-populism is not that of the Other; it is much closer to home. It is the fear, socially and economically, of falling *downwards*. A fear of the loss of status inevitable in downwards social mobility. And it is a fear amplified when governments are thought to be using "tax-payers' money" to unfairly "level-up" the underserving at the expense of the deserving. After all,

---

[5]One practical initiative of the Obama administration was equally revealing. They offered Cathy O'Neill, a hedge-fund QUANT who had aligned herself with OWS, a job at the Securities and Exchange Commission (SEC). (She turned it down on realizing those making the offer had no interest in OWS concerns, but were seeking a public relations coup) (see Langston 2017 [Epilogue]).

[6]This is the view of the Australian analyst of PHON, David Marr, for whom it is clear that "One Nation will never be dealt with until the major parties find the courage to address the issue that haunts this country: race" (Marr 2017).

for the undeserving to obtain assistance denied to the deserving is to disadvantage the latter. Pauline Hanson's views on Indigenous welfare are representative of this attitude:

> Along with millions of Australians, I am fed up to the back teeth with the inequalities that are being promoted by the government and paid for by the taxpayer under the assumption that Aboriginals are the most disadvantaged people in Australia (Hanson, in Clarke 2016).

This moralized, status-centered, downwards blaming is far easier politically, socially, and psychologically, than blaming the other way. It is easier because such blaming reasserts a superior status to those blamed; to blame upwards at the rich and powerful as a class might close off any hopes of rising into that elite class, and, perhaps just as importantly, undermine the perennial hope of someone from it riding to one's rescue and re-righting the world.

It is precisely because these are the drivers of discrimination, rather than simple racism, that the targets of such "racism" may change, and in striking ways. Thus (to take just one example) while Pauline Hanson sprang to notoriety by attacking Indigenous Australians, that focus has now pretty much vanished. There is today no entry or policy for Indigenous Australians in PHON's national policies. The only reference to Indigenous Australians to be found in a policy document is one concerning Crocodile Management, where we find ourselves reassured that PHON will "ensure that the importance of crocodiles in Aboriginal culture and nature is well known"! (PHONP n.d.).[7] What there is now is a focus on "Islam", as first there had been a focus on Indigenous Australians, then one on "Asians", and later on South Africans as HIV carriers.

Given the lability of the target populations, what we would appear to have is not some essentialist racist hatred, but an anxiety-driven fear of those people and groups that are seen as clear and present threats from below, from a lower-status position, to one's rightful standing in the world.

3.5 Billionaire Populism

This leads into the second matter—the fact that so many right-populist leaders are themselves of the neoliberal elite. These are the "Millionaire/Billionaire Populists". They claim to be both successful business leaders and/or entrepreneurs, with "a demonstrated track record of innovation and success", and anti-establishment political mavericks or outsiders.

---

[7]There is one mention of Indigenous Australians in PHON's "Principles and Objectives":

> 3. To acknowledge and respect the Aboriginal and Torres Strait Islanders as the first peoples of this land. However, One Nation opposes acknowledging Aboriginal and Torres Strait Islanders in the preamble to the Australian Constitution, as One Nation believes that all Australians are owners and custodians of this land and should work toward unification, not segregation, under the one law for all.

Here we find such right-populists as Donald Trump (US), Andrej Babis (Czech Republic), and Emmanuel Macron (France). Babis's Action for Dissatisfied Citizen (ANO) manifesto is characteristic:

> Today we already have experience, and if you give us a chance, we will show you that the government can be so different from what traditional politicians have so far demonstrated. We want to show that we can be active, economic, and loyal employees of this great family business, which is called the Czech Republic and belongs to you (Babis, in Swain 2017).

This is "top-down" right-populism that, at the same time as seeking to exploit the status anxiety of those who fear downwards mobility, pushes for the ultimate embedding of neoliberalism by reducing government to logic of corporate management. It is the populism of the strong leader, benevolent and competent, who will (as Andrej Babis put it) "run this country like I run my business" (Babis, in Swain 2017).

The trouble with this "Billionaire Right-Populism" (not least for those attracted to such a populist leader) is that what it promises is inherently contradictory, and so always deceptive. This contradiction, this deception, doesn't mean that such right-populism will not encourage blaming downwards, and actively respond to such blaming with discriminatory measures. On the contrary, this is what it will do. But in the end, and however successful the distractions, it can never assuage the status anxiety of those whose insecurities it exploits (which is one reason to expect it to spiral downwards into ever-growing Spectacle and Hypocrisy.) This is because "Top-Down Billionaire Right-Populism" is committed to just that open financialized economic nationalism of cross-border competition, free trade, deregulation, and privatization that creates status insecurity and anxiety in the first place.

3.6   The Bottom-Up Right-Populism of PHON

Pauline Hanson is not a billionaire, and her populism, while clearly of the Right, is not of this kind. This does not mean it is "kinder" or "fairer", but it does make it a different, more "bottom-up" than "top-down", style of right-populism.

Pauline Hanson is not a neoliberal-embedding "Billionaire Right-Populist". Politically she is of the sensible "middle class".[8] She has, and makes, no claims to political excellence based on a history of corporate management, financial speculation, or ostentatiously successful entrepreneurship, nor does she—and so nor does PHON—embrace what Margaret Thatcher labelled as the "There is NO Alternative" (or "TINA") logic (see Berlinski 2011) of neoliberal economic modernization. Quite the contrary.

In the 31 "Principles and Objectives" PHON sets itself, none sings the praises of economic globalization, transnational finance, free trade, or privatization. Instead we find the following:

---

[8]Though a diminished and stressed middle class that, 40 years into neoliberalism and the abandonment of the working class by their traditional parties, now tends to view itself as that group made up of all "hard-working families".

15. [We aim…] To stop foreign ownership of Australia's agriculture land and established housing. Oppose the sale of public assets without the consent of Australians and repeal United Nations treaties that are detrimental or of no benefit to Australia.

16. To restore tariff protection where appropriate, revitalise and encourage Australian industry and manufacturing and initiate financial support for small business and the rural sector, in particular in the interest of creating national wealth and employment.

18. To re-establish a publicly-owned people's bank like the Commonwealth Bank used to be, prior to it being privatised to create true competition, value and benefit Australians.

27. [And…] One Nation opposes the privatisation of essential services such as water, gas, electricity, telecommunications and defence. This must and should remain in the hands of our governments and not foreign ownership and control. We oppose Agenda 21 and its push for 'sustainable development'.

28. One Nation is committed to protecting the farming sector in time of drought, flood and foreign takeover. If we cannot feed ourselves we will starve. We cannot allow other countries to use our land to feed their own when we should be growing the food and exporting it.

29. One Nation will repeal or review the 1953 Double Taxation Agreement Act that provides for foreign investors not to pay tax in Australia. Foreign investors take out more in unpaid taxes than Australian companies operating in other countries, bring in (PHONP 2017).

With these Principles and Objectives we find ourselves face to face with that closed economic nationalism undone under neoliberal modernization, and we find this undoing framed in an especially revealing way. For what holds the policy package together is a basic commitment. It is:

> To support and advocate traditional family values and uphold the institution of the family in its fight against the many who aim to breakdown this important unit of any decent society (PHONP 2017).

As we shall see, the historical and ideological roots of this commitment to a closed economic nationalism of "traditional family values" is that of the pre-neoliberal Liberal Party formed and successfully led by Robert Menzies as Prime Minister from 1949 until 1966.

Figuratively speaking, Pauline Hanson and PHON are Menzies' status-anxiety-riven children.

Hanson's and PHON's populism is, ultimately, an anguished expression of the traditional Australian Liberal party base in an age of neoliberalism that hollows out the "middle class" and makes it more precarious, just as much as it lays waste to the ALP's traditional working-class base. And so it is not a left-populism of class and class conflict. It is, rather, as Menzies put it in 1942 as he sought to bring the anti-Labor conservative base to political self-consciousness, a politics of "homes material, homes human, homes spiritual".

3.7 PHON'S Liberal Personnel

The idea that Hansonism expresses, under the inhospitable conditions of neoliberalism, the politics of Robert Menzies' Liberal Party base, will seem peculiar to those who view PHON as some kind of deviant, intrinsically racist, aberration from politics as usual, but it is suggested by some pretty obvious facts.

The first is something we have already mentioned. We do not have, under hegemonic neoliberalism, democratic politics as usual; instead we have an elite commitment to a bipartisan neoliberalism that tends to disenfranchize traditional party bases, left and right. The second fact has also been mentioned: the ease and facility with which many PHON policies have been co-opted by both the Coalition and the ALP. A third fact lies in PHON's history in parliament of supporting Coalition policies (to the tune of around 85% of the time). And a fourth in its willingness to enter into preference deals with the Liberals, and the latter's recent willingness in the 2017 state elections in both Western Australia and Queensland to accept, even encourage, this. But it is the fifth and sixth facts that are the most telling.

The first of these revealing facts is that PHON is a constituency, a voting bloc, of born-in-Australia voters, and disproportionately so. As Marr (2017) pointed out, looking at the 2016 federal election data:

> One Nation voters in 2016 were almost entirely native-born Australians. Not even newcomers from the UK or New Zealand were drawn to Hanson's party. Her people are absolutely ours and One Nation is the most Aussie party of them all.

Liberal	78% native-born
Labor	79%
Greens	82%
National	91%
One Nation	98%

Now add to this generational and nativist orientation the sixth fact: that *all* of the key party/organization figures involved in furthering of Hanson's political career were and are, like Hanson herself, figures with a Liberal Party history. Thus it was with her initial political adviser as an independent and author of her attention-grabbing maiden speech, John Pasquarelli (1996); her conspiratorial Svengali, David Oldfield, the Deputy Leader of PHON (1997–2000); and is today (since 2015), with the party's General Secretary, James Ashby.[9]

Hanson, Pasquarelli, and Oldfield have all stood (or been endorsed to stand) as Liberal Party candidates for state or federal election: Pasquarelli in the 1987 federal election for the Victorian seat of Jagadaga; Oldfield for the seat of Manly in the 1995 NSW state election; and Hanson, before dis-endorsement, but still as a Liberal on the ballot paper, in 1996 in the Queensland seat of Oxley; while Ashby, as a Liberal Party member and political advisor, worked as Media Adviser for the long-term Liberal member for the Division of Fisher, Peter Slipper (2011–2012).

In terms of their backgrounds this Liberal pedigree is unsurprising. Pasquarelli's father was a well-off professional—a doctor who, a fellow student with Pasquarelli at

---

[9]Hanson (for reasons, as we shall see, I take to be associated with her commitment to the Mensian politics of home) seems compelled to organize PHON around herself and a strong male figure. These men exhaust that list thus far.

Melbourne University recalls, "would drop by monthly in a Rolls Royce or Bentley with money for John" (Birnbauer et al. 2002). Oldfield's father, after distinguished war service, became CEO of the Australian Household Goods company Samuel Taylor Pty. Ltd., his mother running a small business in Manly; while Hanson's parents were small business operators, running a milk bar/take-away in Ipswich. Each of the three, Hanson, Pasquarelli, and Oldfield, at various times themselves ran small businesses—Hanson, like her parents, a fish and chip shop, Pasquerelli various import/export ventures, and Oldfield a sporting goods retail outlet—while Ashby, after a peripatetic prior career as a radio shock jock, now runs a printing business (indeed, the business PHON uses for its own printing requirements).

Their profiles—parents and offspring—are professional, small business, and entrepreneurial. They are, all of them, members of the traditional Liberal Party base, as were unionized wage-laborers of the traditional, pre-neoliberal, ALP.

It follows that if we are to understand the origins of Hanson's right-populism and its basic ideological and rhetorical logic, we need to understand the political ideas, the political ideology, of this traditional, Australian, Liberal constituency. And this we can do if we understand that this constituency—whilst it had, in one sense always been there, and been committed to the anti-Labor side of Australian politics—was called into self-consciousness as a mass political party base by Robert Menzies in 1942. At that time he was seeking to create a unified anti-ALP party from the dysfunctional remains of a United Australia Party that had been formed over a decade earlier from a union of fiscally conservative and pro-Empire former ALP members and the Nationalist Party.

3.8 Upon This Rock—Menzies' Liberal Party and the Forgotten People

Menzies faced a number of concerns of varying degrees of severity. He was worried about the future political impact of the wartime Curtin Labor Government and the clear demonstration of competent and far-reaching state action. He was concerned to consolidate a secure foundation for conservative opposition to socialism (one that did not rely on the whims of conservative ALP defectors). And he was despairing of the organizational capacity and popular appeal of United Australia Party (he had been UAP leader and Prime Minister from 1939 to 1941, before internal party ructions had led him to resign). Consequently Menzies sought to construct a committed and self-aware party base that could match the ALP's union and working-class base's scale, enthusiasm, an intellectual coherence.

He began his project in revealing fashion by denying the political reality of class at the same time as drawing on it:

> In a country like Australia the class war must always be a false war. But if we are to talk of classes, then the time has come to say something of the forgotten class—the middle class—those people who are constantly in danger of being ground between the upper and

the nether millstones of the false war; the middle class who, properly regarded represent the backbone of this country (Menzies, in Menzies Foundation n.d.).[10]

This class-that-was-not-a-class that Menzies invoked—this "forgotten class", these "forgotten people", whose values and interests were supposedly lost and ignored in the battle between organized Labor and capitalist plutocrats—was, in fact, a status group in precisely the sense Max Weber meant when he distinguished class from status.

What defines a class is essentially economic, but a status group (however entwined with matters economic) is a value grouping in a broader sense. It is a "moral class" rather than simply an economic, or only an economic, class. To think economic interests more fundamental than the rankings, honor, and privileges of status (as, Menzies feels, so often do the very rich and the laborious poor) is "one of the great blots on our modern living"; it "is the cult of false values", it is nothing more than a "a repeated application of the test of money".

This class-that-is-not-a-class is not the class of the capitalist, nor is it that of the proletariat. It is the middle class, and it consists of "salary-earners, shopkeepers, skilled artisans, professional men and women, farmers and so on". These people are not obsessed with money as, in their differing ways, are the rich and the politically organized working class. Certainly they take money seriously—they are frugal, they are savers—but it is not the most important or fundamental value. That important, that fundamental, value, is the *home*, and so all that goes into being at home. "I do not believe", Menzies said:

> that the real life of this nation is to be found either in great luxury hotels and the petty gossip of so-called fashionable suburbs, or in the officialdom of the organised masses. It is to be found in the homes of people who are nameless and unadvertised, and who, whatever their individual religious conviction or dogma, see in their children their greatest contribution to the immortality of their race. The home is the foundation of sanity and sobriety; it is the indispensable condition of continuity; its health determines the health of society as a whole (Menzies, in Menzies Foundation n.d.; emphasis added).

Nothing is more central to Menzies' understanding of the Liberal middle class than the idea of home, and so the importance of being, of truly feeling, *at home*. For the forgotten people politics is not a revolutionary project, nor even, on the most basic level, a competition for (scarce) resources ("the class war must always be a false war"); it is rather a matter of ensuring the conditions for the healthy existence and expression of that "best instinct" for "a home of our own".

It is this idea, articulated in terms of "homes material, homes human and homes spiritual" that holds the middle class together and that founds and informs their status politics, and it is the first—the material home—that holds all three notions together:

> The material home represents the concrete expression of the habits of frugality and saving 'for a home of our own.' Your advanced socialist may rave against private property even while he acquires it; but one of the best instincts in us is that which induces us to have one little piece of earth with a house and a garden which is ours; to which we can withdraw,

---

[10]Menzies' 1942 speech is widely available. I take all the quotations that follow from the copy to be found at the Menzies Foundation (n.d.).

in which we can be among our friends, into which no stranger may come against our will. If you consider it, you will see that if, as in the old saying, 'the Englishman's home is his castle,' it is this very fact that leads on to the conclusion that he who seeks to violate that law by violating the soil of England must be repelled and defeated. National patriotism, in other words, inevitably springs from the instinct to defend and preserve our own homes (Menzies, in Menzies Foundation n.d.).

As Menzies sees it, the basis of meaningful citizenship and civility lies in the middle class's "instinct to defend and preserve our homes". Here, indeed, is the very origin and point of political sovereignty itself. Its core manifestation is, as we might put it in explicitly political terms, border defense and control ("into which no stranger may come against our will"). And the point of this defense and control is that through it we, the householders, the citizens, ensure that "we can be among friends", among those, that is, who "share our values", the values of "Real Australians", "ordinary, hardworking, taxpayers". Equally, it is just because proper politics is the politics of home that government—as with any home—must run a tight budget, avoid debt, "balance the books", and avoid wasteful expenditures on those who will inevitably expect any assistance to reflect an entitlement.

The human home amplifies this conception:

Then we have homes human. A great house, full of loneliness, is not a home. 'Stone walls do not a prison make,' nor do they make a house. They may equally make a stable or a piggery. Brick walls, dormer windows and central heating need not make more than a hotel. My home is where my wife and children are. The instinct to be with them is the great instinct of civilised man; the instinct to give them a chance in life – to make them not leaners but lifters – is a noble instinct (Menzies, in Menzies Foundation n.d.).

The material home—that which, through frugality, savings, and effort, a man may acquire as his own family kingdom—is both a private domain and, as such, the productive source of those social ambitions for betterment and improvement that constitute the essential virtue of middle class as "lifters," not "leaners". For:

If human homes are to fulfil their destiny, then we must have frugality and saving for education and progress.

Put together the material and the human home, Menzies says, and:

we have homes spiritual… Human nature is at its greatest when it combines dependence upon God with independence of man. We offer no affront… when we say that the greatest element in a strong people is a fierce independence of spirit. This is the only real freedom, and it has as its corollary a brave acceptance of unclouded individual responsibility… The home spiritual…is not produced by lassitude or by dependence; it is produced by self-sacrifice, by frugality and saving (Menzies, in Menzies Foundation n.d.).

We may summarize the social politics of Menzies' middle class as follows: it is not a revolutionary or utopian politics, for its core ideal is one of *home*—and so of the virtues and values of the *home owner*. Even the notion of freedom must respect this more fundamental value. (As the PHON website says under "What We Stand For": "**Freedom**. Freedom of thought, expression, initiative, association, and exchange is essential for efficient collaboration and risk taking that is respectful of others' rights including property rights.") It is therefore a conservative politics in the sense that it is the natural politics of those who are already, or anticipate being, home owners at home, and so with a stake in the system worth defending. Here, in this place, with these people, lie the roots of *sovereignty* across all its personal, social, and political dimensions. The home owner, in being at home in their home, is in control of that home, its access and restriction rights and policies, and its standards of expected and required behaviors and comportment. As the ultimate or true ground of sovereignty, the home owner rightfully expects and demands that their virtues be given the respect they deserve, and such respect demands a conservative, frugal, self-reliant politics.

While the very rich must, at a minimum, pay lip service to these virtues, and certainly not actively thwart them, the laboring poor pose the real problem, for their lower status ensures resentment and hostility, and so powers a willingness to capture political power to express this resentment and envy through ruinous taxation and redistribution policies. Thus the task of middle class respecting government is not to do anything that furthers, as Menzies put it, "our greatest political disease—the disease of thinking that the community is divided". After all, nothing is more obvious than that a house divided against itself cannot stand.

It is here that Menzies' middle class reaches, in its own way, to a notion of the general good or public interest, and so becomes, in the Aristotelian sense, a genuine kind of politics, and not the "pressure politics" of this or that sectional interest. Whilst withering in his assessment of the supposed vices and venality of the traditional Labor constituency, Menzies speaking for the middle class (and speaking in the midst of a war fought with the laboring class as its troops and producers) is clear on one thing:

> We cannot exclude them from problems of social progress, for one of the prime objects of modern social and political policy is to give them a proper measure of security, and provide the conditions which will enable them to acquire skill and knowledge and individuality (Menzies, in Menzies Foundation n.d.).

This "proper measure of security" reflects "the warmest human compassion toward those whom fate has compelled to live upon the bounty of the State", but its coin is not monetary or financial (giving a man what he has not earned, but has, through political activity, extracted from others, is corrupting on every level). What compassion demands from the middle class is not to corrupt the working class and the destitute, but policies that encourage in them "a fierce independence of spirit". "This", Menzies says, "is the only real freedom, and it has as its corollary a brave acceptance of unclouded individual responsibility". What is required is the opportunity for people to rise into the middle class where they will realize (hopefully forever) that partisan and class-based politics is a grievous error. For "the moment a man seeks moral and intellectual refuge in the emotions of a crowd, he ceases to be a human being and becomes a cipher".

3.9 PHON and the Politics of Home Under Neoliberalism

It takes no great expertise or insight to see just how much the ideology of PHON reflects and draws on Menzies' middle-class politics of home. The personal and nationalistic pride in being at home, and having worked hard for that home; the sense of hard-won entitlement this founds; the insistence on border control and rigid control of access so that those who enter do so at our invitation, and share and respect the values of the household and its occupants; the antipathy to government redistribution downwards to those who have not managed, or have no desire, to trust their lives to a "fierce independence of spirit"; and a fundamental need to divide the deserving from the undeserving on the basis of the amount of pride one takes in one's home, its maintenance, cohesiveness.

All of this in its status fixation and moralistic analysis is there in what otherwise, and mistakenly, might appear to be a politically incoherent mess of knee jerk reactions, racism, and prejudice.

But if the ideological package that is PHON is as coherent as a class-denying conservative politics ever can be, it finds itself now in a far different world than that in which Menzies lived, or would have wanted to live. For while clever neoliberals, like Margaret Thatcher in the UK, exploited the idea of home ownership to undermine working-class identity and to privatize public housing stock, in the end neoliberalism is no respecter of the politics of home. It is a politics of the kind Menzies condemned as a "cult of false values, a repeated application of the test of money". It is a politics of globalization, where capital can flow anywhere and labor arbitrage—the loss of jobs to places where business costs are lower, and the importation of low-cost labor to the domestic economy—is the rule. It is a politics oriented not to the virtuous middle class, but to the big end of town, and so to transnational corporate interests. It is a politics built on "cheap money", and so a willingness to assume debt, not on frugality and saving. As such, it is a politics that tends of its nature to impact adversely on precisely those who value the security of home and home ownership above all, for it pressures them into asset-inflating debt that makes it ever harder for the next generation to obtain their own home at the same time as it renders their hold on their own home a hostage to economic conditions largely outside national political control.

So where are these people, this middle class with its politics of home, to look when neoliberalism is a bipartisan project? They cannot look to the ALP, even the neoliberalized ALP we have today, for that would mean voluntarily accepting an equality of status with those who have too little respect for the necessities of self-reliance, and an ALP that, despite its recent history, is still too closely associated with "unionism" to be trusted. But nor can they look with any security or faith to the Liberal Party or the Coalition as a champion. Certainly the latter may—and does—find it a little easier than the ALP to give expression to much of the status anxiety of threatened home owners, for punching down has always been an element in the middle class's sense of superior status. But, like "Billionaire Right-Populism", it can't—or won't—do anything that will alleviate the ultimate driver of this anxiety, the neoliberal regime of globalized money, profit, and markets.

When the then Coalition Federal Treasurer Hockey (2012) said "The Age of Entitlement is over. We should not take this as cause for despair. It is our market based economies which have forced this change on unwilling participants"[11] it may have seemed he was speaking only of those "deplorables" conservatives have traditionally identified as welfare dependents, as leaners not lifters. But the necessity he invoked and celebrated hits also the status entitlements of the traditional Liberal party base, and they feel it. Their tragedy as "unwilling participants" then is a double one, for what they feel they cannot express in any meaningful political way. To do that they would have to think in terms of class, and this—given their ideology and values—they cannot do. And so it is that right-populism, whatever the noise and shouts of racism and fascism, poses no existential threat to neoliberal politics, even as it chafes against it. What it does, and what it can do, is provide avenues for neoliberal political entrepreneurs—or, like Hanson, despairing remnants of a disappearing base with its roots in the receding pre-neoliberal era—to incite and indulge the passions of status anxiety as they, just as much as the neoliberal elites, do all they can to close off the one real threat: a Populism of the Left.

3.10   Is Right-Populism Fascism?

Right-populism of all stripes, and very obviously so with PHON in Australia, draws on the class-repressing, status-elevating, middle-class ideology of home. Traditionally this ideology and this commitment defined the status of the conservative middle classes as patriotic and self-reliant: frugal savers whose status demanded government refuse the entitlement claims of the more feckless and less prudent in the community,

---

[11] Strikingly, but unsurprisingly, Hockey's words resemble those of Labour Party Prime Minister Tony Blair's Leader's Speech to the Labour Party Conference, Winter Gardens, Blackpool, 1 October 2002.

> Now with globalisation, a new era has begun. People are no less individualist, but they are insecure. Modern prosperity may be greater but modern life is pressure and stress. 20th Century collective power was exercised through the Big State. Their welfare was paternalistic, handing down from on high. That won't do today. Just as mass production has departed from industry, so the monolithic provision of services has to depart from the public sector. People want an individual service for them.
>
> They want Government under them not over them.
>
> They want Government to empower them, not control them. And they want equality of both opportunity and responsibility. They want to know the same rules that apply to them, apply to all. Out goes the Big State. In comes the Enabling State. Out goes a culture of benefits and entitlements. In comes a partnership of rights and responsibilities. That's why we need reform (Blair 2002).

and protect them from the philistine monetary aspirations of those Menzies derided as occupants of "great luxury hotels".

After the Second World War and through to the late 70s and early 80s this ideology held together the base of the major anti-Labor, anti-socialist political parties of the right. It could do this, in great part, because the other threat to this politics—that from "the upper … millstone of the false war"—was largely defused because of the political power of Labor, the real ideological conflict of the Cold War, and the continuing and largely crisis-free levels of widespread economic growth. But with the oil price shock and stagflation that emerged in the 1970s, this elite class, with its distinctive interest in maximizing its share of economic profits at the expense of Labor, returned to the political center with the willing collaboration of traditional Left and Right party elites as neoliberal reform, draped in the language of a beneficent inevitability, became the shared policy orientation.

What this meant for the Left and its traditional base is a familiar story[12]; but it is what it meant for the Right and its traditional base that explains the emergence of right-populism. For no longer could that base find the security it sought in a policy environment that set no store at all in the traditional certainties of home and of being at home, but instead valorized competition, change, innovation, and debt-funded risk-taking in a world of rising inequality and the consequent hollowing out of the affluent middle. The traditional base of the Right was unable, because of its class-repressing, status-emphasizing ideology of home, to launch a anything more than a moralistic critique of those big money interests neoliberalism unleashed and served, and it was saddled with a moralism that was deeply ambivalent about such elite interests. Many of this now anxiety-riven base therefore sought the maintenance of their traditional self-image in the only way the neoliberal bipartisanship made available—through, and in, the search for a Leader, a Champion, who spoke openly of their fears and promised, however objectively unlikely it might be,[13] to restore them to their traditional place as, in Menzies' foundational words, "the backbone of this country".

It seems natural for many, at this point, after all the talk of home, status anxiety, and the need for Leadership, to view right-populism as kind of fascism, a fanatical politics of Heimat, Patrie, Homeland, just as, for related reasons, many have seen it as an inherently racist politics. But just as the easy claim of racism isn't quite right, neither is that of fascism. The point, as with racism, isn't that right-populism might not flow along such lines, but that if this is what it does, then the full explanation lies elsewhere. For if right-populism becomes an explicitly fascistic politics, then it will only be because of neoliberalism, because a neoliberal world now *needs* such a politics.

---

[12]For my own account of this story, see Lynch (2016).

[13]One might, with an ironical hat tip to Obama's (2006) Oprah Winfrey-endorsed bestseller, call this line of thought, *The audacity of hope*; a hat tip even more deserved with the title's completion: *reclaiming the American dream*.

3.11 Neoliberalism and a Right-Populist Fascism

When might this be the case? There would seem to be two obvious situations. The first would be if a powerful left-populist movement were to arise, for this would mean the return of class politics and the threat of systemic and revolutionary change. And this threat would be especially worrying if, as perhaps with Corbyn's Labour Party, it threatened to effectively mobilize a mass political base sufficient to take power through the ballot box. In such circumstances, sponsoring an extra-democratic right-populism might be a very attractive option to neoliberal elites, and especially to those of its members that, like our "Billionaire Right-Populists", have a lust for power, a certain charisma, and a capacity to deploy the appearance of "the common touch".

The second possibility is even bleaker. On the basis of current trends, one can imagine that stagnating or negative economic growth, in the context of intra-elite competition for the income and wealth, might see that competition extend to the political domain as various "oligarchs" seek to maintain and further their powers of accumulation and extraction, and do so in an environment resolutely hostile to class politics, and to any kind of democracy that might allow such a politics. This, after all, is not too far from Tony Blair's notorious declaration: "I wouldn't want to win from a traditional leftist platform. Even if I thought it was the route to victory, I wouldn't take it" (Blair, in Sky News 2015).

However things turn out Pauline Hanson's One Nation is not likely to provide such a fascist politics. She is not a member of the neoliberal elite, and she is not a "Top-Down Billionaire Right-Populist". She is not—while undoubtedly a source of some fascination—a powerfully charismatic figure. And she has very few, if any, organizational skills and capacities. PHON is not the danger. The real danger would arise if a charismatic billionaire populist were to emerge to harness and exploit the despair and anguish of those who (and rightly) see their status, their homes, and so their lives, slipping away, and who—just because of their focus on the home—cannot react to this loss through class analysis or class politics.

This inability is the tragedy of right-populism.

References

Berlinski, C. (2011). *There is no alternative: Why Margaret Thatcher matters* (2nd ed.). London: Basic Books.
Birnbauer, B., Elias, D., & Graham, D. (2002). The amazing man behind Pauline Hanson. *The Age* [month and day unknown]. http://www.exkiap.net/articles/miscellaneous/pasquarelli.htm. Accessed 18 June 2018.
Blair, T. (2002). Leader's speech, Blackpool 2002. In *British Political Speech, Speech archive*. http://www.britishpoliticalspeech.org/speech-archive.htm?speech=185. Accessed 19 June 2018.
Clarke, A. (2016, July 5). Here's a bunch of things Pauline Hanson has said about Indigenous Australians. *Buzzfeed*. https://www.buzzfeed.com/allanclarke/pauline-hanson-and-indigenous-australia?utm_term=.uxBjqgZw9#.qrX4YaNAz. Accessed 18 June 2018.

Conley, T. (2013, June 12). Revisiting the banana republic and other familiar destinations. *The Conversation*. https://theconversation.com/revisiting-the-banana-republic-and-other-familiar-de stinations-15088. Accessed 18 June 2018.

Grant, B. (Ed.). (1997). *Pauline Hanson, One Nation and Australian politics*. Armidale: UNE Press.

Halper, D. (2011, October 18). Obama on Occupy Wall Street: "We are on their side". *The Weekly Standard*. https://www.weeklystandard.com/obama-on-occupy-wall-street-we-are-on-th eir-side/article/598251. Accessed 18 June 2018.

Hockey, J. (2012, April 17). *The end of the age of entitlement*. Address to the Institute of Economic Affairs, London. http://www.joehockey.com/the-end-of-the-age-of-entitlement/. Accessed 19 June 2018.

Johnston, M. (2013, November 10). Failed asylum asker policy among Julia Gillard's regrets as prime minister. *Herald Sun*. https://www.news.com.au/national/failed-asylum-seeker-policy-am ong-julia-gillards-regrets-as-prime-minister/news-story/6c4d902162b15dfceaf6f2ded3abe5e1. Accessed 18 June 2018.

Kelly, P. (2000). The politics of economic change in Australia in the 1980's and the 1990's. In *Reserve Bank of Australia 2000 Conference, after-dinner address*. https://www.rba.gov.au/publi cations/confs/2000/kelly-address.htm. Accessed 18 June 2018.

Langston, T. S. (2017). *Ideologues and Presidents [Epilogue]*. London: Routledge.

Lynch, T. (2016). Now is the turn of the Right: "Ditch the base". *Social Alternatives, 35*(2), 56–61.

Maddox, G., Moore, T., & Bourke, S. (2002). Australia and the emergence of the modern two party system. *Australian Journal of Politics and History, 44*(1), 17–31.

Marr, D. (2017, March 27). Looking back, and angry: What drives Hanson's voters. *The Guardian*. https://www.theguardian.com/australia-news/2017/mar/27/looking-back-and-angry-what-drives-pauline-hansons-voters. Accessed 18 June 2018.

Menzies Foundation. (n.d.). *Menzies virtual museum. The forgotten people*. Chapter 1—The forgotten people. https://menziesvirtualmuseum.org.au/transcripts/the-forgotten-people/59-chapter-1-the-forgotten-people. Accessed 19 June 2018.

Obama, B. (2006). *The audacity of hope: Thoughts on reclaiming the American dream*. New York: Crown/Three Rivers Press.

PHONP [Pauline Hanson's One Nation Party]. (2017). *Principles and objectives*. http://www.onen ation.com.au/principles. Accessed 18 June 2018.

PHONP [Pauline Hanson's One Nation Party]. (n.d.). *Crocodile management*. http://www.onenati on.com.au/policies/qldpolicies/CrocodileManagement.pdf. Accessed 18 June 2018.

Sky News. (2015, July 22). *Blair and Corbyn's battle: The best quotes*. https://news.sky.com/stor y/blair-and-corbyns-battle-the-best-quotes-10351682. Accessed 18 June 2018.

Swain, D. (2017, October 11). The avoidable rise of Andrei Babis. *Jacobin*. https://www.jacobinm ag.com/2017/11/andrej-babis-czech-republic-election. Accessed 18 June 2018.

Young, S. (2016). *70 years of election campaign slogans*. Election Watch. University of Melbourne. https://electionwatch.unimelb.edu.au/australia-2016/articles/70-years-of-campaign-slogans. Accessed 18 June 2018.

Chapter 4
Pauline Hanson, One Nation (PHON) and Right-Wing Protective Popular Nationalism: Monocultural Tendencies at the Expense of Social Cohesion

Belinda J. Flannery and Susan E. Watt

Stop having a go at me [be]cause I'm a patriotic Australian, I love being Australian and I want to protect my country.

(Hanson 2016b)

Abstract This chapter offers a new conceptualization of popular nationalism in Australia, termed *right-wing protective popular nationalism* (RWPPN). Taken from theoretical underpinnings which suggest that the rise of popular nationalism in Australia links with the Hanson phenomenon, RWPPN concerns a desire to protect and preserve the national culture and way of life. It associates strongly with a sense of national identity that is defined, at least in part, by opposition to multiculturalism and prejudice to non-white/Anglo ethnic groups. To understand the interplay between RWPPN and 12 other psychological profiling variables (which we argue are related to Hansonism and a broader discourse of ethnic inclusion and exclusion), we present a cluster analysis. Cluster analysis is commonly used in audience segmentation studies to show how the population divides naturally into different groups. The analysis revealed three clear segments in participants' level of RWPPN sentiment and responses to ethnic groups in Australia, which we labelled "inclusive" (low RWPPN), "guarded" (med RWPPN), and "exclusive" (high RWPPN). The "exclusive" group is strongly emotive and quite large, but is nonetheless outnumbered by the "inclusive" group. Based on these results, we conclude that RWPPN relates to monocultural tendencies and that it does so at the expense of social cohesion.

B. J. Flannery (✉) · S. E. Watt
School of Psychology and Behavioural Sciences, University of New England, Armidale, NSW 2351, Australia
e-mail: bflanner@myune.edu.au

S. E. Watt
e-mail: sue.watt@une.edu.au

© Springer Nature Singapore Pte Ltd. 2019
B. Grant et al. (eds.), *The Rise of Right-Populism*,
https://doi.org/10.1007/978-981-13-2670-7_4

Keywords Cluster analysis · Monoculturalism · Multiculturism
Popular nationalism · Right-wing protective popular nationalism

4.1 Introduction

Monoculturalism can be defined as a policy or process of supporting and advocating the expression of a single culture, and is often seen as the antithesis of multiculturalism (Mclennan 2001; Shaw et al. 1999). Although Australia has celebrated and embraced its multicultural heritage for several decades, the white/Anglo roots of colonization have never been far from its collective consciousness. As such, a pull toward monocultural tendencies can at times be felt. This is especially evident when sections of the populace perceive threat, either to resources that underlie standards of living, such as employment opportunities, or to something more symbolic, such as a threat to culture and societal norms. Focusing on symbolic threat, this chapter explores the state of play between monocultural and multicultural tendencies in contemporary Australia. We make particular reference to Pauline Hanson's emergence and re-emergence in the political sphere and the repercussions this has incurred.

Rewind to 1997 and John Pasquarelli, Pauline Hanson's former media advisor, is delivering a speech to the Council for the National Interest (Pasquarelli 1997). Pasquarelli was Hanson's original spin-doctor and is often credited with having written her well-known maiden speech to the House of Representatives (e.g., Pasquarelli 1998, pp. 13–136). Pasquarelli's (1997) speech reflected on the ordinariness of Hanson. Fish and chip shop owner who left school at the age of 15. Barmaid. Battling single Mum. Unremarkable. Yet, Pasquarelli argued, she was a *phenomenon*. Pasquarelli claimed that not only did this politically naïve individual, with no real background in politics, take on the political establishment and win, but she did so by relating to and claiming to represent ordinary Australians. Hanson existed far from the mainstream of the political elite and regarded herself as *untarnished* and a *non-politician*, a voice of the people. Pasquarelli succeeded in his brief; the phenomenon that was to become *Hansonism* gained traction not only in the Australian political landscape but also in the awareness of the Australian people.

During the early years of her political career, Hanson also forged a political identity based on anti-intellectual sentiment and the notion that "common sense" and having had one's "fair share of life's knocks" were the cornerstones to effective policymaking. Urging economists to "get their heads out of textbooks and get a real job", Hanson implied that the deliberate acquisition of knowledge was no match for life experience. She was "fed up" with elitist rhetoric which, in her opinion, did not meet the true needs of the Australian people (see House of Representatives Official Hansard (Parliamentary Debates 1996) for a full transcript of Hanson's maiden speech). Determined to stand up for her beliefs and speak her mind, Hanson considered her views to be the unspoken and suppressed views of the majority of Australians. Indeed, her supporters have validated and continue to validate such claims. Despite often regarding their leader as "outlandish" and at times "out of line", Hansonites consider Hanson brave to speak the words that many are supposedly thinking (Marr 2017, p. 6). Therefore, as Hanson's rhetoric was of the people, her political approach was that of populism.

As several authors of this edited volume note, populist political expression can align with both sides of the traditional political spectrum. Research has demonstrated that Australians regard the political ideology of Hanson's One Nation as both right (for example, when addressing issues of race and ethnicity), and left (when concerned with issues of employment and trade—see, for example, Murray 2005). However, for scholars within the social sciences, where race relations and issues such as ethnicity are pertinent to their field of inquiry, Hansonism is viewed as a political ideology of right populism. Wells (1997) cogently argued the case for this view. He joined these two concepts by highlighting the interplay between One Nation ideologies and the mechanisms of right populism. Wells (1997, p. 20) articulated potential issues of right populism, including its tendency to pave the way for a "politics of disappointment and resentment" which eventually equates to a "politics of fear". He suggested that this is more likely when populist rhetoric is perceived as originating from the emotive "gut-feelings" of those leading the populist charge (such as Hanson). Wells (1997, p. 21) pointed out that this fear can appear in "divisive and xenophobic tendencies", for example, Hanson's rise was accompanied by increased racial vilification. Wells also concluded that, given Hanson's limitations in character and political nous, right populism was unlikely to become embedded in the Australian landscape, but also warned that this was contingent on major political parties resisting the temptation to play the "populist card".

Nonetheless, the "populist" card was subsequently drawn. Wear (2008) referred to Canovans' (1981) "politician's populism", whereby politicians borrow and use populist techniques within the mainstream political arena to garner popularity and to stifle the competition of emerging populist parties. Wear argued that the Howard Government adopted this approach throughout their four terms in office by embedding Hanson's populism into the fabric of its political repertoire. He further suggested that this tactic led Howard to promote the status of white/Anglo Australian identity (which Hanson upheld and defended) and also to commit to policies that were advocated by One Nation. Therefore, the strategic use of populist rhetoric by Howard may have assisted in securing his government's successive terms in office. However, the cost was high. As Wear concludes, it resulted not only in the alienation of some sectors of the community but encouraged community suspicion towards democratic institutions.

Analysis has shown that Hanson's right populism did merge into the mainstream (see, for example, Broinowski 2017; Grant 1997; Gray and Winter 1997; Leach et al. 2000; Markus 2001). This may not have been intentionally planned by Hanson, but it was achieved nonetheless. A parallel can be found in the study of nationalism and how Hansonism likewise provided a foundation for the emergence of a specific form of popular nationalism. It is to this that we now turn.

4.2   From Hanson's Right Populism to Australian Popular Nationalism

I believe we are in danger of being swamped by Asians. (Hanson 1996b)

In its most basic formulation, populism is an overarching expression that seeks to represent the vision of "the people" in their shared agency to rise against the establishment and in so doing oppose privileged elites. Nationalism, on the other hand, is more specific. Encompassing a range of national-oriented expressions, behaviors and beliefs, nationalism is concerned with promoting the interests of "the nation"; however, it is defined and manufactured (see, for example, Anderson 1983; Brubaker 2004; Gellner 1983). Popular nationalism arises when nationalism is characterized by populist sentiment.

Australian sociologist Gale (2004, 2005) conceptualized and described a specific form of popular nationalism, which we refer to as Australian popular nationalism (APN). APN "places an emphasis on what is seen as a threat to national culture and the Australian way of life" (Gale 2004, p. 322). It is built into Gale's overall thesis, wherein he, like Wells (1997), spoke of *a politics of fear*. For Gale, a politics of fear referred to the notion that racism and the generation of fear has become entrenched in the contemporary politics of western nation-states. What underpins this fear is a sense of threat that derives from changes to Australia's predominately white social and cultural foundations brought about by increased Asian immigration in the 1980s and 1990s. Gale (2005, p. 5) described Hanson's (1996b) comment "*I believe we are in danger of being swamped by Asians*" (HR Deb 1996) as igniting a "politics of discontent". He claimed that it promoted sentiments of fear that focused on race and immigration such as concerns about "*how many?*" and "*where from?*" (see also Markus 2001) . These concerns reflected a broader discourse of "Anglo-decline" (Hage 1998, p. 20). In this discourse, core contemporary Australian values were believed to be at risk of being watered down because of the intrusion of other cultures into a primarily white/Anglo Australian cultural landscape.

Gale (2004, 2005) claimed that Pauline Hanson employed a racist political dialogue centered on cultural differences rather than physical superiority. Regarded as expressions of *new racism*, this political discourse replaced blatant expressions of racial superiority and inferiority with symbolic boundaries of inclusion and exclusion. Comments such as, "*I'm not racist but ...*" are a prime example of this (see also Soutphommasane et al. 2015 for an in-depth analysis of race relations in Australia). As Gale (2004, p. 323) stated:

> Within this 'racial discourse', immigrants, especially those categorized as 'non-whites', are not labelled as being racially inferior. Nonetheless, their cultures and values are commonly represented in media discourse as 'alien' and a threat to whiteness, and western, core values or democracy itself.

Therefore, Gale (2005) proposed that populist rhetoric and the media played a central role in the development of APN. This language contributed to the construction of national identity and how belief systems of race and nation define Australianness, and therefore who is Australian and who is not.

It is in this context that Gale (2005) made specific mention of the interplay between Hansonism and the Howard Government. Political themes such as border protection (the primary focus of Howard's 2001 campaign encapsulated in the catch cry, *"we will decide who comes to this country"*) and events such as the Tampa crisis and the terrorist attacks of 9/11 further served to fuel this climate. Symbolic markers of Australian identity, derived from a culture of fear instigated by Hanson and perpetuated by Howard, entered everyday discourse concerning the preservation of cultural heritage, the maintenance of traditional values, and the promotion of heightened national identity in the form of *"Aussie pride"*. Such sentiment paved the way for establishing an *"us"* (we grew here) versus *"them"* (you flew here) mentality, whereby *"us"* (the ingroup: white/Anglo Australians) were to fear and exclude *"them"* (the outgroup: non-white/Anglo Australians). Within this intergroup dynamic, the outgroup is often regarded as a threat to things held dear by the ingroup with reference to national identity and culture, and more specifically the Australian way of life.

The term *"the Australian way of life"* refers to a particular view of Australian national identity. *"The Australian Way of Life"* was the title of Hanson's 2007 Senate Federal Election campaign theme song, which Hanson co-wrote (Callaghan and Hanson 2007). The song included the sentiment that the Australian way of life will never change, and that we must all come together, stand proud, and fight for our country. It was also the main theme in the 2003 Howard Government's national security information campaign: *Let's look out for Australia: protecting our way of life from a possible terrorist attack* (Abetz 2003). In both cases, the Australian way of life featured many cultural stereotypes (for example, the Aussie digger, true blue, the beach, our shores, backyard cricket, and barbeques). The rhetoric claimed to welcome anyone from anywhere, but the "Australian way of life" that was described upheld traditional white/Anglo values and was resilient to outside cultural influences. This was especially evident in the national security information campaign, which has been critiqued as propagandist in nature (Gleeson 2016; Porter 2003; Younane 2006). By using the threat of terrorism to further cement national identity, rhetoric based around the Australian way of life and all that is *good* encouraged a level of vigilance by white Australians in response to the threat of the "terrorist other" and all that is *bad* (Gleeson 2016).

Gale's conceptualization of APN offers insight to intergroup dynamics drawn partly from Hansonism. Extending on this, we suggest that APN is based on right populist ideations, where cultural differences and the perceived threat from these differences are heightened. These concepts seem to explain events in Australia, but whether it is a distinct phenomenon in the Australian population, separate from other forms of nationalism has not been empirically measured—and in any event is a complex theoretical and historical question. We recently developed an empirically derived scale, drawing on social psychology measures and principles, to address this (Flannery and Watt 2017) . Focusing on the core characteristic of APN, namely that outgroup cultural differences pose a threat to the ingroup's way of life (Gale 2004), we reasoned that feeling threat would motivate ingroup members to want to *protect* their way of life from the outgroup. Hence, we extended the concept of

APN to include a concern with national protection. That is, there would be a desire to protect and preserve the national culture and way of life from cultural variation. We labelled this construct "Right Wing Protective Popular Nationalism" (RWPPN). We then developed and validated a measure of RWPPN, which we called the "Right Wing Protective Popular Nationalism Scale" (RWPPN Scale). Having a measure of RWPPN would allow us to further explore this concept within the Australian population.

Ten items make up the RWPPN Scale and center on the protection of Australian culture, values, traditions, and way of life from the outgroup. Example items from the RWPPN Scale include *"in regards to Australian culture we need to protect what we've got"*, *"we need to ensure Australian values are not replaced by the values of other countries"*, and *"all Australians need to stand guard to maintain our traditional ways"*. A validation study was conducted to determine the reliability and validity of the RWPPN Scale and if RWPPN is a unique construct (Flannery and Watt 2017). The results of this study indicated that, when taken together, the ten items of the RWPPN Scale have been shown to be both a reliable and valid measure of RWPPN. In addition, RWPPN was found to correlate with similar constructs, such as nationalism, patriotism, symbolic threat, and ethnocentrism, but it did not completely overlap them. This empirically supported that RWPPN is its own separate construct.

4.3 Protecting Our Way of Life: Further Cementing the Notion of *"Us"* Versus *"Them"*

Not happening, not interested in Halal. Thank you. (Hanson 2016a)

As RWPPN is concerned with a desire to protect and preserve the Australian culture and way of life, and considered to be part of a right populist discourse of inclusion and exclusion, we argued that RWPPN sentiment, as measured on the RWPPN Scale, would relate to national identity and intergroup relations. Findings from our preliminary study (Flannery and Watt 2017) suggested this may be the case. RWPPN sentiment significantly correlated with relevant phenomena. These included opposition to multiculturalism, the tendency to identify as Australian over and above identifying as a member of humanity, national flag displays, and perceptions of threat from ethnic minorities. High RWPPN sentiment also correlated with negative behavioral, emotional, and attitudinal responses to ethnic groups, including high levels of prejudice, fear, anger, aggression, and avoidance (Flannery and Watt 2017).

The phenomena that RWPPN correlates with opposition to multiculturalism is also characterized in events such as the 2005 Cronulla riots, the subsequent Australia Day riots, the more recent clashes between the far right and far left, and the emergence of various right nationalist groups such as Reclaim Australia and Patriot Blue (just to name a few). In particular, the use of national symbols by white/Anglo Australians, specifically the Australian national flag, have played a role by symbolizing a message of ethnic exclusion (Dunn 2009). Consistent with this, Fozdar et al. (2015) found that displaying the Australian flag was associated with support for the White Australia policy and negativity towards Muslims and asylum seekers. It is important to note that national flags mean many things to many people. We are not suggesting that the Australian flag has been reduced to only represent such narrow views of national identity and inclusion; we are merely acknowledging a shift where the Australian flag has become ensconced within a surge of right populist sentiment.

Our discussion so far has focused on intergroup dynamics when RWPPN senti-ment is prevalent. However, people differ in their level of RWPPN sentiment, and also in their level of support for multiculturalism or their belief that ethnic groups pose a threat to Australia (and so on and so forth). Audience segmentation studies seek to identify, within a population, distinct clusters of people who have features in common. We used this method to discover whether there are distinct clusters in Australian society based on RWPPN and, if so, to characterize them through the use of profiling variables. This is explained below.

While there are many clustering methodologies available (see Hartigan 1975 for a summary) the overarching principle is to create homogenous groups (taxonomies) within complex data sets. Similarities in people's responses to a set of profiling variables are used to determine the groups. The resulting groups comprise people who are as similar as possible to each other (high within-group homogeneity) while being as different as possible to those in other groups (low between-group homogeneity) (Clatworthy et al. 2005).

Basing our analysis on three expected levels of RWPPN sentiment (low, medium, and high), we sought to identify response patterns within an Australian sample across 13 psychological profiling variables. Exploratory K-means cluster analysis was used (this is required when there is a pre-determined number of audience segments). The profiling variables measured individual tendencies to:

- support multiculturalism
- identify primarily as an Australian
- identify primarily as a member of humanity
- perceive ethnic groups as posing a threat to Australia (*threat*)
- display the national flag (either at home, on one's car, or on one's person)
- hold negative attitudes towards ethnic groups (*prejudice*)
- respond to people belonging to ethnic groups with anger
- respond to people belonging to ethnic groups with fear
- aggress against people belonging to ethnic groups
- avoid people belonging to ethnic groups
- be influenced by the media (TV, print, online) regarding the views one holds about ethnic groups
- be influenced by populist rhetoric that highlights fear and concern for Australia should ethnic groups be allowed to live here
- support RWPPN sentiment.

4.4   Segmenting an Australian Audience Based on Low, Medium, and High Levels of RWPPN

To survive in peace and harmony, united and strong, we must have one people, one nation, one flag. (Hanson 1996b)

4.4.1   Method

Participants and Procedure

A nationally representative sample of 657 adult Australian citizens was recruited by an online panels company (The Online Research Unit). Their ages ranged from 18 to 86, with an average age of 48. Slightly over half (51%) were males, and 49% were females. Eighty-four percent identified as Caucasian (white). Concerning political orientation (independent of political party preference), 35.6% reported a central political orientation, 26.3% a somewhat to strongly left political orientation, 23.5% a somewhat to strongly right political orientation and 14.5% a disinterest in politics. The education levels of the sample were as follows: 33% had partially or fully completed tertiary education, 29.2% had partially or fully completed vocational training or a diploma and 30.1% had completed secondary school, while 7.3% had not completed secondary school.

Participants were invited to complete an online questionnaire of randomly ordered items for a small reimbursement.

Audience Segmentation Variables

Participants were classified into *"like-minded"* groups based on their responses to a questionnaire that measured the profiling variables listed in Sect. 4.3. The question-naire also included demographic variables of gender, age, identifying as Caucasian (white), political orientation, and level of education. For further detail pertaining to the questionnaire items, see Flannery and Watt (Flannery and Watt 2017) , where a larger questionnaire was used for scale validation purposes.

4.4.2   Results

The cluster analysis was conducted using SPSS computer software. Before running the analysis, all variables were standardized so that each had a mean (average) of 0 and a standard deviation of 1. By doing this, the variables were now on the same scale and could easily be compared and interpreted. The three-segment solution provided adequate interpretability. The characteristics of the three audience segments are illus-trated in Fig. 1.1 and described. We describe each segment (group) by comparison with the overall sample average.

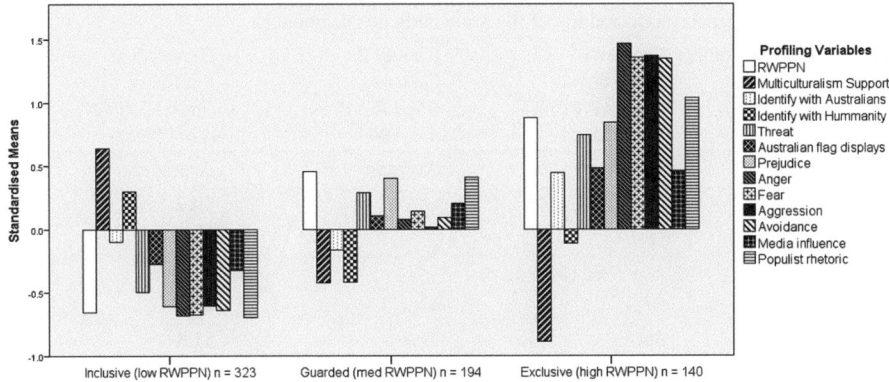

Fig. 4.1 Results of the cluster analysis showing psychological characteristics of the three RWPPN groups (low, med, high)

As shown in Fig. 1.1, the first audience segment, with low RWPPN sentiment, included 323 participants, or 49% of the sample. Based on their psychological profile, this group was labelled "*Inclusive*". The group showed moderately above average support for multiculturalism, and somewhat above average identification with humanity. Their identification with Australians was slightly lower than average. For this group, the remaining profiling variables were all moderately below average, with flag displays and media influence slightly less low than the other variables.

The second audience segment, with medium RWPPN sentiment, comprised 194 participants, or 30% of the sample. Based on their psychological profile, this group was labelled "*Guarded*". The group was close to the overall average on most of the profiling variables; this was especially so for anger, aggression, avoidance, and flag displays. Fear was slightly elevated, and support for multiculturalism and identification with humanity were both below the overall mean. *Guarded* participants also had below average identification with Australians, and their average identification with all of humanity was even lower.

The third segment, characterized by high RWPPN sentiment, included 140 participants, or 21% of the sample. This group was labelled "*Exclusive*". The pattern of responding across all the profiling variables from this audience segment was opposite to that of the low RWPPN group. Support for multiculturalism was well below average (almost one standard deviation). They had the strongest identification with Australians of all groups, and slightly below average identification with humanity. The mean scores for anger, fear, aggression, avoidance, and populist rhetoric were all more than one standard deviation above the mean.

In addition to examining the psychological profile of each cluster, we examined the demographic characteristics of each cluster. These are shown in Table 4.1, and are further elaborated in the following section.

Table 4.1 Demographic information of the three audience segments

Demographic variable	Cluster 1 Inclusive (low RWPPN) n = 323	Cluster 2 Guarded (med RWPPN) n = 194	Cluster 3 Exclusive (high RWPPN) n = 140
	Average	Average	Average
Age	45.5	48.7	50.7
	%	%	%
Gender			
Female	53.3	42.3	48.6
Male	46.7	57.7	51.4
Caucasian identity			
Yes	80.1	86.6	86.4
No	19.2	13.4	13.6
Political orientation			
Left	33.4	22.2	15.7
Center	35.9	32.5	39.3
Right	17.3	27.8	32.1
Don't care	13.3	17.5	12.9
Level of education			
Did not complete secondary	4.6	7.7	12.9
Completed secondary	25.7	35.6	32.9
Vocational	12.4	22.7	14.3
Undergraduate diploma	12.7	11.9	17.1
Bachelor degree	30.7	16.0	15.7
Higher degree	13.9	6.2	7.1

Notes Age is given as an average
Other variables are percentages (%) within the cluster

4.5   The Cost of Protecting a Nation: Monocultural Tendencies and Social Cohesion in Australia

Please explain. (Hanson 1996a)

The cluster analysis revealed clear patterns of responding across a wide range of psychological profiling variables. The profiling variables were selected because they underpin some of the key themes introduced by Hansonism and espoused by Howard, and they are representative of a discourse concerning ethnic inclusion and exclusion in Australia. The results provide increased understanding of what aligns like-minded people in relation to RWPPN sentiment; however, before we highlight these we will first discuss the demographic characteristics of the three groups as shown in Table 4.1.

Regarding political orientation, the right and left orientation percentages were almost mirror opposites when comparing the *inclusive* and *exclusive* groups. As we would expect, a higher percentage of members in the *exclusive* group were right in their political orientation (the percentage was double that of left-oriented members), while the *inclusive* group comprised a higher percentage of left members (here the percentage was almost double that of right-oriented members). In contrast to these two groups, the *guarded* group held a more balanced composition of right- and left-oriented members.

Trends in the level of education were also found across the groups. Participants who had received higher levels of education were clustered together in the *inclusive* group, while participants who had received lower levels of education were clustered together in the *exclusive* group. This pattern reflects a consensus within the literature that low levels of education are associated with prejudice and other forms of negativity towards minority groups. The patterns of percentages across the clusters for age and gender were not as noteworthy. The mean age for each cluster was somewhat similar to the mean age for the entire sample, so age did not characterize the clusters. The percentages for the male-to-female ratios in each of the three groups were relatively representative of the sample as a whole. The only group that contained more females to males was the *inclusive* group. This suggests that females may be more likely to portray such psychological characteristics when compared with males. Lastly, and as expected, the *inclusive* group comprised the largest percentage of people who did not identify as Caucasian, with equal and larger percentages of Caucasians respectively found in the *guarded* and *exclusive* groups.

The key findings of the cluster analysis are as follows. First, *inclusive* people characteristically show a below average desire to protect and preserve the Australian culture and way of life. When compared with the average, they are more supportive of multiculturalism and tend to have a broader sense of identity as belonging to all of humanity, as opposed to a narrow sense of being Australian. They are less likely to display the national flag and are less influenced by the media or populist rhetoric in developing their views regarding ethnic groups or consequently Australia's wellbeing. They are less likely to feel that ethnic groups pose a threat to Australia and display less prejudice, anger, fear, aggression, or avoidance towards people belonging to ethnic groups.

In contrast, *exclusive* people, who most strongly endorse the desire to protect and preserve the Australian culture and way of life, show the opposite pattern, but with more gusto. By this, we mean their scores on most variables tend to be more extreme than those of the other groups. Emotions are especially prevalent in this group. They are substantially more angry, fearful, aggressive, and avoidant of ethnic groups than the sample average and they strongly oppose multiculturalism. Populist rhetoric influences them and, compared with the other groups, they demonstrate the strongest identification with Australians. They are also most likely to display the national flag.

Finally, *guarded* people who moderately endorse RWPPN sit somewhere in the middle. While they show above average need to protect the Australian way of life, below average support for a multicultural society, and are somewhat prejudiced toward ethnic groups, they do not show the same strong emotional responses as the *exclusive* group. The influences of media and populist rhetoric on this group are above average. Compared with the rest of the sample, this group does not show elevated identification with humanity, nor with Australians.

More generally, we would like to highlight that, while the exclusive group may have demonstrated more extreme scores across the psychological profiling variables than the other groups, they were the minority, albeit an emotive one. This does seem to challenge Hanson's notion that populist rhetoric such as hers is representative of the people at large. Perhaps as a nation we are not as fearful, concerned, or fed up as the tabloids and politicians claim us to be. Indeed, a recent survey on social cohesion in Australian has offered data to support the idea that Australian is a relatively cohesive society and that the majority of Australians agree that multiculturalism has been good for Australia (Markus 2015).

On the flip side however, this does not deter from the primary result reported in this chapter: that people can be classified into like-minded groups according to how much they desire to protect and preserve Australian culture and the Australian way of life. The psychological profile of those who highly desire this suggests that monoculturalism is their preference and comes so at the expense of social cohesion. As we have explored in this chapter, it is this form of popular nationalism that has been promoted by Hanson and taken up by other key players within mainstream Australian politics. Should this *protective* baton of nationalism continue to be passed on, what will become of our multicultural heritage? So, for the sake of further enhancing social cohesion and ensuring that the pull towards monoculturalism is less felt, we ask Pauline Hanson and like-minded people not only to "*please explain*", but also to "*please refrain*".

References

Abetz, E. (2003). *Let's look out for Australia: Protecting our way of life from a possible terrorist threat*. Canberra: Attorney-General's Department.

Anderson, B. (1983). *Imagined communities: Reflections on the origins and spread of nationalism*. New York: Verso.

Broinowski, A. (2017). *Please explain: The rise, fall and rise again of Pauline Hanson*. Sydney: Penguin Random House Australia.

Brubaker, R. (2004). In the name of the nation: Reflections on nationalism and patriotism. *Citizenship Studies, 8*(2), 115–127.

Callaghan, C., & Hanson, P. (2007). *Pauline Hanson's theme song: The Australian way of life*. https://www.youtube.com/watch?v=-bCx7cA7se8. Accessed December 21, 2017.

Canovan, M. (1981). *Populism*. New York: Harcourt Brace Jovanovich.

Clatworthy, J., Buick, D., Hankins, M., Weinman, J., & Horne, R. (2005). The use and reporting of cluster analysis in health psychology: A review. *British Journal of Health Psychology, 10*(3), 329–358.

Dunn, K. M. (2009). Performing Australian nationalisms at Cronulla. In G. Noble (Ed.), *Lines in the sand: The Cronulla riots, multiculturalism and national belonging* (pp. 76–94). Sydney: Institute of Criminology Press.

Flannery, B., & Watt, S. (2017). Development and validation of the protective nationalism scale. *In Preperation.*

Fozdar, F., Spittles, B., & Hartley, L. K. (2015). Australia Day, flags on cars and Australian nationalism. *Journal of Sociology, 51*(2), 317–336.

Gale, P. (2004). The refugee crisis and fear: Populist politics and media discourse. *Journal of Sociology, 40*(4), 321–340.

Gale, P. (2005). *The politics of fear : Lighting the Wik*. London: Pearson Education.

Gellner, E. (1983). *Nations and nationalism*. Oxford: Blackwell.

Gleeson, K. (2016). *Australia's 'war on terror' discourse*. London: Routledge.

Grant, B. (Ed.). (1997). *Pauline Hanson, One Nation and Australian politics*. Armidale: UNE Press.

Gray, G., & Winter, C. (Eds.). (1997). *The resurgence of racism: Howard, Hanson and the race debate*. Melbourne: Monash Publications in History.

Hage, G. (1998). *White nation : Fantasies of white supremacy in a multicultural society*. New York: Routledge.

Hanson, P. (1996a). *Channel 9 Sixty Minutes interview (video recording)*. http://australianpolitics.com/1996/10/20/pauline-hanson-please-explain-interview.html. Accessed July 27, 2018.

Hanson, P. (1996b). *House of Representatives Official Hansard, 208*, 3860–3863. http://parlinfo.aph.gov.au/parlInfo/download/chamber/hansardr/1996-09-10/toc_pdf/H1996-09-10.pdf;fileTyp e=application%2Fpdf#search=%22BK6))%22. Accessed June 10, 2018.

Hanson, P. (2016a). Channel 7 television commentry. Cited in https://www.news.com.au/national/federal-election/pauline-hanson-loses-it-over-halal-snack-packs/news-story/a52ed6c717833bdc 81c14839e5de9518. Accessed June 10, 2018.

Hanson, P. (2016b). *The Kyle and Jackie O Show*. Cited in https://www.news.com.au/national/fed eral-election/pauline-hanson-says-she-has-no-problems-with-asians-saying-one-nation-member s-have-asian-wives/news-story/eb2ac8435ae68a49dbf120d83010efe3. Accessed June 10, 2018.

Hartigan, J. A. (1975). *Clustering algorithms*. Hoboken: Wiley.

Leach, M., Stokes, G., & Ward, I. (Eds.). (2000). *The rise and fall of One Nation*. Brisbane: Queensland University Press.

Markus, A. (2001). *Race: John Howard and the remaking of Australia*. Syndey: Allen & Unwin.

Markus, A. (2015). *Mapping social cohesion*. http://monash.edu/mapping-population/. Accessed July 11, 2018.

Marr, D. (2017). The white queen: One Nation and the politics of race. *Quarterly Essay, 65,* 139.

Mclennan, G. (2001). Can there be a "critical" multiculturalism? *Ethnicities, 1*(3), 389–422.

Murray, G. (2005). Pauline Hanson's One Nation: Extreme right, centre party or extreme left? *Labour History, 89,* 101–119.

Parliamentary Debates. (1996). *House of Representatives Official Hansard, 208*, 3860–3863. http://parlinfo.aph.gov.au/parlInfo/download/chamber/hansardr/1996-09-10/toc_pdf/H1996-09-10.pdf;fileType=application%2Fpdf#search=%22BK6))%22. Accessed June 10, 2018.

Pasquarelli, J. (1997). The Pauline Hanson phenomenon. *Australia & World Affairs, 33,* 5–8.

Pasquarelli, J. (1998). *The Pauline Hanson story by the man who knows*. Sydney: New Holland.

Porter, E. (2003). Security and inclusiveness: Protecting Australia's way of life. *Peace, Conflict and Development* 3. http://www.brad.ac.uk/social-sciences/peace-conflict-and-development/issue-3/ Security-and-inclusiveness.pdf. Accessed June 10, 2018.

Shaw, K. M., Valadez, J. R., & Rhoads, R. A. (1999). *Community colleges as cultural texts: Qualitative explorations of organizational and student culture*. New York: State University of New York Press.

Soutphommasane, T., Clarke, M. B., Chocka, B. C., Law, B., Pung, A., & Tsiolkas, C. (2015). *I'm not racist, but—Forty years of the Racial Discrimination Act*. Sydney, Australia: UNSW Press.

Wear, R. (2008). Permanent populism: The Howard Government 1996–2007. *Australian Journal of Political Science, 43*(4), 617–634.

Wells, D. (1997). One Nation and the politics of populism. In B. Grant (Ed.), *Pauline Hanson One Nation and Australian Politics* (pp. 18–28). Armidale: University Press of New England.

Younane, S. (2006). *Protecting "our way of life": Constructions of national identity in government anti-terrorism advertising*. Refereed paper presented to Australasian political Studies Association Conference, University of Newcastle, 25–27 September. http://citeseerx.ist.psu.edu/viewdoc/download;jsessionid=D6595B90F13E2C1F8E7C5222 0DECE4A4?doi=10.1.1.497.6638&rep=rep1&type=pdf. Accessed June 10, 2018.

Part II
Election

Chapter 5
One Nation and the Heartland's Cleavage: An Exploratory Spatial Data Analysis

Ben Reid and Gang-Jun Liu

Abstract The considerable variation in One Nation's 2016 federal election results reflects many social and spatial factors. The party's policies and increased acceptance, on a national scale, are another reflection of the deep anxieties that some voters feel about Islam, race, and immigration. These sentiments have found periodic political expressions in Australian and other societies. One Nation's resurgence has also followed an international trend of increased support for right-populist politics. Some parallels exist between the social and spatial characteristics of One Nation's electoral constituency and these other national contexts. This study of the electoral geography of One Nation utilizes newer methods of spatial analysis to examine these processes.

Keywords Australia's heartland · Geo-spatial analysis · Hansonism

5.1 Introduction

There is no precise definition of right-populism. Its forms of expression vary considerably across European, North American, and other contexts (Bruter and Harrison 2013). Right-populist politics as a whole, however, appeals to both notions of resistance to "established power" and prejudices against ethnocultural, religious, gendered, or sexuality defined "others" (Lazaridis et al. 2016). A range of international processes corresponded with the recent growth in its political support. The ongoing impacts of the Great Recession and the long stagnation of the North Atlantic economies (Judis 2016) occurred alongside increased political insecurity in the Middle East and other majority Muslim regions of the world. One consequence was an

B. Reid (✉) · G.-J. Liu (✉)
Geo-Spatial Sciences, School of Science, Royal Melbourne Institute of Technology (RMIT),
124a La Trobe St., Melbourne, VIC 3000, Australia
e-mail: ben.reid@rmit.edu.au

G.-J. Liu
e-mail: gang-jun.liu@rmit.edu.au

© Springer Nature Singapore Pte Ltd. 2019
B. Grant et al. (eds.), *The Rise of Right-Populism*,
https://doi.org/10.1007/978-981-13-2670-7_5

increase in "Islamophobia", consisting of exaggerated fears over so-called Muslim culture(s) and communities (Kundnani 2014).

Although different from the emergence of other right-populist electoral formations, Donald Trump's election as the United States President and the "Brexit" vote in the United Kingdom arguably represent the movement of some right-populist political themes into the political mainstream (Inglehart and Norris 2016). While the most intense expressions of right-populism have been the emergence of newer parties, there has also been a percolation of these themes into more mainstream and center-right-based groups.

In Australia, an initial rise in electoral support for One Nation occurred in the late 1990s. Its right-populist character consisted of appeals to "Anglo-Celtic" and so-called "battler" voters, combined with the exploitation of fears over levels of "Asian" immigration. It also cultivated resentment towards the modest policies that existed to redress disadvantages amongst the Indigenous minority population (Leach et al. 2000). Despite the absorption of some One Nation policies by mainstream political parties—notably surrounding asylum seekers and Indigenous rights—the popularity of right-populism again increased in the 2016 Federal election (Marr 2017).

Both the established and more recently arrived immigrant Muslim communities are well integrated into Australian society. An intense policy and media focus on so-called Islamic "radicalization", however, has contributed to a sense of marginalization amongst these populations. There has also been an associated upsurge in exaggerated fears over so-called Islamic culture(s) (Dunn et al. 2015). As the analysis below demonstrates, though, the proportional popularity of right-populist voting was often greatest in places with a lower presence of these minorities.

Indeed, the rising levels of electoral support for right-populism in Australia and internationally has often followed distinctive spatial trends. An intensifying spatial and social-based "cleavage" emerged between the so-called "heartlands" of different countries and their more urban centers. The term heartlands has, historically, been employed by geographers in many different ways (Higbie 2014). The contemporary notion of the heartlands implies distinctive spatial, political, and affective aspects. In the United States, its use emerged to define a strategy of political conservatives and business boosters to typically represent a region as rural (see Frank 2004: 16) . It has more recently been applied to designate places with a strong propensity to support right-populist electoral groups in a range of national contexts.

Indeed, we argue One Nation's increased electoral support during and after the 2016 federal election was proportionately much stronger in heartland areas (especially in regional and outback Queensland). Using methods of exploratory spatial data analysis (ESDA), electoral geography, and geographical information systems (GIS), this chapter presents an analysis of the social and spatial characteristics of high One Nation voting areas. The first section examines some of the main trends in election studies and their implications for the Australian context. We then outline the methods derived from innovations in spatial analysis, presenting a detailed analysis and visualization of Senate voting trends on a national scale. A subsequent grouping analysis of Queensland's polling booths presents a typology of five socio-spatial zones based upon variations in levels of support for One Nation.

5.2   The "Heartland Cleavage"

Historically, considerable research has investigated the spatial analysis of elections. It has often focused on the locational dimensions of social cleavages underpinning voting preferences. Like most countries, elections in Australia reflect both these international trends and distinctive facets of the countries' historical development. One Nation's disproportionate popularity in some areas mirrors these historical and geographical processes.

The formal analysis of relationships between social cleavages and election processes and outcomes started in the early 1960s (Johnston 2005; Lijphart 1990). It appeared then that the main patterns in electoral support within higher-income and liberal-democratic countries had been "frozen" since the 1920s. The electoral preferences of groups tended to reflect four distinct social divides: between social classes (owners and labor), land (countryside and cities), secularism (church and state), and location (core and periphery) (Lipset and Rokkan 1967). A predominantly social class-based pattern of voting existed in many countries, which often resulted in competition between loosely center-left versus center-right ideologically based political parties.[1] Electoral geography differs from political sociology as it is more explicitly concerned with both the compositional and contextual (place-based) processes underpinning election outcomes (Johnston and Pattie 2006). It focuses more on how and why people voted ways in different *places*.

In some ways, the cleavage-based framework's explanatory power seemed to increasingly wane after the 1970s. First, the intensity of some cleavages decreased, such as the association between social classes and voting choices (Bartolini and Mair 1990). Second, newer cleavages emerged over ethnicity, gender, sexuality, and other issues (Webster et al. 2010). Third, some older cleavages—such as between the countryside and urban-based areas—reasserted themselves in new and revived forms.

Arguably, the emergence of right-populist politics in many developed countries was one reflection of these trends. The far-right made few electoral inroads during the 1950s and 1960s (Childers 1985). The emergence of some political groups in the 1970s, however, changed this. Debates arose over the social composition and location of these newer parties' bases of electoral support (Lazaridis et al. 2016). One of the most persistent trends underpinning the emergence of right-populism was a deepening of social and spatial-based cleavages between rural/regional and urban-based constituencies.

In the United States, the changing geographies of election outcomes became a focus of discussion (Chinni and Gimpel 2010; Morrill et al. 2007). These studies, however, were not particularly concerned with the rise of newer right-populist parties.[2] Instead they focused mostly on how an increasingly right-wing Republican

---

[1]These are not the only approaches to election analysis. There are other influential approaches based on markets and changing values, for instance (see Norris 1998).

[2]The predominance of proportionally representation-based election systems in Europe is less exclusive to new entrants in electoral competition.

Party attracted rising support amongst lower-income voters. "red versus blue state" cleavage became a popular frame of reference.[3] The low-income populations of the heartland states increasingly shifted support to the Republicans (Frank 2004) . The Republicans successfully utilized appeals to white racial identity and social conservatism to attract their support (Webster et al. 2010).

In contrast, the analyses undertaken outside of the United States focused more on the newer and independent right-populist parties. Whether studied from an explicitly spatial perspective or not, many contextual themes were present. Shin and Agnew (2002) demonstrated that support for the *Liga Nord* in Italy remained largely confined to the country's northern region and outside of major cities. Studies in Switzerland suggested that right-populism's largest base was in rural cantons with "locally cohesive" populations (Fitzgerald and Lawrence 2011). Similar social and locational-based cleavages underpinned the emergence of right-populism elsewhere. There were other common features, such as a low presence of ethnocultural minorities and lower levels of indicators for socio-economic disadvantage. While in rural areas incomes were often lower than in urban areas, there was higher asset ownership and lower unemployment.

Most recently, Donald Trump's unexpected election as United States President and the United Kingdom's "Brexit" vote in 2016 provided more examples of these patterns. First, Trump's constituency was overwhelmingly in the "red states", while a majority of voters in the urban and coastal areas opted for Hillary Clinton (Cohn 2017; Kilibarda and Roithmayr 2016). Second and accordingly, the United Kingdom's vote over leaving the European Union polarized between urban and non-urban electorates. "Euroscepticism" has been associated with right-populism in Britain since the 1980s (Gifford 2014). Almost all of the major cities in England and Wales (except Birmingham) voted to remain in the EU (*The Guardian* 2017), while regional areas opted to leave.[4]

Australia has also experienced similar processes. Political scientists have conducted most of the research into its elections (Goot 2007; McAllister 2011). Australia's electoral and party-based systems largely followed a social-class-based cleavage, although its strength has progressively declined (McAllister 2011, p. 176). The spatial analysis of elections in Australia—examining population variables and their relationships to outcomes—was less prominent. There have been, however, some insightful analyses of state and federal elections (Davis and Stimson 1998; Stimson and Shyy 2013; Stimson et al. 2006) .

Indeed, Stimson and Shyy (2013, p. 640) identified a four-fold "socio-political" typology of areas and their association with party support. Although not formulated with explicit reference to electoral geography, a pattern of socio-spatial cleavages is apparent. First, support for the Liberal Party's (LP)—the main party of the center

---

[3]The geography of election outcomes has altered several times over the last century. Most recently the "sun-belt"-based (south-western versus north-east cleavage) has given way to the blue and red state' based division (Johnston 1982; Lewis 2012; Phillips 2015).

[4]There was an additional factor, however, of a division between England and Wales and Scotland and Northern Ireland.

right—was strongest in areas with both higher levels of income and asset ownership (and less ethnocultural diversity). Second, support for the (notionally) center-left Australian Labor Party's (ALP) was highest in places with both lower incomes and levels of asset ownership (and more ethnocultural diversity). Third, Greens-voting areas had higher incomes and lower levels of asset ownership (and more ethnocultural diversity). Fourth and finally, an ageing regional population exhibited a contradictory combination of lower incomes, higher levels of asset ownership, and less presence of ethnocultural minorities.[5] These areas largely supported the National Party of Australia (NPA) (originally the Country Party) that has usually governed in coalition with the LP.

"Well-to-do" farmers established the NPA in the 1920s, although it had a broader electoral base amongst different sectors in the countryside (and sometimes in cities). It, therefore, historically reflected a cleavage between town and countryside. The NPA's share of the national vote, however, has consistently declined since the 1970s. Its shrinking voter base has reflected economic changes and the related demographic stagnation or decline in many rural areas (Botterill and Cockfield 2009) . In the late 1960s and early 1970s, the party still obtained just under ten percent of the first preference lower-house vote. By 1996 it received just under six percent. The decline contributed to an eventual merger between the NPA with the LP in Queensland (the state where it historically has its greatest base of support), becoming the Liberal and National Party (LNP) in 2008.[6]

The rise, fall, and rise again of One Nation occurred in the context of these shifts in rural and regional voting. One Nation's initial emergence was generally attributed to the NPA's decline in popularity and disappointment over the then new LP and NPA coalition to federal government in 1996. One Nation voters shifted away from supporting the LP and NPA at a rate of more than twice that of the ALP (Leach et al. 2000; Marr 2017, p. 59). Researchers debated the interpretations of survey data and the party's initial surge in popularity. Using the 1998 *Australian Election Study* (AES), Goot and Watson (2001, p. 159) argued One Nation voters were motivated by "opposition to 'new class' values, particularly around race" rather than "economic insecurity". Their critics, while conceding that the depth of opposition to immigration was important, claimed economic vulnerability remained a factor (Turnbull and Wilson 2001). Goot and Watson (2001) conceded that there were limits to their regression-based analysis, as less-educated and regional voters were possibly under-represented in survey results.

Indeed, much of this earlier research paid only cursory attention to the spatial concentrations of One Nation's voters. There were some exceptions. Grant and Sorenson (2000) applied a factor analysis to the 1998 federal poll results and the underlying socio-economic characteristics of electorates in Queensland and New South Wales. They found evidence of a correlation between the incidence of "rural poverty" and levels of One Nation support. The choice of an electorate-based scale of analysis,

---

[5]The Northern Territory's Country-Liberal Party is an exception.

[6]Queensland was traditionally NPA's strongest state and the only place where it was the larger of the two center-right coalition parties (Whitton 1993).

however, aggregated away many of the finer scale aspects of regions. It was difficult to identify differences within such large-scale units of analysis.

In contrast, Davis and Stimson (1998) had earlier examined the results of the Queensland state election using booth and census collection district data (the [then] highest resolution of spatial data). Employing GIS and stepwise regression analysis, they identified some of the predominant features of higher One Nation voting districts. Clustered on the "fringes" of regional urban areas, the One Nation vote corresponded with:

> [B]lue collar industries, percentage employed in agricultural and unskilled workers… Those who own their own homes or are in the process of buying them are also more inclined to the views of the One Nation Party. Finally, areas with higher percentages of non-mainstream (fundamentalist) Christian groups are also more inclined to support the … party (Davis and Stimson 1998, p. 11)

There was already, therefore, a strong regional component of the One Nation vote, although it was lower in the agricultural and farming-based heartlands in comparison to peri-urban areas.

To date, much of the analysis of the June 2016 federal election has, understandably, been conducted by journalists (although there was little coverage of One Nation before the vote).[7] A few articles focused on whether coal-industry industrialist Clive Palmer's right-populist party would again run candidates and, if not, who voters would opt to support (Walker 2016). One Nation's success resulted in more investigative reporting. As in the late 1990s, much of the party's support was disproportionately from traditional NPA voting and regional areas. Considerable attention focused on the decline of large capital expenditures in the mining sector and its impacts on economic growth and regional employment (Murphy and Wade 2016). Other right-populist parties also registered gains.

An extended essay by journalist Marr (2017) drew on—among other sources—material from the 2016 *AES*. He concluded One Nation voters in 2016 were:

> [A]bsolutely Australian: the Aussie children of Aussie parents. They identify as proudly working class. Despite its reputation as a bush party, half One Nation's strength lies in big cities. Almost all Hanson's voters left school early but went on to make a good fist of their lives". (Marr 2017, p. 112)

Other in-depth interviews with One Nation supporters reached similar conclusions. Some focused on older voters outside capital city regions, who voiced concerns about immigration levels and Islam (Madigan and Honnery 2016). Additional accounts from more urban-based supporters also emphasized these fears (Jabour 2016). None, however, deployed systematic qualitative data analysis. The 2016 *AES* had limited value, with One Nation supporters comprising just 70 (32 from Queensland) of 2818 respondents. A disproportionately high proportion (62.5%) of these lived in either a city or large towns (Bean et al. 2003). These biases may account for Marr's observations on One Nation's strength in urban areas.

---

[7] A search of Factiva (2018) revealed just four articles in major Australian newspapers that mentioned the ONP in March 2016. This increased to 952 after the election in July.

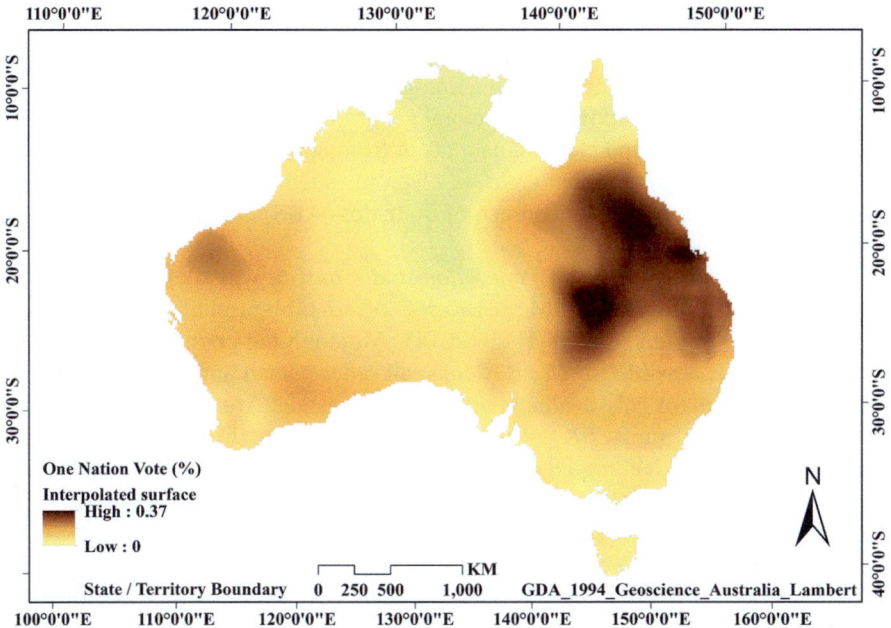

Fig. 5.1 One Nation's 2016 Senate vote percentage heat map. *Source* Derived from AEC (2016)

Claims about the extent of its current urban base notwithstanding, the earlier research emphasized the regional character of One Nation's electoral base. It followed an international trend where rising support for right-populism reflected resurgent rural and urban-centered electoral cleavages.

5.3 Spatial Analysis and Visualization

We conducted a more detailed spatial analysis of One Nation's electoral performance using ESDA and GIS. There were four main steps in the process. The first step involved identifying how and where One Nation's vote varied across Australia. A list of "expected polling places" with (mostly accurate) location address data was matched with booth-level voting outcomes (AEC 2016). These polling places were geo-coded as point data using ArcMap 10.4.1. The first-preference voting data for the Senate was spatially joined to each polling booth. Senate voting was used as One Nation stood in only a limited number of lower house seats across the country. They did not run candidates in the Northern Territory.

The second step involved generating a heat map to visualize the spatial variation of One Nation's proportional vote on a national scale. As Fig. 5.1 illustrates, Queensland was the location with the greatest proportional concentration of One Nation support. It became the focus of subsequent more detailed analysis of socio-spatial characteristics.

The third step involved conducting a fine-grained analysis of relevant spatial and social datasets. As noted above, the electoral geography literature has often used GIS to compare population and election data taken from administrative regions, such as counties, municipal government areas, or electorates (Morrill et al. 2007; Shin and Agnew 2002). Even Australian Bureau of Statistics (ABS) collection districts were defined administratively.

The ABS (2011) *Census on Population and Housing* was the main source of social data used in the study. "Mesh Blocks" of 30–60 households are the smallest spatial units of data storage (Hugo 2014). Although the counts of persons and households are accessible for Mesh Blocks, all other person and household census characteristics remain only available at larger—Statistical Areas Level One (SA1s) and greater—spatial units. SA1-scale records were accessed using the ABS table builder "pro" facility. Taking Davis and Stimson's (1998) earlier work as a starting point, we examined variables to identify characteristics of areas, with some being amalgamated (see Table 5.1).

We assumed that most electors voted close to their usual place of residence and that associations were possible between booth-level results and their surrounding areas' population characteristics. Hence, we examined the characteristics of voting areas with booth catchment level data, aggregated from the Mesh-Block level data, which in turn were disaggregated from the SA1 level data. The allocation of the social data into polling booth catchments followed three sub-steps:

- Each mesh block was allocated its SA1 population proportions. As household and person counts were available for mesh blocks, it was possible to get an estimate of proportional social characteristics at this scale.
- Polling catchments were created using ESRI ArcMap 10.4.1 through closest facility analysis, in which Mesh Block centroids were used as incidents, Polling booth locations were used as facilities, and each Mesh Block was allocated to its nearest polling booth.
- The counts for the mesh blocks and their proportional social characteristics were merged for each polling catchment. Figure 5.2 features an example of the resulting allocation of mesh blocks, routes, and polling booths.

We also geocoded locational data for a range of facilities: schools and education facilities, hospitals and medical centers, commercial centers, places of worship, post offices, and banks (Queensland Government n.d.a). Network-based closest facility analyses were conducted to measure the travel distances from each mesh block centroid to its closest facilities. These travel distances represent the levels of accessibility to these facilities for voters residing in different Mesh Blocks. Both the mean and sum of travel distances from Mesh Block centroids to different types of facilities were calculated for each polling catchment.

The process provided a rich source of data from which to undertake further exploratory spatial data analysis. The main variable of interest was the percentage

Table 5.1 Socio-economic and cultural variables

Variable	Explanation
Employed	Employed full time
Unemployed	Unemployed
Not_in_the_labor_force	Not in labor force
Employ_NA	Employment not applicable
AU_NZ	Australian and New Zealand born
ATSI	Aboriginal and Torres Strait Islander
Non_Muslim_Asia	Origins in non-Muslim majority Asian culture or country
Other_non_Muslim	Origins in non-Muslim majority culture or country
Maj_Muslim_cultures	Muslim majority Asia culture or country
Less20	Employer with 20 or less employees
Btwn20_49	Persons aged more than 50 years old
Over_50	Persons aged between 20 and 50 years old
Income_less200	Income less than $200 a week
Income_bwtn200_599	Income between $200 and $600 a week
Income_greater_600	Income greater than $600 a week
Agriculture__Forestry_and_Fishing	Labor force in agriculture, forestry and fishing
Mining	Labor force in mining
Manufacturing	Labor force in manufacturing
Other_industry	Labor force in other industry
Distribution	Labor force in distribution
Services	Labor force in hospitality
Managers	Managers
Professionals	Professionals
Skilled	Skilled Labor force in technology specialists
Blue	Labor -force that are labourers or machine operators
Christianity	Christian
Islam	Islamic
Rel_oth	Other religions
Year_12_or_equivalent	Year 12 qualifications or equivalent
No_Internet_connection	No internet connection
Owned_outright	Housing owned outright
Owned_with_a_mortgage	Housing owned with a mortgage
Rented	Housing rented

Source Authors

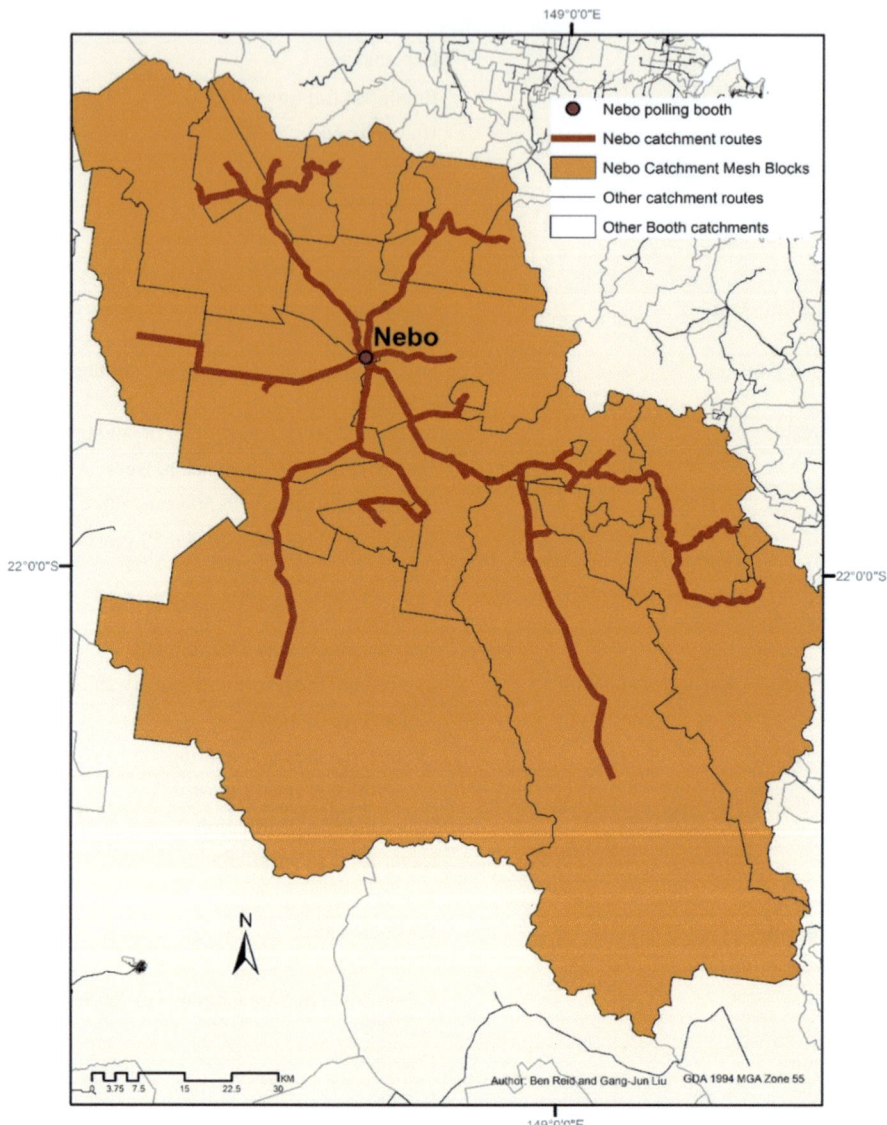

Fig. 5.2 Nebo polling booth 2016 catchment area. *Source* Authors

vote for One Nation, and more important explanatory locational and social variables were identified using a bivariate Pearson correlation matrix.

The fourth step used a grouping analysis to develop an analysis of spatially differentiated voting regions in Queensland. It first identified three categories of voting zones, before two further sub-categories were identified with a set of zone-specific location quotients (LQ) for each of the selected variables, calculated with the following equation:

$$LQ_{ij} = \left[\frac{\left(v_{ij}/p_{ij} \right)}{V_{is}/P_{is}} \right] \tag{1}$$

where:

LQ_{ij} is the location quotient in zone j for variable i
v_{ij} is the number of people in zone j for variable i
p_{ij} is the total population of zone j
V_{is} is the number of people in state s for variable i
P_{is} is the total population in state s for variable i

These location quotients measure the differences between each region in comparison to the mean of a larger area (Stimson et al. 2014). In this case, the mean for the state of Queensland was the comparison. The resulted areas were mapped and represented with separate "radar" diagrams (Figs. 5.3, 5.4, 5.5, 5.6 and 5.7) to visualize the contrasts. An arbitrary upper ratio limit of two was applied.

5.4 One Nation and the 2016 Election

It was clear that pronounced spatial-based trends underpinned both the national and Queensland-based One Nation's Senate vote. The party's proportionate vote was much higher in certain areas.

Figure 5.1 and Table 5.2 summarize the 2016 election outcome for One Nation across the country. The area of the greatest concentration of One Nation voting was the interior of Queensland.

Examining Fig. 5.1 and Table 5.2, the percentage vote was far lower in other states and in urban and more densely settled regional areas. One Nation's primary Senate vote in Queensland was 9.2%, and the national average was 4.2%.

Figure 5.3 shows the spatial variation of One Nation's votes within Queensland. One Nation's percentage vote was far lower in the state's south-east, far north and major urban centers. A larger portion of the state's population did not vote for One Nation. The largest percentage votes for One Nation occurred in Queensland's less densely settled interior and regional areas.

There was a strong positive correlation (0.516) between One Nation vote and a lack of proximity to most services.[8] The exception was with schools, where there was no relationship. Paradoxically, perhaps, a strong negative correlation (−0.614) was found between the population with Year 12 or equivalent qualifications and One Nation vote. Regarding sectoral employment, a higher proportion of One Nation vote was from the labor force employed in Mining (0.265) and Agriculture and

---

[8]Correlation is significant at the 0.01 level (2-tailed).

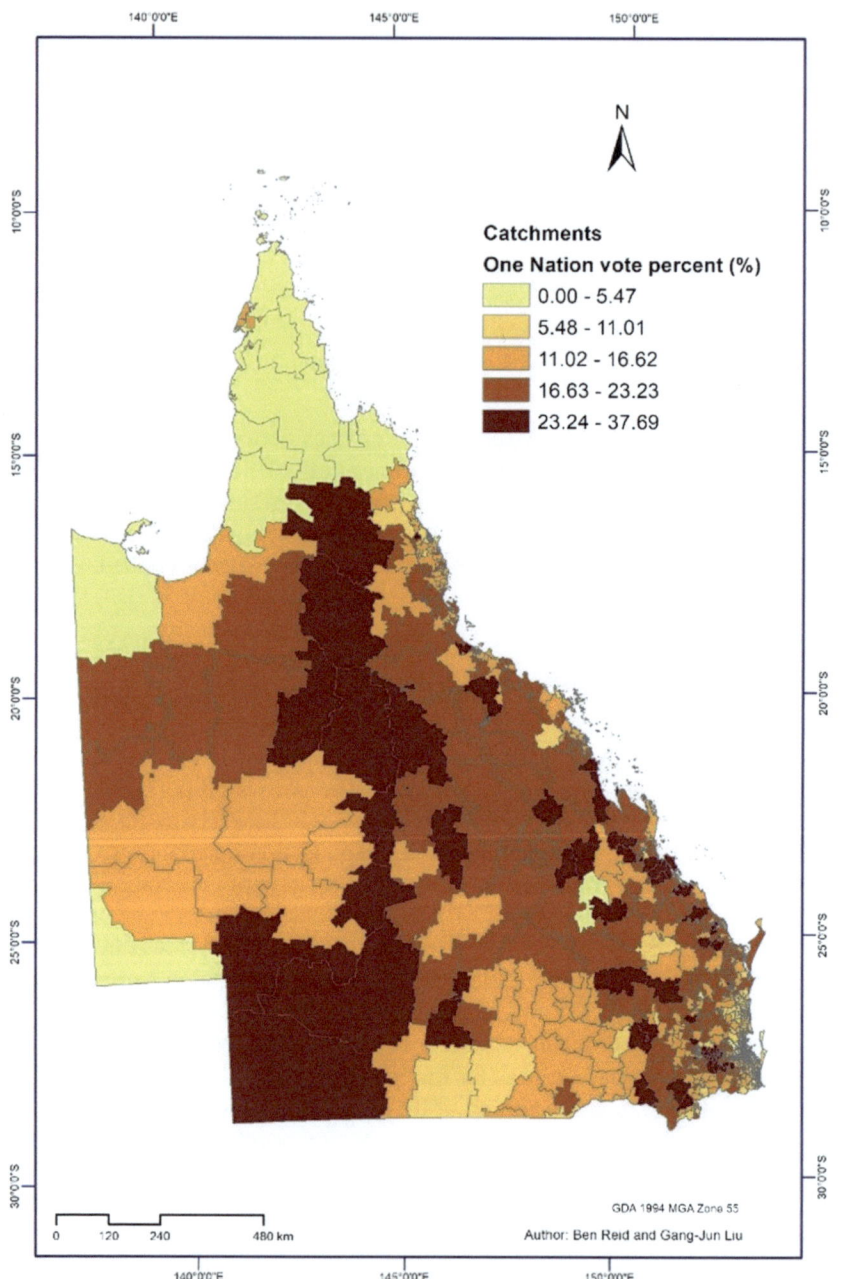

Fig. 5.3 Spatial distribution of One Nation 2016 Senate vote percentage in Queensland. *Source* Authors

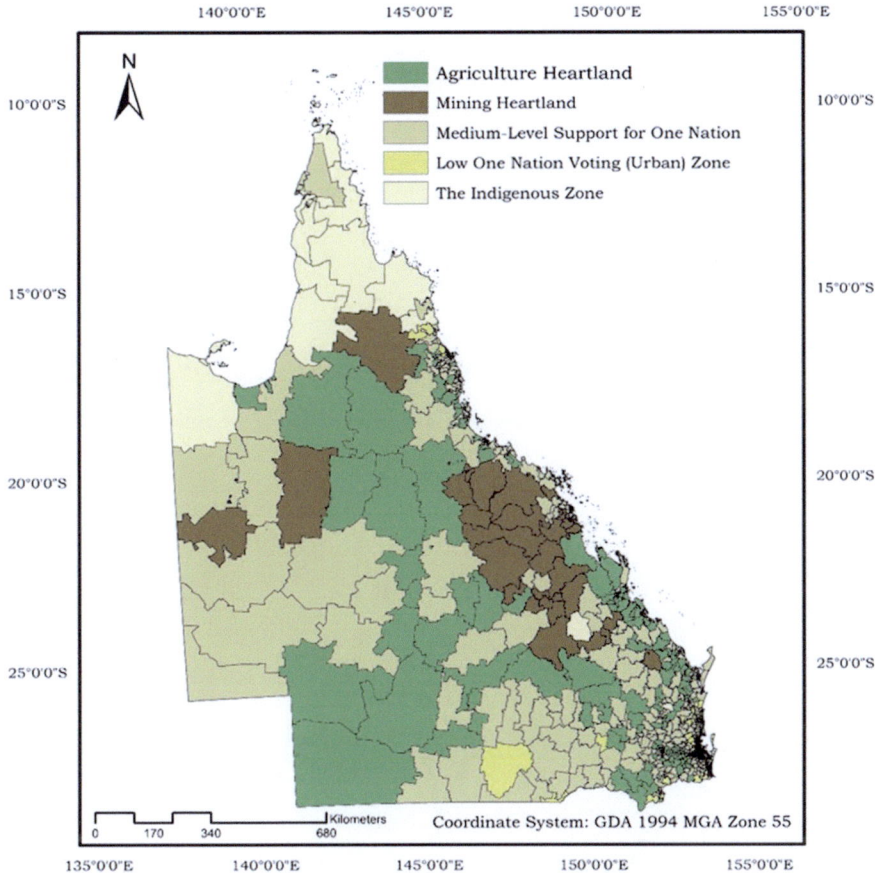

Fig. 5.4 Typology of zones by voter type in Queensland. *Source* Authors

Fisheries (0.426). Employment in services corresponded with a lower One Nation vote. There were contradictory trends with occupations. The presence of blue collar workers (0.554), on the one hand, correlated with a higher One Nation vote, but the relationship between One Nation vote and employment in manufacturing was not significant. A higher presence of professionals correlated with a lower One Nation vote (−0.568), while a prevalence of managers (0.261) corresponded with higher support.

There was a contradictory relationship between levels of support for One Nation and income and asset ownership. A presence of more people with below-average incomes corresponded with higher One Nation support (0.318). Higher level of out-right home ownership, on the other hand, was also associated with areas with greater

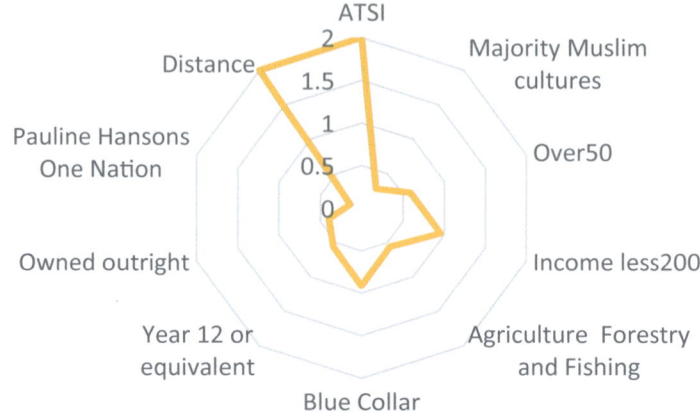

Fig. 5.5 The Indigenous Zone. *Source* Authors

Fig. 5.6 Low One Nation voting (urban) zone. *Source* Authors

One Nation support (0.242). The presence of larger proportions of the population aged over 50 also corresponded with higher One Nation support (0.248).

As indicated above, a lot of attention focused on the One Nation vote and its relationship to the growth in unemployment in regional Queensland. The relationship between support for One Nation and unemployment was difficult to determine as the 2011 census was dated and more recent surveys covered only large-scale labor market regions. The 2011 data showed no significant correlation with One Nation vote (−0.257). While the ABS (2016a, b) employment data for June 2016 suggested there was a much higher level of overall unemployment across the state, finer resolution spatial trends were difficult to discern. The "Queensland-Outback" region,

Fig. 5.7   Medium One Nation supporting zone. *Source* Authors

Table 5.2   One Nation 2016 electoral results

States	Lower house candidates	Senate candidates	% lower house vote	% senate primary vote	Senators elected
ACT	0	0	0	0.0	0
NSW	3	3	0.68	4.1	1
NT	0	0	0	0.0	0
QLD	12	4	5.87	9.2	2
SA	0	2	0	3.0	0
TAS	0	2	0	2.6	0
VIC	0	2	0	1.8	0
WA	0	3	0	4.0	1

Source AEC (2016)

for instance, encompasses both historically high unemployment rate areas like Cape York and low-rate areas such as the western Darling Downs.

The presence of ethnocultural minorities was the main socio-cultural variable of interest. There was a negative association (-0.464) between the incidence of persons from majority Muslims cultures or countries and levels of One Nation support. There was little relationship between One Nation vote and the presence of Aboriginal and Torres Strait Islander (ATSI) people (-0.030).

The identification of these spatial and social factors provided the foundations for developing a more detailed analysis of how different regions voted. We focused on identifying commonalities across socio-economic and cultural variables, and their occurrence as spatial aggregates. Location quotients (LQs) were calculated to measure the variation between different polling catchments from state averages for Queensland. Thirteen main indicators were selected: Aboriginal and Torres Strait Islander population (ATSI), presence of people of Majority Muslim cultures, population aged over 50, households with income less than $200 a week, agricultural employment, mining employment, services employment, managers, professionals, blue collar workers, Year 12 or equivalent, outright home ownership levels, and proximity to services.

The grouping analysis identified three initial zones and subsequently distinguished two additional subcategories with distinct characteristics. The resulting five zones (Fig. 5.4) are described in Sects. 5.4.1, 5.4.2, 5.4.3, 5.4.4 and 5.4.5.

5.4.1 The Indigenous Zone

First, the most remote and disadvantaged areas of Queensland exhibited very low average percentage of One Nation vote. Their defining factor was a much higher proportional prevalence of Indigenous populations (with a LQ of 2 or greater), although the approximate total number of people residing in the Indigenous Region was small (around 80,500). As Fig. 5.4 reveals, these areas were mostly in the state's far north, although other settlements (such as reserves) exist throughout the state. The LQs for the Indigenous Zone are featured in Fig. 5.5.

The results in Fig. 5.5 illustrate several points. First, there was a high LQ (2 or greater) for travel distances, meaning that these polling catchments were on average considerably more remote from commercial centers and services. Second, many of their socio-economic characteristics imply higher levels of economic insecurity. The LQs for Year 12 education (0.6), outright home ownership (0.4), and low-income earners (1.0) were all lower than or close to the state averages. Third, in contrast to the LQ for the presence of Indigenous populations, the LQ for the presence of persons from Majority-Muslim cultures was low (0.3). Finally, the LQ for the age category was low (0.6). The most prominent element, however, was the LQ for the One Nation vote (0.14), which was also the lowest of any region.

Therefore, the prevalence of economic insecurity or remoteness was not in itself a strong predictor of an area having a higher or lower percentage of One Nation vote. While there was no correlation between higher levels of unemployment and higher One Nation votes overall, the Indigenous areas did feature far higher levels of joblessness compared with the heartlands.

5.4.2 Low One Nation Voting (Urban) Zone

The other zone where the proportional One Nation Senate vote was low comprised mostly urban areas. These areas have shorter travel distances, lower than average employment in agriculture or mining, and a much larger share of Queensland's population (over 3 million of the state's 4.3 million inhabitants). This zone includes Queensland's major urban and population centers, such as Brisbane, Logan, the Sunshine and Gold coasts, Toowoomba, Rockhampton, Gladstone, Townsville, and Cairns. There are also "outlier" catchments in the southern interior of the state.

Figure 5.6 illustrates these points. The LQ for the average percentage of One Nation vote in each catchment was 0.8. It had a travel distance LQ of 0.15, and the largest proportional population with Year 12 or above formal qualifications (LQ 1.3). The LQ for employment in the service sector was 1.3. The socio-economic indicators were contradictory, with an average proportional presence of lower-income earners (LQ 1.0), but a lower prevalence of outright home ownership (LQ 0.9). In other words, higher incomes were combined with lower levels of asset ownership. The population was younger, with a LQ of 0.9 of the proportion of the population over the age of 50.

However, the biggest contrasts of all were the socio-cultural indicators for religion and ethnicity. There was, on the one hand, a lower proportional presence of Indigenous minority populations (LQ 0.2). The main difference was the results for the indicators of the presence of Majority-Muslim culture populations, with a LQ of 1.7. It also suggests that these ethnocultural populations resided largely in urban areas with greater proximity to services and commercial centers. The Zone's catchment counts suggest over 94% of Queensland's (just under) 37,800 Muslim-identifying people resided in these areas in 2011.

A greater presence of these ethnocultural minorities corresponded with a much lower percentage of One Nation vote. They, moreover, constituted a small proportion of the population in the Urban Zone. It also suggests that much of the non-ethnocultural minority population in the urban Region was not overly concerned about the presence of minorities, at least not enough to vote for One Nation's Senate candidates.

5.4.3 Zone of Medium Level Support for One Nation

Polling catchments for the zone with a medium level of support for One Nation (with 10–19% of the vote) were quite scattered spatially (see Fig. 5.4), covering large areas of the state's more northern and coastal areas and large parts of the mining, pastoral, and broadacre farming-based interior.

However, these areas had marked differences with the two low One Nation voting zones, as indicated in Fig. 5.7.

Figure 5.7 shows that in this Zone the LQ for One Nation Voting was 1.2. The distance LQ of 1.2 was much higher than the urban-based low One Nation voting zone and lower than the Indigenous zone. Other important contrasts were higher LQs for employment in agriculture and fisheries (1.5), mining (1.2), and blue-collar occupations (1.2). This Zone had slightly lower than average prevalence of low-income earners (LQ 0.9) and high levels of outright home ownership (1.1). The proportion of people with Year 12 education was lower than the low One Nation voting areas (LQ 0.8) and the presence of people aged over 50 was the same as the state's average (LQ 1.0). These areas were, therefore, more remote from services with a slightly below average presence of low-income earners and higher prevalence of home ownership and agricultural and mining-based employment.

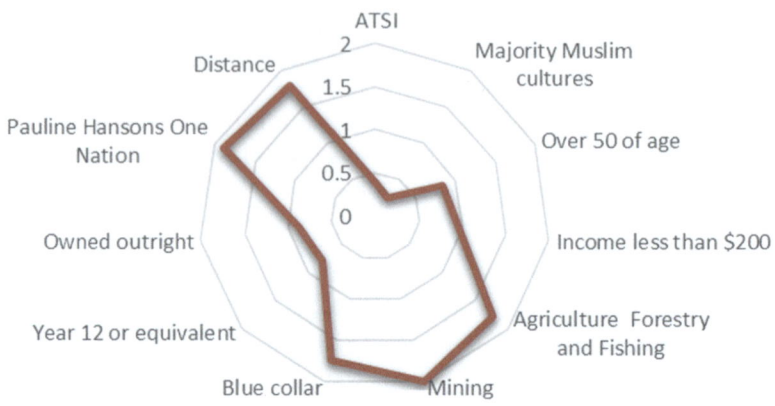

Fig. 5.8 The mining heartland. *Source* The Authors

A lower presence of these minority groups corresponds with a higher level of support for One Nation. LQs for the presence of Indigenous and Muslim culture of origins minority populations (0.4 and 0.5) were much lower than in the low One Nation voting areas.

5.4.4 The Mining Heartland

The high One Nation voting area was based more on mining and agriculture. The Zone had a strong "heartland"-based character, with a combined population of around 752,000 people (out of the state's total population of 4,780,700; Queensland Treasury 2016). The percentage of the One Nate vote ranged between 19.3 and 37.7% in these polling catchments. They can be sub-divided into predominantly mining or agricultural zones.

In the mining-based catchments, employment in mining was more than 50%, higher than the state average. As Fig. 5.4 shows, most of its 205,766 people reside in areas with large numbers of mining leases (DNRM undated.). These mining areas were more likely to be (although not entirely) centered around the Galilee, and Bowen and Styx coal basins of inner and coastal central Queensland (Queensland Government n.d.b). The mining areas with medium levels of One Nation support were more iron ore-, bauxite-, and petroleum-based.

As Fig. 5.8 indicates, the LQ for One Nation voting was 1.9—that is, the mean Senate primary vote for One Nation in this zone was almost twice the state average. The large distance LQ (greater than 1.8) indicates spatial remoteness from commercial centers and other services for the populations residing in the zone.

These mining-based catchments exhibited a smaller proportion of low-income earners (LQ 0.9) and outright home ownership (LQ 0.9), as was the case with the low One Nation supporting urban areas, but much higher proportions of employment in

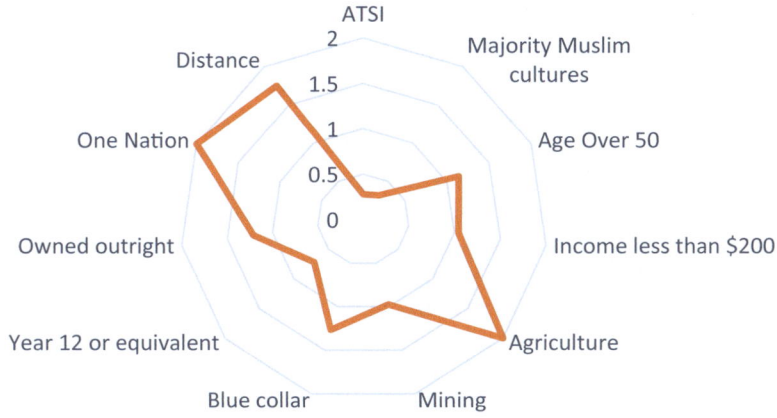

Fig. 5.9 The agricultural heartland. *Source* The Authors

mining (LQ 2.0 or greater) and agriculture (LQ 1.8), as well as blue-collar occupations (1.7). They also had a smaller proportion of the population aged 50 and over (0.8), and of the population with Year 12 qualification (0.8).

Contrasts also existed around the socio-cultural indicators for religion and ethnicity. There was a similar proportional presence of Indigenous minority populations (LQ of 0.4) to the middle-range One Nation supporting zone. The presence of Majority Muslim culture populations (LQ of 0.3) was lower than both the low and mid-ranged One Nation voting areas, but higher than the Indigenous zone.

5.4.5   *The Agricultural Heartland*

The Agricultural Heartland displayed a prevalence of agricultural employment, defined as having a proportional agricultural labor force that was greater than the state's average (LQ greater than 1), and the absence of a large mining-based labor force.

The LQs for its main characteristics are featured in Fig. 5.9. First, this was the Zone with the highest mean percentage vote for One Nation (LQ ≥ 2.0). Second, it followed a trend of the One Nation vote being higher in areas with both lower incomes (LQ 1.1) and higher levels of home asset ownership (LQ 1.2), along with a larger proportion of the population aged over 50 (LQ 1.2). Third, the large LQ of 1.8 for distance also suggests that the region's inhabitants were more likely to reside in areas further away from services and urban centers. Fourth, the LQ for Year 12 education qualifications (0.71) was well below the state's average. Fifth and finally, the LQs for the presence of Indigenous (0.27) and Muslim majority culture populations (0.31) were also low.

The region conformed to the definition of a heartland as it is an interior area of the state, where conservative political parties like One Nation and the NPA had their largest base of support. It is also overwhelmingly composed of the type of socio-political areas that Stimson and Shyy (2013) identified as traditionally supportive of the NPA, with older populations, higher levels of asset ownership, and lower incomes. There was also considerable ethnocultural homogeneity with a low presence of minorities.

Of course, there were variations from the overall trends. Some areas reasonably close to urban centres—such the Lockyer Valley near Toowoomba—had very high percentage of One Nation vote (over 30% in the seat of Wright). There was an additional complication when reviewing both the mining and agriculture-based heartland regions, where other right-populist candidates and parties also received substantial percentage of the Senate vote, including Family-First, Shooters, Fishers and Farmers, and—most notably—(Bob) Katter's Australia Party, most of which allocated preferences to One Nation.

We can see that both heartland regions were high right-populist voting zones, comprising a considerable land area, and yet had a smaller proportional share of the state's total population. They also on average exhibited a greater distance from commercial centres and services. The percentage of One Nation vote was higher, moreover, despite the low presence of ethnocultural and Indigenous minorities.

5.5 Summary and Conclusions

Overall, the analysis of social and spatial trends—on a national scale and in these different areas of Queensland—and their relationship with Senate voting results is revealing. Support for One Nation candidates varied considerably and corresponded with distinctive features of different places. The results followed the international trend of deeper levels of support for right-populism in heartland-based areas in developed country contexts with liberal-democratic institutions.

Competition between rural and urban areas has been a persistent social cleavage that has historically underpinned election outcomes in many countries. The higher proportional support for right-populism within these heartland zones is an expression of these processes that has emerged since the 1970s. The largest social and spatial concentrations of right-populist voters in many parts of the developed world tend to be interior areas with larger resource- and agriculture-based labor forces that are bedrocks of support for the far-right. Although these regions often have a lower presence of ethnocultural minorities, some of the main political and emotional themes of populism have increasingly received considerable support.

Historically, electoral processes in Australia have reflected both these general and distinctive characteristics. The party-based and electoral systems—based primarily on constituencies of competing urban and rural social classes—have proven to be very resilient over time. Australia's history as a settler-colonial society, increasing concentration of the population in urban areas, and changing patterns of sectoral employment have had important impacts. The rural-based NPA, which emerged in the early 20th century, has experienced declining support due to the demographic and economic stagnation of many rural areas.

The results of GIS-based ESDA suggests that, as in the 1990s, proportional support for One Nation varied according to geographically distinct constituencies. As Fig. 5.1 indicates, the greatest support for One Nation was in the heartland areas of Queensland. A social cleavage has arguably deepened between these areas and the more urbanized regions that contain a larger proportion of Australia's population. A comparison of the AEC booth-level votes and ABS census data reveals the extent and character of this social and spatial concentration. The application of network-based closest facility analysis and an aggregation of social data variables from the mesh block level allow for accurate estimates of population characteristics in polling booth catchments.

On the one hand, the analysis suggests a heartland zone with higher levels of One Nation support. The heartland, in turn, can be loosely divided into two sub-regions within the state's interior with differing population characteristics. Both regions contained booth catchments with an average One Nation Senate vote that was 50% higher than the overall average for the state. One region had higher than average employment in agriculture, a population, on average, older than much of the state, and a paradoxical combination of lower incomes and higher levels of asset ownership. The other component of the Heartland had high levels of employment in agriculture, in combination with a substantial workforce in the mining sector. Both agricultural and mining areas were characterized by higher levels of remoteness from commercial centers and services, a low presence of Majority Muslim culture of origin and Indigenous minorities. One exception, however, was the Lockyer Valley in the state's south-east.

Factors such as distance from services, lower incomes, and little presence of ethnocultural minorities did not automatically translate into higher votes for One Nation. The catchments in the most remote areas of Queensland—above all surrounding the Cape York Peninsular and the Gulf of Carpentaria—featured the lowest percentage Senate vote for One Nation. These and other areas had very high proportions of Indigenous people in their populations. One Nation remained unpopular with this constituency.

The more urbanized areas within the state, where the largest share of the population resides, also exhibited much lower levels of support for One Nation. It was also a more formally educated and younger population. There was, on average, a combination of higher incomes with lower levels of asset ownership. It was also—crucially—the only area in the state with a large presence of non-Indigenous ethnocultural minorities. An intermediate zone also exists that supported One Nation at levels above the average for Queensland as a whole. Its employment and social characteristics were in between those of the Urban and Indigenous zones and the Heartland. There was a similarly low proportional presence of ethnocultural minorities.

It follows then that a considerable social cleavage has emerged between a section of the population in these heartland regional areas and those that inhabit the more populated and urban-based areas. It also forms the basis of the higher proportional support for One Nation in these areas. There appears to be a direct relationship between higher levels of support for One Nation and the absence of ethnocultural minority groups. As with right-populism internationally, the One Nation's appeal appears to rely on the "othering" of minority groups that few One Nation voters probably encounter on a day to day basis. While the heartland zones exhibit some signs of locational and socio-economic disadvantage, voters in the most remote and lowest income areas of the state did not support One Nation in any significant way. There was, perhaps, a secondary cleavage within these regional areas between these concentrations of mostly Indigenous populations and the larger heartland. These were populated—by and large—by a less impoverished or socially excluded population.

References

Australian Bureau of Statistics (ABS). (2011). *Australian Census of Population and Housing.* https://auth.censusdata.abs.gov.au/webapi/jsf/dataCatalogueExplorer.xhtml. Accessed 25 September 2017.

Australian Bureau of Statistics (ABS). (2016a). *Australian Census of Population and Housing.* https://auth.censusdata.abs.gov.au/webapi/jsf/dataCatalogueExplorer.xhtml, Accessed 25 September 2017.

Australian Bureau of Statistics (ABS). (2016b). *Labour force, Australia, detailed electronic delivery*, Aug 2016. http://www.abs.gov.au/AUSSTATS/abs@.nsf/DetailsPage/6291.0.55.001Mar2017?OpenDocument. Accessed 7 May 2017.

Australian Electoral Commission (AEC). (2016). Senate downloads—AEC Tally Room. http://results.aec.gov.au/20499/Website/HouseDefault-20499.htm. Accessed 9 October 2016.

Bartolini, S., & Mair, P. (1990). *Identity, competition and electoral availability: The stabilisation of European electorates 1885–1985.* Cambridge, New York: Cambridge University Press.

Bean, C., McAllister, I., Gibson, R., & Makkai, T. (2003). Australian election study 2001. http://www.australianelectionstudy.org. Accessed 11 April 2017.

Botterill, L. E. C., & Cockfield, G. (Eds.). (2009). *The National Party: Prospects for the great survivors.* Crows Nest, NSW: Allen & Unwin.

Bruter, M., & Harrison, S. (2013). *Mapping extreme right ideology: An empirical geography of the European extreme right.* Basingstoke: Palgrave Macmillan.

Childers, T. (1985). *The Nazi voter: The social foundations of fascism in Germany, 1919–1933.* Chapel Hill, NC: University of North Carolina Press.

Chinni, D., & Gimpel, J. (2010). *Our patchwork nation: The surprising truth about the "real" America.* New York, NY: Gotham Books.

Cohn, N. (2017). *A 2016 review: Turnout wasn't the driver of Clinton's defeat.* https://www.nytimes.com/2017/03/28/upshot/a-2016-review-turnout-wasnt-the-driver-of-clintons-defeat.html?_r=0. Accessed 6 April 2017.

Davis, R., & Stimson, R. (1998). Disillusionment and disenchantment at the fringe: Explaining the geography of the One Nation party in the Queensland election. *People and Place, 3,* 1–12.

Dunn, K. A., Atie, R., Mapedzahama, V., Ozalp, M., & Aydogan, A. F. (2015). *The resilience and ordinariness of Australian Muslims.* Western Sydney University. http://apo.org.au/node/59176. Accessed 11 June 2018.

Factavia. (2018). *Search results.* One Nation Party, 01/01–30/09/2016., https://global-factiva-com.ezproxy.lib.rmit.edu.au/ha/default.aspx#./!?&_suid=15295454714550929291748336428. Accessed 21 June 2018.

Fitzgerald, J., & Lawrence, D. (2011). Local cohesion and radical right support: The case of the Swiss People's Party. *Electoral Studies, 30*(4), 834–847.

Frank, T. (2004). *What's the matter with Kansas? How conservatives won the heart of America*. New York, NY: Metropolitan Books.

Gifford, C. (2014). *Making of Eurosceptic Britain*. London: Ashgate Publishing Ltd.

Goot, M. (2007). Election studies. In *Oxford companion to Australian politics*. Oxford: Oxford University Press. Retrieved 13 July 2018, from http://www.oxfordreference.com.ezproxy.lib.rm it.edu.au/view/10.1093/acref/9780195555431.001.0001/acref-9780195555431-e-110.

Goot, M., & Watson, I. (2001). One Nation's electoral support: Where does it come from, what makes it different and how does it fit? *Australian Journal of Politics and History, 47*(2), 159–191.

Grant, B., & Sorenson, T. (2000). Marginality, regionalism and the One Nation vote: Exploring regional socio-economic correlations. In M. Simms & J. Warhurst (Eds.), *Howard's agenda: The 1998 Australian election* (pp. 193–211). St. Lucia: University of Queensland Press.

Higbie, F. (2014). Heartland: The politics of a regional signifier. *Middle West Review, 1*(1), 81–90.

Hugo, G. (2014). Using census data: An Australian example. In R. Stimson (Ed.), *Handbook of research methods and applications in spatially integrated social science* (pp. 103–123). London: Edward Arnold.

Inglehart, R. F., & Norris, P. (2016). *Trump, Brexit, and the rise of populism: Economic have-nots and cultural backlash*. John F Kennedy School of Government, Faculty Research Working Paper Series No. RWP16-026.

Jabour, B. (2016). Meeting Pauline Hanson's voters: Silent screamers find their voice | Australia News. *The Guardian*. https://www.theguardian.com/australia-news/2016/sep/17/meeting-paulin e-hansons-voters-silent-screamers-find-their-voice. Accessed 30 March 2017.

Johnston, R. J. (1982). The changing geography of voting in the United States: 1946–1980. *Transactions of the Institute of British Geographers, 7*(2), 187–204.

Johnston, R. (2005). Anglo-American electoral geography: Same roots and same goals, but different means and ends? *Professional Geographer, 57*(4), 580–587.

Johnston, R., & Pattie, C. (2006). *Putting voters in their place*. Oxford: OUP.

Judis, J. (2016). *The populist explosion: How the great recession transformed American and European politics*. Columbia: Columbia Global Reports.

Kilibarda, K., & Roithmayr, D. (2016). *The myth of the Rust Belt revolt*. Slate. http://www.slate.com/articles/news_and_politics/politics/2016/12/the_myth_of_the_rust_belt_revolt.html. Accessed April 6 2017.

Kundnani, A. (2014). *The muslims are coming! Islamophobia, extremism, and the domestic war on terror*. London: Verso.

Lazaridis, G., Campani, G., & Benveniste, A. (2016). *The rise of the far right in Europe: Populist shifts and "othering"*. London: Palgrave Macmillan.

Leach, M., Stokes, G., & Ward, I. (2000). *The rise and fall of One Nation*. St. Lucia: University of Queensland Press.

Lewis, M. (2012). Changes in U.S. electoral geography from 2000 to 2012: A renewed North/South Divide? *GeoCurrents*. http://www.geocurrents.info/geopolitics/elections/changes-in-u-s-elector al-geography-from-2000-to-2012-a-renewed-northsouth-divide. Accessed 7 April 2017.

Lijphart, A. (1990). The cleavage model and electoral geography: A review. In R. J. Johnston, F. M. Shelley, & P. J. Taylor (Eds.), *Developments in electoral geography* (pp. 143–150). London: Routledge.

Lipset, S. M., & Rokkan, S. (Eds.). (1967). *Party systems and voter alignments: Cross-national perspectives*. New York, NY: Free Press.

Madigan, C., & Honnery, M. (2016, July 9). Swamped by One Nation. *Courier Mail*, p. 49.

Marr, D. (2017). The white queen: One Nation and the politics of race. *Quarterly Essay, 65*, 1–102.

McAllister, I. (2011). *The Australian voter: 50 years of change*. Kensington: University of New South Wales Press.

Morrill, R., Knopp, L., & Brown, M. (2007). Anomalies in red and blue: Exceptionalism in American electoral geography. *Political Geography, 26*(5), 525–553.

Murphy, D., & Wade, M. (2016, November 26). One Nation feeds on rural rumblings. *The Sydney Morning Herald*, p. 26.

Norris, P. (1998). *Elections and voting behaviour: New challenges, new perspectives*. Aldershot: Ashgate.

Phillips, K. (2015). *The emerging Republican majority*. Princeton: Princeton University Press.

Queensland Government. (n.d.-a). Datasets. https://data.qld.gov.au/dataset. Accessed 26 February 2017.

Queensland Government. (n.d.-b). Queensland Coal Map. from http://www.ohsa.com.au/assets/oh sa_documents/MAP/map-assets/qld_coal_map_08.pdf. Accessed 1 May 2017.

Queensland Treasury (2016). Population and growth highlights and trends, Queensland, 2016 edition. Queensland Government Statistician's Office. http://www.qgso.qld.gov.au/products/reports/ pop-growth-highlights-trends-qld/pop-growth-highlights-trends-qld-2016-edn.pdf. Accessed 11 July 2018.

Shin, M. E., & Agnew, J. (2002). The geography of party replacement in Italy, 1987–1996. *Political Geography, 21*(2), 221–242.

Stimson, R. J., & Shyy, T.-K. (2013). And now for something different: Modelling socio-political landscapes. *The Annals of Regional Science, 50*(2), 623–643.

Stimson, R. J., Shyy, T., Azeezullah, I., Azeezullah, I., & Murray, A. (2014). Classification for visualizing data: Integrating multiple attributes and space for choropleth display. In R. J. Stimson (Ed.), *Handbook of research methods and applications in spatially integrated social science* (pp. 265–286). Northampton: Edward Elgar.

Stimson, R., McCrea, R., & Shyy, T. K. (2006). Spatially disaggregated modelling of voting outcomes and socio-economic characteristics at the 2001 Australian federal election. *Geographical Research, 44*(3), 242–254.

The Guardian. (2017). EU referendum full results—find out how your area voted | Politics | The Guardian. https://www.theguardian.com/politics/ng-interactive/2016/jun/23/eu-referendu m-live-results-and-analysis. Accessed 12 January 2017.

Turnbull, N., & Wilson, S. (2001). The two faces of economic insecurity: Reply to Goot and Watson on One Nation. *Australian Journal of Politics & History, 47*(4), 512–515.

Walker, T. (2016, May 21). Turnbull's Senate nightmare. *Australian Financial Review*, p. 16.

Webster, G. R., Chapman, T., & Leib, J. (2010). Sustaining the "societal and scriptural fence": Cultural, social and political topographies of same-sex marriage in Alabama. *The Professional Geographer, 62,* 211–229.

Whitton, E. (1993). *The hillbilly dictator: Australia's police state*. Sydney, NSW: ABC Books.

Chapter 6
Pauline Hanson, Personality, and Electoral Fortunes

Raphaella Kathryn Crosby

Abstract Queensland Senator Pauline Hanson is acknowledged globally as the quintessential populist leader, not for her commitment to populist ideology, but because of her dictatorial control and personality-based leadership of the party. But what are people voting for? Is it populism—the movement intractably associated with right-wing nationalism, hatred, and bigotry? Is it populist campaigning, a framing tactic of posing the candidate as being at one with the ordinary people, in opposition to a (stylized) undemocratic and self-serving elite, irrespective of ideology or partisan leaning? Or is it the rise of the personality or celebrity candidate, who appeals personally to voters more than, and differently from, any message from a political party or ideology? Election results are not always clear, as a candidate may attract voters for all these, or indeed other, reasons, so trying to interpret meaning from vote data is ambiguous at best. To know what voters are voting for, we must determine vote causality. This chapter looks at the difference between populism, populist campaigns, and personality candidates, examines whether there is evidence of support for any of them (with specific reference to Pauline Hanson's One Nation) by comparing 2013 and 2016 federal election Senate results, and discusses the likely performance of Pauline Hanson's One Nation in the upcoming federal election.

Keywords Campaigning · Elections · One Nation · Pauline Hanson · Populism

6.1 Introduction

The cascade of electoral results that political professionals, commentators, and election polls failed to predict—from Brexit (Curtice 2016; Hobolt 2016; Hübner 2016), to Trump (Azari 2016; Loukissas and Pollock 2017; Lusinchi 2017), to the 2015 British general election (Curtice 2015; Sturgis et al. 2016; Wring and Ward 2015),

R. K. Crosby (✉)
College of Arts, Society and Education (CASE), James Cook University & Voter Choice Project, James Cook Drive, Queensland 4814 Douglas, Australia
e-mail: rk.crosby@my.jcu.edu.au; rkc@voterchoice.com.au

© Springer Nature Singapore Pte Ltd. 2019
B. Grant et al. (eds.), *The Rise of Right-Populism*,
https://doi.org/10.1007/978-981-13-2670-7_6

the 2015 Israeli election (Navot et al. 2017; Peters and Pinfold 2015; Rahat et al. 2016), and even the Greek bailout referendum (Silver 2015; Tsatsanis and Teperoglou 2016)—have led to intense conjecture as to whether or not a fundamental shift has occurred in an assortment of political landscapes, and whether or not these shifts amount to a reconfiguration of politics (see, for example, Inglehart and Norris 2016; Parvu 2016; Schmidt 2017; Zakaria 2016). For some, a rise in populism—linked to unhappy, disempowered electorates eager to blame inter alia immigration and globalization for their woes, with a corresponding uptick in nationalist, hate-filled rhetoric—is a reasonable theoretical conclusion (see, for example, Altman 2017; Inglehart and Norris 2016; McDougall 2016; Mols and Jetten 2016; Zakaria 2016). In Australia, the discussion has revolved around the rapid return of Pauline Hanson after 20 years in the political wilderness (see, in particular, Chap. 10 of this book by Jo Coghlan) and the many and varied possible causes of this second meteoric (see, for example, Altman 2017; Marr 2017; Mols and Jetten 2017). There is certainly evidence there is something going on here, a "phenomenon" of a type or types, but what exactly is it?

In this chapter, I posit that there are three different ways one can examine the phenomenon of populism. First, psephologically, that is, just looking at electoral return numbers. From this perspective, we can map support for personality candidates by seeing the significant lifts in support where those candidates stand, contrasted with their party's level of support elsewhere. Second, from the perspective of political communication. Examined as such, it is possible to conduct a campaign effects study to test the success of a populist campaign compared with other campaign frames deployed by strategists, such as the "ideal candidate" frame that I discuss below. Third, we can discuss populism from an ideological approach, incorporating a definition of what populism means, and analyze the success of those parties that adhere to those ideological principles. To determine if Pauline Hanson and Pauline Hanson's One Nation (PHON) is a personality, populist campaigner or advocate, or populism, I analyze both her/their content and electoral performance in the 2013 and 2016 elections in comparison with other micro political parties contesting the Senate.

6.2   The Psephological Approach—Personality Candidates

In Australian politics there is solid evidence to suggest that simply being a well-known personality will boost a candidate's vote. Australian psephologist Malcolm Mackerras analyzed swing deviations, in combination with data from Aitkin's (1982) Australian Survey Project panel, to identify the value of the personal vote for long-standing, popular, or well-known candidates in both of his Ph.D. attempts (Mackerras 1974, 1976). Mackerras argued that country seats and ministers are more likely to benefit from personal vote (Mackerras 1976, pp 47, 447); that this benefit is highest in Tasmania and higher than average in Queensland; and that Victoria has the lowest personal vote variation (Mackerras 1976, pp. 217, 345, 415, 447). Clive Bean (1990) and Ernie Chaples (1997) have since confirmed the benefit of the personal vote, with estimates ranging anywhere from three to ten percent above the party base level of support being achieved by a prominent candidate. This psephological approach to examining populism aligns with Weyland's (2001, p. 14) definition of populism as "a political strategy through which a personalistic leader seeks or exercises government power based on direct, unmediated, uninstitutionalized support from large numbers of mostly unorganized followers".

The personality candidate is one of the indicative characteristics of populism. Populism is generally associated with a strong leader whose charismatic personal appeal, rather than ideology or policy program, is the basis of their support (Abts and Rummens 2007; Mudde and Rovira Kaltwasser 2017; Weyland 2001). Populist parties are often constructed entirely around a personality, such as Emmanuel Macron's party in France or Pauline Hanson's One Nation. Emmanuel Macron is an example of the personality candidate purportedly "rising above" ideology or party in his defeat of right-wing populist Marine Le Pen; in another result that defied polling and expectations, Macron won the 2017 French presidential elections by more than 10 points than was commonly predicted (Barbieri 2017; Enten 2017). In the context of the Australian Senate, the personality candidate may be all the voter knows about that party. In the case of (say) Queensland maverick lower house MP Bob Katter and Katter's Australian Party, or New South Wales state parliamentarian and (former[1]) Reverend Fred Nile and the Christian Democratic Party, these particular individuals—personalities—might not even be candidates. Yet they may be the only person (indeed, they might be the only piece of *information*) that the voter associates with that political party.

Table 6.1 lists those micro parties that contested the 2013 or 2016 Australian federal elections and that had a prominent figure or personality candidate associated with the party. They have been categorized into two groups. Group A (in bold) are personalities who stood for the Senate and, as such, their personal vote should be reflected in voting figures. Group B are personalities that are prominent within what I am deeming as their personal sphere of influence, but they are not prominent media figures, or they did not personally stand for the Senate.

My analysis of their success is presented in Sect. 6.5. At this point, it is worth noting that since the 2016 election there has been considerable change in what is arguably one of the most volatile periods in Australian political history, and that many of these personalities and parties have either changed or have simply exited the political landscape (Butler 2018). Before moving on to consider populism from the perspective of political communication, it is worth providing an account of the current Section 44[2] Constitutional Crisis and how this has had an impact upon the personality politics of the Australian federal parliament; indeed, more generally. The crisis—a bizarre turn of events which has seen many members of parliament

---

[1] Fred Nile still uses the title Reverend but he resigned from the Uniting Church that ordained him in 2003 because they decided to ordain gay and lesbian ministers. Nile and the Church had a long history of being at odds on many issues before and after his resignation.

[2] Section 44 of the Constitution sets out restrictions on who can be a candidate for federal parliament. In full it reads:

Table 6.1 Personalities associated with AEC registered micro parties 2013 and 2016

Party	Personality	Group
Australian Liberty Alliance	**Kirralee Smith**, Angry Anderson	A
Australian Motoring Enthusiast Party	**Ricky Muir**	A
Australian Sex Party	**Fiona Patten**	A
Derryn Hinch's Justice Party	**Derryn Hinch**	A
Family First	**Bob Day**	A
Glenn Lazarus Team	**Glenn Lazarus (2016)**	A
Jacqui Lambie Network	**Jacqui Lambie**	A
John Madigan's Manufacturing & Farming Party	**John Madigan**	A
Liberal Democrats (LDP)	**David Leyonhjelm**	A
Nick Xenophon Team	**Nick Xenophon**	A
Palmer United	Clive Palmer, **Glenn Lazarus** (2013)	A
Pauline Hanson's One Nation	**Pauline Hanson**	A
The WikiLeaks Party	**Philip Nitschke**	A
Voluntary Euthanasia Party	**Julian Assange**	A
Australia First Party	Jim Saleam	B
Christian Democratic Party	Fred Nile	B
CountryMinded	Peter Mailler (2016)	B
Drug Law Reform	Greg Chipp	B
Katter's Australian Party	Bob Katter, Peter Mailler (2013)	B
Renewable Energy Party	Peter Breen	B
Rise Up Australia Party	Daniel Nalliah	B
Shooters, Fishers and Farmers	Robert Brown	B
Socialist Equality Party	Nick Beams	B
Sustainable Australia	Sandra Kanck	B

Source Author

found ineligible to sit in the parliament—has claimed many political scalps: at the time of writing, 15 had been disqualified (or compelled to resign) on citizenship grounds in violation of part i, two of whom were re-elected in by-elections and a further four are currently facing by-elections.[3] One (PHON Senator for Western Australia, Rod Culleton), was disqualified for being convicted of theft at the time of his nomination, in violation of part ii, one (New South Wales Liberal Hollie Hughes, who was to replace Deputy Nationals leader Fiona Nash) for holding an office of profit under the crown in violation of part iv, and one (Bob Day) for pecuniary interest in violation of part v. While both Bob Day and Rod Culleton have been declared bankrupt, which renders them ineligible to sit under part iii of the disqualification categories of Section 44 (and thus would make it a clean sweep of the all options for disqualification under Section 44), they were not disqualified as electoral candidates by the High Court on the grounds of their bankruptcies (Byrne and Doran 2017; Castello and Shepherd 2017; Harris 2017).

Liberal Party Senator for South Australia Cory Bernardi quit the Liberal Party and formed the Australian Conservatives shortly after the 2016 election (Bernardi 2017)

---

44. Any person who

(i) Is under any acknowledgement of allegiance, obedience, or adherence to a foreign power, or is a subject or a citizen or entitled to the rights or privileges of a subject or citizen of a foreign power: or

(ii) Is attainted of treason, or has been convicted and is under sentence, or subject to be sentenced, for any offence punishable under the law of the Commonwealth or of a State by imprisonment for one year or longer: or

(iii) Is an undischarged bankrupt or insolvent: or

(iv) Holds any office of profit under the Crown, or any pension payable during the pleasure of the Crown out of any of the revenues of the Commonwealth: or

(v) Has any direct or indirect pecuniary interest in any agreement with the Public Service of the Commonwealth otherwise than as a member and in common with the other members of an incorporated company consisting of more than twenty-five persons:

shall be incapable of being chosen or of sitting as a senator or a member of the House of Representatives.

But sub-section iv. does not apply to the office of any of the Queen's Ministers of State for the Commonwealth, or of any of the Queen's Ministers for a State, or to the receipt of pay, half pay, or a pension, by any person as an officer or member of the Queen s navy or army, or to the receipt of pay as an officer or member of the naval or military forces of the Commonwealth by any person whose services are not wholly employed by the Commonwealth.

[3] Scott Ludlum (Greens Deputy Leader, Senator for Western Australia) and Barnaby Joyce (Deputy Prime Minister, Nationals Leader, Member for New England, New South Wales) held New Zealand citizenship; Larissa Waters (Green Deputy Leader, Senator for Queensland) held Canadian citizenship; Fiona Nash (Nationals Deputy Leader, Senator for New South Wales), Malcolm Roberts (One Nation, Senator for Queensland), Stephen Parry (Liberal, Senator for Tasmania, President of the Senate), Jacqui Lambie (Jacqui Lambie Network, Senator for Tasmania) John Alexander (Liberal, Member for Bennelong, New South Wales—resigned), Skye Kakoschke-Moore (NXT, Senator for SA), Katy Gallagher (Labor, Senator for ACT), David Feeney (Labor, Member for Batman, Victoria), Susan Lamb (Labor, Member for Longman), Justine Keay (Labor, Member for Braddon), Josh Wilson (Labor, Member for Fremantle) and Rebekha Sharkie (NXT, Member for Mayo) were UK citizens (Doran 2018). Barnaby Joyce and John Alexander won their respective by-elections in late 2017; Susan Lamb, Justine Keay, Josh Wilson, and Rebekha Sharkie all recontested and retained their seats in by-elections held on July 28, 2018 (Koziol 2018).

and Family First merged with Bernardi's new party (Owen 2017; Yaxley 2017). At precisely the same time, Senator Bob Day, also of South Australia, resigned from the Senate due to his bankruptcy. Following that, the High Court ruled that he was never eligible to stand as a candidate due to his pecuniary interest, thus the candidate next on the ticket would be declared elected rather than Family First (or Bernardi) being able to nominate a candidate of their choosing (Harris 2017). However, Day's replacement, Lucy Gichuhi, who survived a challenge to her own eligibility on the grounds of citizenship (Doran et al. 2017), opted not to join the party and sat as an independent (Owen 2017), before joining the Liberal Party in February 2018 (Belot 2018). Kirralee Smith, a vocal anti-Halal food campaigner with a large online following who contested the 2016 New South Wales Senate race, quit the Australian Liberty Alliance and also joined Bernardi's Australian Conservatives (O'Malley 2017).

Fraser Anning, who replaced PHON's second senator from Queensland, Malcolm Roberts, after he was disqualified on citizenship grounds, was also obliged to prove that he was not bankrupt before taking his seat (Gartrell 2017). In a twist typical of the overall atmosphere of instability and in PHON particularly, Fraser Anning either quit (Hanson's version of events) or was kicked out (Anning's version of events) of the party on the day he was sworn into the Senate, thereby reducing the PHON presence from four senators to three (Bickers and Killoran 2017). Anning later joined Katter's Australia Party, throwing his lot in with the rebel lower house personality from North Queensland, Bob Katter (Australian Associated Press 2018). PHON's numbers were further reduced to two, with NSW Senator Brian Burston seeking a new political home, having split with Pauline Hanson over tax issues (Barbour 2018; Coorey 2018; Remeikis 2018). Discounting West Australian Rod Culleton still claiming he is a Senator and his disqualification and replacement by brother-in-law Peter Georgiou is somehow illegal (McLeay 2018), this leaves Pauline Hanson as the only remaining PHON senator actually elected in 2016.

Jacqui Lambie resigned after discovering she had inherited UK citizenship and has repeatedly stated her intention to contest the next election in the Senate, after sacking her replacement Steve Martin, former mayor of the north-west Tasmanian town of Devonport, from the party for refusing to stand aside so she could return immediately. Martin has since joined the Nationals, and the Jacqui Lambie Network fared very badly in the Tasmanian State election (Clark 2018; Kempton 2018). Nick Xenophon was cleared by the High Court, but resigned anyway to contest the South Australian state election in March 2018 for his state party SA Best—a strategically poor move that resulted in his effective exit from politics. The national NXT party has now been renamed Centre Alliance, and it is not clear if he will return to run again for the Senate (Langenberg 2018; MacLennan 2018). Additionally, a legal battle ensued over his replacement as the next on the ticket was no longer a member of the party, but wanted Xenophon's seat (Murphy and Remeikis 2017). Tim Storer got there in the end by replacing the UK dual citizen Skye Kakoschke-Moore, reducing the party's numbers to three (Holderhead 2018). Peter Mailler, leader of CountryMinded, could have been a beneficiary of the s44 crisis, but performed poorly in the by-election in New England against former Deputy Prime Minister and National Party Leader

Barnaby Joyce (who was declared ineligible by the High Court due to holding New Zealand citizenship), securing just 2.42% of the vote (Murphy 2017), and his party has since been deregistered due to lack of membership (McArthur 2018).

On this account, it is clear that the Section 44 Constitutional Crisis has affected the standing of many individuals across the party political spectrum. Yet it can be understood more systemically and in relation to my discussion of populism as a psephological/personality candidate phenomenon. Viewed in this light, as well as being an unholy constitutional mess, it has further *individuated* Australian federal politics. Not only are the candidates and the political parties obliged to check eligibility for standing, it has also forced the gaze of the electorate, and certainly the media, toward individual politicians and away from substantive policy issues and the institutionalized conflict for which parliaments are designed. This is demonstrated in the handling of Barnaby Joyce's alleged extra-marital affair and the confirmed breakdown of his marriage (and other rumors), in which the fifth estate of bloggers, opinion writers, and voters were interested (anoukeblackheart 2017; Crosby 2017; Jones 2017; Markson and Devine 2017), but Joyce's colleagues and the Canberra Press Gallery wrestled with their standing convention that it was not their business and voters did not need to know (Neate 2017; Wilson 2017). Certainly at play are tacit ideas of authenticity, associated by some with populism generally (see, for example, Birks 2011) and as such virtue, grounded in not merely nationalism understood in an ideational sense, but as defined by the basic law of the Australian federation. This is notwithstanding claims that the constitution is "out of date" (see, for example, Strom 2017).

Other changes affecting personalities listed above but not affecting the current Senate cohort include a rebranding and base-broadening exercise of the Australian Sex Party, moves that are in essence trying to entice other small progressive parties to merge with them and become "Reason" (Preiss 2017). Former Victorian Senator John Madigan, who was not returned at the 2016 election, deregistered his own party and joined the Australian Country Party (Australian Country Party 2016). The Australian Motoring Enthusiasts Party, Palmer United, Glenn Lazarus Team, and The Wikileaks Party have all been deregistered as political parties by the Australian Electoral Commission.

Again, I turn to analyse the results of the 2013 and 2016 Senate elections in Sect. 6.5 of the chapter.

6.3 The Political Communication Approach—Populist Campaigning

From a political communication approach, populism is a communication frame that appeals to and identifies with the people, and claims to speak in their name (Block and Negrine 2017; Canovan 1999; Jagers and Walgrave 2007). This correlates with Laclau's (1977, 2005) conceptualization of populism as a discursive frame, or what has also been referred to as the "political style" understanding of populism (Aslanidis 2015; Canovan 1982; Laclau 1977, 2005; Moffitt and Tormey 2013; Weyland 2001). Populism as a communication frame is commonly characterized by simplistic solutions to complex problems communicated in very direct language, appealing to the "common sense" of the people, while attacking the established elites (Abts and Rummens 2007). The populist frame is one frequently deployed by political strategists. For example, Rick Ridder of RBI Strategies, who worked with the Australian Democrats in the 1990s and the NSW Labor party from 1998 to 2008, argues that straight-talking candidates who can simplify policy and avoid "process-speak" are successful because they come across as "a genuine person with whom most voters can relate" (Ridder 2016, p. 131). On this account, populist *campaigning* is not a strategy just for proponents of populism; it is a strategy for anyone who wants to win.

Grabe and Bucy (2011) define the "populist campaigner" frame used by political strategists in similar terms to those theorists who define populism as an ideology—namely as the ordinary people standing in opposition to the self-serving elite. The cues deployed by the populist campaigner have two main qualities: mass-appeal and ordinariness. Mass appeal[4] is achieved through the visuals of the candidate amongst large, adoring crowds and celebrities transferring their popular appeal through endorsements. Ordinariness[5] is achieved through appearances with "regular folks", displays of athletic ability (in "ordinary" sports), and the quintessential appearances without jacket and tie, shirtsleeves rolled up. Language style is an essential component for effective execution of any populist campaign; conversing with audiences in simple and often fragmented sentences. Bill Clinton, widely regarded as the best natural campaigner in American politics, excelled in the populist style of campaigning (Grabe and Bucy 2009, 2011; Napolitan 2003).

The populist campaigner frame is defined against the "ideal candidate" and the "sure loser". The ideal candidate frame is based on research that shows voters have an idea of what they expect a politician to be—physical appeal, the right personality and background, leadership abilities, honesty, intelligence, and a principled stance on issues that align with voters' attitudes. Additionally, voters will assess job performance using cues on decisiveness, competence, and speaking style. From all this, there are two traits that dominate: statesmanship and compassion. Statesmanship[6] is effectively represented through projecting power and control: speaking from the podium backed by flags or other symbolic backdrops (such as a parliament house); appearing surrounded with high-ranking peers (as opposed to the populist's adoring ordinary people); almost always dressed in suit and tie, in contrast to the casual, populist dress; speaking in reassuring but authoritative tones, that is, speaking *to* an audience in contrast to the common language speaking *with* the conversational tone

---

[4]The visual frame coding set used for mass appeal is: celebrities; large audiences; approving audiences; interaction with crowds.

[5]The visual frame coding set used for ordinariness is: informal attire; casual dress; athletic clothing; ordinary people; physical activity.

[6]The visual frame coding set for statesmanship is: elected officials and other influentials; patriotic symbols; symbols of progress; identifiable entourage; campaign paraphernalia; political hoopla; formal attire.

of the populist. Compassion[7] is often conveyed through interaction with children, or other strategies to show a candidate's softer side—the kissing of a supporter's baby being the most clichéd construction of compassion on the campaign trail. Surrounding the candidate with children (their own or others), particularly during economic hard times, can also signal messages of "father" of the nation (Grabe and Bucy 2011).

The "sure loser" is the Stephen Bradbury[8] of elections—someone who gets to the finish line through the missteps and poor judgment of otherwise leading candidates. Sure loser[9] framing is applied by others, rather than constituting a deliberate strategy, and is often associated with unfavorable news coverage because of some problem with the candidate's position, profile, reputation, or character that causes them not to fit the "ideal candidate" standard, and thus makes them an easy target for attack. More commonly, it is generated from the inability of the candidate to connect with the voters, poor polling, and repeated calls for the candidate to stop wasting the voters' (and media's) time and to just give up—in the US Presidential context, to drop out of the race—so the "real" candidates can be heard. Visual cues are predominantly the opposite of the ideal and populist frames. Coverage of campaign events may be described as protest events or may highlight the poor turnout (in contrast to the populist's large crowd) rather than issues of substance (Grabe and Bucy 2011) . Donald Trump was framed as a sure loser as no one—including his own team—thought he was going to win.

In Australia, an additional frame must be added to Grabe and Bucy's theory: that of the maverick. Borrowing from Peter Tucker's (2011) Ph.D. on the Australian maverick, which defined the maverick candidate within the party context, I would submit that the maverick frame[10] is of the unpredictable, celebrity candidate with their own issue agenda at odds with the mainstream. Pitching themselves as a "conviction politician", they intentionally, aggressively, and in a media attention-grabbing way, "buck the system". Ignoring convention and breaking the rules so as to appear to be "not a politician", their dress is rarely conforming, often adopting a signature physical attribute or item of apparel, such as Bob Katter's hat. Their style of speech is blunt, bordering on brash, and at times is downright offensive. A maverick does not try to appear informed about serious issues; they only care about their issues, their people, and are harshly dismissive to those who question their ability or commitment. Mavericks do exist in party structures—Barnaby Joyce is the most prominent current

---

[7]The compassion framing set includes four visual and three behavioral measures: children; family associations; admiring women; religious symbols; and affinity gestures; interaction with individuals; physical embraces.

[8]Steven Bradbury was an Australian ice skater who won an 'accidental' gold medal in the 1000 m short-track speed skating final at the Salt Lake City 2002 Winter Games after his four rivals all collided and sprawled around the ice, leaving him to skate alone past the finish line (Gordon 2003). The term "doing a Bradbury" has since entered the Australian lexicon to mean 'become the unlikely winner' (Gwynn 2014).

[9]The sure loser coding set is: small crowds; disapproving audiences; displays of weakness; defiant gestures; inappropriate nonverbal displays.

[10]The maverick coding set I developed was unconventional dress; standing alone; aggressiveness; defiance; blunt speech; disengagement from broader agenda; behaving like a celebrity.

example—but they currently thrive on the Senate cross bench. The maverick is a concept associated with populism, but mavericks need to be offering anti-establishment appeal to be populist (Barr 2009; Vraga 2017).

Note here that the language of these frames is demonstrably masculine. That is not an error, nor a failure to update old theories and make them gender neutral. Politics is still a masculine domain. Ask a voter to define their ideal candidate and the phrases which most use are masculine, even if they have no intention of inferring that the ideal candidate should be a man, as the stereotypes of traits needed for electoral success favor masculine over feminine traits (Dolan 2013; Vraga 2017). For example, Moore and Dewberry (2012) analyzed the use of sport by presidential candidates to communicate to voters that they are a "man's man", physically superior to other men, and (as noted above) a key component of the "ordinariness" aspect of populist campaigning is engaging in ordinary (male) sports. Moore and Dewberry conclude that female candidates must also communicate their "masculinity" via sports to be successful. This presents an invasive conundrum for female candidates when being sporty: it can also result in the double-edged whisper of questions about her sexuality (Krane and Kaus 2014).

It is important to underscore that all four types of campaign framing as I have discussed them are not tied to particular sides of politics. On the contrary; any of these frames can be deployed by, or applied to, any candidate—and in Australia almost all parties do, to some extent, deploy populist campaigning techniques. It is also worth noting that a campaigner can fall foul of any framing strategy, by choosing the wrong frame. Miscasting a candidate in an ill-fitting frame, such as casting an ideal candidate in a populist campaign frame, will generally result in an election loss: for example, George H. W. Bush's 1988 re-election campaign attempted to portray the Yale educated, foreign policy focused, aristocratic style President in a populist frame with a "down home" American feel, with many missteps that only served to amplify how out of touch he was with ordinary Americans (Grabe and Bucy 2009, 2011). For an Australian example: the portrayal of Tony Abbott—a Rhodes Scholar best known with voters for his staunch Catholicism, blue ties and eviscerating attacks in parliament—as a sportsman and "friendly bloke" you could have a beer with was the source of great mirth and undermined his credibility (Garton 2011; Holmes et al. 2012). To this day, the now ex-Leader of the Liberal Party is depicted by cartoonists in his tiny red "budgie smugglers" Speedo swimwear (Glover 2016), despite righting his personal framing to an authentic, hardline, ideal candidate frame (Hurcombe 2016).

6.4   The Ideological Approach—Populism

At a more abstract level, and as discussed in Part I of this book generally, populism has numerous contested definitions. It has been referred to as an ideology, a style, a discourse, a worldview, a movement, and a syndrome (Barr 2009; Moffitt and Tormey 2013; Mudde and Kaltwasser 2017, pp. 2, 5). For my purposes in this chapter, one of these definitions is of more relevance. Mudde and Kaltwasser (2017, p. 6) define populism as "a thin-centered ideology that considers society to be ultimately separated into two homogenous and antagonistic camps, 'the pure people' versus 'the corrupt elite', and which argues that politics should be an expression of the general will of the people". Thin-centered ideologies such as populism rarely appear in a pure form, and it is frequently argued that, by itself, populism simply lacks the complexity to answer the political questions of modern society (Mudde and Kaltwasser 2017, pp. 6–7; Stanley 2008). Importantly, populism is neither left nor right, and can attach itself to an ideology anywhere on the ideological spectrum (Abts and Rummens 2007; Albertazzi and McDonnell 2008; Bakker et al. 2016; Mudde and Kaltwasser 2017, p. 8). Mudde and Kaltwasser (2017, p. 14) perhaps controversially contend that nationalism is a thin ideology that is often prone to completely merge with populism. The opposites of populism according to this account are defined as elitism and pluralism. Elitism holds the same dualistic worldview but contends that the people are the destructive force to be opposed, instead of the elite; pluralism is the direct opposite of the dualistic view, holding that society is divided into a variety of partly overlapping social groups, seeing diversity as a strength rather than a weakness (Mudde and Kaltwasser 2017, p. 8; see also Schoor 2017).

This widely cited view of populism as a thin-centered ideology is arguably the current dominant theoretical paradigm, yet it has been subject to numerous criticisms (see, for example, Aslanidis 2015; Canovan 1999; Moffitt and Tormey 2013; van Kessel 2014). If we broadly accept (if only for the sake of argument) this view of populism as ideology, there are two pure populist parties in Australia: Online Direct Democracy (ODD; previously called Senator Online) and Flux. Both propose the same solution to the problem of the elite: give the people complete control by allowing them to vote on every piece of legislation. Both these political parties have no policies of any kind. The major differences are that ODD is a relatively long-lived organization, registered with the Australian Electoral Commission (AEC) in August of 2007, and its voting system is a simple website and app (Online Direct Democracy 2017). Alternatively, Flux was new at the 2016 election, their preferred method of political decision-making is based on a "blockchain" system where unused votes can be traded with other members for credits, enabling those who care more about certain issues to have a greater say on them (Flux 2017; Lander and Cooper 2017).

Defining the other micro parties as having an ideology of populism—as distinct from nationalism, protectionism, or any other ideology combined with some other populist aspect—is quite a challenge and rightly cause for debate. For instance, having a populist *leader* is not a necessary component for a party to be a proponent of populism, nor does populist *campaigning* denote populism (Abts and Rummens 2007; Inglehart and Norris 2016; Weyland 2001). Moreover, populism can be top down, that is, formed around a personality; or bottom up, that is, formed around a movement; or both, formed around a party (De La Torre 2016; Inglehart and Norris 2016; Mudde and Kaltwasser 2017, p. 42).

Analyzing primarily a party's manifesto, supplemented by an examination of their website (archived versions where those parties no longer exist), and where available, campaign materials, policies, first speeches, and press coverage quoting leaders, I have applied three tests:

- The first test seeks *defined language* using the three core ideas in populism—"the people", "the elite", and "the general will" (or equivalents)—as rhetorical devices;
- The second test examines *political strategies* that seek to undermine societal norms by attacking whatever is defined as the "other" to unite the "people" to their cause;
- The third test searches for *a clear anti-establishment or anti-elite narrative*, as indicated by regular attacks on the entire political system or all other political players, or alternatively big business, and/or cultured or educated people or their institutions, and/or the media.

The parties that fit all three tests of language, strategy, and narrative are listed in Table 6.2, alongside examples of their rhetoric. Examining Table 6.2, we can see that in all the examples listed the rhetoric matches the tests applied. For example, the Australia First Party (row 1) refers to the "people" as Australians or men and women; the elite are labelled as the "traitor class"; and they call upon those men and women to unite to their "general will" of "regime change". Their anti-elite narrative is clear, as are their attacks on big business. Similarly, Katter's Australian Party (row 7) refers to the people as "fellow Australians"; the elite are identified as "foreign-owned corporations", "big business" and "monopolistic companies" (several examples are listed) as well as the Chinese. It implores the people to "wake up and stand up" to join the (less clearly defined) general will of protecting Australian jobs and to stop major parties from "selling out your country from underneath you". Similarly, the Socialist Alliance (row 12) refers to the people as "ordinary" or "working people" pitched against the "ruling" and "capitalist elite"; uniting for a clear "general will" of "a democratic society run by and for working people". This is consistent with their attacks on the entire current political system and big business (called "union bashers" in the quote). The Socialist Alliance had the most consistent presentation of populism using these tests, with almost every post, page, and press release clearly using the language of the people against the ruling elite, with little use of ambiguous phrasing.

Despite Pauline Hanson herself being pointed to as an exemplar of a populist leader (see for example Denemark and Bowler 2002; Mason 2010; Mudde and Kaltwasser 2017, pp. 69–70), Pauline Hanson's One Nation (PHON), the political party, is a challenging case study. The party passes the three tests, but their stated "general will" is inconsistent. Their strategy certainly attacks their "others" of Aboriginal and Torres Strait Islander (ATSI) people, immigrants, and Islam, but the "uniting the people" factor is not always evident as part of those attacks. And the anti-establishment or anti-elite narrative is not as consistent in the party content as it is on Hanson's personal platforms, especially on her Facebook page (Hanson 2017). As an organization, it can be argued that PHON has weak underlying foundations, with a number of contradictory statements in its manifesto. In particular, the top six points of Australian values, Federalism, Honesty and Integrity, Fairness, Freedom, and Human Progress are both supported and contradicted by the 31 numbered Principles and objectives (listed on the same webpage) which, for example, imply that Freedom is a pleasure

Table 6.2 AEC registered parties with observed populism characteristics that contested the 2013 or 2016 federal elections

1. Australia First Party	… what the prevailing traitor class advocates is against the interests of Australians, and is undermining our civilization. Their globalist doctrines will see the Australian People perish. The Australia First Party is committed to a regime change from this traitor class, and offers a beacon for men and women to step forward, and to join in this challenge (Australia First Party Victorian Branch 2017)
2. Australian Liberty Alliance	As civic-minded Australians we cannot remain passive while damage is done to our nation, our communities and our families … There is no place for big government, racism, political correctness, moral relativism, divisive multiculturalism or tolerance for the intolerant … Australian Liberty Alliance is inclusive and seeks to unite individuals and groups for a common cause (Australian Liberty Alliance 2017)
3. Australian Protectionist Party[a]	Australia's way of life needs protecting from the destructiveness of Multiculturalism and Political Correctness … APP is a party for ordinary Australians seeking to defend the Australian way of life … an alternative to the Establishment's internationalist policies, and aims to protect Australia's national interests (Australian Protectionist Party 2017)
4. Citizens Electoral Council	For 28 years the CEC has fought as an independent political party for the principles of the common good and national sovereignty … We have fought to free Australia from the Crown-City of London-Wall Street apparatus of banks and multinational corporations, which seized control of our economy under the policies of deregulation and privatization that the Hawke-Keating ALP started, and the Liberals continued (Citizens Electoral Council 2016) The presently ruling policies of globalisation, privatization, deregulation and free trade, together with the enforcement of "environmentalist" policies so radical that they are best described as "green fascism", are plunging the vast majority of Australians—along with most of the rest of the world—into poverty and misery; destroying our once-great nation; and eliminating any meaningful future for our children (Citizens Electoral Council 2012)
5. Health Australia Party	The Health Australia Party (HAP) will create a new paradigm, a middle ground where Australians can come together … The left/right polarization, perceived dishonesty, the litany of broken promises, accusations, abuse and the general tone of the political debate has created a "trust deficit" which has further alienated many Australians (Health Australia Party 2017) To promote the political, social, and economic order of a democratic national community, free from the powerful national and international vested interests of big business and big unions (Health Australia Party 2015)

(continued)

Table 6.2 (continued)

6. John Madigan's Manufacturing and Farming Party[b]	This is a party to unite all Australians behind that which has and will continue to make this country great (John Madigan's Manufacturing and Farming Party 2016) At a time of increasing anger and disillusionment with politics and political parties we say "Don't get mad. Get Madigan!" So if you're tired of Turnbull, sick of Shorten or browned off with the Greens—then help us out (Madigan 2016)
7. Katter's Australian Party	It is clear that foreign owned corporations and big business have a capacity and will to undermine Australian pay and conditions … KAP will pursue policies that increase demand for Australian products and support Australian jobs and that will aggressively wind back the market share and/or market power of monopolistic companies that control access to markets for Australian small business, like Coles, Woolworths, Graincorp, Glencore and CBH (Katter's Australian Party 2016b) Please … fellow Australians wake up and stand up. The LNP and ALP are selling out your country from underneath you. You will have no resources that can earn you any money and you will be under the iron fist of Chinese corporations, almost all of who [sic] are controlled by the Chinese Government (Katter's Australian Party 2016a)
8. Nick Xenophon Team[c]	Every couple of years the major political parties have expected us to walk into a polling booth and put a number one in the box of the political party we dislike the least. Voters are sick of parties that promise one thing before an election and do the opposite afterwards … Politicians should listen to the people instead of walking all over them. And they should respect the fact that they are here to serve, not to rule (Xenophon 2014) Politicians must be open and up front with the Australian people. And governments should deliver value-for-money for the services you deserve. Australians who speak out against corrupt practices deserve to be protected. Corporations—particularly multi-nationals—must pay their fair share of taxes (Nick Xenophon Team 2017)
9. Palmer United Party[d]	The main issue facing Australia today is not just balancing our budget, but what Australians can do to regain Australia's status as the lucky country. Sadly, the Liberal and Labor parties are devoid of ideas… We are all on Struggle Street together, but it's our country and it's our responsibility to do all we can to make the lives of all our citizens better than it is today (Palmer 2015, p. 4) How long can parliament remain indifferent to the needs of all Australians? How long can government be deaf to the everyday struggles of all Australians? They must be on top of the national agenda (Palmer 2015, p. 18)

(continued)

Table 6.2 (continued)

10. Pauline Hanson's One Nation (additional quotes in text below)	We believe that our country's future wealth and the prosperity of all Australians can be assured only through listening and then caring enough to openly address the problems that Liberal-Labor-Nationals-Greens created politically and continue to make … One Nation opposes acknowledging Aboriginal and Torres Strait Islanders in the preamble to the Australian Constitution, as One Nation believes that all Australians are owners and custodians of this land and should work toward unification, not segregation, under the one law for all (Pauline Hanson's One Nation 2017h) There is only One Nation left to oppose them, a party that is not funded by and subservient to the multinationals; but instead represents the farmers and the hopes of the Australian people (Pauline Hanson's One Nation 2017e)
11. Rise Up Australia	Rather than uniting the country under one flag, multiculturalism has had the completely opposite effect. Australia is a multi-ethnic country comprising, many races, many skin colours—but one culture—Australian! (Rise Up Australia 2017b) The goal of Rise Up Australia is to limit and reduce foreign ownership of our assets (including the media), to repay our foreign debt and to reduce the influence of overseas organisations … Foreign ownership and external influences may not always have the best interests of the Australian people at heart, so Rise Up Australia will work to ensure these issues are not detrimental to the wellbeing of our citizens (Rise Up Australia 2017a)
12. Socialist Alliance	The Socialist Alliance stands for socialism—a democratic society run by and for working people, not the greedy, destructive capitalist elite that now rules … in order to bring about such a society, we have to replace the institutions that protect and defend this ruling elite (such as parliament, government administration, police and the military) with institutions under the democratic control of ordinary people … The Socialist Alliance is made up of people who, like millions of others, are sick of being ruled by the warmongers, racists, union-bashers, and capitalist politicians (Socialist Alliance 2017)
13. Uniting Australia Party[e]	Our aim is to bring back some common sense into politics. It is about real people and the real issues facing everyday Australians. It is about listening, hearing, and acting on what real Australians need. It is about putting Australians first (Uniting Australia Party 2013)

Notes
[a] Australian Protectionist Party was deregistered by the AEC on 18 June 2015 (AEC 2015). They still operate as an organization
[b] John Madigan's Manufacturing and Farming Party no longer exists; it was a vanity party only for John Madigan's re-election, who has since joined the Australian Country Party (Australian Country Party 2016)
[c] Nick Xenophon Team has been renamed to Centre Alliance (MacLennan 2018)
[d] Palmer United Party was voluntarily deregistered on 5 May 2017 (AEC 2017b; Silva 2017)
[e] Uniting Australia Party was deregistered for failing to respond on 23 July 2015 (AEC 2015). There is very little remaining of the Uniting Australia Party, some of the best resources are social media commentary and individual voter's reviews of such as this YouTube video https://youtu.be/s6fFX2 3snB8

only for law abiding, Christian, Australian citizens who are prepared to give up some of that freedom to measures such as an Australian Identity Card to access government services (Pauline Hanson's One Nation 2017h).

The picture becomes more confusing if one delves into the policies of PHON published at the time of the 2016 election. For example, principle and objective number 6, "To actively pursue and promote treaties, investment and development as deemed appropriate and in the national interest and repeal those that are not in our best interests" is somewhat complicated by point 15's commitment to repeal United Nations (UN) treaties that are detrimental to Australia (Pauline Hanson's One Nation 2017h). This "actively pursue" principle is then contradicted by the Manufacturing and Primary Industry policies which evince strong opposition to globalization, free trade, a commitment to withdraw from all trade agreements, impose tariffs and protectionist measures, and ban certain imports. It goes so far as to state: "Australia is capable of producing any agriculture [sic] product needed for use or consumption by its people" (Pauline Hanson's One Nation 2017d, e). Picking up the anti-UN thread, the Economics and Tax policy proposes that Australia exit the UN entirely and "Investigate 7000 foreign treaties and commitments signed by Liberal-Labor-Nationals governments with a view to revoking all but those beneficial to Australia and Australians" (Pauline Hanson's One Nation 2017b).

It is these anti-UN positions, not notably advanced in election campaigns, which have nevertheless dominated PHON's parliamentary contributions. The now former Senator Malcolm Roberts advocated these positions strongly—with further inconsistencies from published policy—in his maiden speech when he called for an "Ausexit" from all international organizations. Pauline Hanson moved a motion, with Australian Conservatives Senator for South Australia Cory Bernardi (and on World Refugee Day in 2017) for Australia to withdraw from the United Nations 1951 Convention relating to the Status of Refugees (Bernardi and Hanson 2017). The motion was swiftly defeated 6-50, with PHON's four votes and that of Cory Bernardi being joined only by fellow cross bench Tasmanian Senator Jacqui Lambie (Butler 2017).

There are also inconsistencies among the same policy, for example, within the anti-Islamic policy. Principle and objective 21 says:

> To stop the teaching and infiltration of Islam and its totalitarian ideology, that opposes our democracy, way of life and laws. To ban the Burqa in public places, government buildings and schools. To make genital mutilation of young girls a criminal offence, carrying heavy sentences. To stop islamists (sic) and their families from receiving welfare benefits; we are a Christian country, only one marriage is recognised. Ban the building of any more Mosques (Pauline Hanson's One Nation 2017h) .

This point is complemented by number 22 which opposes the introduction of Sharia Law; number 24 includes a commitment to "stop the practice of Halal Certification on all products, service, and machinery in Australia, other than for export", and 25 which states Australia should only take Christian refugees (Pauline Hanson's One Nation 2017h). The policy on Islam expands on these principles and objectives, stating that the religious aspect of Islam is a fraud: "it is rather a totalitarian political system, including legal, economic, social and military components, masquerading as a religion"; before proposing the specific measures, namely:

- Call for an inquiry or Royal Commission to determine if Islam is a religion or political ideology
- Stop further Muslim Immigration and the intake of Muslim refugees until we can assure the safety of Australians
- Ban the Burqa and Niquab in public places
- Driver's licence cannot be obtained without showing the full face and having photo ID on driver's licence
- Surveillance cameras to be installed in all Mosques and schools. Mosques to be open to the public during all opening hours
- No more mosques to be built until the inquiry is held
- Oppose the introduction of Sharia Law
- Investigate welfare payments paid to Muslims who may be in multiple marriages, having multiple children
- Ban Halal certification. Halal certified food not to be provided in prisons or the armed services. Companies may comply for export but no monies must be paid
- Call for a referendum to change Sect. 116 of the Australian Constitution
- Muslims will not be allowed to be sworn into Parliament under the Qur'an
- Female genital mutilation to carry lengthy jail term (Pauline Hanson's One Nation 2017c).

Note this policy language changes the "stopping of welfare" to "investigating welfare recipients". It also advocates new measures: the installation of security cameras in mosques; opening mosques to the public, restrictions on what can be worn for photos for drivers' licences and Muslim members of parliament not being sworn in on the Qur'an. Further, it changes the Halal certification ban to include a ban on export companies paying any fees for Halal certified products. It rejects the provision of Halal-certified food in prisons and the armed services (arguably, this contradicts the principle of statement 13 which commits the party to "supporting our defence forces and personnel"). It introduces a halt to the immigration of Muslim people *in toto*, yet implies that Muslim refugees (blocked under the Christian requirement of principle 25) might be permitted to enter Australia if safety can be assured. It proposes a change to Section 116 of the *Australian Constitution* by referendum, which would be necessary to implement most of these policies—Section 116 prohibits any law that limits the free exercise of any religion.

The 2016 campaign flyer differed again in taking a softer line than the policy in some areas (see Fig. 6.1): banning the burqa in public and government buildings (as opposed to public places generally); implying that Halal certification would be allowed (just the fee would be banned) and (interestingly) adding Islamic schools to the list of banned institutions. The latter does not appear in either the policy or the principle statements (Pauline Hanson's One Nation 2016) .

Possibly the most viewed campaign item on the issue was the graphic shared on Pauline Hanson's personal Facebook page (see Fig. 6.2). This gave a simplified version of the policy, and became a news story in itself (see Pauline Hanson's Facebook

Fig. 6.1 2016 PHON campaign flyer: Halal certification and Islam section. *Source* Excerpt from Pauline Hanson's One Nation (2016). Bringing Back Australian Values: Federal Policy Guide, pamphlet. Downloaded from Pauline Hanson's One Nation Website, 10 August 2017, http://www. onenation.com.au/LiteratureRetrieve.aspx?ID=155063

Post on Muslims Gains Support 2015). It would be an interesting research question to determine what proportion of Hanson supporters had based their decision to support the party on the various sources of content, given the demonstrable contradictions and inconsistencies, although it is likely the vast majority of PHON voters were voting for the personality of Pauline Hanson. PHON also does not hide its history of internal disruption, with references to "dissidents" and Pauline Hanson's absence from the party noted on multiple pages, and a section on the party History page actually titled "Internal disputes" (Pauline Hanson's One Nation 2017a, f, g). Given that Hanson was absent from the party for some 13 years (Pauline Hanson's One Nation 2017g), these inconsistencies in language style and content are arguably not surprising, and may resolve over time. Indeed, a recent website upgrade has stripped many of them back to a paragraph or just a sentence, if they remained at all. However, the disputes and instability between members of PHON, as most notably demonstrated in the defection or sacking of Fraser Anning and resignation of Brian Burston mentioned earlier, appear to be going nowhere.

6.5   Which "Populism" Is Gaining Support?

To try to determine whether it is populist personalities, populist campaigning, or populism gaining support, there are few to no suitable data sources available in Australia. The ideal way to demonstrate causality of vote is via a multi-wave panel study, which interviews the same respondents multiple times throughout the campaign, thus enabling capture and measurement of media effects and campaign influence or the effects of other events and influences on vote decision (Andreß 2017; Eveland and Morey 2011; Lazarsfeld 1941, 1948; Ruspini 2002). The last time a two-wave panel study was conducted was the 1990 election (Bean 1994; Bean and Kelley 1995) ; there has been only one three-wave panel study ever conducted, and that focused solely on the influence of a single Prime Ministerial speech in 1963 using a small sample in Canberra (Hughes and Western 1966). We simply do not have current

 Pauline Hanson's Please Explain is with Jeshurun Rajadurai   •••
and 9 others.
6 October 2015 · 🌐

A vote for me at the next Federal Election will be your insurance, the major parties will have absolute opposition to any more Mosques, Sharia Law, Halal Certification & Muslim Refugees. NO MORE!

Share if you agree.

#PaulineHanson #OneNation #FedUp #Islam #AusPol

NO MORE
- **MOSQUES**
- **SHARIA LAW**
- **HALAL CERTIFICATION**
- **MUSLIM REFUGEES**

QLD SENATE CANDIDATE

PAULINE HANSON'S
one
NATION

Share

Fig. 6.2 "No More" Facebook post on Pauline Hanson's Please Explain page (Hanson 2015)

causal data on Australian voting behavior. However, this situation will change with the first Columbia model multi-wave panel scheduled to be conducted on the next Federal election in 2018 or 2019.[11] I have chosen to undertake a simple aggregate analysis comparing the 2013 and 2016 Senate election results.[12]

Electoral support can be demonstrated either by the number of votes received, or by seats won. Electoral success can also be defined in two ways: electoral breakthrough (winning enough votes to enter parliament) or electoral persistence (the ability to develop into a stable force within the political system) (Mudde and Kaltwasser 2017, p. 59). For example, the performance of PHON in the 2017 Queensland election can be deemed successful in terms of electoral breakthrough: they did win the seat in Mirani, despite it being well below expectations (Miragliotta 2017). However, party leader Steve Dickson, who had defected from the Liberal National Party, lost his seat of Buderim, and thus the result cannot be seen as a success by the measure of electoral persistence as they are not developing into a stable force within the political system (Chang 2017). Additionally, we need to distinguish between a rise in a particular party from a rise in an ideology. The collapse of one party being replaced by another party does not necessarily indicate a rise in that ideology if the net result of votes for that ideological position is flat or in decline.

First, analyzing our list of personality-led parties as identified above, there is a figure in the bottom line of Table 6.3 that rightfully warrants due attention: personality-led parties account for the entire Senate cross bench.

If we drill down to the state level figures to assess the performance of those specific personalities, focusing only on those parties that contested both 2013 and 2016 and polled above 1% of the vote, we can infer a significant influence of personality candidates. As shown in Table 6.4, the collapse of the PUP vote in Queensland was almost directly matched with the rise of the PHON vote and the vote for Lazarus, the net gain across all three in 2016 being 26,799 votes or 0.59% of the Queensland vote. Mackerras (1976) found a higher personal vote for Queensland candidates than the national average, so it may be reasonable to surmise that there is a culture of voting for personalities (aligning with direct election for all local government mayors—see Grant et al. 2015) and that this "personality vote" shifted from Palmer to Hanson in 2016. In Victoria, it can be argued that the Sex Party paid a price for not having their standard bearer Fiona Patten as a candidate in 2016. In South Australia the NXT vote fell 3.14% (their national gain of 1.34% attributable to standing candidates

---

[11] The Voter Choice Project is this author's Ph.D. research. The Columbia model is the multi-wave panel devised by Paul Lazarsfeld and colleagues at the Columbia Office of Radio Research (later Bureau of Applied Social Research) deployed on the Erie County study in the 1940 presidential election (see Lazarsfeld et al. 1968 [1944]) and the Elmira study in the 1948 presidential election (see Berelson et al. 1954).

[12] The Australian Election Study data set is too small for a meaningful comparison of voters for most of these micro parties. We do not have panel data addressing the specific question, and not all parties contest House seats, thus Senate results are the best available data set. As noted by Antony Green (2017) in his review of the election, using the figures from the 2014 Senate re-run in Western Australia is not really useful for this purpose, so I am using the 2013 election figures; thus these swing figures will not correlate with the AEC tally room site but should correlate with Antony Green's figures.

Table 6.3 2013 and 2016 Australian Senate elections: parties with personality figures compared

Party	2013 Vote	2013%	2013 Seats	2016 Vote	2016%	2016 Seats	Var.	Swing	Net
Australia First Party	10,157	0.08	0	3,005	0.02	0	−7,152	−0.06	0
Australian Liberty Alliance	0	0	0	102,982	0.74	0	102,982	0.74	0
Australian Motoring Enthusiast Party	67,560	0.5	1	53,232	0.38	0	−14,328	−0.12	−1
Australian Sex Party[a]	183,731	1.37	0	94,262	0.68	0	−89,469	−0.69	0
Sex Party/HEMP[a]	0	0	0	76,744	0.55	0	76,744	0.55	0
Christian Democratic Party	72,544	0.54	0	162,155	1.17	0	89,611	0.63	0
CountryMinded	0	0	0	5,989	0.04	0	5,989	0.06	0
Derryn Hinch's Justice Party	0	0	0	266,607	1.93	1	**266,607**	**1.93**	**1**
Drug Law Reform	10,189	0.08	0	61,327	0.44	0	51,138	0.36	0
Family First	149,306	1.11	1	191,112	1.38	1	41,806	0.27	0
Glenn Lazarus Team	0	0	(PUP)	45,149	0.33	0	45,149	0.33	0

(continued)

Table 6.3 (continued)

Party	2013 Vote	2013%	2013 Seats	2016 Vote	2016%	2016 Seats	Var.	Swing	Net
Jacqui Lambie Network	0	0	(PUP)	69,074	0.5	1	69,074	0.5	1
John Madigan's Manufacturing and Farming Party	0	0	1 Sitting (DLP)	5,268	0.04	0	5,268	0.04	*−1*
Katter's Australian Party	119,920	0.89	0	53,123	0.38	0	−66,797	−0.51	0
Liberal Democrats (LDP)	523,831	3.91	1	298,915	2.16	1	−224,916	−1.75	0
Nick Xenophon Team	258,376	1.93	1	456,369	3.3	3	*197,993*	**1.37**	**2**
Palmer United Party	658,976	4.91	3[b,c]	26,210	0.19	0	*−632,766*	*−4.72*	*−3*
Pauline Hanson's One Nation	70,851	0.53	0	593,013	4.29	4^	**522,162**	**3.76**	**4**
Renewable Energy Party	0	0	0	29,983	0.22	0	29,983	0.22	0

(continued)

Table 6.3 (continued)

Party	2013 Vote	2013%	2013 Seats	2016 Vote	2016%	2016 Seats	Var.	Swing	Net
Rise Up Australia Party	49,341	0.37	0	36,424	0.26	0	−12,917	−0.11	0
Shooters, Fishers and Farmers	127,397	0.95	0	192,923	1.39	0	65,526	0.44	0
Socialist Equality Party	9,774	0.07	0	7,865	0.06	0	−1,909	−0.01	0
Sustainable Australia	12,671	0.09	0	26,341	0.19	0	13,670	0.1	0
The WikiLeaks Party	88,092	0.66	0	0	0	0	−88,092	−0.66	0
Voluntary Euthanasia Party	21,854	0.16	0	23,252	0.17	0	1,398	0.01	0
TOTAL Personality vote	2,434,570	18.15	8	2,881,324	20.81	11	**446,754**	**3.02**	**3**

[a]The Sex Party and HEMP ran on a joint ticket in Qld, WA, SA, Tas, and NT in 2016

[b]The third PUP Senator Dio Wang, was from Western Australia. He was elected on the first count, lost to Wayne Dropulich on the second count, and was safely elected in the re-election in 2014

[c]Senators quit the party after the election

Sources AEC (2013) Federal Election Senate First Preferences by Group by Vote Type Version 9.1.17.21449 (AEC 2013, 2016) Federal Election Senate First Preferences by Group by Vote Type Version (AEC 2016)

Table 6.4 2013 and 2016 Australian Senate elections: Micro parties with Group A personalities that contested both elections polling over 1%, State figures where personality was candidate

Party/Group name	2013 Vote	2013%	2016 Vote	2016%	Var.	Swing
New South Wales						
Liberal Democrats	415,901	9.5	139,007	3.09	−276,894	−6.41
Queensland						
Glenn Lazarus Team	0	0	45,149	1.66	45,149	1.66
Palmer United Party	258,944	9.89	4,816	0.18	−254,128	−9.71
Pauline Hanson's One Nation	14,348	0.55	250,126	9.19	235,778	8.64
Victoria						
Australian Sex Party	63,883	1.89	54,128	1.55	−9,755	−0.34
South Australia						
Nick Xenophon Team	258,376	24.88	230,703	21.74	−27,673	−3.14
Family First	39,032	3.76	30,464	2.87	−8,568	−0.89

Sources AEC (2013) Tally Room 2013 Federal Election Senate First Preferences By Group By Vote Type By State version 9.1.17.21449 (AEC 2014, 2016) Tally Room 2016 Federal Election Senate First Preferences By Group By Vote Type By State Version 10.5.84.43192 (AEC 2017a)

in other states for the first time); Family First also suffered a loss of 0.89% in a hotly contested state Senate race. It is worth noting that the South Australian contest does have some of the Senate's biggest personalities: in addition to Xenophon, Cory Bernardi, Labor Senate Leader Penny Wong, and Greens Senator Sarah Hanson Young were all battling to be returned in in 2016. Liberal, Labor, and Greens all increased their vote share in South Australia in 2016. The fall in David Leyonhjelm Liberal Democrats' vote in New South Wales needs to be seen in the context of the 2013 aberrant result: the Liberal Democrats drew the "donkey vote" position of column A in 2013 and it was generally accepted that their large result was a result of name confusion with the Liberal Party (Colebatch 2013; Green 2014) . The 2016 Liberal Democrats vote is simply a correction.

Second, as discussed above, almost all parties in Australia deploy some populist campaigning strategy during any campaign. Using a sampling of images and stories from the 2016 campaign, my brief analysis[13] is that Pauline Hanson and Jacqui Lambie were pitching themselves as "mavericks" but were framed by the media as "sure losers". While there was little doubt, particularly in Lambie's case, that they would win their individual seats, coverage of both women regularly focused on their opposition and lack of organised support—for example, Lambie needing to use crowd funding to pay for her campaign and only being able to raise $60 (Smith 2016). Images of both women most frequently showed them alone and exhibiting negative

---

[13]For comparison: Labor Leader Bill Shorten and his 100 Policy bus, nearly always in a blue suit (except when taking in his daily run), was framed an ideal candidate; wearing leather jacket, wandering through the markets or at the beach Prime Minister Malcolm Turnbull and skivvy-wearing Greens Leader Richard Di Natale were populist campaigners.

facial expressions, such as frowns or scowls, waving hands or pointing fingers which are images clearly identified in the sure loser coding framework (Grabe and Bucy 2009, p. 292).

Glenn Lazarus was the textbook example of a personality candidate: often dressed in his casual clothes, surrounded by adoring fans, and with many stories referencing his football past (see, for example, Atfield 2016; Harrison 2016). In the past Nick Xenophon has been famed for his populist stunts (Manne 2015), but in the 2016 campaign he was very much playing the role of party leader: a disciplined "ideal candidate". His 2013 signature bright orange shirt with sleeves rolled up was in 2016 traded for a black suit, with just one significant stunt involving a three-wheeled motorcycle starting at a shock-absorber manufacturer (O'Malley 2016). Derryn Hinch certainly tried the ideal candidate, aside from never wearing a tie and mentioning he had been to jail (Wright 2014); he was arguably a borderline "ideal-maverick". New South Wales Senator and Liberal Democrats leader David Leyonhjelm was an "ideal candidate", always in a tie and usually pictured only at a desk or other formal setting, aside from the occasional picture with a motorbike or gun (see, for example, Selmes 2016). Victorian independent Senator John Madigan was a definite "maverick", using his blacksmith skills to make a steel Ned Kelly bushranger suit to raise money for his campaign (Hamer 2016).

Many of the smaller parties either did not campaign, did not campaign enough, or were not covered by the media in a way that is archived and accessible after the election so that their tactics can be assessed using the visual framing content analysis method. Regardless, we cannot objectively assess campaign framing strategy performance using electoral return statistics. To conduct a proper analysis of campaign framing strategies and their success would require a detailed campaign and media content analysis (such as the method used by Grabe and Bucy 2009; or alternatively Jagers and Walgrave 2007), and a corresponding voter impact and saliency survey of some kind to see which strategies resonated and influenced voters. One could then correlate those results with electoral statistics for confirmation.

Third, I compare the parties that promoted a populist ideology (as discussed earlier) across the 2013 and 2016 elections. This reveals that electoral support changed less than 1% in most cases and many cases changed less than 0.1% (see Table 6.5). For only three parties was there substantial change: Nick Xenophon Team (NXT) and PHON gaining 1.37% and 3.76%, respectively, and Palmer United Party (PUP) losing 4.72%.

From 2013 to 2016 the total net gain in votes for all parties exhibiting ideas characteristic of populism as I have defined it above was 223,271 or 1.34% (see Table 6.5). The 2016 election also yielded two additional seats. However, this would not have been the case if it were not a double-dissolution election. After the election, the AEC conducted a re-count under Section 282 of the *Commonwealth Electoral Act 1918* which simulated the outcome as if only six senators were elected. This saw Victorian Senator Derryn Hinch and Pauline Hanson elected (but none of the other PHON candidates), and four Greens, with the rest from the Coalition and Labor. Theoretically a NXT candidate in South Australia and a Jacqui Lambie Network candidate in Tasmania would have been elected, but note that neither Nick Xenophon

Table 6.5 2013 and 2016 Australian Senate elections: ALL micro political parties with observed populism platforms compared

Party	2013 Vote	2013%	2013 Seats	2016 Vote	2016%	2016 Seats	Var.	Swing	Net
Australia First Party	10,157	0.08	0	3,005	0.02	0	−7,152	−0.06	0
Australian Liberty Alliance	0	0	0	102,982	0.74	0	102,982	0.74	0
Australian Protectionist Party	3,379	0.03	0	0	0	0	−3,379	−0.03	0
Citizens Electoral Council	1,708	0.01	0	9,850	0.07	0	8,142	0.06	0
Health Australia Party	0	0	0	85,233	0.62	0	85,233	0.62	0
John Madigan's Manufacturing and Farming Party	0	0	1 Sitting (DLP)	5,268	0.04	0	5,268	0.04	−1
Katter's Australian Party	119,920	0.89	0	53,123	0.38	0	−66,797	−0.51	0
Nick Xenophon Team	258,376	1.93	1	456,369	3.3	3	197,993	1.37	2

(continued)

Table 6.5 (continued)

Party	2013 Vote	2013%	2013 Seats	2016 Vote	2016%	2016 Seats	Var.	Swing	Net
Online Direct Democracy	9,625	0.07	0	11,857	0.09	0	2,232	0.02	0
Palmer United Party	658,976	4.91	3[a]	26,210	0.19	0	−632,766	−4.72	−3
Pauline Hanson's One Nation	70,851	0.53	0	593,013	4.29	4[a]	522,162	3.76	4
Rise Up Australia Party	49,341	0.37	0	36,424	0.26	0	−12,917	−0.11	0
Socialist Alliance	2,728	0.02	0	9,968	0.07	0	7,240	0.05	0
Uniting Australia Party	5,423	0.04	0	0	0	0	−5,423	−0.04	0
Flux	0	0	0	20,453	0.15	0	20,453	0.15	0
TOTAL National Populist	1,190,484	8.88	5	1,413,755	10.22	7	223,271	1.34	2

Sources AEC (2013) Federal Election Senate First Preferences by Group by Vote Type Version 9.1.17.21449 (AEC 2013, 2016) Federal Election Senate First Preferences by Group by Vote Type Version (AEC 2016)
[a]Senators quit the party after the election

Table 6.6 2013 and 2016 Australian Senate elections: right wing micro parties with observed populist platforms vote compared

Party/Group name	2013 Vote	2013%	2016 Vote	2016%	Var.	Swing
Australia First Party	10,157	0.08	3,005	0.02	−7,152	−0.06
Australian Liberty Alliance	0	0	102,982	0.74	102,982	0.74
Australian Protectionist Party	3,379	0.03	0	0	−3,379	−0.03
Citizens Electoral Council	1,708	0.01	9,850	0.07	8,142	0.06
John Madigan's Manufacturing and Farming Party	0	0	5,268	0.04	5,268	0.04
Katter's Australian Party	119,920	0.89	53,123	0.38	−66,797	−0.51
Palmer United Party	658,976	4.91	26,210	0.19	*−632,766*	*−4.72*
Pauline Hanson's One Nation	70,851	0.53	593,013	4.29	**522,162**	**3.76**
Rise Up Australia Party	49,341	0.37	36,424	0.26	−12,917	−0.11
Uniting Australia Party	5,423	0.04	0	0	−5,423	−0.04
TOTAL Right Wing Populist Parties	919,755	6.86	829,875	5.99	−89,880	−0.87

Sources AEC (2013) Federal Election Senate First Preferences by Group by Vote Type Version 9.1.17.21449 (AEC 2013, 2016) Federal Election Senate First Preferences by Group by Vote Type Version (AEC 2016)

nor Jacqui Lambie themselves were facing re-election if it were a normal election, so it is debatable whether that would have eventuated (Green 2017) . Applying this "normal election" re-count, the "net seat" (i.e., column 10) for Table 6.5 would read John Madigan −1, NXT 1 + 1 continuing, PHON 1, PUP 1 continuing; otherwise stated a total of 4 populist cross bench Senate seats, with a loss of one seat, despite the increase in votes. Thus, there was a small increase in votes for populism, but a false indicator of increased support in the one seat gain, in that the net increase in seats was only a by-product of the double dissolution election.

If we break down the populist vote by the imperfect left/right spectrum, we see something else that goes against the dominant narrative: the vote for right wing populism actually fell 0.87%, while left wing and centre populism increased (see Tables 6.6 and 6.7).

What I have defined as the "pure" populist parties do not fit on the spectrum as they have no policies or positions of any kind, and arguably 32,310 votes (see Table 6.8) will not make a substantive difference to any overall trend and are not worth overstating. Of all these ideologically populist parties, only NXT can be argued to have demonstrated electoral success, electoral breakthrough, and electoral persis-

Table 6.7 2013 and 2016 Australian Senate elections: Left wing center micro parties with observed populism platforms compared

Party/Group name	2013 Vote	2013%	2016 Vote	2016%	Var.	Swing
Health Australia Party	0	0	85,233	0.62	85,233	0.62
Nick Xenophon Team	258,376	1.93	456,369	3.3	**197,993**	**1.37**
Socialist Alliance	2,728	0.02	9,968	0.07	7,240	0.05
TOTAL Left or Center Populism	261,104	1.95	551,570	3.99	**290,466**	**2.04**

Sources AEC (2013) Federal Election Senate First Preferences by Group by Vote Type Version 9.1.17.21449 (AEC 2013, 2016) Federal Election Senate First Preferences by Group by Vote Type Version (AEC 2016)

Table 6.8 2013 and 2016 Australian Senate elections: parties with observed pure-populist (indirect voting) platforms compared

Party	2013 Vote	2013%	2016 Vote	2016%	Var.	Swing
Online Direct Democracy	9,625	0.07	11,857	0.09	2,232	0.02
Flux	0	0	20,453	0.15	20,453	0.15
TOTAL Pure Populist Vote	9,625	0.07	32,310	0.24	22,685	0.17

Sources AEC (2013) Federal Election Senate First Preferences by Group by Vote Type Version 9.1.17.21449 (AEC 2013, 2016) Federal Election Senate First Preferences by Group by Vote Type Version (AEC 2016)

tence through both increased votes and increased numbers of seats in parliament over subsequent elections.

Finally, if we overlay the personality and populism analyses (see Table 6.9) to look for any pattern, we can see that the two parties with significant gains—NXT and PHON—are both proponents of populism *and* have personality candidates. However, they did not predominantly engage in populist campaigning. As mentioned previously, Nick Xenophon primarily pitched himself as an "ideal candidate" and Pauline Hanson was a "maverick" framed by the media as a "sure loser". There is nothing about posting YouTube videos from inside your own plane (or, as Hanson claims, her chief of staff James Ashby's plane, branded with PHON and possibly used for campaigning, but not donated to the party by a millionaire property developer[14]) that communicates *"I'm one of the common people like you"*. This is a celebrity approach to campaigning, a similar approach to that employed by former lower house MP and leader of the Palmer United Party, Clive Palmer, where the leader or candidate makes little attempt to make it appear like their life is similar to those of their constituents,

---

[14]The Australian Electoral Commission is investigating PHON's failure to declare the donation of the plane used by Pauline Hanson during the campaign by property developer Bill McNee (McGhee 2017). Senator Hanson has defended herself by insisting the plane belongs to staffer James Ashby (Bickers 2017).

Table 6.9 2013 and 2016 Australian Senate elections: micro parties with both observed populist platforms and personality figures compared

Party	2013 Vote	2013%	2013 Seats	2016 Vote	2016%	2016 Seats	Var.	Swing	Net
Australia First Party	10,157	0.08	0	3,005	0.02	0	-7,152	-0.06	0
Australian Liberty Alliance	0	0	0	102,982	0.74	0	102,982	0.74	0
John Madigan's Manufacturing and Farming Party	0	0	1 Sitting (DLP)	5,268	0.04	0	5,268	0.04	−1
Katter's Australian Party	119,920	0.89	0	53,123	0.38	0	-66,797	-0.51	0
Nick Xenophon Team	258,376	1.93	1	456,369	3.3	3	**197,993**	**1.37**	**2**
Palmer United Party	658,976	4.91	3[a,b]	26,210	0.19	0	-632,766	-4.72	−3
Pauline Hanson's One Nation	70,851	0.53	0	593,013	4.29	4[b]	**522,162**	**3.76**	**4**
Rise Up Australia Party	49,341	0.37	0	36,424	0.26	0	-12,917	-0.11	0
TOTAL populism + Personality vote	1,116,721	8.71	5	1,276,394	9.22	7	**108,773**	**0.51**	**2**

[a]The third PUP Senator, Dio Wang, was from Western Australia. He was elected on the first count, lost to Wayne Dropulich on the second count, and was safely elected in the re-election in 2014

[b]Senators quit the party after the election

Sources AEC (2013) Federal Election Senate First Preferences by Group by Vote Type Version 9.1.17.21449 (AEC 2013, 2016) Federal Election Senate First Preferences by Group by Vote Type Version (AEC 2016)

but rather is one more like a movie star's. Much is known about celebrities and others with significant name recognition moving into politics; in particular that they will enjoy a boost from the reality that voters will vote for "somebody" over a "nobody" regardless of platform (Wood et al. 2016; Zwarun and Torrey 2011). Whether a candidate can conjure a celebrity effect by simply behaving like a celebrity, without the pre-existing name recognition, is not clear (for a discussion of the literature on celebrity politicians, see Wood et al. 2016). Xenophon's shift from the far more populist campaigning style in 2013 to the "ideal" frame in 2016 is a possible reason for the decline in the South Australian figures shown in Table 6.4, but cannot be determined on this data alone.

The other parties that used the combination of populism and personality need to be considered in their individual context, but overall the combination analysis does not yield additional insight. Some parties gained, some lost, some were flat; there is no discernible pattern.

6.6 Conclusion

Pauline Hanson is certainly a brand, a known quantity with extraordinary name recognition. Yet there is a significant tension between her somewhat protectionist, nationalist, and not definitively populist party, and her personal rhetoric, which indicates a weakness in her personal, dictatorial-style leadership. This is most readily observable in the infighting and lack of discipline: dirty laundry that is frequently, if not eagerly, aired. Her personal campaigning is effective, she definitely connects with voters, but it is not classically populist: she's a maverick, hard to handle, impossible to control, unpredictable. And that is okay, it works well with her audience, but she will never be Prime Minister. Looking at the votes only from the psephological approach, she is clearly a solid personality candidate… but that maverick aspect of her campaigning style and her extremist policies means she has probably peaked. Again. Never forgetting the bulk of PHON's success was due to the double dissolution math lowering the bar, and given that PHON will also be facing a serious contender in Cory Bernardi's Australian Conservatives, which will be perceived as a more stable option for conservative voters to park their protest votes with, it is unlikely any success will be repeated in the 2018/2019 federal election without the pull of Pauline Hanson's name on the ticket.

References

Abts, K., & Rummens, S. (2007). Populism versus democracy. *Political Studies, 55*(2), 405–424. https://doi.org/10.1111/j.1467-9248.2007.00657.x.

AEC [Australian Electoral Commission]. (2013). *2013 Federal election senate first preferences by group by vote type. 2013 Virtual Tally Room*. http://results.aec.gov.au/17496/Website/Downloads/SenateFirstPrefsByGroupByVoteTypeDownload-17496.csv. Accessed January 14, 2017.

AEC [Australian Electoral Commission]. (2014). *2013 federal election Senate first preferences by group by vote type by state*. http://results.aec.gov.au/17496/Website/Downloads/SenateFirstPrefsByStateByGroupByVoteTypeDownload-17496.csv. Accessed January 14, 2017.

AEC [Australian Electoral Commission]. (2015). *Uniting Australia party*. http://www.aec.gov.au/Parties_and_Representatives/Party_Registration/Deregistered_parties/uniting-australia.htm. Accessed August 28, 2017.

AEC [Australian Electoral Commission]. (2016). *Vote type breakdown by state: 2016 federal election tally room (as at the return of the writs)*. http://results.aec.gov.au/20499/Website/HouseVoteTypeBreakdownByState-20499.htm. Accessed June 27, 2017.

AEC [Australian Electoral Commission]. (2017a). *2016 federal election Senate first preferences by group by vote type by state (as at the return of the writs)*. http://results.aec.gov.au/20499/pre-cdr/Website/Downloads/SenateFirstPrefsByStateByGroupByVoteTypeDownload-20499.csv. Accessed June 27, 2017.

AEC [Australian Electoral Commission]. (2017b). *Palmer United Party: Notice under s 135(1) of the Commonwealth Electoral Act 1918*. http://www.aec.gov.au/Parties_and_Representatives/Party_Registration/Deregistered_parties/palmer.htm. Accessed August 28, 2017.

Aitkin, D. (1982). *Stability and change in Australian politics* (2nd ed.). Canberra: Australian National University Press.

Andreß, H.-J. (2017). The need for and use of panel data. *IZA World of Labor, April*. https://doi.org/10.15185/izawol.352. Accessed July 13, 2018.

Albertazzi, D., & McDonnell, D. (2008). Introduction: The sceptre and the spectre. In D. Albertazzi & D. McDonnell (Eds.), *Twenty-first century populism* (pp. 1–11). New York: Palgrave Macmillan.

Altman, D. (2017). Discontents: Identity, politics, institutions. *Griffith REVIEW, 57*, 80–92.

anoukeblackheart. (2017, November 19). Barnaby Joyce: Peeling back the rumours. *Reddit thread*. https://www.reddit.com/r/australia/comments/7dws0k/barnaby_joyce_peeling_back_the_rumours/. Accessed February 23, 2018.

Aslanidis, P. (2015). Is populism an ideology? a refutation and a new perspective. *Political Studies, 64*(1_suppl), 88–104. https://doi.org/10.1111/1467-9248.12224.

Atfield, C. (2016, May 27). Federal election 2016: Glenn Lazarus keen to run his own show. *Sydney Morning Herald*. http://www.smh.com.au/federal-politics/federal-election-2016/federal-election-2016-glenn-lazarus-keen-to-run-his-own-show-20160527-gp5ucr.html. Accessed August 18, 2017.

Australia First Party, Victorian Branch. (2017). *Our vision*. http://australiafirstparty.net/our-policies/policies-explored/our-vision/. Accessed August 15, 2017.

Australian Associated Press. (2018, June 4). Former One Nation senator Fraser Anning joins Katter party. *The Guardian*. https://www.theguardian.com/australia-news/2018/jun/04/former-one-nation-senator-fraser-anning-joins-katter-party. Accessed June 9, 2018.

Australian Country Party. (2016). John Madigan joins the Country Party. http://countryparty.org.au/john-madigan-joins-country-party/. Accessed August 28, 2017.

Australian Liberty Alliance. (2017). Values and core policies. https://www.australianlibertyalliance.org.au/values-and-policies/values-and-core-policies.html. Accessed August 15, 2017.

Australian Protectionist Party. (2017). *About*. http://www.protectionist.net/about/. Accessed July 15, 2017.

Azari, J. R. (2016). How the news media helped to nominate Trump. *Political Communication, 33*(4), 677–680. https://doi.org/10.1080/10584609.2016.1224417.

Bakker, B. N., Rooduijn, M., & Schumacher, G. (2016). The psychological roots of populist voting: Evidence from the United States, the Netherlands and Germany. *European Journal of Political Research, 55*(2), 302–320. https://doi.org/10.1111/1475-6765.12121.

Barbieri, P. (2017, April 25). The death and life of social democracy. *Foreign Affairs*. https://www. foreignaffairs.com/articles/europe/2017-04-25/death-and-life-social-democracy. Accessed May 14, 2017.

Barbour, L. (2018, June 1). Pauline Hanson asks Brian Burston to leave One Nation. *ABC News*. http://www.abc.net.au/news/2018-06-01/pauline-hanson-asks-brian-burston-to-leave-one-nation/9825896. Accessed June 9, 2018.

Barr, R. R. (2009). Populists, outsiders and anti-establishment politics. *Party Politics, 15*(1), 29–48. https://doi.org/10.1177/1354068808097890.

Bean, C. (1990). The personal vote in Australian federal elections. *Political Studies, 38*(2), 253–268. https://doi.org/10.1111/j.1467-9248.1990.tb01491.x.

Bean, C. (1994). The 1993 election and Australian electoral studies in the 1990s. *Australian Journal of Political Science, 29*(sup1), 1–9. https://doi.org/10.1080/10361146.1994.11733423.

Bean, C., & Kelley, J. (1995). The electoral impact of new politics issues: The environment in the 1990 Australian federal election. *Comparative Politics, 27*(3), 339. https://doi.org/10.2307/42 2062.

Belot, H. (2018, February 2). Lucy Gichuhi, independent senator, joins Liberal Party. *ABC News*. http://www.abc.net.au/news/2018-02-02/lucy-gichuhi-independent-senator-joins-liberal-party/9392018. Accessed February 2, 2018.

Berelson, B. R., Lazarsfeld, P. F., & McPhee, W. N. (1954). *Voting*. Chicago: University of Chicago Press.

Bernardi, C. (2017). *Cory Bernardi launches Australian conservatives*. https://www.conservatives. org.au/update_9_australian_conservatives_launched. Accessed August 17, 2017.

Bernardi, C., & Hanson, P. (2017). *Refugee convention*. Motion to the Senate, Australian Parliament House. https://parlwork.aph.gov.au/motions/026879bc-f254-e711-9ed4-005056a40008. Accessed November 18, 2017.

Bickers, C. (2017, May 2). Pauline Hanson says the plane at the centre of a donation probe belongs to her staffer, not her. *news.com.au*. http://www.news.com.au/national/politics/pauline-hanson-s ays-the-plane-at-the-centre-of-a-donation-probe-belongs-to-her-staffer-not-her/news-story/f217 25d96acf947dfcb7f3fb07022633. Accessed August 17, 2017.

Bickers, C., & Killoran, M. (2017, November 13). Citizenship saga: Fraser Anning quits One Nation as new senators, Senate President sworn in. *news.com.au*. http://www.news.com.au/nat ional/citizenship-saga-new-senators-senate-president-sworn-in/news-story/f5ee15a0ae2793762 5636ee1dc37d245. Accessed November 13, 2017.

Birks, J. (2011). The politics of protest in newspaper campaigns: Dissent, populism and the rhetoric of authenticity. *British Politics, 6*(June), 128–154. https://doi.org/10.1057/bp.2011.5.

Block, E., & Negrine, R. (2017). The populist communication style: Toward a critical framework. *International Journal of Communication, 11,* 20.

Butler, J. (2017, June 20). Senate squashes Pauline Hanson and Cory Bernardi motion trashing the refugee convention. *Huffington Post*. http://www.huffingtonpost.com.au/2017/06/20/senate-squa shes-pauline-hanson-and-cory-bernardi-motion-trashing_a_22491097/. Accessed November 19, 2017.

Butler, J. (2018, June 8). A quarter of the Senate has resigned or changed parties since 2016 election. *Ten Daily*. https://tendaily.com.au/news/politics/a180605rwm/a-quarter-of-the-senate-has-resigned-or-changed-parties-since-2016-election-20180608. Accessed June 9, 2018.

Byrne, E., & Doran, M. (2017, February 3). Rod Culleton's election invalid: High Court orders special recount of WA senate vote. *ABC News*. http://www.abc.net.au/news/2017-02-03/rod-cul leton-election-invalid-high-court-finds/8238104. Accessed February 3, 2017.

Canovan, M. (1982). Two strategies for the study of populism. *Political Studies, 30*(4), 544–552. https://doi.org/10.1111/j.1467-9248.1982.tb00559.x.

Canovan, M. (1999). Trust the people! Populism and the two faces of democracy. *Political Studies, 47*(1), 2–16. https://doi.org/10.1111/1467-9248.00184.

Castello, R., & Shepherd, T. (2017, April 26). Former Family First senator and Homestead Homes owner Bob Day is officially bankrupt. *The Advertiser.* http://www.news.com.au/national/south-a ustralia/former-family-first-senator-and-homestead-homes-owner-bob-day-is-officially-bankru pt/news-story/9273884a519238ee6f03572d9bea30bb. Accessed November 19, 2017.

Chang, C. (2017, December 10). One Nation threat fails to materialise in Queensland election. *news.com.au*. Accessed July 13, 2018.

Chaples, E. (1997). The Australian voters. In R. K. Smith (Ed.), *Politics in Australia* (3rd ed., pp. 354–371). Allen & Unwin: St. Leonards.

Citizens Electoral Council. (2012). *The future of Australia: Develop, or die*. http://cecaust.com.au/ resolution/. Accessed September 4, 2017.

Citizens Electoral Council. (2016). *Election 2016. Campaign material*. http://www.cecaust.com.a u/election2016/. Accessed September 4, 2017.

Clark, N. (2018, March 4). Lambie lashes pokies after disappointing performance. *The Mercury*. https://www.themercury.com.au/news/politics/jacqui-lambie-lashes-pokies-lobby-after-her-part y-flopped-in-its-first-state-election/news-story/2e4820f63d8ef48345e565f39626f4d6. Accessed June 9, 2018.

Colebatch, T. (2013, October 5). How mistaken identity and luck won on the day. *Sydney Morning Herald*. http://www.smh.com.au/national/how-mistaken-identity-and-luck-won-on-the-day-201 31004-2uzse.html. Accessed September 18, 2017.

Coorey, P. (2018, June 6). Brian Burston to defy Pauline Hanson and vote for income tax cuts. *Financial Review*. https://www.afr.com/news/brian-burston-to-defy-pauline-hanson-and-vote-fo r-income-tax-cuts-20180605-h110mx. Accessed June 9, 2018.

Crosby, R. K. (2017, December 3). Results of the New England by-election exit poll. *Medium* (blog). https://medium.com/@ktxby/results-of-the-new-england-by-election-exit-poll- a2ec09d98f1. Accessed July 13, 2018.

Curtice, J. (2015). General election 2015: Business as usual or new departure? *Political Insight, 6*(2), 4–7. https://doi.org/10.1111/2041-9066.12092.

Curtice, J. (2016). Brexit: Behind the referendum. *Political Insight, 7*(2), 4–7. https://doi.org/10.1 177/2041905816666122.

De La Torre, C. (2016). Left-wing populism: Inclusion and authoritarianism in Venezuela, Bolivia, and Ecuador. *Brown Journal of World Affairs, 23*(1), 61–76.

Denemark, D., & Bowler, S. (2002). Minor parties and protest votes in Australia and New Zealand: Locating populist politics. *Electoral Studies, 21*(1), 47–67.

Dolan, K. (2013). Gender stereotypes, candidate evaluations, and voting for women candidates. *Political Research Quarterly, 67*(1), 96–107. https://doi.org/10.1177/1065912913487949.

Doran, M. (2018, May 9). What is it about Section 44 that keeps tripping up our politicians? *ABC News*. http://www.abc.net.au/news/2017-11-17/constitution-section-44-what-it-says-abou t-disqualification/9161180. Accessed July 13, 2018.

Doran, M., Belot, H., & Crothers, J. (2017, August 16). Family First senator Lucy Gichuhi survives ALP challenge over citizenship concerns. *ABC News*. http://www.abc.net.au/news/2017-04-19/l abor-party-to-challenge-eligiblity-of-sa-senator-elect/8452514. Accessed September 15, 2017.

Enten, H. (2017, May 8). Macron won, but the French polls were way off. *FiveThirtyEight*, Vol. 2017. https://fivethirtyeight.com/features/macron-won-but-the-french-polls-were-way-off/. Accessed August 28, 2017.

Eveland, W. P., Jr., & Morey, A. C. (2011). Challenges and opportunities of panel designs. In E. P. Bucy & L. R. Holbert (Eds.), *Sourcebook for political communication research: Methods, measures, and analytical techniques* (pp. 19–33). New York: Routledge.

Flux. (2017). *The Flux voting system explained*. https://voteflux.org/about/how/. Accessed August 24, 2017.

Gartrell, A. (2017, October 3). One Nation's Fraser Anning avoids bankruptcy, cleared to replace Malcolm Roberts. *The Sydney Morning Herald*. http://www.smh.com.au/federal-politics/politi cal-news/one-nations-fraser-anning-avoids-bankruptcy-cleared-to-replace-malcolm-roberts-201 71002-gyt35r.html. Accessed November 19, 2017.

Garton, M. B. (2011). Abbott's budgie-smuggler blues. *Eureka Street*, Vol. 21, p. 30.

Glover, S. (2016). Their body politics: Malcolm, John and the junk in Tony's trunks. *Griffith REVIEW, 53,* 28–38.

Gordon, H. (2003). *Steven Bradbury.* http://corporate.olympics.com.au/athlete/steven-bradbury. Accessed August 28, 2017.

Grabe, M. E., & Bucy, E. P. (2009). *Image bite politics: News and the visual framing of elections.* New York: Oxford University Press.

Grabe, M. E., & Bucy, E. P. (2011). Image bite analysis of political visuals: Understanding the visual framing process in election news. In E. P. Bucy & R. L. Holbert (Eds.), *Sourcebook for political communication research: Methods, Measures, and analytical techniques* (pp. 209–237). New York: Routledge.

Grant, B., Dollery, B. E., & Kortt, M. (2015). Is there a case for mandating directly elected "semi-executive" mayors in Australian local government? Lessons from the 2012 Queensland local government elections. *Australian Journal of Public Administration, 74*(4), 484–494.

Green, A. (2014, February 3). Should 'Liberal' and 'Labor' be quarantined as politi-cal party names? *Antony Green's Election Blog*. https://web.archive.org/web/2015090800 3822, http://blogs.abc.net.au/antonygreen/2014/02/should-liberal-and-labor-be-quarantined-as-political-party-names.html. Accessed May 3, 2017. Archived copy accessed from Internet Archive Wayback Machine.

Green, A. (2017, April 3). (A bit late but a) post-2016 federal election pendulum plus results summary. *Antony Green's Election Blog*. https://web.archive.org/web/2017061109 4430, http://blogs.abc.net.au/antonygreen/2017/04/a-bit-late-but-a-post-2016-federal-election-p endulum-plus-results-summary.html. Accessed May 4, 2017. Archived copy accessed from Way-back Machine.

Gwynn, M. (2014). *Doing a Bradbury—an Aussie term born in the Winter Olympics*. http://ozwor ds.org/?p=5912. Accessed August 28, 2017.

Hamer, A. (2016, July 8). Senator John Madigan's greatest hits. *The Courier*. http://www.thecouri er.com.au/story/4019664/senator-john-madigans-greatest-hits/. Accessed September 12, 2017.

Hanson, P. (2015). *A vote for me at the next election will be your insurance …* https://www.facebo ok.com/PaulineHansonAu/posts/405136729690645:0. Accessed September 12, 2017.

Hanson, P. (2017). *Pauline Hanson's please explain*. https://www.facebook.com/pg/PaulineHans onAu. Accessed August 10, 2017.

Harris, B. (2017, April 5). Explainer: Why the High Court ruled Bob Day's election to the Senate invalid. *The Conversation*. https://theconversation.com/explainer-why-the-high-court-ruled-bob-days-election-to-the-senate-invalid-75556. Accessed November 19, 2017.

Harrison, J. (2016, April 29). Three reasons Senator Glenn Lazarus will be back for another term. *Brisbane Times*. https://www.brisbanetimes.com.au/national/queensland/three-reasons-senator-g lenn-lazarus-will-be-back-for-another-term-20160429-goi5sm.html. Accessed August 18, 2017.

Health Australia Party. (2015). *Constitution*. https://www.healthaustraliaparty.com.au/index.php/c onstitution/. Accessed July 15, 2017.

Health Australia Party. (2017). *Preamble*. https://www.healthaustraliaparty.com.au/index.php/prea mble/. Accessed July 15, 2017.

Hobolt, S. B. (2016). The Brexit vote: A divided nation, a divided continent. *Journal of European Public Policy, 23*(9), 1259–1277. https://doi.org/10.1080/13501763.2016.1225785.

Holderhead, S. (2018, January 23). Banished NXT candidate Tim Storer makes grab at Skye Kakosche-Moore's seat. *The Advertiser*. https://www.adelaidenow.com.au/news/banished-nxt-c andidate-tim-storer-makes-grab-at-skye-kakoschemoores-seat/news-story/ef554216acadc2dcf6 0e2795415d6535. Accessed June 9, 2018.

Holmes, B, Fernandes, S., & Department of Parliamentary Services. (2012). *2010 federal election: A brief history* (Vol. 2011–12). Canberra: Parliament House.

Hübner, K. (2016). Understanding Brexit. *European Policy Analysis, 2*(2), 4–11. https://doi.org/1 0.18278/epa.2.2.1.

Hughes, C. A., & Western, J. S. (1966). *The Prime Minister's policy speech: A case study in televised politics*. Canberra: Australian National University Press.

Hurcombe, E. (2016). The making of a captain: The production and projection of a political image on the Tony Abbott Facebook page. *Communication, Politics & Culture, 49,* 19–38.

Inglehart, R., & Norris, P. (2016). Trump, Brexit, and the rise of populism: Economic have-nots and cultural backlash. *HKS Working Paper No. RWP16-026.* https://doi.org/10.2139/ssrn.2818659.

Jagers, J. A. N., & Walgrave, S. (2007). Populism as political communication style: An empirical study of political parties' discourse in Belgium. *European Journal of Political Research, 46*(3), 319–345. https://doi.org/10.1111/j.1475-6765.2006.00690.x.

John Madigan's Manufacturing and Farming Party. (2016). What we stand for. *Party document.* http://pandora.nla.gov.au/pan/151832/20160704-0833/www.manufacturingandfarmingpa rty.org/welcome/index.html. Accessed July 15, 2017. Accessed via Pandora web archive.

Jones, R. (2017, November 19). Exclusive! Barnaby Joyce: Peeling back the rumours. *Independent Australia* (blog). https://independentaustralia.net/politics/politics-display/exclusive-barnaby-joy ce-peeling-back-the-rumours,10942. Accessed July 13, 2018.

Katter's Australian Party. (2016a). *Don't 'kid' yourself Australia—The LNP will sell Kidman to the Chinese.* https://www.ausparty.org.au/news/media-releases/view/3. Accessed September 5, 2017.

Katter's Australian Party. (2016b). *Protecting Australian jobs and Australian business.* https://www.ausparty.org.au/page/attachment/45/protecting-australian-jobs-and-australia n-business. Accessed July 15, 2017.

Kempton, H. (2018, May 29). Steve Martin becomes state's First Nationals senator. *The Mercury.* https://www.themercury.com.au/news/politics/steve-martin-becomes-states-first-natio nals-senator/news-story/d9a19acc8f3158c3151a5fdd0aa52076. Accessed July 12, 2018.

Koziol, M. (2018, May 9). Four dual citizen MPs Resign in wake of High court ruling, sparking by-elections. *The Sydney Morning Herald.* https://www.smh.com.au/politics/federal/four-dual-citizen-mps-resign-in-wake-of-high-court-ruling-sparking-byelections-20180509-p4ze89.html. Accessed June 9, 2018.

Krane, V., & Kaus, R. J. (2014). Gendered social dynamics in sport. In M. R. Beauchamp & M. A. Eys (Eds.), *Group dynamics in exercise and sport psychology* (2nd ed., pp. 335–349). Florence: Taylor and Francis.

Laclau, E. (1977). *Politics and ideology in Marxist theory: Capitalism, fascism, populism.* London: NLB.

Laclau, E. (2005). *On populist reason.* London: Verso.

Lander, L., & Cooper, N. (2017). *Promoting public deliberation in low trust environments: Australian use cases.* Paper presented at the Proceedings of the Workshop on Linked Democracy: Artificial Intelligence for Democratic Innovation co-located with the 26th International Joint Conference on Artificial Intelligence (IJCAI 2017), Melbourne, August 19, 2017.

Langenberg, A. (2018, March 18). Deflated Xenophon rules out return to Canberra. *Adelaide Now.* http://www.adelaidenow.com.au/news/sa-election-2018/election-2018-after-his-personal-defea t-sa-best-leader-nick-xenophon/news-story/1c07e88ddb746e68068430c47884bd79. Accessed June 9, 2018.

Lazarsfeld, P. F. (1941). Repeated interviews as a tool for studying changes in opinion and their causes. *American Statistical Association Bulletin 2,* 3–7. http://www.jstor.org/stable/42731708.

Lazarsfeld, P. F. (1948). The use of panels in social research. *Proceedings of the American Philosophical Society, 92,* 405–10. http://www.jstor.org/stable/3143053.

Lazarsfeld, P. F., Bernard B., & Gaudet H. (1968). *The people's choice: How the voter makes up his mind in a presidential campaign* (3rd ed.). Columbia University Press.

Loukissas, Y., & Pollock, A. (2017). After big data failed: The Enduring allure of numbers in the wake of the 2016 US election. *Engaging Science, Technology, and Society, 3,* 16. https://doi.org/10.17351/ests2017.150.

Lusinchi, D. (2017). "Clinton defeats Trump" 2016 polls and the shadow of 1948. *Significance, 14*(4), 8–9. https://doi.org/10.1111/j.1740-9713.2017.01049.x.

Mackerras, M. (1974). *The role of the candidate in the electoral process in Australia* (Thesis (Ph.D.)). Canberra: Australian National University.

Mackerras, M. (1976). *Incumbency as an electoral advantage: The influence of the sitting member on constituency voting patterns in Australian Federal and State elections, 1953–76* (Thesis (Ph.D.)). Canberra: Australian National University.

MacLennan, L. (2018, April 10). Nick Xenophon's federal party drops his name. *ABC News.* http://www.abc.net.au/news/2018-04-10/nick-xenophons-party-drops-his-name/9636598. Accessed June 9, 2018.

Madigan, J. (2016). *Tired of big party politics?* http://pandora.nla.gov.au/pan/159328/20160705-0037/www.johnmadigan.com.au/campaign2016/2016/3/31/a-message-from-the-campaign-to-re-elect-john-madigan.html. Accessed September 5, 2017. Accessed via Pandora web archive.

Manne, A. (2015, November). Joker in the pack: On the road with the irrepressible Nick Xenophon. *The Monthly.* https://www.themonthly.com.au/issue/2015/november/1446296400/anne-manne/joker-pack. Accessed August 24, 2017.

Marr, D. (2017). The white queen: One nation and the politics of race. *Quarterly Essay, 65,* 1–102.

Markson, S., & Devine. M. (2017, October 21). The dirty war on Barnaby. *The Daily Telegraph.*

Mason, R. (2010). 'Pitbulls' and Populist Politicians: Sarah Palin, Pauline Hanson and the use of gendered nostalgia in electoral campaigns. *Comparative American Studies: An International Journal, 8*(3), 185–199.

McArthur, J. (2018, May 22). The party's over: CountryMinded deregistered by electoral commission. *The Land.* https://www.theland.com.au/story/5420580/the-partys-over-countryminded-deregistered-by-electoral-commission/. Accessed July 12, 2018.

McLeay, B. (2018, March 20). 12 months later and Rod Culleton still refuses to accept he's not a senator. *Pedestrian TV.* https://www.pedestrian.tv/news/rod-culleton-senator-high-court-crikey/. Accessed March 20, 2018.

McDougall, D. (2016). Australia and Brexit: Déjà vu all over again? *The Round Table, 105*(5), 557–572. https://doi.org/10.1080/00358533.2016.1233759.

McGhee, A. (2017, May 26). Pauline Hanson's One Nation to be investigated by Electoral Commission over plane ownership. *ABC News.* http://www.abc.net.au/news/2017-05-26/electoral-commission-investigates-one-nation-plane/8560062. Accessed August 28, 2017.

Miragliotta, N. (2017, December 10). Pauline Hanson: What the Queensland election tells us about One Nation. *ABC News.* http://www.abc.net.au/news/2017-11-30/pauline-hanson-one-nation-queensland-election-conservative/9209944. Accessed July 13, 2018.

Moffitt, B., & Tormey, S. (2013). Rethinking populism: Politics, mediatisation and political style. *Political Studies, 62*(2), 381–397. https://doi.org/10.1111/1467-9248.12032.

Mols, F., & Jetten, J. (2016). Explaining the appeal of populist right-wing parties in times of economic prosperity. *Political Psychology, 37*(2), 275–292. https://doi.org/10.1111/pops.12258.

Mols, F., & Jetten, J. (2017). One Nation's support: Why 'income' is a poor predictor. *Australasian Parliamentary Review, 32*(1), 92–100.

Moore, A. J., & Dewberry, D. (2012). The masculine image of presidents as sporting figures. *SAGE Open, 2*(3). https://doi.org/10.1177/2158244012457078.

Mudde, C., & Kaltwasser, C. R. (2017). *Populism: A very short introduction.* New York: Oxford University Press.

Murphy, J. (2017, December 6). How did the other New England by-election candidates go? *The Northern Daily Leader.*

Murphy, K., & Remeikis, A. (2017, October 6). Nick Xenophon resigns from Senate to run for state parliament. *The Guardian Australia.* https://www.theguardian.com/australia-news/2017/oct/06/nick-xenophon-resigns-from-senate-to-run-for-state-parliament. Accessed October 6, 2017.

Napolitan, J. (2003). Napolitan's rules: 112 lessons learned from a career in politics. In R. A. Faucheux (Ed.), *Winning elections. Political campaign management, strategy and tactics* (pp. 26–58). New York: M. Evans and Company.

Navot, D., Rubin, A., & Ghanem, A. (2017). The 2015 Israeli general election: The triumph of Jewish skepticism, the emergence of Arab faith. *The Middle East Journal, 71*(2), 248–268. https://doi.org/10.3751/71.2.14.

Neate, N. (2017, October 23). Who is waging the 'dirty war' on Barnaby? *Independent Australia (blog)*. https://independentaustralia.net/politics/politics-display/who-is-waging-the-dirty-war-on-barnaby,10851. Accessed February 23, 2018.

Nick Xenophon Team. (2017). *Our focus*. https://nxt.org.au/whats-nxt/our-focus/. Accessed September 5, 2017.

O'Malley, N. (2016, July 1). Election 2016: Nick Xenophon ready for the SuperShock of polling day. *Sydney Morning Herald*. http://www.smh.com.au/federal-politics/federal-election-2016/election-2016-nick-xenophon-ready-for-the-supershock-of-polling-day-20160701-gpwkv9.html Accessed August 28, 2017.

O'Malley, N. (2017, April 8). Anti-halal leader Kirralie Smith joins Cory Bernardi's Australian Conservatives. *The Sydney Morning Herald*. http://www.smh.com.au/federal-politics/political-news/antihalal-leader-kirralie-smith-joins-cory-bernardis-australian-conservatives-20170407-gvgb8f.html. Accessed November 19, 2017.

Online Direct Democracy. (2017). *How the party works and FAQs*. https://www.onlinedirectdemocracy.org/how-the-party-works/. Accessed August 21, 2017.

Owen, M. (2017, April 25). Bernardi and Family First join forces. *The Weekend Australian*. http://www.theaustralian.com.au/national-affairs/bernardi-and-family-first-join-forces-for-conservative-vote/news-story/c2604388c3b1c7b1b320d7e9678f8b3d. Accessed November 19, 2017.

Palmer, C. (2015). *Vision for Australia*. Maroochydore: Palmer United Party.

Parvu, C. A. (2016). Populism, cosmopolitanism and the reconfiguration of contemporary politics. *Annals of the University of Bucharest, Political Science Series, 18*(1), 103–119.

Pauline Hanson's One Nation. (2016). *Bringing back Australian values: Federal policy guide*. Albion: Pauline Hanson's One Nation. http://www.onenation.com.au/LiteratureRetrieve.aspx?ID=155063 Accessed August 10, 2017.

Pauline Hanson's One Nation. (2017a). *About Pauline Hanson's One Nation*. http://www.onenation.com.au/about. Accessed August 10, 2017.

Pauline Hanson's One Nation. (2017b). *Economics and tax policy: Additional information*. http://www.onenation.com.au/policies/economics/economics-2. Accessed September 6, 2017.

Pauline Hanson's One Nation. (2017c). *One Nation Policies: Islam*. http://www.onenation.com.au/policies/islam. Accessed August 20, 2017.

Pauline Hanson's One Nation. (2017d). *One Nation policies: Manufacturing*. http://www.onenation.com.au/policies/manufacturing. Accessed September 6, 2017.

Pauline Hanson's One Nation. (2017e). *One Nation Policies: Primary industries*. http://www.onenation.com.au/policies/primary-industries. Accessed September 6, 2017.

Pauline Hanson's One Nation. (2017f). *Our history*. http://www.onenation.com.au/history. Accessed August 10, 2017.

Pauline Hanson's One Nation. (2017g). *Pauline Hanson*. http://www.onenation.com.au/paulinehanson. Accessed August 10, 2017.

Pauline Hanson's One Nation. (2017h). *Principles and objectives*. http://www.onenation.com.au/principles. Accessed September 6, 2017.

Pauline Hanson's Facebook post on Muslims gains support. (2015, October 8). *news.com.au*. http://www.news.com.au/national/politics/pauline-hansons-facebook-post-on-muslims-gains-support/news-story/9b13b3c6dbb5ada004ea4ba55c54a39a. Accessed September 12, 2017.

Peters, J., & Pinfold, R. (2015). Consolidating right-wing hegemony: The Israeli election 2015. *Mediterranean Politics, 20*(3), 405–412. https://doi.org/10.1080/13629395.2015.1084146.

Preiss, B. (2017, August 22). Australian Sex Party to become the Reason Party. *The Sydney Morning Herald*. http://www.smh.com.au/federal-politics/political-news/australian-sex-party-to-become-the-reason-party-20170821-gy185f.html. Accessed September 15, 2017.

Rahat, G., Hazan, R. Y., & Ben-Nun Bloom, P. (2016). Stable blocs and multiple identities: The 2015 elections in Israel. *Representation, 52*(1), 99–117. https://doi.org/10.1080/00344893.2016.1190592.

Remeikis, A. (2018, June 4). Brian Burston says he's still a member of One Nation. *The Guardian*. http://www.theguardian.com/australia-news/2018/jun/04/brian-burston-says-hes-still-a-member-of-one-nation. Accessed June 9, 2018.

Ridder, R. (2016). *Looking for votes in all the wrong places*. New York: Radius Book Group.

Rise Up Australia. (2017a). *Foreign ownership policy*. http://riseupaustraliaparty.com/our-policies/foreign-ownership-policy/. Accessed August 10, 2017.

Rise Up Australia. (2017b). *Multi cultures. Policy document*. http://riseupaustraliaparty.com/our-policies/multi-cultures/. Accessed August 10, 2017.

Ruspini, E. (2002). *An introduction to longitudinal research*. Abingdon, Oxon, US: Taylor and Francis.

Schmidt, V. A. (2017). Britain-out and Trump-in: A discursive institutionalist analysis of the British referendum on the EU and the US presidential election. *Review of International Political Economy, 24*(2), 248–269. https://doi.org/10.1080/09692290.2017.1304974.

Schoor, C. (2017). In the theater of political style: Touches of populism, pluralism and elitism in speeches of politicians. *Discourse & Society*. 0957926517721082. https://doi.org/10.1177/0957926517721082.

Selmes, J. (2016). AHP #115 Liberal Democrats Senator David Leyonhjelm. In J. Selmes (Ed.), *Australian hunting podcast: Hunting, shooting and fishing radio*. http://australianhuntingpodcast.com.au/ahp-115-liberal-democrats-senator-david-leyonhjelm/. Accessed September 20, 2017.

Silva, K. (2017, April 19). Clive Palmer disbands Palmer United Party, with federal registration to be cancelled. *ABC News*. http://www.abc.net.au/news/2017-04-19/clive-palmer-disbands-palmer-united-party/8452760. Accessed August 28, 2017.

Silver, N. (2015, July 7). The polls were bad in Greece. The conventional wisdom was worse. *FiveThirtyEight: Polling*. https://fivethirtyeight.com/datalab/the-polls-were-bad-in-greece-the-conventional-wisdom-was-worse/. Accessed April 20, 2017.

Smith, M. (2016, April 20). Senator Jacqui Lambie bid to crowdsource campaign funding falls flat. *The Hobart Mercury*. http://www.themercury.com.au/news/politics/senator-jacqui-lambie-bid-to-crowdsource-campaign-funding-falls-flat/news-story/6338e00e1380110c4da3ad8614ef9ec5. Accessed August 28, 2017.

Socialist Alliance. (2017). *About*. https://socialist-alliance.org/about. Accessed September 4, 2017.

Stanley, B. (2008). The thin ideology of populism. *Journal of Political Ideologies, 13*(1), 95–110. https://doi.org/10.1080/13569310701822289.

Strom, M. (2017, August 18). The Constitution is broken and out of date—we should abolish it and start again. *ABC News*, http://www.abc.net.au/news/2017-08-18/abolish-the-constitution-and-start-again/8816488. Accessed December 9, 2017.

Sturgis, P., Baker, N., Callegaro, M., Fisher, S., Green, J., Jennings, W., et al. (2016). *Report of the inquiry into the 2015 British general election opinion polls* (p. 115). London: Market Research Society and British Polling Council.

Tsatsanis, E., & Teperoglou, E. (2016). Realignment under stress: The July 2015 referendum and the September parliamentary election in Greece. *South European Society and Politics, 21*(4), 427–450. https://doi.org/10.1080/13608746.2016.1208906.

Tucker, P. E. (2011). *The consequences and impacts of maverick politicians on contemporary Australian politics* (Ph.D. Thesis). Hobart: University of Tasmania.

Uniting Australia Party. (2013). *About*. https://web.archive.org/web/20130825131818, http://www.unitingaustraliaparty.com.au:80/. Accessed July 12, 2017. Accessed from the Internet Archive Wayback Machine.

van Kessel, S. (2014). The populist cat-dog: Applying the concept of populism to contemporary European party systems. *Journal of Political Ideologies, 19*(1), 99–118. https://doi.org/10.1080/13569317.2013.869457.

Vraga, E. K. (2017). Which candidates can be mavericks? The effects of issue disagreement and gender on candidate evaluations. *Politics & Policy, 45*(1), 4–30. https://doi.org/10.1111/polp.12192.

Weyland, K. (2001). Clarifying a contested concept: Populism in the study of Latin American politics. *Comparative Politics, 34*(1), 1–22. https://doi.org/10.2307/422412.

Wilson, J. (2017, October 24). Politicians, sex and the press gallery. *No Place for Sheep (blog)*. https://noplaceforsheep.com/2017/10/24/politicians-sex-and-the-press-gallery/ Accessed Feberuary 23, 2018.

Wood, M., Corbett, J., & Flinders, M. (2016). Just like us: Everyday celebrity politicians and the pursuit of popularity in an age of anti-politics. *The British Journal of Politics and International Relations, 18*(3), 581–598. https://doi.org/10.1177/1369148116632182.

Wright, J. (2014, March, 7). Derryn Hinch released from prison after failing to pay contempt of court fine. *Sydney Morning Herald.* http://www.smh.com.au/entertainment/tv-and-radio/derryn-hinch-released-from-prison-after-failing-to-pay-contempt-of-court-fine-20140306-34au1. Accessed September 12, 2017.

Wring, D., & Ward, S. (2015). Exit velocity: The media election. *Parliamentary Affairs*, 68(suppl_1), 224–240. https://doi.org/10.1093/pa/gsv037.

Xenophon, N. (2014). *Party launch*. https://nxt.org.au/party-launch/. Accessed August 10, 2017.

Yaxley, L. (2017, April 26). Cory Bernardi's Australian Conservatives to amalgamate with Family First. *ABC News.* http://www.abc.net.au/news/2017-04-25/cory-bernardi-australian-conservatives-family-first-to-merge/8471244. Accessed September 19, 2017.

Zakaria, F. (2016, November–December). Populism on the march: why the West is in trouble. *Foreign Affairs.* https://www.foreignaffairs.com/articles/united-states/2016-10-17/populism-march. Accessed September 8, 2017.

Zwarun, L., & Torrey, A. (2011). Somebody versus nobody: An exploration of the role of celebrity status in an election. *The Social Science Journal, 48*(4), 672–680. https://doi.org/10.1016/j.soscij.2011.06.005.

Part III
Politics and Policy

Chapter 7
One Nation and Indigenous Reconciliation

Simon Burgess

Abstract Hanson and her party believe in Australia: They believe in our common culture, in our identity as Australians, and in giving one another a "fair go". They themselves, however, have not consistently afforded everyone a fair go, and their divisive and alienating approach to leadership is hardly conducive to the kind of national unity that they would like Australia to have. Reconciliation between Indigenous and non-Indigenous Australians was never going to be easy. But as I seek to explain, it is possible to see how progress can been made; it is also clear that significant progress has been made. Many of us tend to assume that political correctness is beneficial to people who belong to oppressed or marginalized groups. But political correctness is unpopular, and One Nation's opposition to it undoubtedly helps to explain some of the support that they enjoy. This chapter advances three concerns about political correctness: that it is intellectually corrupting, psychologically enfeebling, and socially divisive. Correspondingly, I suggest that in the interests of genuine reconciliation between Indigenous and non-Indigenous Australians it would be better to favor various familiar virtues, norms, and practices. These include, for example, good humor, a generosity of spirit, patience, politeness, and the kind of genuine conversation that is sustained by mutual curiosity.

Keywords Identity · Leadership · One Nation · Pauline Hanson
Political correctness · Racism · Reconciliation

7.1 Introduction

It can be tempting to dismiss Hanson's One Nation party as a loose line-up of squabbling bumblers and opportunists. But there are dangers in such contempt. While Hanson and her party do not articulate their beliefs or concerns very well, some

S. Burgess (✉)
University of New England Business School, University of New England,
Armidale, NSW 2351, Australia
e-mail: sburge27@une.edu.au

© Springer Nature Singapore Pte Ltd. 2019
B. Grant et al. (eds.), *The Rise of Right-Populism*,
https://doi.org/10.1007/978-981-13-2670-7_7

of their core convictions are readily discernible, reasonably formidable, and quite widely shared. Briefly summarized, they represent the view that we have a vitally important sense of identity as Australians, that we belong together as the people of a nation, and that we have an inherited common culture worth maintaining. They could presumably be prompted to say that if we ever lose that sense of unity in culture, belonging, and nationhood, then we shall have no hope of ever becoming a truly reconciled nation.

In this chapter I do not take issue with such convictions. But I do highlight Hanson's impoverished sense of what it is to be Australian, along with her divisive and alienating approach to leadership. She has not even tried to engage proactively and productively with Indigenous,[1] Asian or Islamic community leaders, and she has failed to afford them a "fair go". These are some of the reasons her efforts have been unconducive to the kind of national unity that she would like Australia to have.

Developing and sustaining an inclusive and unified nation is not easy, and we do need to see the challenge of reconciliation in perspective. It is 230 years since Captain Arthur Phillip arrived in 1788 and reconciliation has still not been achieved. Yet by thinking about what it is to be Australian, about the history of interaction between Indigenous and non-Indigenous Australians, and about the ways in which we live and see ourselves today, it is possible to see how genuine progress can be made. It is also evident that significant progress *has* been made.

One Nation's opposition to political correctness is worth discussing. It is not that they have offered a finely expressed critique of political correctness; their objection amounts to little more than an inchoate gut instinct. But their inability to formulate the relevant arguments does not imply that the arguments do not exist.

It is not surprising that many of us assume political correctness to be beneficial to people who belong to oppressed or marginalized groups. Nonetheless, I outline certain concerns about it, and argue that it is not something with which we should rest content. I contend instead that we should favor various familiar virtues, norms, and practices, at least some of which are essential to the ethos of a fair go. We should favor good humor, for example, along with a generosity of spirit, patience, politeness, and the kind of genuine conversation that is sustained by mutual curiosity.

7.2   One Nation and the Ethos of a Fair Go

One of the more renowned accounts of Australian colonial culture is still that written by George Nadel, a "Dunera boy" of cultivated Viennese sensibility.[2] To him, our

---

[1]In accordance with current convention I use the term "Indigenous" here in relation to both Aboriginal Australians and Torres Strait Islanders. In many historical contexts the term is anachronistic although I have generally favored it here given that it is both inclusive and concise. Admittedly, like any term of such broad scope, it is not one that all Indigenous Australians will readily use to describe themselves.

[2]The Dunera boys comprised around 2500 internees who were sent from Liverpool to Australia on the HMT *Dunera* in July 1940. Although most were Jewish males of German or Austrian birth who

colloquial talk of "mateship" was *gauche*; he probably had similar misgivings about our talk of giving one another a fair go. But he admired the robust sense of equality, independence, acceptance, and trust with which Australians relate to one another. He recognized that to be Australian is to embrace that ethos, and he saw it as our great unifying strength (Nadel 1957).

Of course, there is room for debate as to what a fair go is supposed to entail. Our major political parties may disagree on whether it compels us to support a large welfare state, for example (compare the pieces by Carmen Lawrence and by John Howard in Hirst (2010b, pp. 161–164)). But everyone—including Hanson and her party—seems to agree that the fair go is something to be held dear,[3] and the reasons for this are easy enough to see. At the very least it is an ethos that has militated against snobbery and pointless displays of deference. It encourages a friendly, easy-going attitude. While never counselling any kind of naiveté, it does urge us to give one another the benefit of the doubt. It gently discourages any needlessly hostile, mean-spirited, or censorious attitudes.

Thanks to our embrace of the fair go, one might expect an inclusive and unifying approach to leadership to come naturally to us. I would suggest that such an approach to leadership generally *does* come naturally to us. Yet it is readily arguable that Hanson's style of leadership is a divisive and alienating one.

She and her party see "a need for Australia to be truly one nation" and they may genuinely wish for "fair and equal treatment" of us all.[4] They want us all to "work toward unification" and for government assistance to be "based on need, not race".[5] Considered in isolation, there is nothing divisive or ignoble in any of this; abstractly stated, almost all of us share such sentiments. And Hanson's concern for Australia "to be truly one nation" can be seen in the context of a broad range of concerns about Australia's social fabric and its state of repair. Social conservatives like Hanson tend to worry about cultural diversity and respect for the law; progressives are usually more concerned about racism, social inclusion, and the acceptance of cultural diversity. It is easy enough to accept that all such concerns are genuine. But whatever one's political convictions, the style of leadership that we bring to such challenges is crucial. Whoever wishes to work on the nation's social fabric has to recognize that there is a world of difference between mending and rending.

In seeking to advance her agenda Hanson has been critical of immigration, of Asian and Muslim immigration in particular, of Indigenous "separatism", the notion of Indigenous disadvantage, and the nature of Islamic faith. Open, honest, and thoughtfully critical discussion about such matters is an important characteristic of a healthy public culture, but there is a strident and rancorous quality to many of Hanson's stunts and interventions. She has failed to engage proactively, seriously,

---

had fled Nazi oppression, they were arrested by the British in fear that they might be enemy spies. For some tantalizing glimpses as to who Nadel was, see Inglis (2010). See also John Mulvaney's reflections in Gare et al. (2003, pp. 165–166).

[3] See proposition 4 under "What We Stand For" (PHONP 2017).
[4] See proposition 1 under "Principles & Objectives" (PHONP 2017).
[5] See propositions 3 and 11 under "Principles & Objectives" (PHONP 2017).

directly, and amicably with those in Australia's Indigenous, Asian, or Islamic communities. She has still never formed personal relationships with credible or influential leaders from those communities. She had never been to an Indigenous community until asked to do so on national television (see 60 Minutes 1996). And she appears unconcerned by the fact that almost all of those who voted for her in 2016 were born in Australia; only 2% of them had been born overseas (Marr 2017, p. 48).[6]

Hanson does not appear vindictive. Although she has been at the center of any number of acrimonious encounters with Indigenous and Muslim community members, in recent times she has publicly expressed a desire to work with certain Indigenous and Muslim community leaders (see, for example, ABC News 2016; Young and Reynolds 2016). But while such a desire is to her credit, she appears not to have given much thought to what she needs to do to develop genuine, firm, trusting, productive, and mutually supportive relationships with such leaders.

Reaching out to them is something that she should always have been doing proactively rather than reactively. Considering all the acrimony of the past, she needs to show some humility and to acknowledge that her strident and divisive rancor of the past has been misguided and pernicious, otherwise she is never going to be able to establish her *bona fides* and suitability as a political partner. She also needs to appreciate that the work required to develop such relationships is best done out of the media spotlight. That happens to be a point that negotiation and conflict resolution specialists routinely make (see, for example: Fisher et al. 2012, p. 38; Shapiro 2010, pp. 634–645, 642). The presence of reporters and camera crews only intensifies the pressure to maintain an established position and posture. It magnifies the threat of embarrassment and humiliation. Honest, open, and genuinely curious explorations of mutual interest become all the more difficult, and the possibility of any concession, apology, or bridge-building becomes far less likely. Of course it strains credulity to think that any of this will ever happen. The kind of transformation that would be required of Hanson could be likened to the Pauline conversion that we associate with the road to Damascus. But if she ever does venture down that Damascene road, she should be applauded all the way.

In fairness to Hanson, her approach to leadership does not embody every form of menace. While she is a demagogue of sorts, she does not mesmerize or manipulate anyone through diabolical charisma or charm. She recognizes the resentment to be found among some socially conservative voters and she takes advantage of it. But her concerns are clearly focused on cultural and religious matters; unlike the ruthless and hateful firebrand politics of a Klansman, she does not generally seek to inflame tensions in plainly racial terms.

Hanson has often been accused of racism, and those who have made the allegation include some of the most intelligent and articulate commentators we have [see, for example: journalist and author Marr (2017), and filmmaker Broinowski (2017)]. Broinowski acknowledges that in order to advance the allegation, the word's meaning does need to be stretched. As she says, "if 'racism' can encompass culture and religion

---

[6]The corresponding percentages for the other significant parties were: Liberal, 78%; Labor, 79%; Greens, 82%; National, 91%.

as well as biology, then Hanson most certainly is racist" (2017, p. 296). Of course Broinowski and Marr regard racism as a truly grave matter, as we all should. But neither acknowledges that when the meaning of so important a word is stretched in this way, it also becomes less precise, less helpful.

Hanson herself, during parliamentary debate over amendments to the Racial Discrimination Act, has maintained that "A racist is a person who believes their race to be superior to another['s]" and that no one has ever been able to provide any evidence to show that she herself has ever held any such belief (Hanson 2016b, p. 3167). While her conception of racism is relatively simple, it is consistent with the principal dictionary definitions.

Marr (2017) recognizes Hanson's approach to the racism question and he provides no serious critique of it (p. 74). He appears to accept One Nation's principle of "government assistance based on need, not race", along with the ideal of being "colour-blind". All this, Marr says, is "fine in theory" (p. 33). Nonetheless, he is determined to convict Hanson of racism. In relation to the principle of assistance being based on need rather than race, he observes that "in Hanson's world this means cheap loans for farmers but no scholarships for black kids" (p. 33). But of course that particular irony does not prove racism; it can just as easily be taken to imply that One Nation need to rethink their approach to industrial policy.

Marr also resorts to a variety of other argumentative maneuvers, not all of which afford Hanson a fair go. Most conspicuously, he refuses to regard the familiar socially conservative concerns about culture and religion as genuine; in his view they are really about race (Marr 2017, p. 31). He appears to accept that such concerns are not about "blood and biology" per se. Nonetheless, they are still concerns that he identifies with a "key racist claim through the ages", that of "not being able to fit into a new country" (p. 31).

Marr later goes on to assert that "she has grown over time into an ideologue of race, one of those with what [Andrew] Markus sees as the distinguishing mark of a racist: a conspiratorial mindset" (2017, p. 74).[7] But again, Marr is viewing "The White Queen" here only through his own looking-glass, and such Dodgsonian maneuvers represent as much intellectual discipline as Humpty Dumpty: "'When *I* use a word,' Humpty Dumpty said, in rather a scornful tone, 'it means just what I choose it to mean—neither more nor less.'" (Carroll 1872, p. 124). Marr is talking about concerns about culture, religion, conspiratorial mindsets, and racism, all of which may be ignorant, confused, malevolent, and pernicious. But however bad they often are, getting them thoroughly mixed up is hardly a good idea. The attempt to bludgeon conspiracy theorists, xenophobes, and Islamophobes with blunt accusations of racism is not likely to teach them anything, and is bound to make them feel even more contemptuous and resentful than they already do.

When accusations of racism are thrown about thoughtlessly, one of the many fears that we should have is that such accusations will ultimately lose their moral gravity. And, at least in certain circles, this is exactly what appears to be happening. Donald

---

[7] Andrew Markus is a professor at Monash University who has written extensively on immigration, race relations, and social cohesion.

Trump's former chief strategist, Steve Bannon, recently addressed the party congress of France's National Front, and in a short speech that appears to have been both well-rehearsed and well received, he encouraged those in attendance to no longer regard an accusation of racism as a truly grave indictment. A view that Bannon likes to encourage is that such accusations are now so meaningless that they can actually be treated with contempt: "Let them call you racist. Let them call you xenophobes. Let them call you nativists. Wear it as a badge of honor. Because every day, we get stronger and they get weaker" (Winsor 2018).

Even if there is no overwhelming evidence of Hanson's alleged racism, her deficiencies and limitations as a leader are manifest. As Hanson herself has admitted, she is unpolished (1996, p. 3860), and her lack of intellectual finesse makes her vulnerable to a range of misjudgments, gaffes, and embarrassments. In her efforts to express her social concerns, judicious discrimination is not one of her strengths.

The journalist Christopher Hitchens often liked to say that the moral flaw of racists is not one of discrimination per se:

> "Discrimination" is something that they just can't manage … A racist is a racist precisely because he can't distinguish between a Jew and another Jew, or an Asian or West Indian or Chechen. The 'out' groups are all made up of generalized amalgams and there can be no exceptions (Hitchens 2007).

Some of us may quibble with Hitchens here: the inability to judiciously discriminate in the way that he describes is perhaps neither necessary nor sufficient for being characterized as a racist. But any such quibbles aside, it is certainly true that at times Hanson has treated entire minority groups as if they were homogeneous, and that she has smeared each of their individual members in the process. In her first speech to the House of Representatives, for example, she spoke of migrants "of Asian origin" and said of them indiscriminately: "[t]hey have their own culture and religion, form ghettos and do not assimilate" (Hanson 1996, p. 3862). By the time of her first speech to the Senate in 2016, Hanson appeared to have dropped the concerns that were specific to *Asian* immigration. In her words:

> Australia has embraced migrants from all different races, making us one of the most multiracial nations on earth. Most have assimilated and are proud to call themselves Australians, accepting our culture, beliefs and laws. I welcome them from the bottom of my heart. As they integrate and assimilate, the disruption caused by diversity diminishes (Hanson 2016a, p. 939).

Her concerns about Islam, however, had certainly come to the fore. So in that same speech she observed that "our leaders continue to tell us to be tolerant and embrace the good Muslims" and then asked rhetorically:

> But how should we tell the difference? There is no sign saying "good Muslim" or "bad Muslim". How many lives will be lost or destroyed trying to determine who is good and who is bad? (Hanson 2016a, p. 939).

Of course if Hanson had been proactively engaging with Muslim community leaders and forming genuine personal relationships with some them, it is very doubtful that she would have been so readily inclined to indulge in such indiscriminate smears.

In March 2017 the journalist Tracy Grimshaw posed an earnest question seeking to better understand Hanson's position: "So, no Muslim is a good Muslim?" In response to this, Hanson did make an acknowledgement of sorts: "I do believe there are some that want to actually live a quiet life, and a, you know, a good life" (Hanson, in *A Current* Affair 2017). But she then simply reiterated her earlier line: "Tracy, you tell me, you line up a number of Muslims, who's the good one? Who's not?" (Hanson, in *A Current* Affair 2017).

Compared to Asian and Muslim Australians, it is arguable that ordinary Indigenous Australians have suffered relatively little from Hanson's lack of judicious discrimination. In her 1996 speech she directed her hostility not towards ordinary Indigenous Australians but to the elites of the "Aboriginal industry", the office bearers within the Aboriginal and Torres Strait Islander Commission, members of the Council for Aboriginal Reconciliation, and other such "fat cats", "bureaucrats" and "do-gooders" (Hanson 1996, p. 3860). One naturally wonders why on earth she would not bother to recognize that many elites within the "industry" were not merely cynical, self-serving, seat-warmers. While her focus there was not on *ordinary* Indigenous Australians, the lack of judicious discrimination was clear.

7.3 Unity Through Mind and Mirth

In presenting her approach to Indigenous issues Hanson has sometimes emphasized her agreement with Paul Hasluck, the former Liberal Party politician and Governor-General. Most notably, she has alluded to his vision of "a single society in which racial emphases were rejected and social issues addressed" (Hanson 1996, p. 3860). Given that Hasluck was the minister responsible for policies of Aboriginal assimilation from 1951 to 1963, his detractors routinely and quite rightly describe him as a paternalist. But in seeking to move beyond the racial concerns and divisions of the past, it has to be acknowledged that he was advancing something that many Indigenous leaders had also long sought.

When Hanson spoke of Hasluck she was undoubtedly sincere. Nonetheless, her admiration falls a long way short of emulation. Hasluck was paternalistic, but he was also known for his humility, propriety, and thoughtful lucidity. Such people serve to remind us that some of the challenges in politics are serious *intellectual* challenges. It is not that the matters involved can be addressed only by an intellectual elite; many of the questions at issue are routinely discussed by school children as part of a decent civics education program, and they should be discussed by as wide a range of people as possible. Many of the questions, however, are intellectually challenging for anyone who thinks seriously about them.

John Hirst, the historian who chaired the Howard Government's Civics Education Group, did as much as anyone to foster the discussion of such questions. When discussing the theme of diversity and unity in modern Australia, Hirst placed *our identity as Australians* at the heart of all considerations. In his own words:

> [H]ow are we to hold together? By being Australian; by celebrating, exploring, criticizing
> and reassessing our Australian heritage, all the things that have defined and still define what
> it means to be Australian and live in this place (Hirst 2010a, p. 213).

This issue of how the nation is to hold together is one in which we may all take an interest. It is central to concerns about multiculturalism, and our responses to it are also bound to inform our thoughts about reconciliation.

As discussed above, the ethos of a fair go is widely embraced in Australia, and it features prominently in accounts of what it is to be Australian. But there are also some philosophical questions to consider, including questions of how one's sense of national identity is supposed to fit with all the other affiliations and identities that we may have. Noel Pearson—prominent intellectual, Aboriginal leader, and founder of the Cape York Institute for Policy and Leadership—has offered an insightful exploration of some of these questions. In his preferred metaphor, individuals and groups possess *layers* of identity:

> These layers include identification with cultural and linguistic groups; religions; places of
> birth, upbringing, residency and death; local and regional geographic communities; regional,
> provincial and national polities; and professional, literary, recreational, philosophical and
> other sub-cultural groups (Pearson 2009, p. 334).

Admittedly, Pearson (2009) says very little about "what it means to be Australian and live in this place". Importantly, however, he does identify himself as an Australian (p. 333) and he situates that quality of "Australianness" amongst the wide range of other qualities, interests, and affiliations that he happens to possess.

While notions of identity have often been exploited in divisive and sectarian ways, Pearson's "layered" account of identity does not readily lend itself to such abuse. As explained by Altman (2017), a former professor of politics:

> Identity politics threaten democratic debate when they become a means of shutting down
> any comment that does not grow entirely out of experience.

But Pearson does not seek to stifle debate in any such way. He explicitly disavows the assumption that we have one principal affiliation with an importance that automatically overrides that of all the others (Pearson 2009, p. 333); his sense of identity cannot be easily reduced to a mere demand for loyalty.[8] In Pearson's multi-layered conception of identity we may hear echoes of Wieseltier's (1994) gnomic reflections on identity and politics: "Not: my identity, but: my identities. There is greater truth in the plural. There is also greater likelihood of decency" (p. 30).

Hanson, like Hirst, would probably agree that a clear sense of *being Australian* is what should hold us together. But a basic point worth emphasizing is that Hirst encouraged a *critical* understanding of what it is to be Australian. While he saw the need to celebrate and explore our heritage, he also saw the importance of criticizing and reassessing it. Hanson, by contrast, seems unwilling to engage in such criticism. Of course she loves Australia; there is much to love. But her sense of being Australian seems not to involve any sustained critical reflection. Her love is blind, complacent,

---

[8]This is a principal concern of Kwame Anthony Appiah (2005) in *The Ethics of Identity*.

and unduly self-satisfied. Her sense of being Australian, along with her patriotism, is of an impoverished form. While she likes to wrap herself in the Australian flag, such jingoistic silliness remains embarrassing to most Australians.

In Hanson's first parliamentary speech in 1996 she complained about "reverse racism", the "terminal mess" of the Aboriginal and Torres Strait Islander Commission, the allowances paid to members of the Council for Aboriginal Reconciliation, and "the privileges Aboriginals enjoy over other Australians" (Hanson 1996, pp. 3860–3861). She showed little understanding of Indigenous disadvantage, and she expressed skepticism about its severity. Yet reconciliation requires curiosity about how we got to where we are now.

We know that first contact between Europeans and Indigenous Australians was not always hostile. As the historian Henry Reynolds explains:

> Contact between explorers and Aborigines was often friendly and mutually satisfactory …
> Explorers have left accounts of many meetings when both whites and blacks behaved with
> decorum and sensitivity thereby reducing the tension of contact (Reynolds 1990, pp. 23–24).

The historian and anthropologist Clendinnen (2003) has described what we know of the interracial dancing, singing, and "clowning pantomimes" that sometimes arose during the early years of European settlement around Sydney Cove (p. 254). As Clendinnen makes clear, the First Fleet journals are full of intriguing observations and reflections, and for many of us her book is apt to whet the appetite for more. But while those instances of early conviviality can sound propitious, we should not overestimate the level of mutual understanding involved. As Clendinnen explains:

> what we are most aware of as we read is that we, like [Judge-Advocate David Collins, one
> of the keener observers], are blind and must be blind to much of what is going on before our
> eyes. The deeper symbolism of movement, gesture, sequence and regalia remained obscure
> to him, as it does to us (2003, p. 254).

It may have been the British Government's "Royal Will and Pleasure" that Captain Phillip:

> endeavour by every possible means to open an Intercourse with the Natives and to conciliate
> their affections, enjoining all Our Subjects to live in amity and kindness with them (United
> Kingdom 1787).

But the cultural gulf was never going to be readily bridgeable; the challenge of living together in amity and kindness was always going to take time to achieve.

The anthropologist W.E.H. Stanner took the view that by the 1830s the Europeans, or at least a small number of them, knew enough about the Indigenous Australians and their ways of life to enable far better racial relations. By the 1830s, however, the major problem was that European settlers and their interests were not open to the kinds of negotiation that would be required (Stanner 2010, p. 195). Stanner once explained that he was concerned to:

> use direct Aboriginal testimony to illumine Aboriginal problems with us, not ours with them.
> My idea was to try to change our perspective in the belief that we might then find credible
> motives for going more than half-way to meet them (Stanner 2010, p. 246).

He then went on to describe a range of contrary approaches that have been tried, generally with lamentable results. One approach he illustrates by the lack of genuine consultation with the Aboriginal people of Yirrkala in the 1960s and early 1970s, before allowing mining interests to be favored over theirs. A second relates to the discouragement and loss of Aboriginal male rites of passage into manhood. A third focuses on the refusal to first teach literacy skills to Aboriginal children in their own first languages. Such examples suggest some of the ways—both conciliatory and practical—that we could still make use of Stanner's work.

Clendinnen and Stanner were in agreement in many respects and neither was inclined to advance anything radical (see Clendinnen 2009, pp. 56–61). While they both saw the serial injustices suffered by generations of Indigenous Australians as being rooted in a "British failure to comprehend, much less to tolerate, legitimate difference" (Clendinnen 2009, p. 58), it is very doubtful that either of them would have ever advocated any form of Indigenous sovereignty or secession.

In the epilogue to her book, Clendinnen reflects:

> Despite our long alienation, despite our merely adjacent histories, and through processes I do not yet understand, we are now more like each other than we are like any other people. We even share something of the same style of humour, which is a subtle but far-reaching affinity. Here, in this place, I think we are all Australians now (Clendinnen 2003, p. 288).

While Clendinnen is not saying that reconciliation has already been achieved, she is surely right to suppose that we are much closer to it now than we were in the days of mutual incomprehension or frontier violence. Research surveys consistently show that the vast majority of Australians consider the relationship between Indigenous and non-Indigenous Australians to be important (see, for instance, Reconciliation Australia 2008, 2010, 2012, 2014, 2016). And as a more subtle matter it is worth noticing that many Indigenous Australians identify themselves as *Indigenous Australians*, and virtually none as *Australian Indigenes*. When the term "Australian" serves as a substantive instead of an adjective, the unifying connotations are definitely more substantial.

Clendinnen does not illustrate her comment about sharing the same style of humor. But given that the point is worth appreciating, consider the recent creation of *Black Comedy*, "A sketch comedy show by Blackfellas. For everyone." (ABC TV 2018). Most of the sketches focus on urban Indigenous Australians. The tone is irreverent and the acting superb. Many of the laughs are generated through wonderfully striking depictions of an increasingly evident fact: within urban Indigenous Australia there are still cultural differences and idiosyncrasies that interested people can identify, but most of them are comically trivial.

In one sketch, a hapless Aboriginal man is charged with not being "black enough" on account of having bought organic vegetables and a Delta Goodrem album (Series 1, Episode 1; see ABC TV 2018). Another man is at serious risk of failing the blackness test until, with real comic relief, he proves his cultural credentials by demonstrating that he was smuggling a couple of mates into the local footy ground in the boot of his car (Series 1, Episode 1; see ABC TV 2018). Perhaps more compelling still is that some tired old tropes common to some of the most repugnant jokes about

Aboriginal people (e.g., those that rest on an image typified by humbugging or laziness) are reversed and ridiculed. In one early sketch, for example, an Aboriginal Moses grandiloquently reads out the Ten Commandments until politely interrupted.

> Um… like, those laws are great. As far as commandments go, they're top notch. But we've got a few of our own … Can I read'em out?…
>
> Thou shalt not go to thy brother's house on pay day to ask for a loan; but if thou does, then thou must pay it back on thine own pay day… (Series 1, Episode 1; see ABC TV 2018).

In another sketch, a whiny caller to the "Black on Track" organization soon finds herself on the receiving end of an hilariously profane lecture, all from a receptionist who has shown himself normally to be impeccably professional and polite. Notwithstanding the profanity, his response was presented as authentic Aboriginality at its best; he had stood up to her insults and attempted bullying, and had refused to capitulate to her demand that the organization send someone out to pick up her 27 year old son from the airport (Series 1, Episode 2; see ABC TV 2018).

If Hanson were to consider the cultural developments that *Black Comedy* represents, she would presumably find herself reassured. And of course—fanciful though all this may be—the adoption some of that same self-depreciatory humor would improve her leadership style.

7.4   Political Correctness

Political correctness is not popular, especially among older Australians (Core Data 2017, p. 61). But even among "millennials" (i.e., those aged 18–35 years old) there appears to be a majority who agree with statements such as "people are getting too politically correct these days", "too much political correctness is ruining society", "always trying to be politically correct is not authentic", and "politically correct people really annoy me" (Core Data 2017, p. 61). There is also evidence to suggest that a majority of Australians find politically incorrect humor to be best described not as "offensive", "boring", or "embarrassing", but rather as either "entertaining" or "secretly funny" (Core Data 2017, p. 59).

Hanson's publicly-expressed concerns about political correctness date back to her 1996 first speech to the House of Representatives, if not earlier. Perhaps her most thoughtful reflections, however, were given more recently when speaking to the Senate about potential amendments to Section 18C of the Racial Discrimination Act. She acknowledged that Aboriginal and Torres Strait Islander Australians were "the first peoples of this land" and she welcomed the fact that many migrants have "come here to join us" (Hanson 2016b, p. 3166). She mentioned having had a Polish-born husband, an Aboriginal mother and child as tenants, and a senior Laotian employee. Yet of most relevance here are Hanson's reflections concerning some former industry colleagues who had migrated to Australia from Greece and Italy. They were often indelicately described as "wogs" although in Hanson's view they were not particularly perturbed by this:

when the Aussies had a go at them in that Aussie way they became part of the community—they assimilated. I remember all the guys at the fish markets—the Greeks and the Italians. We all had jokes together and it was taken in a good sense of humour. I think we have lost that in Australia. I think people have become so precious that you cannot say or do anything anymore. Otherwise, you will be dragged off to the law courts (Hanson, 2016b, pp. 3166–3167).

Hanson's words here may well come across as being more like casual chit-chat than rigorously developed social analysis. Arguably, however, they show Hanson in one of her more genial and astute moments. The kind of sensitivity that is polite, earnest, and politically correct certainly provides one way of getting along with strangers. But as Hanson recognizes, it is not the only way, it is hardly the way of the fish market, and it is not really the Australian way. In fact anyone who reads Christie Davies's (1996, 2002) celebrated sociological work on ethnic jokes and ethnic humor could well conclude that such sensitivity is simply not the way of the world.

Some of Davies's most extensive treatment is given to jokes about the supposedly stupid Irish, Poles, and Newfoundlanders. He also devotes some attention to boastful Americans, militaristic Germans, coarse Australians, and backward Tasmanians. As Davies explains, the butts of such jokes are often:

distant provincials, familiar and related neighbors, or all but assimilated immigrants. In consequence the joke tellers tend to regard them as comic anomalies, as ambiguous, transitional, wavering peoples (TWPs) who are a suitable subject for humor (Davies 1996, p. 313).

In telling these jokes, we may well play with aggression, but this is not to be confused with real aggression. Americans may joke that the history of Polack culture is the thinnest book ever written, and this can certainly be regarded as the humor of superiority and condescension, but it is not the humor of hostility or resentment. As Davies explains:

The joke tellers see the local TWP not as a powerful alien group that is feared or hated, but as a poor imitation of themselves, a group whose culture or language is an imperfect version of their own (Davies 1996, p. 55).

So as Hanson dimly suggests, it may well be that these jokes and the like have a role to play in processes of acculturation, integration, or assimilation; they can even be precursors to friendship.

All that said, it must be emphasized that not all forms of ethnic humor are conducive to the needs of nationhood. Those who have heard some of the vulgar and truly racist jokes through which Indigenous Australians are sometimes disparaged will immediately recognize that they are far from playful or innocuous. Quite to the contrary, they are thoroughly distasteful and can be deeply pernicious. Yet even when confronted with such forms of racism, it is not clear that political correctness offers anything worthwhile. There are some impressive, evidence-based ways by which to deal with racist beliefs and attitudes. But as has been found by those who work with racially motivated offenders, didactic moralizing about the evils of racism tends to be counter-productive (see, for example, Burgess 2016, esp. pp. 89–91).

Many of us have to deal with the "crazy uncle" problem around Christmas time, and it can be tempting to get on one's high horse and to "call him out" by simply telling him that his politically incorrect words are unacceptable. But if we wish to actually persuade him of anything, a more empathetic approach tends to be more effective. Righteous indignation is no substitute for thoughtful discussion. We often need to take on the role of the good listener, as well as that of the good teacher or explainer (see Collett 2017).

This is not to say that clear, calm, and empathetic rational persuasion is the only good way by which to engage with those who hold boorish, racist, or bigoted views. Warm and good-natured humor appears to be profoundly challenging to racists, and most defenders of political correctness could presumably agree that there is much to be said for some gentle mocking, satirizing, or teasing. In recent decades there have been some hilarious instances in which clowns and other brightly-dressed activists have undermined white supremacists and their public rallies through nothing but peaceful acts of joyful irreverence. As Sarah Freeman-Woolpert explains, such humor:

> puts white supremacists in a dilemma in which their own use of violence will seem unwarranted, and their machismo image is tainted by the comedic performance by their opponent. Humor de-escalates their rallies, turning what could become a violent confrontation into a big joke (Freeman-Woolpert 2017).

Yet even when confronted with racists, it may be that lampooning them with great hostility tends not to be wise. Nelly Thomas is a comedian who comes "from Hanson country". As she explains "my roots are there, my family are there and I know *this* Australia intimately" (Thomas 2016). But while Thomas is deeply opposed to Hanson and her views, she has come to think that lampooning Hanson, at least in certain ways, is misguided: it "does nothing more than make those of us who already despise Hansonism feel better. *And Superior*" (Thomas 2016). Good-natured humor, by contrast, along with tact and a generosity of spirit, can help to create the kind of atmosphere in which racists are willing to reconsider their belligerent views and attitudes.

Clive Hamilton is a broad-ranging intellectual and professor of public ethics at Charles Sturt University who has sought to defend political correctness, appearing to concede only that it has sometimes been deployed with regrettable zealotry. According to his characterization:

> To be politically correct is to choose words (and sometimes actions) that avoid disparaging, insulting or offending people because they belong to oppressed groups. Oppressed groups are those subject to prejudice, disrespect or discrimination on the basis of their race, ethnicity, gender, sexual orientation or physical disability (Hamilton 2015).

But even on this highly sympathetic account of what political correctness is, one has to question whether it is likely to give everyone a fair go. It can appear that we need to be apprised even of those words or actions that merely *might* be taken to be disparaging, insulting, or offensive by those who belong to an oppressed group. It seems then to require us to have the eloquence and urbanity to avoid using such words and to refrain from such actions.[9]

---

[9] Hamilton would presumably accept that those who take offense (or feel disparaged or insulted) are not *necessarily* justified in doing so. And it is possible that he also accepts that when another

Eloquence and urbanity are not amongst Hanson's strengths, and perhaps that helps to account for her frustration with political correctness. But a great many of us lack such qualities, and surely it is neither necessary nor realistic to expect all of us to develop them. I suggest that if it were not for the somewhat distracting, misplaced concerns associated with political correctness it is doubtful that the particular words that people use would often be thought crucial. We could instead pay more attention to what our interlocutors *mean*, and whether their *intention* and *tone* is innocent and friendly.

Hamilton is undeniably intelligent and well-motivated. Yet he gives no consideration to the importance of charitable interpretation, and writes as if all ordinary human conversations are earnest occasions for meticulous rule-following. He must have noticed that the kinds of human interaction that are actually enjoyable and relationship-forming often involve endlessly playful rule *violations*. Yet he does not assure us that those who believe in political correctness are obliged to remain attentive to a speaker's sense of irony and good humor. He says nothing about the need to be sensitive to the tone with which a person's words are expressed. He is silent on whether we should wish to retain that basic feature of good-natured, civil conduct: the belief that until evidence to the contrary is overwhelming, everyone should be assumed to have the best of intentions.

Hamilton recognizes that political correctness has prompted a backlash. As he explains:

> The backlash began in the United States in the early 1990s when conservative intellectuals began to use 'political correctness' to criticize the left for imposing their views on others and suppressing dissenting opinion.

> In universities, more traditional subjects were being augmented or replaced by others dealing with feminism, queer politics, post-colonial history and so on. Leading conservatives began to attack the liberal-left for making certain topics of study 'off-limits'.

> … For conservative activists losing the culture war rankled deeply (Hamilton 2015).

Concerns about political correctness, however, amount to far more than mere expressions of conservative resentment. Some critics of political correctness readily accept that it is well-motivated, and many—myself included—share certain interests and hopes that are more commonly associated with the political left. Not all of us could be regarded as callous towards the poor, and some of us are especially interested in ways by which to foster mutual understanding, resilience, social cohesion, and reconciliation, for example. Nonetheless, our concern is that the influence of political correctness—or something very much like it—has been intellectually corrupting, psychologically enfeebling, and socially divisive.

Some aspects of the *intellectual corruption* involved are simply instances of what John Stuart Mill famously discussed in his defense of liberty in thought and discussion. Most obviously, by effectively making certain topics "off limits" we lose the ability to correct each other's misapprehensions, wishful delusions, false assumptions, and other such errors. Moreover, in absence of any critical discussion, many

---

person's behavior has not been *intentionally* or *heedlessly* offensive, then *taking offense* is wrong. These are fairly basic concerns in my view, although Hamilton does not address either of them.

an important conviction—entirely true though it may be—is likely to be held merely "in the manner of a prejudice, with little comprehension or feeling of its rational grounds" (Mill 1859, Ch. 2).

The kind of intellectual corruption associated with political correctness has been widely seen to follow a certain pattern. It was over 35 years ago that Peter Biskup lamented the emergence of Australian historical writing that is a mere caricature of the real thing. In his words: "This inverted racism which peoples the Australian landscape with black goodies and white baddies tends to be not only boring but is ultimately self-defeating ..." (Biskup 1982, p. 30). For a variety of other examples of well-motivated absurdities, fallacies, and myths relating to Indigenous Australia, particular works by Hirst (1994), Pearson (2009), the journalist Neill (2002), or the anthropologist Sutton (2009) may be consulted. Of course some of the errors are more egregious than others; some are more pernicious than others. But for those who remain unpersuaded about the need for something better than political correctness, such works are essential reading.[10]

In North America one of the more prominent academic opponents of political correctness is Jordan Peterson, a professor of psychology at the University of Toronto. He explores political correctness in some detail, seeing it as a form of ideology that radically simplifies the world. Within this ideology differences in individual levels of human achievement are of course acknowledged; within any area of human activity "winners" and "losers" can be identified. But these differences are explained simply by assuming that "the losers are losing because they are oppressed by the winners". Of course it can hardly be denied that in many areas some such form of oppression will exist. But neither the existence of such oppression nor its extent can be known a priori, and assertions about them should not be accepted simply as a matter of ideological faith. It is because of this ideological kind of thinking that Peterson takes political correctness to involve a lack of intellectual discipline. In his view it constitutes an easy alternative to actual critical thinking and wisdom, while giving nothing more than an illusion of understanding, a claim of allegiance with the oppressed, and a morally reassuring feeling about one's own position in the world (see, for example, Peterson 2016).

In his lectures and interviews Peterson's usual style is forthright and pugnacious (see Peterson n.d.). He is notably less combative, however, than some of the "social justice warriors" who, in his words, "weaponize compassion" (see, for instance, Peterson in Tucker and VandenBeukel 2016). As can be seen in the available online videos, the strident moral hectoring of some of those who confront him is plainly uncharitable and ill-conducive to rational persuasion and mutual understanding (see, for example, Flemming 2016).

---

[10]Further discussion of this problem, along with a much broader range of examples, can be found on the website of the Heterodox Academy at: https://heterodoxacademy.org/. The Academy (of which I am a member) is an international association of "progressives, conservatives, libertarians, and centrists who have coalesced around the need to create a credible counterforce to entrenched orthodoxies". Its mission is "To improve the quality of research and education in universities by increasing viewpoint diversity, mutual understanding, and constructive disagreement".

Peterson can appear unwilling to recognize anything admirable in the motives of those who believe in political correctness. When he contends that the "authoritarian left" is actually motivated not by compassion but resentment (see Peterson in Tucker and VandenBeukel 2016), one can hear echoes of the supposed "slave revolt" in morality that Nietzsche so excitedly described (see 1886, §195; then the three essays of 1887). But in any case, Peterson's analysis does have some clear merits. First, it shows how easily political correctness—conceived of as an ideology—can be applied. Second, it explains the consistent pattern that can be discerned in the political causes with which political correctness has been associated. Third, it succinctly describes how political correctness both encourages and exploits what Philip Roth once called "the ecstasy of sanctimony" (Roth 2001, p. 2).

The concern that political correctness—perhaps in combination with various other forms of over-protectiveness—has been *psychologically enfeebling* is one that has met with some attention in recent years (see, for example, Haidt and Haslam 2016; Haidt and Lukianoff 2017; Lukianoff and Haidt 2015). In essence, the concern is that we are seeing a generation of young people who have come to think of themselves as unable to cope with the kind of challenging discussion and robust debate that has traditionally been central to education, particularly at universities. In association with this concern further topics and phrases are being placed off-limits, controversial speakers are being "no platformed" or shouted down, various discussions are prefaced with "trigger warnings", some critical discussions are being described as "violence", and certain violations of the new expectations are being regarded as "microaggressions". Thus far, most of these developments have been less conspicuous in Australia than in the UK or the USA. But while the resilience of Indigenous Australians is commonly noted (see Griffiths et al. 2017), the psychological danger posed by political correctness is also being recognized.

Noel Pearson has described the crushing and insidious burden of racism with articulate passion and insight. Yet he has also seen good reason to reject the temptation to characterize racism as a *disability* (Pearson 2009, p. 161). Similarly, academic researcher Anthony Dillon has long been alerting his fellow Indigenous Australians to the danger of facilitating one's own disempowerment in this way: a danger that involves unnecessarily—and perhaps unconsciously—taking on the role, status, and self-image of a victim (Dillon 2013, pp. 88–89). Dillon is not one to deny injustice, blame victims, or absolve governments of their responsibilities. Reinforced by his academic expertise in positive psychology, however, he is entirely unimpressed when, for example, people of "minimal" Aboriginal ancestry claim to be offended by questions about precisely why they identify themselves as Aboriginal Australians (pp. 88–89). And in contrast to those whose "obsession" with Aboriginal identity leads them to adopt an "'us versus them' mentality" (pp. 88–89), he emphasizes the various ways in which "all of life is interconnected" (p. 80). As he explains:

> Many traditional Aboriginal people (and some other groups) do not see themselves as special, and hence different from others (in the spiritual sense), instead they see equality, oneness, and unity of life all originating from one spiritual source (p. 80).

With regard to reconciliation in Australia, Dillon is "gladdened by what could be our future if we can do away with political correctness and victimology" (p. 90).

As Hamilton appears to acknowledge, one of the distinctive characteristics of those who are politically correct is a willingness to sacrifice conversation and persuasion in favor of suppression, imposition, and a new form of censorship (Hamilton 2015). The concern that political correctness is *socially divisive* comes from the thought that such efforts are needlessly abrasive and alienating.

Of course it would be comically hypocritical for *Hanson* to complain about people who are all too abrasive and alienating. But it is perfectly coherent to call for a "plague o' both your houses!"; we can be critical of Hanson's socially divisive tendencies while also being critical of others of comparable tendency.

Admittedly, the art of moral critique is a subtle one. Sometimes it is difficult to listen to someone with genuine empathy and curiosity. The temptations of sanctimony and contempt can be great. For most of us, good humor, charm, judgment and tact are difficult to sustain. In spite of the difficulties, however, my suggestion is that those familiar virtues, norms, and practices give us an approach to moral critique that is vastly preferable to that of political correctness. Rather than settle for political correctness, my view is that we shall be better off if we take good humor, a generosity of spirit, patience, politeness, mutually curious conversation, principled thinking, and a fair go, for example, and embrace them all anew.

The desire to suppress a wide range of obnoxious expressions, beliefs, and opinions is readily understandable. In an important sense, however, it is actually very doubtful that the form of censorship imposed by political correctness is successful. What seems more likely is that each opposing group—both the One Nation supporters and their politically correct critics, for example—will continue to talk amongst themselves and to thereby reinforce their existing views. The One Nation supporters will be silenced only in the sense that they will cease talking to those of the opposing group, especially about the serious issues over which they disagree.

Hamilton (2015) suggests that political correctness has been effective in reducing the extent to which people who belong to oppressed groups are needlessly disparaged, insulted, or offended. While he is presumably right about that, we should not overstate it as an achievement. If he believes that simply scolding each other over the use of certain words has had any deep and welcome influence over our *thinking*, he gives us no reason to share that belief. He seems barely to even recognize what appear to be insidious side-effects of political correctness. And he makes no effort to show that political correctness is the only viable way by which any of its modestly positive results could have been achieved.

We must remember that regardless of what defenders of political correctness may imply, conversations between politically diverse people can be many good things all at once: warm, enjoyable, stimulating, enlightening, hilarious, transgressive, and relationship-forming. Moreover, such conversations are important,[11] and when political correctness inhibits them, it is also at risk of inhibiting reconciliation.

---

[11]This point has been recently made with unusually thoughtful urgency by Jacobs (2017).

7.5 Conclusion

Hanson and her party have some core convictions that are quite widely shared. They believe that we have a sense of identity as Australians, that we belong together as the people of a nation, and that we have an inherited common culture worth maintaining. If prompted to think about reconciliation, we could expect them to say that some such sense of unity in culture, belonging, and nationhood is something that reconciliation must involve. I have not contested any of these convictions here. I have, however, taken issue with Hanson's sense of what it is to be Australian, along with her divisive and alienating approach to leadership. She has not engaged proactively or congenially with Indigenous, Asian, and Islamic community leaders, and she has failed to give them a fair go. We have long expected more from our politicians, and we should continue to do so.

Hanson is constantly dogged by allegations of racism. As discussed, the evidence in support of these allegations appears weak, and so there is a clear sense in which she herself is commonly denied a fair go. Of course because her political work has been so divisive and alienating, that unfairness that she suffers does not engender universal sympathy. Yet regardless of how free of sympathy for her we may be, we should not press those allegations of racism without overwhelming evidence. To throw them around lightly is to treat them as being of little moral gravity. Moreover, they are allegations that badly misstate the case against her and are likely to make many of her supporters feel even more contemptuous and resentful than they already do.

It is possible to see how genuine progress towards an inclusive, unified, reconciled nation can be made. As was argued by John Hirst, there is much to be said for the view that we are best held together by having a clear sense of *being Australian* (2010a). The necessary sense of national identity does need to be both appreciative and critical of our history and cultural heritage. But a great deal of serious work has been put to that task over the years, and it is clear that serious progress towards reconciliation has been made.

Although my view of Hanson and her party is largely critical, like so many others I do share their antipathy towards political correctness. It seems basically well-motivated but it provides a very poor solution to the kind of problems that it is supposed to address. If the concerns outlined here are well founded, political correctness is intellectually corrupting, psychologically enfeebling, and socially divisive. And counter-intuitive though this may be, I suggest that genuine reconciliation between Indigenous and non-Indigenous Australians requires something quite different. Importantly, none of the arguments or contentions that I have presented here serves as any kind of apologia or encouragement for those who are boorish, racist, or bigoted. Quite to the contrary; my view is that we should make greater use of certain familiar virtues, norms, and practices to engage with such people and challenge them in ways of suitable depth and warmth. Rather than settle for political correctness, I suggest that we take good humor, a generosity of spirit, patience, politeness, mutually curious conversation, principled thinking, and a fair go, for example, and truly put them to work.

References

60 Minutes [Television] (1996). The Hanson phenomenon. https://www.9now.com.au/60-minute s/rewind/clip-cisgujra700110hp4h13jno2f/dbd76eaf-3e7a-4510-b6c2-5eed55475b3e. Accessed December 5, 2017.

ABC News. (2016). Pauline Hanson fields attack from Aboriginal leader Murrandoo Yanner while visiting Cairns. July 17. http://www.abc.net.au/news/2016-07-17/aboriginal-leader-murrandoo-yanner-yells-at-pauline-hanson/7635506. Accessed December 5, 2017.

ABC TV (2018). Black Comedy. http://www.abc.net.au/tv/programs/black-comedy/. Accessed December 5, 2017.

A Current Affair (2017). Pauline Hanson on Islam. Republished via *News Bite Global* and available at: https://www.youtube.com/watch?v=u-vuXUxeksI. Accessed June 23, 2018.

Altman, D. (2017). How conservatives use identity politics to shut down debate. *The Conversation*. 12 December. https://theconversation.com/how-conservatives-use-identity-politics-to-shut-dow n-debate-89026. Accessed June 23, 2018.

Appiah, K. A. (2005). *The ethics of identity*. Princeton: Princeton University Press.

Australia, Reconciliation. (2008). *Australian reconciliation barometer: Comparative report*. Sydney: Auspoll.

Biskup, P. (1982). Aboriginal history. In G. Osborne & W. F. Mandle (Eds.), *New history: Studying Australia today*. Sydney: George Allen and Unwin.

Broinowski, A. (2017). *Please explain. The rise and fall and rise again of Pauline Hanson*. Melbourne: Penguin Random House.

Burgess, S. (2016). The rocky road to reconciliation. *Journal of Australian Indigenous Issues, 19*(3), 77–94.

Carroll, L. (1872). *Through the looking glass, and what Alice found there*. London: Macmillan and Co.

Clendinnen, I. (2003). *Dancing with strangers*. Melbourne: Text Publishing.

Clendinnen, I. (2009). The good soldier. *The Monthly*, April, 56–61.

Collett, M. (2017). A guide to dealing with offensive remarks at Christmas lunch. *ABC News*, 24 December. http://www.abc.net.au/news/2017-12-24/a-guide-to-dealing-with-offensive-rema rks-at-christmas-lunch/9277002. Accessed 16 January 2018.

Core Data (2017). The Australian seniors series: Modern Australian manners. June. https://www.s eniors.com.au/news-insights/modern-manners-survey. Accessed January 11, 2018.

Davies, C. (1996). *Ethnic humour around the world: A comparative analysis*. Bloomington and Indianapolis: Indiana University Press.

Davies, C. (2002). *The mirth of nations*. New Brunswick, New Jersey: Transaction Publishers.

Dillon, A. (2013). No more victims. In R. Craven, A. Dillon, & N. Parbury (Eds.), *In black and white: Australians all at the crossroads* (pp. 75–90). Ballan: Connor Court.

Fisher, R., & Ury, W. with Patton B. (Ed.). (2012). *Getting to yes: negotiating an agreement without giving in* (3rd ed). London: Random House Business Books.

Flemming, K. (2016). Professor Jordan Peterson swarmed by narcissistic SJW Ideologues after UofT Rally [YouTube video]. https://www.youtube.com/watch?v=O-nvNAcvUPE. Accessed June 23, 2018.

Freeman-Woolpert, S. (2017). Why Nazis are so afraid of these clowns. *Waging Non-Violence*, 25 August. https://wagingnonviolence.org/feature/nazis-afraid-clowns/. Accessed January 16, 2018.

Gare, D., Bolton, G., Macintyre, S., & Stannage, T. (2003). *The fuss that never ended: The life and work of Geoffrey Blainey*. Carlton: Melbourne University Press.

Griffiths, B., Russell, L., Roberts, R. (2017). A story of rupture and resilience: When did Australia's human history begin? *The Conversation*, 17 November. http://www.abc.net.au/news/science/201 7-11-17/when-did-australias-human-history-begin-conversation/9158202. Accessed January 12, 2018.

Haidt, J., & Haslam, N. (2016). Campuses are places for open minds—not where debate is closed down. *The Guardian*, 10 April. https://www.theguardian.com/commentisfree/2016/apr/10/stude nts-censorship-safe-places-platforming-free-speech. Accessed January 12, 2018.

Haidt, J., & Lukianoff, G. (2017). Why it's a bad idea to tell students words are violence. *The Atlantic*, 18 July. https://www.theatlantic.com/education/archive/2017/07/why-its-a-bad-idea-to-tell-stud ents-words-are-violence/533970/. Accessed January 12, 2017.

Hamilton, C. (2015). Political correctness: Its origins and the backlash against it. *The Conversation*. 31 August. https://theconversation.com/political-correctness-its-origins-and-the-backlash-again st-it-46862. Accessed December 5, 2017.

Hanson, P. (1996). Maiden speech, *House of Representatives: Official Hansard*, No. 208, Tuesday, September 10, 3860–3863.

Hanson, P. (2016a) First speech, *Senate: Official Hansard*, Wednesday, September 14, 937–944.

Hanson, P. (2016b). *Senate: Official Hansard*, Thursday, 24 November, 3166–3168.

Hirst, J. (1994). Five fallacies of Aboriginal policy. *Quadrant*, No. 308, July-August, 11–16.

Hirst, J. (2010a). *Looking for Australia: Historical essays*. Melbourne: Black Inc.

Hirst, J. (2010b). *The Australians: Insiders and outsiders on the national character since 1770* (2nd ed.). Collingwood: Black Inc.

Hitchens, C. (2007). Martin Amis is no racist. The Guardian, Wednesday 21 November. https:// www.theguardian.com/uk/2007/nov/21/race.religion. Accessed December 5, 2017.

Inglis, K. (2010). From Berlin to the bush. The Monthly, August, 48–53.

Jacobs, A. (2017). *How to think: A survival guide for a world at odds*. New York: Currency.

Lukianoff, G., & Haidt, J. (2015). The coddling of the American mind. The Atlantic, September. https://www.theatlantic.com/magazine/archive/2015/09/the-coddling-of-the-americ an-mind/399356/. Accessed January 12, 2018.

Marr, D. (2017). The white queen: One Nation and the politics of race. Quarterly Essay, 65.

Mill, J. S. (1991 [1859]). *On Liberty*. In H. B. Acton (Ed.), *John Stuart Mill: Utilitarianism, on liberty, considerations on representative government* (pp. 69–185). London: Everyman.

Nadel, G. (1957). *Australia's colonial culture: Ideas, men and institutions in mid-nineteenth century eastern Australia*. Melbourne: F.W. Cheshire.

Neill, R. (2002). *Black out: How politics is killing black Australia*. Crows Nest: Allen and Unwin.

Nietzsche, F. (1998 [1887]). *On the genealogy of morals*. Translated by Douglas Smith. Oxford: Oxford University Press.

Nietzsche, F. (2008 [1886]). *Beyond good and evil*. Translated by Marion Faber. Oxford: Oxford University Press.

Pearson, N. (2009). *Up from the mission: Selected writings*. Melbourne: Black Inc.

Peterson, J. (2016). Part 3: The PC game (and some counter-tactics). online lecture https://www.y outube.com/watch?v=W2u62u4entc. Accessed December 5, 2017.

Peterson, J. (n.d.). Jordan B. Peterson [website home]. https://jordanbpeterson.com/. Accessed June 23, 2018.

PHONP (Pauline Hanson's One Nation Party) (2017). Principles and objectives. http://www.onen ation.com.au/principles. Accessed June 18, 2018.

Reconciliation Australia, (2010). *Australian reconciliation barometer 2010*, Auspoll.

Reconciliation Australia (2012). *Australian reconciliation barometer 2012*, Auspoll.

Reconciliation Australia (2014). *Australian reconciliation barometer 2014*, Polity Research and Consulting.

Reconciliation Australia (2016). *2016 Australian reconciliation barometer*, Polity Research and Consulting.

Reynolds, H. (1990). *The other side of the frontier*. Ringwood: Penguin.

Roth, P. (2001). *The human stain*. London: Vintage.

Shapiro, D. L. (2010). Relational identity theory: A systematic approach for transforming the emotional dimension of conflict. *American Psychologist, 65*(7), 634–645.

Stanner, W. E. H. (2010). *The Dreaming and other essays*. Collingwood: Black Inc.

Sutton, P. (2009). *The politics of suffering: Indigenous Australia and the end of the liberal consensus.* Carlton: Melbourne University Press.

Thomas, N. (2016). Understanding Pauline. *The New Matilda*, 9 October. https://newmatilda.com/2016/10/09/understanding-pauline/. Accessed January.

Tucker, J., & VandenBeukel, J. (2016). "We're teaching university students lies"—An interview with Dr Jordan Peterson. *C2C Journal*, 1 December. http://www.c2cjournal.ca/2016/12/were-teaching-university-students-lies-an-interview-with-dr-jordan-peterson/. Accessed December 5.

United Kingdom (1787). Governor Phillip's instructions, 25 April. *Historical records of Australia.* https://www.foundingdocs.gov.au/resources/transcripts/nsw2_doc_1787.rtf. Accessed December 5, 2017.

Wieseltier, L. (1994). Against identity. *The New Republic*, 28 November, 24–32.

Winsor, M. (2018). Steve Bannon: "Let them call you racist… Wear it as a badge of honor". *ABC News*, 10 March. https://abcnews.go.com/Politics/steve-bannon-call-racist-wear-badge-honor/story?id=53656814. Accessed 28 June 2018.

Young, M., & Reynolds, E. (2016). Pauline Hanson reveals she "wants to work with Muslims". *News.com.au*, 29 August. http://www.news.com.au/finance/work/leaders/pauline-hanson-reveals-she-wants-to-work-with-muslims/news-story/3cc9f522bf5a5b825cfe080749f80693. Accessed 5 December 2017.

Chapter 8
"Manning Up" with Pauline Hanson: Playing the Gender Card, Again

Jim Jose

Abstract Pauline Hanson's strategy of "manning up" provides an opportunity to explore a different view of what it means to play the gender card. Hanson presents herself as an anti-politician, an ordinary woman whose claim to political authenticity is as someone who stands outside the circuits of the so-called political class of professional politicians. At the same time, she positions herself explicitly within a recognizably masculinist style of politics. Hence her embrace of an anti-political identity is argued here as a particular politics of embodied power predicated on playing the gender card. A brief discussion of the idea of "playing the gender card" provides a background context for the subsequent discussion of her views as expressed within Pauline Hanson's One Nation's political platform in 1998 and 2016, and the relevant parts of her debut speeches to the House of Representatives and the Senate, respectively. This establishes a degree of continuity in her politics as well as how she has positioned herself politically, and hence demonstrates the centrality of her "manning up" strategy as a form of playing the gender card.

Keywords Australian politics · Gender card · Gender politics · Manning up Pauline Hanson

8.1 Introduction

Pauline Hanson's first term in the Australian parliament as a Member of the House of Representatives (MHR) from 1996 to 1998 proved to be a watershed moment for Australia's political culture. Her first three years in parliament served as a lightning rod for openly expressed intolerance and racism to gain respectability within mainstream political discourse. Those three years heralded "a form of politics of the future not the past" (Curthoys and Johnson 1998, p. 97) . Since her vacating

J. Jose (✉)
Newcastle Business School, University of Newcastle, 409 Hunter St, Newcastle, NSW 2300, Australia
e-mail: jim.jose@newcastle.edu.au

© Springer Nature Singapore Pte Ltd. 2019
B. Grant et al. (eds.), *The Rise of Right-Populism*,
https://doi.org/10.1007/978-981-13-2670-7_8

the (then) seat of Oxley in the House of Representatives in 1998 the discourses of intolerance to which she gave substance in her first speech as an MHR in 1996 and the launch speech for the Pauline Hanson One Nation (PHON) in 1997 have become normalized across significant parts of Australia's national political culture (Wear 2008). As filmmaker Anna Broinowski noted, Hanson's One Nation launch speech today reads as "no more incendiary than a 2017 press release from the hard-right faction of the Turnbull government" (Broinowski 2017, p. 52). Hanson's election to the Senate in 2016 would seem to bear this out because this time she was joined by three other PHON members. This four-person political bloc meant that she was no longer a solitary voice facing a more-or-less indifferent parliament. Even though two of the original four senators have left the PHON they, along with Pauline Hanson and the other remaining PHON member, still occupy a political space in a Senate that has been shaped by a slow-burning disaffection with the seemingly unresponsive mainstream political culture. PHON and the other independent and non-aligned Senators are products of increasing dissatisfaction with the political mainstream, a dissatisfaction that has only intensified in the intervening 20 years since her first appearance in the parliament.

Hanson has extended her appeal beyond those who make race and immigration the scapegoats for their economic and social situations (initially a core PHON constituency) to those who have been adversely affected by the dynamics of Australia's willing engagement with neoliberal policy settings and the concomitant globalizing dynamics (Johnson 1998; McSwinney and Cottle 2017; Moore 1997) . In 2016, Hanson continued to present herself as she did in her debut speech to the parliament in 1996, as an "anti-politician" (Brett 1998), thereby capitalizing successfully on the manifest alienation of voters from the mainstream political process. Both mainstream political parties recognize this political alienation and manipulate it for partisan advantage, while continuing to pursue the very policies and practices that sustain its growth. Hanson has also continued to frame her political appeal around an explicitly xenophobic politics, which for most of her critics remains a key marker of her politics. But where in 1996 she railed against a so-called "flood" of Asians and supposedly inequitable privileges for Indigenous Australians, in 2016 she eschewed her previous anti-Asian rhetoric to pursue an anti-Islam ethnocentrism. This latter strategy has had the perverse effect of enabling her to garner support from those she once vilified (Broinowski 2017). Hanson herself has denied that she is racist because "a racist means a person who considers their race to be superior to others", a position she has stated that she does not hold or subscribe to (Kingston 2001, p. 124) . Yet it is difficult to escape the conclusion, her comments notwithstanding, that Hanson remains "an ideologue of race" (Hill 1998; Marr 2017, p. 74) .

Almost as deeply embedded in her political discourse as her ethnocentric and racist pronouncements is her similarly contradictory approach to being a woman in politics, an approach best described as "manning up". This was a distinctive feature of her first term in politics and has remained so in the 2016 version. For present purposes, the strategy of "manning up" is understood here to be "a stereotypically masculine approach or course of action" (Dictionary.com 2016; EOLD 2016). In 1996, she presented herself as a woman "articulating what is commonly thought to

be a 'masculinist' political agenda" (Deutchman and Ellison 1999, p. 47), manifest-
ing her political presence as a form of "embodied power" (Hawkesworth 2016) that
was masculinist in orientation but conveyed via a feminized body. Thus, in the 1990s
Hanson was described in terms of being a "man's woman" (Lake 1998, p. 114), a
"feminized battler" speaking up for disaffected and alienated masculinity (Probyn
1999, pp. 166–167). At that time she presented a variation on "emphasised feminini-
ty" framed and calibrated according to the dominant masculinist tropes of Australian
politics and culture, in particular that of "hegemonic masculinity" (Connell 1987,
pp. 183–188).

Her embrace of a strategy of "manning up", in particular her conscious deployment of her sexuality, was recognized at the time as "an essential factor in her
success" (Curthoys and Johnson 1998; Deutchman and Ellison 1999, 2004; Ellison
and Deutchman 1997, p. 142; Lake 1998; Probyn 1999). It guaranteed her media
attention that in turn secured, as well as reinforced, ongoing political support from
her core base of non-urban voters, predominantly aging white men (Goot 1998).
However, the projection of a sexualized anti-political political identity is one that
is fraught with contradictions, as numerous scholars noted at the time of her first
parliamentary foray (Curthoys and Johnson 1998; Deutchman and Ellison 2004;
Ellison and Deutchman 1997; Lake 1998; Probyn 1999). Some of these contradictions will be noted only briefly to the extent that they bear on the central argument
of this chapter, namely that Hanson's anti-political approach is a particular politics
of embodied power predicated on playing the gender card, and in particular that her
strategy of "manning up" gives a different view of what it means to play the gender
card.

In the late 1990s the notion of "playing the gender card", as an explicitly articulated strategy, had little or no currency within Australian political discourse. Yet
key characteristics of Pauline Hanson's strategy throughout her political career have
been framed around a conscious deployment of the dominant tropes of the prevailing masculinist gender regime at the core of Australian politics. Since she is not
objecting to or complaining about the sexism embedded within masculinist forms
of politics, partly because she negotiates this sexism by embracing and endorsing
masculinist political practices, this is currently not recognized as playing the gender
card. However, as Johnson (2015) has perceptively argued, calibrating appropriate
masculinities for political advantage has long been a feature of Australian (if not all)
politics, and this is itself playing the gender card *par excellence*.

In this chapter I argue that being a woman (anti-) politician aligning herself explicitly and outspokenly with a masculinist political agenda is a version of playing the
gender card. Before looking at Hanson's views (in both 1996–1998 and from 2016)
and the manner in which she articulates them, it is necessary to say something about
the idea of "playing the gender card". This provides the context to situate the subsequent discussion of Hanson's views and how she has positioned herself politically.
The argument then proceeds to provide a brief critical overview of her policy positions as expressed within Pauline Hanson's One Nation's political platform in 1998
and 2016 , including a discussion of some of the relevant parts of her debut speeches

to the House of Representatives and the Senate, respectively. This establishes the degree of continuity in her politics and demonstrates the centrality of her "manning up" strategy as a form of playing the gender card.

8.2 On the Idea of Playing the Gender Card

Politics—or political activity—is often likened to a game in which participants vie for advantage and dominance. In this context, the use of the phrase "playing the gender card" aims to invoke the idea that the gender card is like a "get out of jail free card" in Monopoly or "a trump card" in a card game; in either metaphorical context "it helps the candidate who plays it" (Falk 2013, p. 201). The gender card (or the race card) can be played to advance the strategic position of those playing. However, in the past it has been assumed that there are some subtle differences in the respective ways in which the gender card and the race card are played, even though both aim to elicit particular responses from supporters and opponents alike. On the one hand, the race card is usually played in such a way as to evoke a race-based response from the supporters of those invoking it, often covertly through the phenomenon of "dog whistling" where "subliminal targeted messages are sent to specific audiences, just as farm dogs rounding up sheep and cattle are directed by whistles, pitched so that only the dogs can hear" (Johnson 2015, p. 297; see also Fear 2007; Goodin and Saward 2005). The gender card, on the other hand, is most commonly understood to be played against an opponent in order to undermine their position of power and their credibility. In many respects, use of the gender card involves less of the dog whistle and more of the wolf as its playing is often far less subtle and rarely left to subliminal messaging. As we shall see, Hanson's approach to playing the gender card aligns more closely with that of the race card.

There are a number of ways in which the gender card might be played, as Falk (2013, p. 200) has shown in the context of US political contests:

(1) by drawing attention to your gender as a woman to make you stand out in a field of men;
(2) by arguing that people should vote for a woman to remediate current underrepresentation;
(3) by campaigning on issues that women are believed to support;
(4) by arguing that sexism plays a role in attacks against you or that you are the subject of sexist attacks; and
(5) by mentioning the fact that women face discrimination in the public sphere (Falk 2013, p. 200).

If a politician, usually a woman, does one or other of these actions, especially one of the last two in the above list, they are accused by their opponents of playing the gender card. The effect of such an accusation is intended to position the person so accused of seeking to gain an unfair advantage or of playing the game unfairly and hence to silence them or negate the legitimacy of their position (Falk 2013, pp. 201–203).

Johnson (2015) has taken Falk's analysis further by arguing that playing the gender card is not restricted to men politicians trying to silence their women opponents; rather, it has been an ongoing, if mostly unnoticed, feature of masculinist politics. Johnson (2015, p. 295) perceptively noted that "there is actually a long history of the gender card being played in Australian politics" and that "it has normally been played by men against men". That is, men have frequently called into question their opponent's masculinity, or at least drawn attention to the presumed lack of some attribute of whatever is assumed at the time to be the prevailing form of "hegemonic masculinity" (Connell 1987, pp. 183–185) relevant for their political standing. Johnson noted that while there may be concerns with "how well leaders perform their masculinity … there are no inherent tensions between being a leader and being masculine, as leadership is coded masculine" (Johnson 2015, pp. 298–299). Women politicians aspiring to be leaders find themselves in a precarious position, since their gender identity is always already not-masculine. They are continually required to negotiate their gendered presence in ways that do not invoke negative references to their gender. Hence Hanson's strategy of playing the gender card.

8.3 Pauline Hanson's One Nation, Gender and Policy Ideas

The policies articulated by Hanson and One Nation are largely populist in aspiration, both in the 1990s and from 2016 onwards. They are also deeply tinged with racist understandings, perhaps best encapsulated by Hanson's statements in her debut speech to the House of Representatives in 1996 where she told the parliament that "We now have a situation where a type of reverse racism is applied to mainstream Australians", in which white Australians are less favorably treated, and that the country was "in danger of being swamped by Asians" (Hanson 1996). The racist strand of Hanson's politics has been well canvassed by others (e.g., Hill 1998; Marr 2017). However, her appeal (and to a lesser extent that of One Nation) is clearly tied to key economic questions arising mostly from the relentless pursuit of internationalization or globalization by successive Australian governments, and which for Hanson and many of her supporters could be exploited in racial terms. She has articulated the significant angst felt within the wider Australian population about the decline of Australian manufacturing, about the need for targeted protective tariffs to protect jobs, about the neglect (if not abandoning) of rural communities, and the plight of Australian workers (by which she meant mainly white Anglo-Saxon men). Within the context of policy formulation these were not women's issues as such but issues of concern for all, and hence she signaled that she was pursuing mainstream issues, not specifically women's, and certainly not feminist, issues. In fact, for many commentators Hanson has positioned herself as anti-feminist, a view that accords with her explicitly stated views (see, for example, Hanson in Broinowski 2017, pp. 72–73). Yet her position on gender issues (and her relationship to feminism more generally) was and remains complex and contradictory, as numerous scholars have pointed out (Broinowski 2017; Curthoys and Johnson 1998; Deutchman and Ellison 2004; Ellison and Deutchman 1997; Lake 1998; Probyn 1999) .

Of the 31 Principles and Objectives currently listed on the party's website, only two cover so-called women's issues:

> #12 To support and advocate traditional family values and uphold the institution of the family in its fight against the many who aim to breakdown this important unit of any decent society.

> # 30 Marriage between two people of the same sex is a social issue, and One Nation believes all Australians should have the right to vote in a referendum, rather than a vote on the floor of Parliament. If it is to be determined by Parliament then One Nation members of Parliament will be allowed a conscience vote. We also acknowledge that same sex couples living in de facto relationships should be afforded the same property rights as heterosexuals [sic] couples. (PHON 2016a)

Here we see the contradictoriness with respect to gender values. On the one hand, PHON is standing up for traditional family values with all the inbuilt heteronormative biases therein, while at the same time acknowledging equal rights for same-sex couples. The populist appeal is still there since the PHON position is for the people, not the parliament, to determine the issue of same sex marriage. Aside from the above two policy issues, the rest of the party's stated policies and objectives speak to mainstream issues of immigration, race, economic nationalism, and defense of Australian industries, all of which positioned her in 1997, and continue to position her in 2016, centrally within the "masculinist culture of Right wing politics" (Ellison and Deutchman 1997, p. 144).

In Hanson's debut parliamentary speech in 1996 her one key comment that might be categorized as a woman's issue concerned the (then) current Family Law Act and issues surrounding child support and custody arrangements. But it needs to be acknowledged that her concern was not how this impacted on women, but on men. Her position was articulated with men's issues at the forefront of her concerns:

> I refer to the social and family upheaval created by the Family Law Act and the ramifications of that act embodied in the child support scheme. The Family Law Act, which was the child of the disgraceful Senator Lionel Murphy, should be repealed. It has brought death, misery and heartache to countless thousands of Australians. Children are treated like pawns in some crazy game of chess.

> The child support scheme has become unworkable, very unfair and one sided. Custodial parents can often profit handsomely at the expense of a parent paying child support, and in many cases the non-custodial parent simply gives up employment to escape the, in many cases, heavy and punitive financial demand. (Hanson 1996, pp. 3861–3862)

When the PHON was founded in 1997 these sentiments were expanded and formalized as part of its policy in 1998 (PHON 1998).

Practically identical sentiments were to be found on the 2016 One Nation webpage where the (then) version of their Family Law Child Support Policy was presented (PHON 2016b). Perhaps the only thing different in the 2016 version is a lower intensity of stridency around the issue of equal parenting. Her debut speech in the Senate, 20 years almost to the day, also stayed close to the stated party policy. However, in her delivery to the Senate the stridency returned: "Family Law would be the most discriminatory, biased and unworkable policy in this country. I referred to it in my maiden speech 20 years ago and still nothing has changed—if anything, it is worse" (Hanson 2016, p. 942):

> … on average, three men, and occasionally a woman, suicide a day due to family breakdowns. … The whole system is unworkable and is in desperate need of change. Children are used as pawns in custody battles where women make frivolous claims and believe they have the sole right to the children. Children have two parents and, until we treat mums and dads with the same courtesy and rights, we will continue to see murders due to sheer frustration and depression and mental illness caused by this unworkable system. (Hanson 2016, p. 942)

Here we see something that appears to be a characteristic trait of Hanson's politics, namely an inability to revise her rhetoric with readily available evidence. There is no acknowledgment that, in the intervening 20 years, reforms to the *Family Law Act* implemented by the Howard Government in 2006 embedded the presumption of shared parental responsibility into the family court framework (see, for example, Flood 2010). The Senator's complaint that the "system" was not "treat[ing] mums and dads with the same courtesy and rights" (Hanson 2016) had no basis in fact. But this was not what Hanson intended to be understood by her invocation of the idea of "the same courtesy and rights". Rather what was meant was the basis upon which parental care and custodial arrangements were to be organized, a position clearly articulated in PHON policy where "Joint custody is the option of choice for ONE Nation" (PHON 2016b).

Despite using words like "balance", "fairness", and "equal" to frame her comments, Hanson makes it quite clear where PHON's sympathies are directed:

> … Their lives having been destroyed and the pain of missing their children are the reasons many end up in a state of depression caused by the trauma and in some cases the blatant vindictiveness from former partners.
>
> Child support is another contentious issue and should be revised. Some parents are left caring and providing for children without any financial help from the other parent. Others refuse to work so they do not have to pay child support. The system needs to be balanced, taking in the age of the child on a sliding scale and both parents' incomes should be taken into account. Non-custodial parents find it hard to restart their lives, with excessive child support payments that see their former partners live a very comfortable life. Make it fair with both custody and child support and most parents will gladly take on their responsibility. (Hanson 2016, pp. 942–943)

For Hanson and her supporters, it is men's lives that are being "destroyed", men who "suffer the pain of missing their children", men who "end up in a state of depression", men who are the victims of "the blatant vindictiveness from former partners", and men who are the "non-custodial parents" finding it "hard to restart their lives". Women on the other hand are the "vindictive" "former partners" who, with the collusion of an "unworkable" family court system, are able to lead "very comfortable [lives]"—even if some women, as Hanson appears to acknowledge, "are left caring and providing for children without any financial help from the other parent" and that perhaps "others [presumably men] refuse to work so they do not have to pay child support".

Hanson and PHON's solution to these problems is, amongst other things, to abolish the Family Court and replace it with a tribunal "consist[ing] of people from mainstream Australia", and to implement a radical overhaul of the "functions and operation of the Child Support Agency" (PHON 2016a). Both of these entities are asserted by PHON to be responsible for problems besetting the family law system. For PHON, "strong functional family units" are the cornerstone of "safe, secure and happy societies"—hence the national government should pursue policies aimed at securing "long term family stability" (PHON 2016a). While PHON also supports same-sex marriage, the ideal family unit for PHON is assumed to be heteronormative in its makeup with men holding a privileged position within it. Hanson's own experiences and occasional statements about men (for instance, she is reported to have said to a young female staffer "men are only good for one thing: use them for their bodies, then move on"—Hanson cited in Broinowski 2017, p. 74) may well contradict the ideal, but it is clear that where one might have expected a greater sensitivity to the problems faced by women such as in the areas of relationship breakdowns, domestic violence, and child support, both Hanson and PHON show a marked propensity to treat women as part of the problem. The aim appears to be to restore to men their "rightful" place of power (and hence sense of entitlement) within family relationships. There is certainly little about Hanson's views and the PHON policies that might be described as even remotely woman-friendly, let alone feminist.

8.4   Hanson, Anti-politics and Playing the Gender Gard

Indeed, Hanson has been at pains to distance herself from the feminist label, declaring to Anna Broinowski that "I am not a feminist at all" (Hanson quoted in Broinowski 2017, p. 72; see also Kingston 2001, pp. 42–43). Elaborating, Hanson explains that:

> I call myself a lady because I like to be treated like a lady, and there are some men out there who like to treat women as ladies, and there are some women out there who don't want the door opened for them and say "I'm equal" and all that, but it's not about that. It's having respect for each other. You're male and you're female. I had a hot meal waiting on the table for my husbands every night when they got home. And I love being treated like a lady. (Hanson quoted in Broinowski 2017, p. 72)

In addition to eschewing any identification with feminism, Hanson explains that it is respect, not difference, that defines who men and women are and the nature of relations between them. At the same time, she reveals that she has willingly played the role of a traditional wife, though whether this was from duty or desire is unclear. Framing her own sense of self in terms of being a lady, of enjoying being treated like a lady, points to a cocquettishness that nevertheless she insists is played out on her terms. Specifically, "I am definitely not a Mrs. I've been there and done that, and I definitely don't belong to anyone" (Hanson cited in Broinowski 2017, p. 74). This is not to say that she is not aware of feminist issues and how gender identities and gender relations shape every human activity. Rather, she represents herself as an anti-feminist in much the same way that she represents herself as an anti-politician.

She acknowledges that she is involved in the game of politics but, to the extent that it is possible, she attempts to engage with it almost exclusively on her terms. Similarly, when it comes to what might be understood as negotiating gender she believes that she does so on her own terms.

Hanson's self-representation as an anti-politician and the brace of policies she espouses clearly articulate traditional gender norms and boundaries. At the same time her very actions push against these boundaries and draw our attention to the ever-present sexist structuring of the world of politics. When it suits her purposes, she plays on the fact that she is a woman. In her first speech to the House of Representatives she began with an opening gambit that she came there, "not as a polished politician but as a woman who has had her fair share of life's hard knocks" (Hanson 1996). This has been a constant theme of her political persona. She is the self-made woman, as both a business operator and politician (Broinowski 2017), beholden to no man, especially a political power-broker, for her success. She sees herself as "an independent, free thinking person" (Hanson cited in Kingston 2001, p. 10) . This has been a major part of her appeal, at least on a personal level. Similarly, her statement that she "has had her fair share of life's hard knocks" has continued to resonate with voters, supporters and non-supporters alike. It has formed a central part of her popular appeal. Everything about her presentation of self could be understood as demonstrating that she was not the product of privilege, wealth or political patronage; her manner of speaking, her dress sense, her bearing, even her seeming lack of sophistication about key policy issues, all bespeak someone ostensibly of the people rather than someone who purported to represent them.

Yet even while appealing to her embodied power as a woman, she has also been adamant that being a woman had no relevance to doing a politician's or any other type of job: "regardless of what sex you are has got nothing to do with it—it is the best person for the job" (Hanson cited in Kingston 2001, p. 123). And even as she spoke those words she followed them up immediately with what appeared to be a feminist-friendly statement, namely that "women look at things totally different and I'd like to see more women there by all means. The men have had hold in this country for too long and see what they've done with it" (Hanson cited in Kingston 2001, p. 124). This is a view that would not be out of place in some strands of modern feminist thought, in which women and men are understood to have specifically different sensibilities and ways of understanding and engaging with the world (e.g., Gilligan 1982). That view notwithstanding, one of the interesting features of both incarnations of PHON has been the presence of key men advisers within the inner circle of the party executive. In the 1990s a number of men (e.g., John Pasquarelli, David Oldfield, David Ettridge) jockeyed for position and power, and were only too eager to project themselves as the architects of Hanson's success while downplaying her contributions to her own speeches, the party's policies, and strategic directions (Broinowski 2017, pp. 125–126; Kingston 2001). Since 2016 the masculinist dominance appears to have been more muted as her key adviser, James Ashby, has been less visible, publicly at least, in managing Hanson and the party's political strategies (Broinowski 2017, pp. 286–298).

When Hanson first began her political odyssey after being disendorsed by the Liberal Party in 1996, she presented herself as an outsider, as someone who did not belong to (indeed was not welcome in) the so-called "political class"—the term used by Hanson and others, usually pejoratively, to describe those who make a living from politics (Allen and Cairney 2017; Cooke 2014). In her 2016 comeback Hanson still invoked an outsider status and, by extension, that of an anti-politician, but she had long moved beyond her 1996 claim of not being "a polished politician". In the intervening 18 years following her defeat in 1998 she unsuccessfully contested seven elections. Her eventual success with the Senate in 2016 was her tenth electoral campaign under her own name. During that time Hanson had also become a media celebrity in her own right through her participation on a number of reality television shows. She had appeared as a regular on *Dancing with the Stars* in 2004, on *Celebrity Apprentice* in 2011, and for many months before the 2016 election had a regular guest spot on Channel 7's *Sunrise* and Channel 9's *Today*. By the time of the 2016 election, she was a polished media performer, a "rolled-gold celebrity" whose "social media following was so large she didn't need to send out media releases, posting instead to Facebook" (Broinowski 2017, p. 33). After contesting ten elections, Hanson is far from being a political neophyte. Even though her self-representation as an anti-politician might have less purchase in 2018, hers is a particular politics of embodied power predicated on playing the gender card. Her success, both as a political performer and a celebrity, rests heavily on her conscious deployment of recognizable gender tropes around which she wraps her populist homilies and broad-based economic nationalist policies.

8.5 Conclusion

In her first foray into national politics Hanson herself did not need to play the gender card overtly, but rather could take advantage of the novelty of her situation. At this time, a (mostly) masculinist media throng focused on her presentation of self as a feisty, provocative woman politician and the gender contradictions inherent in her political position to drive their media representations of her (Deutchman and Ellison 1999). Since 2016, the political landscape has changed. Hanson has continued to position herself as a "manned up" woman politician, but media receptivity no longer appears to be taken with the novelty of the gender contradictions. Over the past two decades there has been a woman Prime Minister, a woman Governor-General, numerous women Premiers, two women Chief Ministers, and until August 2018 both the Liberal Party and the Australian Labor Party had women Deputy Leaders, and there is a woman presiding as Chief Justice of the High Court. Women occupying positions of political power, doing so-called masculinist things within the political system, does not carry the novelty value it did in 1996.

In her discussion of playing the gender card in Australia, Johnson (2015, p. 313) observed that scholars needed to develop "a more sophisticated understanding of when politicians are merely playing the gender card to reinforce traditional gender norms and when they are raising legitimate issues about sexism in public life". This is an appropriate observation, because raising legitimate issues about sexism in public life should not be understood as playing the gender card. Yet in Hanson's case, her playing of the gender card cannot be easily fitted into one or other of these alternatives. Rather, her politics encompasses and extends beyond both of these possibilities. At every turn, she draws attention to the fact that she is a woman operating in a so-called man's world. Paradoxically, while her objective is to minimize perceptions of her transgressions of the prevailing masculinist gender regime in Australia politics, she ends up embodying the sorts of challenges that would undermine the central stereotypes of that regime even as she articulates and defends them as part of the PHON's policies.

For Pauline Hanson, playing the gender card is not an incidental matter. But in playing the gender card she is not aiming to seek an unfair advantage. It is a necessary consequence of negotiating the masculinist structures that make up the Australian political system. It is not simply something exclusive to Pauline Hanson or the Hanson phenomenon. It is something that confronts all women politicians attempting to succeed in politics. Women politicians are by definition caught on the horns of the gender dilemma since the political system, its values, measures of achievement, and qualities of leadership are calibrated according to masculinist codes. And herein lies the significance of considering Hanson in the context of playing the gender card.

References

Allen, P., & Cairney, P. (2017). What do we mean when we talk about the "Political Class"? *Political Studies Review, 15*(1), 18–27.

Brett, J. (1998). Representing the unrepresented: One Nation and the formation of the Labor Party. In R. Manne (Ed.), *Two nations: The causes and effects of the rise of the One Nation Party in Australia* (pp. 26–37). Melbourne: Bookman Press.

Broinowski, A. (2017). *Please explain: The rise, fall, and rise again of Pauline Hanson*. Melbourne: Penguin Random House.

Connell, R. (1987). *Gender and power: Society, the person and sexual politics*. Sydney: Allen and Unwin.

Cooke, R. (2014). The people versus the political class. *The Monthly* June. https://www.themonthly.com.au/issue/2014/june/1401544800/richard-cooke/people-versus-political-class. Accessed November 30, 2017.

Curthoys, A., & Johnson, C. (1998). Articulating the future and the past: gender, race and globalisation in One Nation's self–construction. *Hecate, 24*(2), 97–114.

Deutchman, I., & Ellison, A. (1999). A star is born: The rollercoaster ride of Pauline Hanson in the news. *Media, Culture and Society, 21,* 33–50.

Deutchman, I., & Ellison, A. (2004). When feminists don't fit the case of Pauline Hanson. *International Feminist Journal of Politics, 6*(1), 29–52.

Dictionary.com (2016). Man Up. http://www.dictionary.com/browse/man–up. Accessed October 8, 2016.

Ellison, A., & Deutchman, I. (1997). Men only: Pauline Hanson and the far right. In B. Grant (Ed.), *Pauline Hanson: One Nation and Australian politics* (pp. 141–150). Armidale: University of New England Press.

EOLD (English Oxford *Living* Dictionary). (2016). Man up. https://en.oxforddictionaries.com/def inition/man_up. Accessed October 8, 2016.

Falk, E. (2013). Clinton and the playing-the-gender-card metaphor in Campaign News. *Feminist Media Studies, 13*(2), 192–207.

Fear, J. (2007). Under the radar: Dog-whistle politics in Australia. Discussion Paper No. 96. Canberra: The Australia Institute.

Flood, M. (2010). "Father's Rights" and the defence of parental authority in Australia. *Violence Against Women, 16*(3), 328–347.

Gilligan, C. (1982). *In a different voice: Psychological theory and women's development*. Cambridge, MA: Harvard University Press.

Goodin, R., & Saward, M. (2005). Dog whistles and democratic mandates. *The Political Quarterly, 76*(4), 471–476.

Goot, M. (1998). Hanson's heartland: Who's for One Nation and why. In R. Manne (Ed.), *Two nations: The causes and effects of the rise of the One Nation Party in Australia* (pp. 51–74). Melbourne: Bookman Press.

Hanson, P. (1996, September 10). First Speech. *Commonwealth Parliamentary Debates* (HR). Thirty-eighth Parliament. First Session—Second Period. pp. 3860–3863.

Hanson, P. (2016, September 14). First Speech. *Commonwealth Parliamentary Debates* (Senate). Forty-fifth Parliament First Session—First Period. pp. 937–944.

Hawkesworth, M. (2016). *Embodied power: Demystifying disembodied politics*. New York: Routledge.

Hill, L. (1998). Pauline Hanson, free speech and reconciliation. *Journal of Australian Studies, 22*(57), 10–22.

Johnson, C. (1998). Pauline Hanson and One Nation. In H.-G. Betz & S. Immerfall (Eds.), *The new politics of the right: Neo-populist parties and movements in established democracies*. New York: St Martin's Press.

Johnson, C. (2015). Playing the gender card: The uses and abuses of gender in Australian politics. *Politics and Gender, 11*(2), 291–319.

Kingston, M. (2001). *Off the rails: the Pauline Hanson trip* (2nd ed.). Crows Nest: Allen and Unwin.

Lake, M. (1998). Pauline Hanson: Virago in parliament, viagra in the bush. In R. Manne (Ed.), *Two nations: The causes and effects of the rise of the One Nation Party in Australia* (pp. 114–122). Melbourne: Bookman Press.

Marr, D. (2017). *The white queen: One Nation and the politics of race. Quarterly Essay*. Melbourne: La Trobe University Press and Black Inc.

McSwinney, J., & Cottle, D. (2017). Unintended consequences: One Nation and neoliberalism in contemporary Australia. *Journal of Australian Political Economy, 79,* 87–106.

Moore, T. (1997). Economic rationalism and economic nationalism. In B. Grant (Ed.), *Pauline Hanson, One Nation and Australian politics* (pp. 50–62). Armidale: UNE Press.

PHON (Pauline Hanson's One Nation). (1998). Family law and child support policy directions. http://www.gwb.com.au/onenation/policy/family1.html. Accessed November 23, 2016.

PHON (Pauline Hanson's One Nation). (2016a). One Nation policies—Principles and objectives. http://www.onenation.com.au/principles. Accessed November 23, 2016.

PHON (Pauline Hanson's One Nation). (2016b). One Nation policies—Family law courts child support scheme. http://www.onenation.com.au/policiess/family-law. Accessed November 23, 2016.

Probyn, F. (1999). That woman: Pauline Hanson and cultural crisis. *Australian Feminist Studies, 14*(29), 161–171.

Wear, R. (2008). Permanent populism: The Howard Government 1996–2007. *Australian Journal of Political Science, 43*(4), 617–634.

Chapter 9
Rebranded Pauline Hanson: A Party of Policy or Protest?

Jo Coghlan

Abstract The title of this chapter comes from David Marr's ongoing interest in Pauline Hanson: an interest I share, having watched her rise in 1996, contemplated what happened to her during her years in the political wilderness, and watched her successful return to politics in 2016. More broadly, the idea of looking at Hanson and Hansonism through the prisms of policy or, alternatively, protest is interesting. It changes how one thinks about her, her Party, its minor electoral successes, and its major electoral failures. Examining Pauline Hanson's One Nation Party (PHONP) as a party of policy focuses our attention upon its impact on the legislative agenda, in both 1996 and 2016. Alternatively, in considering PHONP as a party of protest, its positions are stripped of the pretense of seeking change and instead become mere rhetoric.

Keywords Pauline Hanson · Policy · Populism · Protest

9.1 Introduction

Adopting this framework of policy and protest, Hanson's stance on a range of social and economic positions unearths as much about Australian politics as it does about Hanson. Hanson is a populist. Populists will always find electoral spaces through which to emerge when there are social and political cleavages. This is particularly the case when there is a sense of the "breakdown between citizens and their representatives" (Moffitt and Tormey 2014, p. 391). In spaces such as these, populists embed themselves in public discourses as the champion of "the people" who have been let down, left behind, ignored, "badly governed", and "rendered powerless" by their political representatives (Moffitt and Tormey 2014, p. 391).

J. Coghlan (✉)
School of Humanities, Arts and Social Sciences, University of New England,
Armidale, NSW, Australia
e-mail: jo.coghlan@une.edu.au

© Springer Nature Singapore Pte Ltd. 2019
B. Grant et al. (eds.), *The Rise of Right-Populism*,
https://doi.org/10.1007/978-981-13-2670-7_9

179

Considering Hanson in this light offers an understanding of why she emerges in 1996 and again in 2016. Cracks in the political consensus between representatives and voters were evident at both junctures. As argued by Tony Lunch in Chap. 3 of this volume, the political compact between voters and, in particular, the three major parties—the Australian Labor Party (ALP) and, on the conservative side of parliamentary politics, the Liberal Party and the National Party—had been in decline for some time. Even though the Howard Government was elected in a landslide election in 1996, 12% of Australian voters did not vote for the ALP or the Liberal Party (Barber and Johnson 2014). In 2013, this rose to over 35%, which may account for the subsequent Turnbull Government's one-seat majority (Barber and Johnson 2014).[1] Voters' increasing disillusionment with the major parties provides a discursive and electoral space for populists to emerge.

Populists like Hanson draw on voter dissatisfaction. They position themselves as one of "the people" opposing the political elites and damning the political system that entrenches power. They condemn the political institutions that deny "the people" their sovereignty. What is surprising is that it was Hanson who became the lightning rod for this populist discourse. Others had come before her, like Graeme Campbell (the former right-wing Labor Federal Member for Kalgoorlie and founder of the Australia First Party), with little success in flaming the discontent felt against political parties. Yet it is Hanson who has been able to craft a resonating and authentic message that articulated and energized the "worries of many citizens, who felt neglected by the federal elite" (Mason 2010, p. 187). Hanson, with her "cultural nostalgia that emphasised individual agency", focused voter anger on the system and its representatives. This denied the need to offer detailed policies for complex social, cultural and economic issues (Mason 2010, p. 188). Such is the appeal and the strategy of populists as discussed in several contributions to this book.

This prefaces the first argument of this chapter: Hanson, I argue, is a populist who is tapping into the fracturing of political support for the major parties. In 2016, 45 minor parties took 3 million votes from the ALP and the Liberal and National parties (Harris, cited in Marr 2017b, p. 143). At the 2017 Queensland state election, only 69% of voters cast their ballot for the ALP or the Liberal-National Party (a formal coalition in that state) (Electoral Commission Queensland 2017).[2] Leadership changes, the dual citizenship fiasco (see Chap. 6 of this volume), and a policy impasse may account for why voters moved away from the major parties at that particular election. Hanson, as with many other minor parties, benefits from voter discontent with the ALP and LNP.

This leads us to a central issue in contemporary Australian politics: To what lengths will Australians tolerate populists? In 1996, the Australian electorate was acquiescent to Howard's popular appeals to the "mainstream" and his promise to govern "For All of Us" (Howard 1996 cited in Brett 2005, p. 30). As Howard said "Our slogan 'For All of Us' brought together in a very effective fashion the mood and the resentments of the Australian people towards the type of government that they

---

[1] All voting data is for primary votes in the House of Representatives
[2] Queensland voting data is primary votes.

had experienced over thirteen years" (Howard 1996, cited in Brett 2005, p. 30). In the Queensland electorate of Oxley, voters were willing to support Hanson's populist appeals for government for "ordinary' people". In both cases, voters were responding to popular appeals that tapped into dissatisfaction. But this is very different from the hardened support for right-wing populism, as represented by Reclaim Australia and the plethora of other far-right political parties and organizations sitting on the fringes of Australian politics, as discussed by Kathryn Crosby in Chap. 6 of this book. Arguably, Australia has little taste for the extremism of European and American leaders on the radical right. But with the election of Hanson, at least, it does suggest that Australians will engage with populism when in narrates positions that are anti-party and anti-parliamentary institutions (Murphy 2016).

In comparing Hanson's ideological position in 1996 to her position in 2016, the argument of this chapter is that Hanson has become more extreme. In the post-Howard period, the competition for votes on the right has become more congested. Facing opposition from parties like the protectionist Katter's Australia Party, the nationalist Rise Up Australia Party, the anti-Islamic Australian Liberty Alliance, and the socially conservative Family First, as well as from individuals like Cory Bernardi and George Christensen, Hanson now has clearly identifiable rivals occupying broadly the same ideological space, all of whom contest elections. In order to sustain her electoral currency in the current period, Hanson has adopted more fanatical positions. This is evident when you compare Hanson's maiden speech in the House of Representatives in 1996 and her first speech in the Senate in 2016. In moving further to the right, Hanson risks rendering mute whatever popular voice she gave to "ordinary" Australians in 1996. Arguably, the hardening of Hanson's ideological position bodes poorly for her electoral future and that of One Nation.

While race remains the central core of Hanson's position, her view has hardened. In 1996, Hanson opposed Asian immigration. In 2016, she wanted Islam banned in Australia. In 1996, Hanson attacked Indigenous Australians. In 2016 Hanson had nothing to say about Indigenous Australians. In 1996, Hanson blamed globalization for the ills facing Australia. In 2016, the list of who to blame was much longer. In shifting her position further to the extreme right, Hanson risks what electoral support she has from the disaffected post-industrial working class and the social conservatives who supported her in 1996. Conversely, while she may appeal to those aligned with organizations like Reclaim Australia, this constituency is not large enough or organized enough to deliver Hanson the votes she needs to claim any sort of mandate for her extremism.

Before moving on to the basis of the claims I have made to date, I want to return to the issue of policy. How much of Hanson's ideological position can be under-stood as policy? To talk of policy suggests a set of targeted changes and outcomes which, via parliamentary processes, seek legislative change. Hanson, at least in 1996, sought changes in government policy, notably in the areas of race politics, specifically Indigenous Affairs and Immigration. Because of Howard's own views, and with one eye on polling, Hanson did have some effect. However, in 2016 Hanson's policy agenda, as at least noted in her first speech to the Senate which calls for the banning of Islam (Hanson 2016), failed to offer a legislative pathway to achieve this and, furthermore, she appears to not recognize the constitutional impossibility of such a task.[3] Without a clear legislative pathway, and more so, without any coherent policy detail, does this leave Hansonism as a party of protest?

If not a policy party, PHONP has come to represent a protest movement. It is a movement that, as I have noted, has hardened since 1996. In 2016, PHONP represented more extreme, intemperate positions. While Howard placated Hanson in 1996 (Wear 2008), and was condemned for it (Brett 2003), the Liberal and National parties continue their dalliances with Hanson (noting the preference deals done between Hanson and the Liberals at the 2017 West Australian election, and the deal done in the Queensland state elections). While current Prime Minister Malcolm Turnbull may not repeat this mistake at the next federal election, he is still enacting policies that Hanson "applaud[s]" as "victories for her cause" (Marr 2017b, p. 144) . Among these are an unwavering opposition to asylum seekers entering Australia, the holding of a Royal Commission into the banking and financial services sector, and allowing machinations (albeit unsuccessful ones) to kill off the changes to marriage laws within his own parliamentary Liberal Party. Shifting the Coalition Government further to the right placates Hanson (as it did in 1996) and emboldens her to call for more extreme change.

The ALP is also complicit in this. In its demand for a banking Royal Commission, its pursuit of legislation to ensure multinationals pay tax on profits made in Australia, its unwavering bipartisanship on opposing asylum seekers entry to Australia, and its dabbling in economic nationalism (still popular in the right-wing of the ALP) it also encourages Hanson. But as Marr (2017b, p. 141) suggests, there is no "reason to "kowtow to her [Hanson]". More so, any policy shifts to the right by the ALP or the LNP will only give Hanson momentum to call for more extreme positions. There is a risk for Hanson here as well. In shifting further to the right, she will alienate those who supported her in 1996 and swap that support for those aligned with extreme racist views on Islam (Reclaim Australia). Placating Hanson will only embolden her to push the policy agenda further to the right. This may hurt her but it will hurt the Australian nation more.

There has been a shift in Hanson's rhetoric since 1996. Less and less is there any sense that Hanson is seeking a pragmatic agenda of social conservatism or economic nationalism as she did 20 years ago. Her positions have hardened as she flirts with organizations on the extreme right in her search for votes. The logical extension is that Hansonism becomes more chaotic in its policy demands, and it becomes more hostile in its views about government. Populism, as Murphy (2016, p. 8) asserts, is already embedded with an "anti-institutionalism" which "downplays party and parliamentary organisations". This was Hanson's view in 1996 but it became much firmer in 2016.

Hanson will claim she is responsible for the shifts to the right in Australian politics; this should be countered. Hanson isn't interested in legislative change. Her role from 2016 has been little more than sitting in parliament as an outsider, the

---

[3] Section 116 of the Australian Constitution prohibits the Commonwealth Government from "prohibiting the free exercise of any religion". See Australian Government (2017).

"anti-politician" (Manne 1998a, p. 89), pointing to the incompetence of the ALP and the Liberal and National parties, all to maintain discontent.

Crystallizing my view about Hanson's lack of interest in policy prescriptions in 2016 has been my observation of another politician, in many ways not dissimilar to Hanson, namely the former Tasmanian Senator Jackie Lambie. Lambie and Hanson share much. They are both "maverick" politicians (for a discussion, see Chap. 6 of this book) who *prima facie* possess an authenticity that appeals to the disaffected (albeit they come from different backgrounds and different perspectives have informed their narratives; see Kurmelovs 2017). Both narrate their positions with voices of outrage that claim to reflect the frustrations "ordinary" Australians have with the major parties and the processes of government. Both are populists, relying on homespun anecdotes as evidence of the failing of public policy and a disintegrating political system. Both rely on media spectacles to give oxygen to their causes. Both, as Alan Scott notes in Chap. 11 of this book, are populists with an "appeal to the people—and to the 'will of the people'—against the elite". But there is at least one fundamental difference between the two: Lambie wanted the federal parliament to fix things; Hanson isn't interested in reform.

Hanson isn't like Lambie, or even Donald Trump. Trump and Lambie share a view that the problem facing their respective nations is not the political system (the Congress or the federal parliament); rather, it is the people who sit in the chambers: self-serving, out of touch, and more interested in protecting special interests. While this may sound like Hanson, Hanson isn't interested in, as Trump puts it, "draining the swamp". Hanson, and what Hansonism represents, is iconoclastic. She represents a revolt against "government"—always unnamed and all to blame for Australia's social, cultural, and economic ills. The Senate response to Lambie's resignation from Parliament (because of her dual citizenship under Sect. 44 of the Constitution—again, see Chap. 6 of this volume) consolidated a view that, regardless of Lambie's policy positions, she was a respected Senator seen as willing to work with legislators to seek better outcomes for her constituency. Is Hanson seen in the same light? I don't think so. This is not a personal view of Hanson, rather it is based on a view that populists like Lambie, Trump, and even John Howard consider the "people" as the arbiters of good governance, as do most democrats. Yet, for Hanson, the "people" have determined that the problem is with the institution of government itself: a view she increasingly advocates.

To understand how I have come to these positions, a broad political and social land-scape needs to be drawn. No discussion of Hanson can begin without acknowledging the shifting national mood that saw the defeat of the Keating Labor Government and the election of the Howard Coalition Government in 1996. This, and a review of Hanson's election to the seat of Oxley in 1996, Hanson's House of Representatives maiden speech (10 September 1996), and the 1998 Queensland state election, pro-vide a context within which to review Hanson's ideological positions—or Hanson 1.0. This is followed with an assessment of Hanson's positions in 2016, drawn from her first Senate speech (14 September 2016)—Hanson 2.0. In between, is a review of Hanson's period in the electoral wilderness. Her period of exclusion from fed-eral politics has drawn little scholarly attention, with studies rightly focused on her time in Canberra. However, I think her time in the electoral wilderness (1998–2016) explains much about Hanson. It is in this period of continual electoral defeats for federal and state seats in Queensland and NSW that Hanson's views harden and point to the contemporary nature of what Hanson 2.0 is.

9.2   1996: Keating and Howard

A set of unique political and electoral circumstances meant that the 1996 federal election was one that saw two leaders with very distinct ideological views of Australia, its past and its future, seek a mandate. Keating probably should have lost the 1993 election, but for Hawke's refusal to hand over the leadership earlier. Keating, however, won the 1993 election on the back of Hewson's disastrous *Fight Back* policy (van Onselen and Errington 2007). Howard's leadership aspirations were killed off in the 1980s by ructions within the Coalition and because of the absurdity of the Joh Bjelke-Petersen for PM campaign (Coleman and Costello 2009). Yet a lack of political alternatives, after the failings of Hewson and Downer, saw Howard's return. Howard himself concedes this (Howard 2010). However, Howard claims the other reason for his return to the leadership was that he was a "conviction politician" who "stood for certain things" (Howard 2010, p. 212). This included ending the "perpetual naval-gazing about [Australian] cultural identity" that emphasized "shame and guilt" over "enterprise and individualism" (Howard 2010, p. 233).

The election of the Howard Government with a 44-seat majority in the House of Representatives (Barber and Johnson 2014) was a rejection of Keating's economic and social agenda for an independent Australia, engaged with Asia, reconciled with Indigenous Australians, and benefitting from an open economy. Yet, apart from changes to taxation policy and the introduction of the GST, Howard maintained Keating's fiscal policies. This itself, and given Howard was to stay in government until 2007, is curious. It is widely accepted that Keating's economic reforms hurt many Australians. Record high unemployment rates, coupled with record high interest rates, had devastating effects on the national economy. In electorates like Oxley, this hurt. The Howard Government though, did benefit from a mining boom that offset unemployment and filled government coffers with tax revenue, a rising Australian dollar that offset national debt, declining interest rates, and rising house prices and real wages growth, all which left Australians feeling less economically vulnerable (see Tiffen and Gittens 2009).

But in the area of social policy, more radical changes would occur. Howard's calls for a more "comfortable and relaxed" Australia (see Lateline 2018) would mean a rejection of political correctness, special interests, and the intelligentsia. Arguably, this was a negative shift in terms of policy. Howard proposed to govern for "All of Us" although this was a dog-whistle for the urban middle and upper class elite to support his attacks on the welfare state and on progressive public policy. As a result, between 1996 and 2007 Australia underwent a period in which social conservatism became the lynchpin of Australian policy. The Republic was defeated. Land rights was moved out of the national spotlight. The Aboriginal and Torres Strait Islander Commission (ATSIC) was dismantled. Marriage was legally defined as between a man and a woman[4]. Australia would introduce some of the harshest immigration restriction policies and punitively deny refugees asylum. Political correctness would be framed as the means of out-of-touch intellectual elites and the chattering classes to deny the common-sense aspirations of "ordinary" Australians.

Others have written at length about the contested nature of Australian identity, and its expressions in the Culture and History Wars of the period. The aim here is not to provide an analysis of the Keating-Howard years and their competing ideological views. Rather the point is to highlight that 1996 marked a distinct conservative turn in the direction of Australian policy which Robert Manne (2001, p. 7) describes as a "closing of minds" and "the hardening of hearts". Manne's view, however, misrepresents the nature of Howard's social conservatism and doesn't explain the nation's apparent acquiescence for Howard's social conservative agenda.

As a social conservative, Howard was able to articulate an orthodoxy that he reflected well in his call for a more "relaxed and comfortable" Australia. This narrative suggested Howard would steer Australia away from the "abstract scheme[s]" embedded in the Keating agenda and, instead, place faith in "pragmatic principles" that would "preserve the things" Howard believed were the most "valuable aspects of Australia" (Melleuish 2009, pp. 44–45). These were the "practices and habits of ordinary people", for they were the "best guardians of their own traditions" (Melleuish 2009, pp. 44–45). Policies that were harmful to the "established practices" of Australia, and that hindered individuals, required reform (Melleuish 2009, pp. 44–45). Conversely, there was no need for state intervention to preserve the common sense of ordinary Australians (Melleuish 2009, pp. 44–45). This was Howard's revival and re-centering of social conservatism in Australian policy.

If Howard was given a national mandate to rid Australian policy of Keating's "abstract schemes", and policy that was "harmful" to the practices and aspirations of "ordinary" Australians, then why did Hanson emerge as such a virulent force in Australian politics in 1996? Surely those voters alienated both economically and socially by what they saw as Keating's governance on "behalf of a politically correct elite … who arrogantly, coercively and disastrously tried to ram his version of a multicultural, pro-Asian, pro-Aboriginal Australia down the throats of an unwilling nation" (Manne 1998b, p. 6) had found their champion in Howard. Howard's "sympathies", including his "detestation of political correctness, his unease with the idea of multiculturalism, his suspicion of the Aboriginal 'industry' [and] his repudiation of the 'black armband' version of Australian history" (Manne 1998b, p. 6), should have negated an ideological space for Hansonism to emerge. A rejection of the Keating Government alone doesn't capture the reason for Hanson's rise. If so, Howard would

---

[4]In 2004 the Howard Government passed the *Marriage Amendment Act (2004)* of the *Marriage Act 1961*. Subsection 5(1) was included stating "marriage means the union of a man and a woman to the exclusion of all others, voluntarily entered into for life" (Australian Government 2004).

have been a voting option for those discontented and alienated. Arguably, there is more to understand about Hanson and Hansonism in 1996. A return to her origins in the seat of Oxley is revealing.

9.3   1996 Oxley Election

Representative government is predicated on parliamentary delegates addressing and alleviating our discontent. Leadership and policy guide a nation through periods of economic and social prosperity and similarly guide us in times of uncertainty. When uncertainty and discontent become the prevailing conditions for daily life, when leadership and policy are missing, it is natural as a society that we begin to question our foundational institutions. In contexts such as these it is reasonable that intellectuals may write about the demise of the nation state. However, for those living in the Queensland electorate of Oxley in 1996, the discussion wasn't about the demise of the nation state. It was something more visceral: an inflamed sense of the failure of governments to do what they are elected to do—govern. There exist, in places like Oxley, those with a view that governments themselves are the problem. These, in 1996, were Hanson's people. To ignore them is to do so at our peril. This is not to be taken as support for Hansonism. It is not. But without attempting to understand what drives Hansonism, then and now, risks responses that will embolden rather than counter the dystopian nation that Hanson seeks.

Pauline Hanson was elected to the Labor-dominated Ipswich City Council in 1994 as an independent. Her short time on council was spent opposing an Indigenous child-care center. In March 1995, following council boundary changes, she was defeated by 132 votes. She claimed to be a victim of candidates putting her last on their how-to-vote cards. Unperturbed, she joined the Liberal Party and secured preselection for the seat of Oxley. She was dis-endorsed by the Liberal Party for her grievances about Indigenous entitlement printed in the *Brisbane Times*. Hanson wrote: "How can you expect this race to help themselves when government showers them with money, facilities and opportunities that only these people can obtain no matter how minute the indigenous blood that is flowing through their veins ..." (Hanson, cited in Jull 2000, p. 206). While a grievance about supposed entitlements, it also articulates Hanson's subjective view about the authenticity of Indigenous identity. There is no policy prescription in this or other Hanson campaign claims. Rather, her campaign for Oxley is a litany of complaints and accusations that "government had neglected *them* in favour of someone *else*" (Brett 1998, p. 36; emphasis added).

By the time of Hanson's dis-endorsement by the Liberal Party, the ballot papers for Oxley were already printed and she appeared as the Liberal Party candidate. However, there is little to suggest that the voters of Oxley were electing a Liberal to the House of Representatives. Past election results show that the voters of Oxley had little taste for the Liberal Party. The Liberal candidate at the 1993 federal election, George Blain, secured only 25% of the primary vote. More so, from 1961 to 1996 Oxley was a safe Labor seat. It had been held by Whitlam and Hawke Cabinet Minister, and later Governor General, Bill Hayden, from 1961 until 1988. Of some interest is that Hayden was the only Queensland MP to retain his seat at the 1975 election, following Whitlam's dismissal (Farnsworth 2018). Les Scott (ALP) replaced Hayden in a by-election in 1988, with a two-party preferred vote of 53%, increasing his margin to 62% (1990 general election) and slightly again, to 62.5% (1993) (Carr 2018). At the 1996 election, Hanson defeated Scott with a two-party preferred vote of 54.5%. What explains this? The voters of Oxley seem to have dismissed Howard's appeal for a more "comfortable and relaxed" Australia and instead, voted for an inexperienced independent politician who offered little by way of policy prescriptions. One explanation for this is that Oxley voters were rejecting both major parties.

The rejection of Keating's Labor Party is relatively straightforward to understand: Keating's policies hurt. As an outer suburban Brisbane electorate, it is, like many others in urban Australia, a mix of small business and light industry that adversely felt the impact of Keating's economic restructuring. High interest rates, welfare cuts, and declining manufacturing jobs were felt by workers and families in Oxley (Wear 2013). Voters there were less concerned with Asian engagement, the Republic, or Indigenous rights and more concerned with paying their mortgages, the rising cost of living, and the specter or reality of unemployment. As Judith Brett (1998, p. 27) puts it, "nearly two decades of economic liberalism has left many people worse off". The economic reforms embedded in Keating's *One Nation* policy and the reframing of Australian culture found in his *Creative Nation* policy did little to stave off mortgage foreclosures or family breakdowns. Voters of Oxley had enough of Labor, but had little appetite for the Liberal candidate. Oxley never had a tradition of voting Liberal, but this doesn't explain much. A number of electorates swung to the Liberal Party in 1996, including other rusted-on Labor seats. In 1996, Oxley voters were rejecting both the major parties. In 1996, they were also rejecting everyone else. The Australian Democrats and the Australian Greens secured less than 9% of the primary vote between them. The three other independents collectively secured less than 3%. Hanson secured 48% of the primary vote (Barber and Johnson 2014).

Hanson, an outspoken councillor, a local businesswoman, who for a while was a Liberal, would do. Her views were well known, but un-crafted. She spoke like them, she was one of them, and she came unencumbered by loyalties to anyone, especially the Liberal Party. Within days of Keating calling the federal election, she made one claim that may have cemented her election. In response to an Indigenous protest (because of her comments in the *Brisbane Times*) held at her fish and chip shop (Marden's Seafoods in Ipswich), Hanson declared, "I will not back down" (Hanson, cited in Marr 2017a, p. 23). Stripped of preselection, Hanson spent the last two weeks of the 1996 campaign as an independent. She did, however, benefit from the Liberal machine that helped her campaign in the final weeks. On reflection, it was a remarkable election result. Australian voters have shown little interest in electing independents to the House of Representatives in any significant numbers. What changed in Oxley in 1996? Hanson herself is one answer, which I address shortly; the other answer is that both the Liberal and Labor parties were being rejected.

9.4   First Speech 1996

On 10 September 1996, Hanson delivered her first speech to the House of Representatives, described as "demonic, blunt and dripping with contempt for Aborigines
and Asians" (Marr 2017a, p. 28). In a quavering voice, an apparent hallmark of her
authenticity, and noting her difference from professional politicians, she unleashed
Hansonism. The grievances she had expressed during the election campaign about
Indigenous entitlements were by then honed into a narrative of discontent being felt
by "ordinary" Australians, forced upon them by an indifferent political system, led
by self-serving out-of-touch politicians. Drawing on racial intolerance (something
neither new or unfamiliar in Australian politics) and giving voice to the "truth" that
the undeserving were being catered to at the expense of deserving "real" Australians,
Hanson's speech was directed to the national electorate, as much as to the voters of
Oxley. For those feeling disenfranchised from party politics, alienated by Keating's
agenda, and dismissive of Howard's promises, Hanson would be their voice and their
champion. Her role in federal politics wasn't to change the system (although, because
of Howard there were policy changes); it was to empower the resentful and fearful.
Here there are similarities to 2016.

A central plank in understanding Hansonism, and it remains a common theme in
2016, is that Hanson and One Nation (in its various names and deliberate authoritarian
structures) is not about policy change. Hanson's demands in 1996, as in 2016, are little
to do with policy reform or legislative change. Any legislative changes—in line with
Hanson's views—that occurred in 1996–1998 or from 2016 onwards are the result
of the federal Coalition (Howard seeking One Nation votes and Turnbull bowing
to conservative pressure within the Coalition). Hanson's positions are not easily
legislated as they lack any detail—instead they are mostly periphrastic. Further, in a
plural parliament there is no political will to embark on Hanson's calls for a radical
reconfiguration of domestic and international policies, treaties, or alliances. Hanson,
in 1996 and 2016, isn't about reform. She isn't about changing policy. She is about
empowering the resentful and the fearful, each with their own set of antipathies
and anxieties that are morphed into a narrative of envy, fear, and anger. This is
why Hanson, rather than Howard, became their champion in 1996. Howard would
engage in pragmatic reform. Hansonism isn't about reform. It is in this context that
it is reasonable to ask, as David Marr (2017a, p. 7) does, is Hansonism a "party of
protest or a party of policy?"

While there is some contestation about who wrote her first speech, that debate
is mostly mute. Hanson stood and delivered a litany of claims, delivered in the
name of "ordinary" Australians. Laying blame with political and intellectual elites
advancing political correctness, Hanson claimed that ordinary taxpayers were not
only funding the elites, but taxpayers were also funding Indigenous privilege. Hanson
attested that government (unnamed) was providing "opportunities, land, moneys
and facilities available only to Aboriginals" (Hanson 1996). Denouncing Indigenous
disadvantage as false, she continued that the "privileges Aboriginals enjoy over other
Australians" is something that "millions of Australians" were "fed up to the back

teeth" with. Her response was to call for the abolishment of ATSIC, which Howard did in 2004. Howard's decision to abolish ATSIC may have been born from his own prejudices, from a lack of understanding about Indigenous politics, or it may have been considered by Howard as part of his pragmatic conservatism to "reform" that which harms "ordinary" Australia. In the latter sense, it may have also been what David Marr (2017a, p. 5) refers to as Howard seeking out "small pockets of [Hanson] voters out on the fringe".

Demands for changes were signaled when Hanson claimed "ordinary Australian" were "kept out of any debate" about immigration and multiculturalism. The dismantling of multiculturalism and a radical review of immigration policy were called for, with the latter also adopted by the Howard Government. The basis for the latter claim was that Australia was in "danger of being swamped by Asians", who "have their own culture and religion, form ghettos and do not assimilate" (Hanson 1996). Acknowledging she would be called a racist for such comments, this itself was an appeal to those who felt silenced because of political correctness. More so, it is compounded by the homespun claim that "if I can invite whom I want into my home, then I should have the right to have a say in who comes into my country" (Hanson 1996). Again, Howard appropriated this position at the 2001 federal election when he said with reference to asylum seekers: "We will decide who comes to this country and the circumstances in which they come" (Howard 2001, p. 4).

High unemployment, rising national debt, falling living standards, declines in real wages, calls for the repeal of the *Family Law Act*, and opposition to the selling of government assets followed, all providing a platform for Hanson to narrate her ideological differences from other politicians (Hanson 1996). In this rhetorical space, and addressing a nation audience via the echo chamber of the mass media that reported the speech at length, Hanson was talking to those resentful and alienated. She was "one of them" who lives in the "real world". On foreign policy, Hanson called for cuts to foreign aid, Australian withdrawal from the United Nations, tearing up of UN treaties signed by Australia, and tariff increases. These demands merged into calls for job creation programs and the introduction of national service. Hanson postulated an isolationist position for Australia that arguably engaged with the discontent associated with globalization, specifically its impact on Australian manufacturing jobs and farmers. Her speech, to an almost empty parliamentary chamber, claims Hanson, reflects "mainstream Australia", for whom she would speak and stand up for because like them she is an "ordinary Australian" (Hanson 1996).

What does this 1996 speech tell us about the politics of Hansonism? Hanson, an independent, represented one electorate in a parliament with a clear government majority. One Nation was yet to be formed and the Queensland state election was two years away. What mandate did Hanson have for such policy calls? Yet, Howard gave Hanson tacit approval, saying: "… people do feel able to speak a little more freely and a little more openly about what they feel … the pall of censorship on certain issues has been lifted … and I think that's a very good thing …" (Howard 1996, p. 4). It was the second time Hanson was given the approval of the Liberal Party.

9.5   1998 Queensland Election

Why the 1998 Queensland election concerned Howard so much is of interest. He had a clear majority in the House of Representatives and wasn't due to face a federal election until 1999 (although he did call the next federal election for 1998). But, with the Queensland state election looming, Howard did a deal with Hanson over preferences. This cost the Liberal Party a significant number of votes and more significantly exposed the Liberal and National parties to internal and national criticisms. As David Marr (2017a, p. 40) notes, Hanson voters—both then and now—pride themselves on their independence. More so, if they are voters with a distaste for both major parties they would likely ignore any preference arrangement anyway, even one to which Hanson agreed. Hanson was pulling Howard's strings; all the more power to her would have been the mantra of her supporters. Queenslanders voted, delivering Hanson 11 seats from the Nationals and the Labor Party, resulting in a hung parliament (Peter Beattie formed a minority ALP government with independent Peter Wellington). (Newman 1998). The Labor Party stayed in power until 2012.

The decision to hold an early federal election (1998 rather than 1999), coupled with the internal backlash from the Queensland poll, meant Howard and the Liberals and Nationals could no longer consider preference deals with Hanson. Putting Hanson last, and a redistribution of the seat of Oxley, left Hanson to contemplate contesting the Senate or the lower house seat of Blair (Queensland). She chose the latter and was defeated after two years in federal politics. While the One Nation vote was high in Blair and almost one million people voted for One Nation in the Senate, preferences kept Hanson out and saw only one One Nation Senator elected, Heather Hill (Barber and Johnson 2014). Hill was later disqualified under Section 44 of the Constitution and was replaced by Len Harris. Harris lost his Senate seat at the 2004 election, securing only 0.2% of the quota (AEC 2004).

9.6   Hanson's Political Wilderness

Preferences hurt Hanson at the 1998 federal election. While One Nation House of Representative candidates received 8% of the national vote, it was not nearly enough for any to be elected. Hanson, contesting the seat of Blair, secured 36% of the primary vote but was defeated by the Coalition by 4600 votes because of ALP preferences (Barber and Johnson 2014). Policy hurt Hanson at the 1998 election. At this poll Howard wanted a mandate to introduce a Goods and Services Tax (GST). With the electorate focused on tax policy, Hanson's fiscally irresponsible 2% flat tax policy was ridiculed by the electorate. Even though the Coalition suffered a two-party preferred swing against them of 4.6% and secured only 49% of the vote (the ALP secured nearly 51%) the Howard Government was returned with a reduced majority (losing 14 seats and the ALP winning 18 seats) (AEC 1998).

Even with the splintering of One Nation (David Oldfield broke from One Nation and formed One Nation NSW), One Nation managed to win three seats at the West Australian state election in 2001. The Tampa Affair and September 11 foreshadowed race as an issue at the 2001 November federal election. Hanson, contesting a Queensland Senate seat, and Howard both wrapped themselves in the national flag and proclaimed various versions of "deciding who will come into the country/their homes". If 1996 was a race election, it paled into insignificance on 10 November 2001. To ignore the Hanson vote in this period would be an oversight. Hanson secured 10% of the vote at the 2001 federal election; however, preferences denied her a return to parliament. Hanson lost the last Senate spot to the Nationals' Ron Bosswell. Hansonism, in its various incarnations, apart from winning seats in WA, won seats at the 2001, 2004, and 2006 Queensland state elections (Moore 2016).

Poor federal electoral returns were likely a result of the jailing of Pauline Hanson and David Ettridge in 2003, which impacted on media coverage; however, the jailing of Hanson likely steeled support for her, especially when Liberals like Bronwyn Bishop claimed Hanson was Australia's first "political prisoner" (Bishop, cited in Kirk 2003, p. 1). Hanson and Ettridge were charged with gaining advantage by registering a political party to recoup electoral costs. They claimed that Pauline Hanson's One Nation party had 1000 members when in fact the party had this number of supporters, rather than members. In order to claim electoral expenses a political party must have 500 members and a member of parliament. One Nation had only three members: Hanson, Ettridge, and Oldfield. Ettridge and Hanson were charged with fraud on 5 July 2001 and jailed for three years on 20 August 2003. Hanson voters identified that it was the "politicians that drove Hanson out of parliament" (Marr 2017a, p. 59). After 11 weeks in jail, the Court of Appeals overturned the convictions and the pair were released (Crime and Misconduct Commission 2004).

The missing years tell us as much about Hanson as the years she sat in the House of Representatives. Her supporters remained loyal to her; her jailing was seen as a political act to silence her. "The system let me down, like it let a lot of people down" proclaimed Hanson on her release from jail (Hanson cited in Marr 2017a, p. 62). Her first statement is one of a failed system. Narratives of failed legal, political, and electoral systems pervade Hanson's time out of politics. For Hanson, her time in the political wilderness was the fault of "government" machinations (government meaning Canberra, the establishment, the political elite, the intelligentsia, the chattering classes, the ABC). The preference deals that put One Nation last, the collusion between 'government' forces, and the jailing of Hanson emboldened her anti-government views.

The period of Hanson's political wilderness tells us a lot about the intensification and trajectory of Hansonism. In the political wilderness, there was a hardening of Hansonism, both the racism that pervaded her period in politics between 1996 and 1998 and hardening of Hanson's anti-government rhetoric. During the 1996–1998 period, Hanson's statements reflected a view that "ordinary" Australians wanted responsible, accountable government. She had faith in the democratic process because of its "capacity to express the voice of the people" (Stokes 2000, p. 31). It was a democratic populism that called for political institutions to be returned to the "people", so that democracy could be "re-invigorated" (Stokes 2000, p. 32). In doing so, power would be taken away from the elites and the major parties who "impaired the working of Australian democracy" (Stokes 2000, p. 30). Under the control of political elites, government "abandoned their responsibilities to the people they are supposed to serve" and they enacted "bad legislation" (gun control) against the "wishes of the people" (Stokes 2000, p. 30). Unresponsive and irresponsible government occurred because of the party system and the "true believers" who placed their party before the "national interest" (Stokes 2000, pp. 30–31). This type of democratic populism is not new—for more detail see the discussion by Tod Moore in Chap. 11 of this book. As Moore makes clear, such populist calls for power to be returned to the people have pervaded the history of Australian politics. However, by the time of Hanson's re-emergence from the political wilderness, she had little to say about a desire for responsible, accountable government, or its return to the people.

Views about governments, unnamed and undefined, and the institutions of the states (the court that jailed Hanson and that she claimed let "people down") solidified. More so, her opposition to organized forms of power consolidated. Anti-union rhetoric pervaded, driven by inflated instances of union corruption. Anti-bank views hardened on the back of revelations of unethical lending and advice practices and skyrocketing profits. Anti-big business views consolidated as the cause of hurt for farmers, light manufacturers, and small shop owners. Hostility emerged towards big mining companies, who were doing deals with native title owners. Anti-competitive practices were lambasted. Opposition to trade deals, especially with China, and foreign ownership (often with racist undertones) were framed into narratives purporting to be evidence of the collusion against "ordinary" Australians—sometimes small business owners, sometimes farmers. These views are evident in Hanson's first Senate speech (see Hanson 2016).

Hostile views about the ABC were widened to include the broader mainstream media, who were operating in some sort of conspiracy to deny Hanson airtime to say what she wanted without interruption. The government, the courts, the unions, the banks, big business, and the media were all acting in unison against the interests of "ordinary" Australians, and only Hanson had the courage to challenge them. There was no sense of the people demanding responsible and responsive government; the narrative had moved to Hanson being the savior of "ordinary" Australians. It is in the political wilderness that a hardening of Hansonism emerges. This is not to deny that race is still a factor. As noted, race is embedded in views about trade, big business, and foreign ownership, but the trajectory of race took a turn in 2007 (Marr 2017a).

Another realization about the Hanson phenomenon is found in the periods when Hanson wasn't in parliament. Hanson's own electoral success is evident when she is in control of One Nation. It doesn't seem to matter to Hanson voters what the party is called: Pauline Hanson's One Nation or the United Australia Party (2007–2010), as long as it was Hanson, front and center, on the news and giving voice to them. As Marr (2017a, p. 6) puts it, "without Hanson there is no party". Hanson herself is Hansonism. Her own identity, her personal narrative, her lived political experiences, her image, and her voice all convey that which informs Hansonism. Hanson is the expression of a form of populism that melds her own narrative with a particularly nostalgic view of Australia, of the individual battling the elites, reminiscent of the Australian Legend or Ned Kelly. It uses language familiar to her voters, in terms they understand, and says what the politically correct elites deny. It gives voice to the grievances held against governments, banks, big business, and the other orga- nized forces that have erred against "ordinary" Australians. It is much more than opposition to Keating or distrust of Howard. It is a form of Australian populism that is embedded with a longing for not just a better economic deal, but for a mythical past. It is in this sense that Marr (2017b, p. 143) is correct to argue that "we need to realize the gloom driving people into Hanson's camp" isn't just economics. But how Hanson appeals to such a miscellaneous set of desires and hard-to-quantify sets of aspirations has puzzled commentators since the 1990s. One way to view Han- son is the consolidation of "brand" Hanson that arguably emerges in the in-between years. As Murphy (2016) notes, populists are not dissimilar to what we associate with the branding of commodities. They are similarly advertised, becoming "media personalities" (as in the case of Donald Trump) and from this platform they emerg- ing as "table thumping pundits delivering a charged mishmash of anti-establishment rhetoric and anger-baiting identity politics" (Murphy 2016, p. 10). As noted below, it is in the in-between years that Hanson remained in the national imagination with notable appearances on reality television.

As a "brand" politician (for a broader discussion of "brand" politicians see Street 2004; Zavattaro 2010), Hanson has a political style that informs her agenda as much as her dogma does. While much of what is written about Hanson focuses on the many inaccuracies of her claims, it sometimes dismisses the woman herself. One example of "Brand" Hanson that can be offered is her voice: its quavering and unsteady inflection, jolting, with long pauses, jumping erratically around half-formed sentences. It is nervous and tense, while at the same time, full of fervor. It is not always what she says—which likely accounts for the diversity of her demographic appeal—it is how she says it. Hanson, her voice, is judged by her supporters as being authentic. Anecdotes of Hanson voters saying things like "I don't always agree with her but I respect her", is a reflection of what they are identifying as an authenticity. Authenticity is a popular and powerful commodity in politics.

Hanson's quavering voice posits her authenticity and marks her as not like one of "those" Canberra politicians. This, coupled with a carefully crafted narrative of strug- gle (as a single mother), a small business operator, a political victim, and victimized because of her political and racial views, and her claims of being an "ordinary" Aus- tralian, posit Hanson as outside of the prism that is used to judge other politicians. She would remain feminine (noted in her choice of dresses and splashes of vivid color), while fighting the old guard of grey-suited men in Canberra. When needed she would wrap herself in the flag. She would make mistakes—the "death video" (Hanson 1997) and the wearing of the burqa in the Senate (Hanson 2017)—but these are media spectacles that elevate "brand" Hanson into the stratosphere (at least for her supporters).

Hanson's time in the political wilderness was not wasted. While without a party and unable to win a state or federal seat, not without trying, "Brand" Hanson stayed in the public view. On reality television, or as a political commentator, she remained in the public gaze, given a megaphone for her particular brand of populism. Social media would also provide Hanson 2.0 with a vehicle unavailable to her in the 1990s. As a politician, Hanson needs the media, yet she loathes journalists' questions and interruptions (Marr 2017a) . What she needed was to speak directly to the "people". Social media allows this. Her Facebook page, established in 2013 (Pauline Hanson's Please Explain), provides a vehicle for Hanson to talk directly to her supporters. No journalists asking questions. One-way communication from Hanson to Hanson voters, supplemented with "likes" and encouragement from her supporters to "keep going".

At the time of writing (July 2018), her Facebook page as Senator for Queensland has almost 229,000 followers (Facebook 2018). While Facebook alone would not get Hanson elected, her last tilt before the 2016 Senate result—standing in the Queensland state seat of Lockyer at the 2015 election—saw her go to within 114 votes of beating the sitting Liberal member, Ian Rickuss. The two-party preferred count was 13,230–13,116: a first preference swing to Hanson of over 26% (ABC News 2015). Anti-Muslim rhetoric, growing since 2007, paid off. The Queensland poll was held weeks after the 2014 Lindt Café shooting in Sydney. Race was back on the agenda.

9.7 Hanson 2.0

In 2016, when Hanson stood to deliver her first speech to the Senate, her voice still quavered, but the Senate was full. She announced, "I'm back—but not alone" (Hanson 2016). Hanson was joined in the Senate by Malcolm Roberts (Queensland), Brian Burston (NSW), and Rob Culleton (WA). Culleton was found to be ineligible and was replaced by Peter Georgiou.

In Hanson's first speech to the Senate (14 September 2016), delivered 20 years and four days after her first speech to the House of Representatives (10 September 1996)—a speech Hanson claimed "shook the nation"—she rose to claim she was just as relevant in 2016 as she was in 1996. However, this time her opening claim was the "problem" with Australian leadership that was "giving away" Australian sovereignty and democracy, resulting in the nation's decline (Hanson 2016). This was evidenced, for Hanson, in "foreign takeovers of our land and assets, out-of-control debt, failing infrastructure, high unemployment … and the destruction of our farming sector" (Hanson 2016). Immigration, "aggressive multiculturalism", and terrorism were evidence of declining trust, social cohesion, and fear (Hanson 2016).

Hanson retreated from her 1996 position on Asian immigration, which she claimed was "not said out of disrespect for Asians" and instead claimed, "we are now in danger of being swamped by Muslims" (Hanson 2016). She called for a stop to Muslim immigration, the banning of the burqa, and a moratorium on the building of mosques in Australia. She cited a litany of assertions about Muslims having a culture and ideology that is "incompatible", and Islam not believing in democracy or free association. It is because of this that Hanson claims that Muslims disrespect Australian courts, jails allow them to radicalize others, they are three times more likely to be imprisoned, unemployed, and relying on welfare, that they are more "prominent" in organized crime and "associated with violence and drug dealing". Muslim men are "hyper-masculine", antisocial, and misogynistic. Muslims seek to aid ISIS. They are under ASIO surveillance (Hanson 2016). If this wasn't convincing enough for her constituents Hanson continued, bemoaning the access of Muslim women to swimming pools and the provision of prayer rooms in public places. Her strongest criticism is against the wearing of the burqa and halal food certification. All of this, posits Hanson, means that "Muslims want to see Sharia law introduced in Australia" (Hanson 2016). Australians, claimed Hanson, are fearful of crime when Muslims live in their suburbs (Hanson 2016).

This denunciation of Islam is much more detailed than her claims about Asians 1996. In 1996, Hanson claimed: "I believe we are in danger of being swamped by Asians. Between 1984 and 1995, 40% of all migrants coming into this country were of Asian origin. They have their own culture and religion, form ghettos, and do not assimilate" (Hanson 1996). This compares with her litany of subjective and extreme claims against Muslims in 2016. There is not only a shift in the target of her racial vilification, but there is a rancor in content and delivery. Calls for various bans and moratoriums are made, but this isn't a speech seeking a change of government policy, this is a speech that seeks to divide communities, incite fear, and stoke prejudices. It doesn't seek policy solutions, instead it appeases and empowers the far-right.

As a critique of immigration specifically and multiculturalism generally, in both speeches Hanson maintains that Australians have been locked out of relevant debates. In 2016, however, Hanson claims links between increased immigration intakes and increased welfare, and that immigration benefits "multinationals, banks and big business" at the expense of "ordinary" Australians. Money spent on immigrant welfare denies Australians jobs, infrastructure, schools, healthcare, and even water (Hanson 2016). Other themes of Hanson 2.0 include opposition to foreign investment, foreign ownership, and foreign "takeovers" of Australian resources (water and agricultural land) to the detriment of small towns and farming communities, and the reason for housing being beyond the reach of "ordinary" Australians. Also included is her opposition to aspects of Family Law and to the child support system: a claim repeated from 1996 but she provided no detail on what type of legislative reform was needed. Government rorts and mismanagement would be solved, claims Hanson, with the introduction of an Australian identity card. Government debt was "out of control" and "must be reined in" (Hanson 2016), though again no policy prescriptions were offered on how this could be done.

While this summary of her 2016 first speech may not have captured completely the shifts from 1996 to 2016, it is offered as one brief example of the hardening of Hanson's position. In rancor, as much as content, Hanson's position hardens, particularly her racial vilification of Muslims, though noting her subtle regret about Asian Australians, and her silence on Indigenous Australians. Her other claims remain mostly consistent with her 1996 claims; however, there isn't a sense that Hanson is proposing a set of concrete policy reforms. Without policy detail, Hanson's 2016 speech can only be seen as a set of extreme, unfounded, and xenophobic claims peppered with crude economic nationalist assertions spoken in the name of "ordinary" Australians.

It is a speech that seeks to divide us, to empower some, and to deny others. Hanson 2.0 isn't seeking to work as a crossbencher with government to address concerns that are obviously being felt in some parts of Australia. Instead the parliament affords Hanson a position to stir up the discontent felt nationally with the party system, and specifically with the LNP and the ALP. As Harris (in Marr 2017b, p. 143) notes, the collapse of the two-party system is the "major political shift of our time". In this collapsing terrain Hanson, as populists do, will sit back and let it implode. It is in the cleavages of discontent that Hanson can be found, and Hansonism understood, in 2016.

9.8 Conclusion

There is discontent evident in Australian society. Enough polls indicate displeasure with politics and politicians, and most of this discontent seems to be directed at the Coalition and the ALP. Hanson is able to articulate this discontent, just as Lambie did. However, to use this discontent for electoral gain is duplicitous: Hanson is also the cause of much discontent. Her speeches not only give voice to the dysfunctional nature of government, without recognizing her own complicity in a policy-void environment, but they empower and legitimize the violence and vilification of mobs like Reclaim Australia. Surely this is not what "ordinary" Australians want in their suburbs, and Australians have no taste for fascism. Hanson may be a populist, but she risks becoming responsible for something much baser.

A concerted effort by the ALP to put Hanson last on federal and state how-to-vote cards, denying her the preferences needed to retain or regain parliamentary office from 1998 to 2016, seems to be its only coherent response to Hansonism. This is a mistake. Similarly, it is a mistake for the Coalition to do preference deals with Hanson, as they did at the 2017 WA and Queensland state elections. At the WA state election, the Coalition recorded a 15% swing against them (WA Electoral Commission 2017) and at the 2017 Queensland state election it was about half that (Electoral Commission Queensland 2017). The LNP-One Nation preference deal in Queensland was toxic, with the LNP-One Nation deal delivering Hanson a lower house seat (Mirani) from the ALP. The waning novelty of One Nation, a congestion of other right-wing parties, a media increasingly bored with Hanson, ongoing problems with One Nation candidates, and ill-thought out policy positions (flat tax and citizen-initiated referenda) posit that both major parties have no need to continue to dabble with Hanson. But to ignore the message and "shoot the messenger" is dangerous. The message from Hanson in 2016 is that the political consensus between the electorate, the Coalition, and the ALP has been contravened. While this status remains, Hanson and others on the right will exploit this. It is to the peril of us all, if the lesson of Hansonism is not learnt.

My last point is one of numbers. Without taking away from the arguments I have made in this chapter, a phenomenon like Hanson always requires a certain amount of caution. To underestimate her appeal is dangerous, to ignore the reasons for her popularity is irresponsible. However, to overstate her popularity is also reckless. Hanson's popularity always requires contextualization. In 1996, Hanson represented one electorate in the House of Representatives. In 2018, she has one vote in the Senate and, as a bloc, One Nation now have only two votes. While the two One Nation Senators have the ability to join with other crossbenchers to defeat or pass legislation, this shouldn't be the measure of One Nation's popularity. At the 2016 federal election One Nation received 584,000 votes from Australia's 14 million voters (Doran 2016). The results of the 2017 Queensland election were hardly optimal for One Nation, losing the state leader and with former One Nation Senator Malcolm Roberts failing to win a seat in the Queensland parliament (Electoral Commission Queensland 2017). There was no electoral landslide, as there was in Queensland in 1998. At the 2017 WA state election, One Nation received only 65,000 primary votes from the state's 1.3 million voters, and secured no seats in the Legislative Assembly. The party did do better in the Legislative Council, however, securing 110,500 votes (8%) and returning three members to the Upper House (WA Electoral Commission 2017).

While some voters may punish the major parties for their dalliances with One Nation, other voters—anywhere from 5% to 25% of the national electorate—have experimented with One Nation. This should be of concern not only to the Coalition and the ALP, but to all of us. Discontent in the heartland (see Reid and Liu in Chap. 5 of this book) never bodes well. The more complex issue that needs further thought is how populists play with voter discontent for their own political and electoral gain. Heartland discontent is one thing but a string of right-wing populists, particularly in Europe and the US as well as in Australia, appear to be tapping into this dissatisfaction for purposes other than addressing the causes of discontent. As a voice for those alienated from politics, those elected on such platforms arguably have a responsibility to seek legislative change to redress the causes of alienation. In the case of Hanson, there is little evidence that she seeks such legislative change. Her policy positions lack specificity and she rejects compromise. That said, her policies more realistically must be seen at best as rhetoric or at worst as obstructionism, with the latter suggesting she represents a party of protest. In any case, Hanson seems unwilling and is unable to deliver her constituency the sorts of policies the discontent seeks. In the sense, Hanson is a populist. Populism, as Wear (2008, p. 623) reminds us, is something "employed strategically and rhetorically" but it rarely "extends to the implementation of policies". It is not policy reform that populist seek. Hanson is no different.

Acknowledgements The author would like to thank Bligh Grant, Angelika Heurich, Greg Melleuish, and Alan Scott for their comments on earlier drafts of this chapter. I fully acknowledge that this Chapter title comes from David Marr and his insightful Quarterly Essay (2017a) titled "The white queen: One Nation and the politics of race", 65, 1–102. The observations in this chapter are informed by a long-standing interest in Hanson and Hansonism. See Coghlan (1999). Pauline Hanson and Paul Keating: A postmodern analysis. Unpublished Honours thesis, University of Wollongong.

References

ABC News. (2015). Election archive: Lockyer 2015. *ABC News Election Archive*. http://www.abc.net.au/elections/archive/qld/results/2015/Lockyer.htm. Accessed December 18, 2017.

Australian Electoral Commission. (1998). 1998 federal election. http://www.aec.gov.au/Elections/Federal_Elections/1998/index.htm. Accessed June 11, 2018.

AEC [Australian Electoral Commission]. (2004). Senate results. https://results.aec.gov.au/12246/results/SenateResultsMenu-12246.htm. Accessed July 26, 2018.

Australian Government. (2004). *Marriage Amendment Act 2004*. https://www.legislation.gov.au/Details/C2004A01361. Accessed July 26, 2018.

Australian Government (2017). *The Constitution*. https://www.legislation.gov.au/Details/C2005Q00193. Accessed December 18, 2017.

Barber, S., & Johnson, S. (2014). Federal election results, 1901–2014. https://www.aph.gov.au/About_Parliament/Parliamentary_Departments/Parliamentary_Library/pubs/rp/rp1415/FedElect. Accessed July 26, 2018.

Brett, J. (1998). Representing the unrepresented: One Nation and the formation of the Labor Party. In R. Manne (Ed.), *Two nations: The causes and effects of the rise of the One Nation Party in Australia* (pp. 26–37). Melbourne: Bookman Press.

Brett, J. (2003). *Australian liberals and the moral middle class: From Alfred Deakin to John Howard*. Cambridge (UK): Cambridge University Press.

Brett, J. (2005). Relaxed and comfortable: The Liberal Party's Australia. *Quarterly Essay, 19*, 1–79.

Carr, A. (2018). *Australian election archive*. http://psephos.adam-carr.net/countries/a/australia/. Accessed July 26, 2018.

Coghlan, J. (1999). Pauline Hanson and Paul keating: A postmodern analysis. Unpublished Honours thesis, University of Wollongong.

Coleman, P., & Costello, P. (2009). *The Costello memoirs*. Melbourne: Melbourne University Press.

Crime and Misconduct Commission. (2004). *The prosecution of Pauline Hanson and David Ettridge: A report on an inquiry into issues raised in a resolution of parliament*. Crime and Misconduct Commission: Brisbane.

Doran, M. (2016). Election 2016: Pauline Hanson's One Nation, Nick Xenophon Team big winners in election funding. *ABC News*. 27 July http://www.abc.net.au/news/2016-07-27/election-2016-hanson-xenophon-big-winners-in-election-funding/7665618. Accessed July 26, 2018.

Electoral Commission Queensland. (2017). *2017 state general election: Election summary*. https://results.ecq.qld.gov.au/elections/state/State2017/results/summary.html. Accessed July 16, 2018.

Facebook. (2018). *Pauline Hanson's Please Explain*. 16 July 2016. https://www.facebook.com/PaulineHansonAu/. Accessed July 16, 2018.

Farnsworth, M. (2018). *1975 Federal election*. http://australianpolitics.com/elections/federal-1975. Accessed July 26, 2018.

Hanson P. (1996). *First speech. House of representatives*. https://www.youtube.com/watch?v=hkV1PkPj7ZA. Accessed June 11, 2018.

Hanson, P. (1997). *I have been murdered*. https://www.youtube.com/watch?v=JSdLNJW0ct4. Accessed July 26, 2018.

Hanson, P. (2016). *First Speech. Senate*. https://www.youtube.com/watch?v=krEPTyYO6l8. Accessed June 11, 2018.

Hanson, P. (2017). *Hanson wearing burqa in Senate*. https://www.youtube.com/watch?v=XExggl6Q-vo. Accessed July 26, 2018.

Howard, J. (1996). *Address to the Queensland Division of the Liberal Party State Council. 22 September*. http://pmtranscripts.pmc.gov.au/sites/default/files/original/00010114.pdf. Accessed June 11, 2018.

Howard, J. (2001). *2001 federal election speech, Sydney, 28 October*. https://electionspeeches.moadoph.gov.au/speeches/2001-john-howard. Accessed July 26, 2018.

Howard, J. (2010). *Lazarus rising: A personal and political autobiography*. Sydney: HarperCollins.

Jull, P. (2000). Hansonism and Aborigines and Torres Strait Islanders. In M. Leach, G. Stokes, & I. Ward (Eds.), *The rise fall of One Nation* (pp. 206–219). St. Lucia (QLD): University of Queensland Press.

Kirk, A. (2003). Hanson Australia's first political prisoner: Bronwyn Bishop. *The World Today*. 25 August. http://www.abc.net.au/worldtoday/content/2003/s931525.htm. Accessed June 11, 2018.

Kurmelovs, R. (2017). *Rogue nation: Dispatches from Australia's populist uprisings and outsider politics*. London: Hackett.

Lateline. (2018). [Australian Broadcasting Corporation; television]. John Howard. Comfortable and relaxed. Youtube. https://www.youtube.com/watch?v=YA8yB9dqtJQ. Accessed July 16, 2018.

Manne, R. (1998a). *The way we live now: The controversies of the nineties*. Melbourne: Text Publishing.

Manne, R. (1998b). Forward. In R. Manne (Ed.), *Two nations: The causes and effects of the rise of the One Nation Party in Australia* (pp. 3–9). Melbourne: Bookman Press.

Manne, R. (2001). *The barren years: John Howard and Australian political culture*. Melbourne: Text Publishing.

Marr, D. (2017a). The white queen: One Nation and the politics of race. *Quarterly Essay, 65,* 1–102.

Marr, D. (2017b). The white queen: Response to correspondence. *Quarterly Essay, 66,* 141–144.

Mason, R. (2010). "Pitbulls" and populist politicians: Sarah Palin, Pauline Hanson and the use of gendered nostalgia in electoral campaigns. *Comparative American Studies, 8*(3), 185–199.

Melleuish, G. (2009). Understanding Australian conservatism: Modern Australian conservatism reworks old conservative themes. *Policy: A Journal of Public Policy and Ideas, 25*(2), 41–46.

Moffitt, B., & Tormey, S. (2014). Rethinking populism: Politics, mediatisation and political style. *Political Studies, 62,* 381–397.

Moore, T. (2016). The rise and fall and rise of Pauline Hanson. *Brisbane Times*, 7 July. https://www.brisbanetimes.com.au/national/queensland/the-rise-and-fall-and-rise-of-pauline-hanson-20160707-gq13fl.html. Accessed July 26, 2016.

Murphy, P. (2016). Populism rising: The new voice of the "Mad as Hell" voter. *Quadrant, 60*(5), 8–15.

Newman, G. (1998). *1998 Queensland election. Current issues brief No. 2. Parliament of Australia*. https://www.aph.gov.au/About_Parliament/Parliamentary_Departments/Parliamentary_Library/Publications_Archive/CIB/cib9899/99CIB02. Accessed July 26, 2018.

Stokes, G. (2000). One Nation and Australian populism. In M. Leach, G. Stokes, & I. Ward (Eds.), *The rise fall of One Nation* (pp. 23–41). St. Lucia (QLD): University of Queensland Press.

Street, J. (2004). Celebrity politicians: Popular culture and political representation. *British Journal of Politics and International Relations, 6,* 435–452.

Tiffen, R., & Gittens, R. (2009). The Howard impact. *Inside Story*. http://insidestory.org.au/the-howard-impact/. Accessed June 11, 2018.

Wear, R. (2008). Permanent populism: The Howard Government 1996–2007. *Australian Journal of Political Science, 43*(4), 617–634.

Wear, R. (2013). A loss in Oxley spell disaster for Labor. *The Conversation*. https://theconversation.com/a-loss-in-oxley-could-spell-disaster-for-labor-17058. Accessed June 11, 2018.

van Onselen, P., & Errington, W. (2007). From vitriolic criticism to ungainly praise: Locating John Howard's political success. *Australian Quarterly, 79*(2), 4–11.

WA Electoral Commission. (2017). *2017 state general election: Results by party*. https://www.elections.wa.gov.au/elections/state/sgelection#/sg2017. Accessed June 11, 2018.

Zavattaro, S. (2010). Brand Obama: The implications of a branded president. *Administrative Theory & Praxis, 32*(1), 123–128.

Part IV
Comparison

Chapter 10
Once as Tragedy and Again as Farce: Hansonism, Backlashers, and Economic Nationalism After 20 Years

Tod Moore

The angry workers, mighty in their numbers, are marching irresistibly against the arrogant. They are shaking their fists at the sons of privilege. … They are massing at the gates … hoisting the black flag, and while the millionaires tremble in their mansions they are bellowing out their terrifying demands. "We are here" they scream "to cut your taxes".

(Frank 2006 p. 109)

Abstract The study of conservative backlash politics reveals a contradiction whereby blue-collar voters who are not doing well in the *laissez-faire* new economy flock to right-wing politicians whose main contributions to future policy are likely to be smaller government, fewer public amenities, more financial deregulation, weaker unions, and greater wealth inequality. In the first part of this chapter I look at conservative backlash politics in the United States in the early to mid-1990s and again in recent times following the financial meltdown of October 2008. In particular, I draw attention to the analysis of Thomas Frank, arguably the best of the US writers on conservative backlash politics. Having examined the US version it will then be possible to look at the Australian variant of this conservative backlash. The latter section of the chapter begins with a brief historical overview of conservative backlashes in Australia, followed by some observations of the Pauline Hanson One Nation (PHON) example, and a few thoughts about comparisons with the US and with earlier Australian ideas in an attempt to explain similarities and differences. In particular I discuss the political origins of the fear and anger driving the backlash, and the self-harming aspect of Hansonist policies embraced by working-class and middle-class Australians. Dismissing the PHON second wave as populism risks dismissing the acute failures of neoliberalism and globalization, which are at the roots of the phenomenon. These failures must be addressed.

T. Moore (✉)
Newcastle Business School, University of Newcastle, 409 Hunter St, Newcastle, NSW 2300, Australia
e-mail: Tod.Moore@newcastle.edu.au

© Springer Nature Singapore Pte Ltd. 2019
B. Grant et al. (eds.), *The Rise of Right-Populism*,
https://doi.org/10.1007/978-981-13-2670-7_10

Keywords Backlashers · Economic rationalism · Hansonism · Populism

10.1 Hansonism in Context

The onslaught of neoliberal policies and global financial deregulation which began
in earnest in the 1980s is ultimately responsible for the conservative backlash (Davis
2008, p. 298) or "populist radical right" (McSwiney and Cottle 2017, p. 88). However,
the fact that the backlash manifested in both the US and Australia in the 1990s, and a
second time after 2008, and the supposition that other countries also demonstrate this
patterning of two episodes separated by a lacuna, requires explanation. The pervasive
and global nature of neoliberal ideology and its profound effects on policy outcomes,
which, in turn, failed populations in the US, Australia, and many other countries,
adequately accounts for the conservative backlashes observed. With large numbers
of citizens negatively affected by the effects of industry closure, infrastructure decay,
shifts to for-profit service provision, reduced access to affordable housing, and demo-
nization of the unemployed, there are large groups of "sectoral losers" available to
create backlasher constituencies (Goodliffe 2012, p. 140). Examples include rural
and regional populations, blue-collar workers in general, the expanding underclass,
and potentially vulnerable populations in the outer suburbs of larger cities. Given
that neoliberalism has been so constant in public policy, why are there two distinct
waves of conservative backlash?

The spatial distribution of backlashers is not uniform, and favors outer suburban
and regional zones, and in the specific case of PHON there is also a Central and South-
east Queensland concentration (McSwiney and Cottle 2017, p. 95). Demographically
the conservative backlasher is likely to be older, male, and without any tertiary qualifications (Goot 1998, pp. 71–72; Marr 2017, pp. 49–51) . Socially, the backlash has
greatest appeal for working-class and middle-class citizens: the chronically unemployed working class which has paid such a high price for neoliberalism; the middle
class which desperately fears falling into the ranks of the working class (Short 2016,
p. 766). The PHON party has been able to access this "reserve of social and material anxiety" within the electorate (McSwiney and Cottle 2017, pp. 96–97). From a
historical materialist perspective there is something wrong, on surface appearances,
because so many of these conservative backlashers ultimately support policies which
favor only elites, the 1% (Short 2016, p. 773). Such self-harming politics can readily
be understood as a form of misdirected anger within an ideological landscape which
lacks a credible left. Anxious and unhappy, many who might otherwise have headed
towards the political left have gone in the opposite direction, something made necessary by the surrender of the center-left (e.g., Democrats, Australian Labor Party)
 to neoliberalism (Frank 2016, p. 120). The unexpected re-emergence of a credible
left associated with Bernie Sanders and Jeremy Corbyn may, of course, change all
of this.

When Pauline Hanson first came to political prominence in Australia in 1996,
with her openly racist remarks unsurprisingly sparking heated controversy, it was

frequently overlooked that there was another aspect to her rhetoric. While one half of Hansonism was merely reheated Australian racism the other half was more interesting because it revolved around a rejection of the free market economic consensus of the preceding period, a consensus which is strangely still present today. In 1997 I described this aspect of Hanson's thinking as economic nationalism as opposed to the prevalent market based and free trade thinking. I described the keen sense of betrayal engendered by decisions of the Hawke and Keating governments when they abandoned the post-war economic consensus and embraced a contrary neoliberal position or "economic rationalism" as it was termed by Hanson in early 1997 (Moore 1997, pp. 56–57; Walter 2010, p. 301). Hence the binary of economic nationalism and economic rationalism remains part of the Hanson appeal to backlashers now as it did then (McSwiney and Cottle 2017, p. 91).

Evidence of Pauline Hanson's economic nationalism can be found in her 1996 and 2016 maiden speeches to the Commonwealth Parliament, the former to the Representatives and the latter to the Senate. In the 1996 speech she devoted almost a third of the space to this area, with complaints against structural unemployment, abandonment of manufacturing, the evils of global financial markets, lack of infrastructure, lack of business lending, and lack of tariffs (Representatives 1996, pp. 3860–3863). In 2016 the concerns raised included globalization and free trade policies, lack of infrastructure, structural unemployment, the evils of multinational corporations, privatization of essential services, and offshore tax avoidance (Senate 2016, pp. 78–82). While both speeches are notoriously racist and "populist" (Mudde 2004) it is this theme of economic nationalism which most concerns us here. In 2017 the PHON official website included a document of "principles" entitled *What We Stand For*. The document contains two policies which are of great interest here, the promise "to restore tariff protection" and renew manufacturing industries, and robust opposition to "privatisation of essential services"; and it also proposes to re-establish a government-owned bank and limit foreign investment in rural and urban real estate (PHON 2017). Whatever else PHON may represent there is no doubt that it continues to advocate economic nationalism.

This aspect of the Pauline Hanson backlash phenomenon is particularly important because it provides a mechanism for explaining the broadening of her support base beyond the predictable extreme right fringe of the electorate. Due to the persistence of neoliberal or postneoliberal policies it may also provide an avenue for explaining why this same conservative backlash has happened twice, separated by a span of two decades. In this context, it is worth remembering that being a notional economic nationalist is not the same as being ready and willing to implement detailed interventionist policies in practice.

10.2   Backlashes of the United States

In order to better understand the conservative backlash it is helpful to consult Thomas Frank, the US cultural and political commentator and editor. His exploration of the backlash in the US offers insights into the social and cultural dynamics of such phenomena in a polity where the two-party system has established a neoliberal economic consensus along lines also seen in Australia. The US parallels can thus be used to advance understanding, but only if it is remembered that US politics is distinctive and partly rests on its own well-developed traditions of both left and right populism (Grant 1997, p. 15) . When discussing recent mutations of conservative populism and the backlash in the US, including the Tea Party, Frank has identified two phases of the rise of the popular right: one in the 1990s (documented in his book *What's the Matter With Kansas?*), the other the Tea Party movement (a low-tax campaign which began in early 2009 and continues to this day, documented in his book *Pity the Billionaire*). These two studies, together with his 2016 book *Listen, Liberal* on neoliberalism in the Democratic Party, help us in turn to appreciate the re-emergence of Hansonist economic nationalism in Australia.

The rise of backlash politics in Kansas in the early 1990s goes to the heart of the paradox whereby blue-collar voters who are not doing well in the *laissez-faire* economy flock to right-wing politicians. These are politicians whose main contributions to policy are smaller government, fewer public amenities, more financial deregulation, weaker unions, tax cuts for the wealthy, and greater inequality. The end result of tax cuts for the wealthy involved the alchemy of religion and the substitution of disputed values for deeper issues of disputed economic policies. Backlashers were drawn into a culture war and a crusade against reproductive rights, rather than seeking to invert the agenda of free trade (e.g., the North American Free Trade Agreement or NAFTA) and neoliberalism. In the backlasher world, neoliberal economic policies are part of the established system of financial accumulation and thus off the table, so all there is left to wrangle over is a diverse array of social policies which are being actively embraced by upper-middle-class reformers. In Kansas angry backlashers battled over policies portrayed as political correctness, and then linked to "elites" working in advertising or the news media. By raging against "elites" of the economically neutered Democratic Party establishment, conservative backlashers in the 1990s found a home in the Republican Party, and they are still there in the so-called "Red States" today. Religion was a pivotal aspect of the backlash in Kansas. It merged with the Republican right wing in a continuum of "affronted middle American victimhood" where evangelical values confronted the teaching of evolution, same sex marriage, and legal abortion on the "cultural war" battleground (Frank 2006, p. 255). Religiosity comprises an integral part of the "Bible and guns" culture in this blue-collar Red State reality, and in the 1990s anti-abortion fever swept moderates out of the top ranks of the Kansas Republican Party (Frank 2006, pp. 96–98, 183). They were vilified as "Bible-thumpers" by wealthy moderate Republicans but, following a 1991 campaign to close down family planning clinics, in 1992 the blue-collar backlashers were able to take advantage of all the righteous enthusiasm to grasp control of chunks of the party (Frank 2006, p. 92). The Republicans who lost power retained their status and wealth, however, because the economic policies supported by conservative backlashers were still neoliberal, even though it was "culture war that gets the goods" in terms of the popular vote (Frank 2006, p. 10).

The culture war extended beyond evangelical dogmas but never beyond values, never into the forbidden realm of economics. A dichotomy between class values and class politics where "cultural grievances" take precedence over "solid material ones" has been at the core of the Kansas backlash (Frank 2006, p. 239). Thus in the 1990s blue-collar precincts wiped out by waves of neoliberal *laissez-faire* policies "responded by lashing out on cultural issues" and flocking to the cause of the Republican right (Frank 2006, p. 4). The adversary in the culture war was not Wall Street, but the assembled upper-middle-class professionals and their values. Tarred with the brush of the "shadowy, cosmopolitan Other" the professionals were found guilty of the greatest crime, that of intellectualism:

> We do not labor under the yoke of some abstraction like market forces, or even flesh-and-blood figures like executives or owners. No, it is *intellectuals* who call the shots, people with graduate degrees and careers in government, academia, law and the professions. (Frank 2006, p. 191)

Sophisticated, secular, urban and urbane, these "elites" became the new class enemy. It was they who were producing all of the "leftist pro-homosexual pro-evolution pro-abortion propaganda" in Hollywood movies and on TV news (Frank 2006, p. 205) . As opposed to conservative backlashers who rarely have tertiary degrees, the "elites" contained all of the professional gatekeepers who discipline the working class in the purest Foucauldian manner, and teachers of political correctness in taxpayer-funded schools. Here is the "treason of the intellectuals" (Frank 2006, pp. 194, 202–203). With economics off the agenda, political correctness became the easiest thing to target (Lynch and Reavell 1997, p. 44). The fact that advanced social policies are promoted by upper-middle-class media manipulators—precisely because capitalism can painlessly endorse such things—is lost on backlashers, and this is "the basic lie of the backlash" (Frank 2006, p. 242) .

The blue-collar underdog in Kansas who identifies cultural "elites" as the enemy does not need to look far to see where these traitors congregate: they are in the Democratic Party. The Democrats had betrayed their blue-collar base and transformed into the party of "the rich and the self-righteous" abandoning interventionist economic positions held since the days of FDR. Democrats became another pro-business party, another party of Wall Street (Frank 2006, pp. 244–245; Frank 2016). The culture war might have been averted except that Democrats chose to "take economic issues off the table" and thus open their once progressive flank to the possibility of attack. Since the late 1980s and the Clinton takedown of the left within the party, particularly through the meddling of a neoliberal front organization called the Democratic Leadership Council, the Democrats were no longer able to advance working-class interests. Clinging to social radicalism and the urban middle-class voters attracted to such things, Democrats were backtracking on employment, wages, welfare, trade, deregulation, privatization, and public services (Frank 2006, p. 243) . By the time of the 1994 mid-term elections this process was complete and the "Third Way" was making the Democrats economically identical to the Republicans, even delivering NAFTA to the electorate. It was hardly surprising when voters in blue-collar precincts were lost to the Republican right (Frank 2006, p. 177).

Given the premise that it was the neoliberal consensus and consequences of *laissez-faire* for elements of the blue-collar electorate which ultimately caused the backlash in the 1990s, it remains to consider the second backlash following the 2008 Global Financial Crisis (GFC). It is in this period that the term "postneoliberalism" emerged around discussions of the impact of the GFC, and a growing understanding that the GFC was not altering the overall trajectory of economic policies (Dean 2014; Peck et al. 2009). In the US, 2009 marked the emergence of the Tea Party or "the newest Right", superseding the 1994 Republican Revolution but retaining many conservative backlasher attributes of the earlier movement (Frank 2012, pp. 10, 154, 100) . While the Obama White House was bailing out Wall Street and maintaining neoliberalism (Frank 2016, p. 157), a regimen of austerity was being enforced by Labour in the UK and by other allegedly progressive governments in Greece, Ireland, and Italy (Blyth 2013; Curtis 2013; Seymour 2016, p. 105). Austerity, via harsh welfare cuts, was also to be rolled out in Australia in 2016 (McSwiney and Cottle 2017, p. 97). In the US, it was as though the collapse of 2008 had never happened. Instead of reacting against neoliberalism, people were embracing "hard-times conservatism" in defense of capitalism and free market dogma (Frank 2012, pp. 11, 153). Like Sarah Palin, the backlashers of the Tea Party saw themselves as victims of a Democrat and "elite" leftist conspiracy (Frank 2012, pp. 170, 124, 138) . It was a narrative in which "there is only one way that believers in freedom can interpret the meltdown of 2008" regardless of evidence to the contrary (Frank 2012, p. 162). This mutation of the backlash was more representative of small businesses and was also "more ideologically concentrated" in the libertarian direction of deregulation and small government (Frank 2012, pp. 98–100, 186). While abortion was off the Tea Party agenda there were some accusations of emergent racism (Frank 2012, pp. 10, 126). Since the rise of Trump, racism and anti-immigration rhetoric has become endemic in US politics.

The second conservative backlash showed no signs of abating during the somnolent last years of the Obama administration. With no end in sight for the decline of US manufacturing and the widening of the divide between the rich and the rest of society, it seemed as though from the Democratic Party's perspective the 2011 Occupy movement had never happened (Moore 2017). The concept that social inequality was a problem, or even that it existed, appeared to be lost on the political class in America. In 2016 Bernie Sanders nearly captured the Democratic nomination by harnessing the energy and ideas of Occupy in a left populist campaign. For whatever reason, the Third Way sidelined Sanders and Donald Trump won the White House in a close and lackluster general election. By the time Trump won the November election Pauline Hanson had already become a Senator (she toasted his win in front of Parliament House), but his backlasher profile in early 2016 may have assisted the PHON party prior to the Australian elections.

10.3   Backlashes of Australia

It can be argued that the two eruptions of political Hansonism in Australia are matched to the two US backlash movements, and that Frank is basically correct about the nature of blue-collar self-harming backlashers. In a broad sense Australia's Pauline Hanson represents an antipodean species of the same type of politician. This is not the whole story of course, and there are significant cultural and historical differences between the two countries. To better understand these similarities and differences it is useful to briefly consider earlier Australian backlash experiences, some dating back to the time just after Federation in 1901. If there exist some distinctively Australian facets of the backlash form of politics, then such a search is warranted, at least in the hope of uncovering clues.

The rise and fall of backlash movements in Australia goes beyond the familiar examples in historical literature such as the 1880s and 1890s *Bulletin* slogan of "Australia for the Australians" and the New Guard circa 1932. The first such conservative backlash movement following Federation was the Kyabram Movement in Victoria in 1902 (Walter 2010, p. 319). Arising from a mass meeting of the disaffected in the town of Kyabram, the resulting movement rapidly spread through rural populations of small farmers, shopkeepers, and workers. It embraced a politics of reducing government spending (except on rural infrastructure), cutting the number of politicians (assumed to be corrupt), and weakening the alleged hold of 'socialistic' unions. Before it faded away the Kyabram Movement influenced the 1902 Victorian elections and secured the election of country-minded conservatives like George Swinburne (Walter 2010, p. 118). This was a time of great support for the rural idyll, and the tales of brave but poor selectors (i.e., small farmers) in the "Dad and Dave" books of Arthur Hoey Davis (Steele Rudd) outsold the English fiction which had been flooding Australia. In 1908 Davis published one of the later titles in this series, *Dad in Politics*, pitting the virtuous rural battler and patriarch against politicians in the state parliament in Brisbane, with the dénouement of Dad furiously turning his back on all of the urban corruption and returning to his farm. None of the themes from Kyabram (Davis 1909) or *Dad in Politics* would be unfamiliar to an American populist of the era.

In 1913 a book on unification entitled *Australian Unity* was published by Albert Church for the Young Australia Party, a little-known nationalist organization with clear populist tendencies. Here the main issue was the need to abolish federalism and form a unitary government for the sake of national survival. With the threat of an unlikely Asiatic invasion weighing on the Australian psyche at this time (Broinowski 1996), defense preparedness was more vital to Church and friends than the constitution. Also highlighted in the volume was the need for better rural infrastructure, and it extolled the virtues of compulsory military training for boys of 14 years and above (Moore 2005). When the Great War broke out it revealed cleavages in Australian society, especially in the conscription referendum campaigns in 1916 and 1917. As the war dragged on and the cost in blood and treasure grew, there was a wave of interest in country-based political representation, including returned soldiers who wanted to stand for election (Page 1917). Until this emerging group of populist lawmakers was united and disciplined by Earle Page in the early 1920s, and transformed into the Country Party as a partner of the conservative Stanley Bruce (thus enabled to trade support for concessions), there was something of the backlash about these representatives. They repeated the Kyabram accusations of city corruption and lack of empathy of elites towards authentic and virtuous country dwellers, while lamenting the poor state of rural infrastructure. Eventually some of this conservative backlash politics returned in the form of a New State Movement filled with bitter resentment (Ellis 1933).

The most rewarding period before the 1990s for students of the Australian backlash is undoubtedly the era of the 1930s Depression, a time of heightened anger and anxiety (Moore 1995). Much has been written about the New Guard and its somewhat comical effort at "Defending the National Tuckshop" in the words of Michael Cathcart (1988). But other evidence abounds in the 1930s for what Peter Loveday usefully terms "anti-political political thought" (Mackinolty 1981). Some conservative backlashers were extreme, like the "One Mind Association", which intended to solve the economic crisis via spiritualist "sublimation" and the use of fake gold to rebuild Sydney (Becker 1932). Others embraced quack remedies such as the social dividend or social credit, and a reinvigorated version of the old Single Tax idea of Henry George, a favorite of US populism since 1880 (Holmes 1932). Many blamed the crisis on corrupt politics and socialistic unions. While economists and politicians upheld the narrow perspective of the private banks in arguing for austerity measures, there were also numerous voices raised against bankers. Writing on behalf of the Financial Reform League in South Australia, Skitch (1931) complained that under austerity the bankers made no sacrifices and the rich gained at the expense of the poor. Austerity was far from being accepted, and the British bondholders became widely demonized. The backlash peaked in the 1936 publication *The Foundations of Culture in Australia* by P. R. (Inky) Stephensen. Here we see British elites and their Australian imitators betraying and attacking honest Australian battlers, the true bearers of virtue. With racism of the anti-Semitic strand and the most violent opposition to foreign ownership, as well as economic nationalist themes, it clearly fits the conservative backlash stereotype (Stephensen 1986). Both the small-government ethos of Kyabram and the economic-nationalist emphasis of Inky Stephensen have re-emerged under the PHON party.

The conservative backlash did not make much headway in Australia in the relatively prosperous period following the Second World War. Immediately after the war, Gearon (1946) published an anti-communist booklet which was a thinly disguised defense of Nazi ideology adapted to Australia. In 1960 the Australian League of Rights was established and, with related groups, it maintained a shadowy fascistic presence on the fringe of politics. Such front groups have frequently contested Australian elections and small ultra-nationalist parties usually receive 2% of the vote or less, compared with Hanson's figures of 8% to over 20% (Hughes and Graham 1974). Since the Hanson phenomenon of the 1990s there have been the infamous Cronulla Riots in 2005 (Soutphommasane 2012) and, more recently still, the Reclaim Australia movement. It could be argued that groups connected to the League of Rights supplied some of the fuel for the 1996 Hansonite fire, and that Cronulla and Reclaim have both been helpful to Hanson in the latest elections. So too can it be argued that the English UKIP success and the early period of Donald Trump's rise in the US provided some international inspiration to Australian conservative backlashers at the time of the 2016 general election. But if it is agreed that the extreme right is limited to around 2% of the total vote, then the bulk of Hanson's support is not coming from this demographic; it is coming from mainline conservative backlashers.

10.4   Please Explain

Even if it is agreed that the most meaningful aspect of backlash politics in both the US and Australia is a class war somewhat misdirected against faux-progressive elites, at least three areas of difference remain to be explained. The differences can be discussed in terms of issues and policies in dispute, the relationship of the backlash to the two-party system, and some cultural differences between the two polities. Political culture in both places is based on settler society dynamics and historical factors, and the US backlash has features not found in Australia, such as extreme religiosity, especially among the rural working class (Bageant 2007). The centrality of anti-abortion and the Bible in classrooms reflects the reality that the US is religious in the extreme—but Australia is secular, and these things have not been core to the rise and return of Hansonism.

The second point of difference which requires analysis is that in Australia the backlash has largely side-stepped the center-right Liberal National Party (LNP) coalition, whereas in the US it has taken control of huge sections of the Republican Party. Thus Pauline Hanson was thrust out from the LNP in 1996 for her racist comments, and she is forced to remain separate from the LNP even though the party once preselected her. Yet Donald Trump is just as racist and he occupies the White House for the Republican Party. In the Australian case the conservative backlash is external to the two-party system but in the US it has become embedded within the party system. In the 1990s backlashers took control of much of the Republican Party, as we have seen, and today Donald Trump is the darling of the backlash and much more popular than Hanson. This suggests that the US party system is significantly further to the right on the spectrum and is able to accommodate backlashers better than the Australian party system, where Hanson is an unpredictable Senate ally of the LNP at best. While the conservative backlash has been able to be folded into the two-party system in the US, Australia is more like France in the sense that the backlash has remained beyond the regular parties. Like the Front National or FN, the PHON Party has resisted assimilation.

The third and final point of difference is at the policy level, specifically that Australia's backlash is superficially more concerned about defects of *laissez-faire* economics, favoring a greater degree of economic nationalism. It appears that Hansonism is more anti-neoliberal in the area of economic policies, notably industry policy (McSwiney and Cottle 2017, p. 90). In her 2016 maiden speech Hanson includes a frontal attack against "leaders" on the basis of their "economic rational-ism" and "free trade" policies, and this is out of step with the US Tea Party position favoring *laissez-faire*, although not free trade. Of course there is the possibility that Hanson is hostile at a theoretical level, but that in policy terms she actually favors tax cuts and other aspects of the neoliberal agenda and that "she doth protest too much". The muted nature of her economic nationalism means that industry policy is largely absent (no rebuilding of the Australian auto industry), and there is a strong focus on rural infrastructure and assistance to rural industries such as the sugar industry. In the Hanson-inspired book *The Truth* she is portrayed as saying that such rural areas have been made into "economic wastelands" by neoliberalism (McSwiney and Cottle 2017, p. 94). Yet, despite the broad protectionist clause in the principles document (PHON 2017), there has been no sign of any industry policy beyond industries like the sugar industry. As in the case of Trump, another notional protectionist, Hanson seems to be more bark than bite when it comes to actually rejecting neoliberalism and globalization, and this reduces the point of difference at the level of intervention-ist policy. It could also be that the direct critique of *laissez-faire* by PHON reflects the independent status of the party and the fact that it has not been folded into the two-party system the way that the conservative backlash has been in the US.

Despite these differences, there are similarities between the Australian and US experiences of the conservative backlash. The one of particular interest is the hiatus between the 1990s backlash and the second backlash following the GFC and the rise of austerity. In both national examples of the backlash there is a need to explain this second rising after a gap of almost 20 years. As much as the advent of Hansonism in 1996 can be regarded as a freak accident of the election, the comparison with the US backlash presents us with too many similarities to be dismissed. Unhappy and apparently abandoned by their former champions, the working-class and middle-class backlashers join the right in an attack on urban educated "elites" who no longer support them (McSwiney and Cottle 2017, p. 92). But if that is the case (and it almost certainly is) then why the gap of 20 years? It is not possible to offer a definitive answer to this but the 2001 terror attacks of 9/11 and the 2003 invasion of Iraq will go part of the way to explaining the diversion of attention away from social and economic concerns, at least for a number of years. A degree of prosperity at this time can further help to explain the deferral of political reaction. This financial upswing after 2001 turned out to be the prelude to the 2008 crash of course, and the lack of an immediate backlash in 2009 can possibly be ascribed to shock and uncertainty. In Australia other special factors had been at play during this period. Almost coinciding with the 9/11 attacks was the Tampa Affair and the start of the long-running saga of asylum seekers and people smugglers which was so useful to the Howard Government. The Howard Government was also seeking to gain backlasher support with its own anti-elite rhetoric (Marr and Wilkinson 2003). It can be argued that, like the terrorism response, this refugee issue took much of the oxygen away from the backlash. Other Australian developments during the hiatus period included the Howard Government's control of the Senate after the 2004 elections, and the ALP victory in the *Kevin 07* election which promised (at least for a brief period) to push against neoliberal policy settings. Finally there was the long Australian mining boom and its continuation beyond the GFC, which provided employment for blue-collar workers and also postponed austerity. There was much to divert attention away from the backlash, but now Pauline Hanson has returned to Canberra and we must return to the topic of popular right-wing movements.

Conservative backlashes like PHON stand out from the rest of the political spectrum by stridently and offensively advancing nativist and xenophobic policies, typically anti-immigration policies. Unfortunately, many commentators and political scientists concentrate almost exclusively on the developing racism of the backlash, tending to overlook or play down those grievances of so many working-class and middle-class voters which push them into the backlash and help to keep them there. Even Mudde, in his ground-breaking 2004 paper on populist movements, is too dismissive of these grievances and too reluctant to expose the problems caused by the neoliberal policy consensus, especially growing social inequality. Accepting his point that much of the literature mistakenly reduces backlashes to nothing more than class protests, this does not warrant his dismissal of the neoliberal consensus as merely an inevitable "transformation to a post-industrial society" (Mudde 2004, p. 547). More recently, David Marr has done something similar, reacting petulantly to the proposition that PHON supporters are victims of neoliberalism and globalization. In particular, he attacks the idea that there is a blue-collar aspect to PHON's support base, and that outer urban and regional centers have been materially damaged by economic trends (Marr 2017, pp. 52–53). To his credit Mudde acknowledges that there is "some truth" to backlasher allegations of people being left behind, but he too dismisses the dynamic of a political class growing aloof and indifferent in the face of inequality (Mudde 2004, pp. 553). Instead he tends to blame an excess of egalitarianism, and poor political understanding of neoliberal reality (Mudde 2004, pp. 561). None of this fits into the picture painted by Thomas Frank (see above). Against Marr in particular, we should focus on the fear and fury which has been motivating both working-class and middle-class voters, who are not already fully paid up members of the lunar right, to suddenly congregate around the PHON banner, not once but twice.

Comparing Australia and the US, there is an underlying structural similarity, with vulnerable voters opting for far-right politics, as has also been observed in respect to the FN in France (Goodliffe 2012, p. 143; McKnight 2005, pp. 78–79). It is therefore unsurprising that, to attract voters, the PHON party places economic nationalism alongside its other positions. However, the tragedy and ultimately the farce encompassed in all of the deeper class issues at stake is that, as Frank observes, the policies likely to flow from backlash politics are things like lower taxes on the rich and cuts to social welfare spending by governments. Such a self-harming and masochistic politics can be explained by a combination of materialist and cultural drives without necessarily going to the extent of applying Freudian social psychology, although that has been attempted (Short 2016). Regardless of whether some form of self-hatred and narcissism may be at play, it can be easily imagined that victims of neoliberalism reject present political elites while cleaving to the system of accumulation itself, oblivious of the subordinate position to which the system relegates them or the connectedness between the capitalist system and neoliberal ideology per se. Unable to let go of the system, these recruits to the conservative backlash seek another salvation, in charismatic leaders and the scapegoating of the "other" (Short 2016, pp. 762–763; see also Laqueur 1979, p. 267). In Australia this search for the charismatic outsider created the Clive Palmer phenomenon in the 2013 elections, yet the "political super-star" who had stood the test of time was Hanson and with the demise of Palmer she became the darling of the backlash once again (Tanner 2011, p. 132). This preference for "the original over the copy" is also seen in France, where FN has prevailed over rivals by taking advantage of the Le Pen name and brand (Goodliffe 2012, p. 151). Economic nationalism may be present in speeches and statements of principle but the backlash always takes easy options, always preferences the politics of xenophobia and nativism. This makes it incapable of addressing the social necessity that underwrites its very existence.

The popularity of the backlash which is encapsulated in the current return of Hansonism in Australia is essentially a manifestation of class warfare. Support by elements of the blue-collar electorate for the backlash is the factor which makes a difference politically and which makes Pauline Hanson potentially influential. It can be asserted that if the political class prove incapable of disavowing neoliberal and globalist policies, and thereby perpetuate the anxiety and anger of blue collar voters, the backlash is likely to expand (McSwiney and Cottle 2017, p. 98). This may seem an alarming prospect, as there is so much for the electorate to be angry about at present and therefore so much scope for PHON to grow. To most educated commentators the blue-collar supporters of the backlash, who have swung right rather than left as might be expected, constitute a threat. But it is a threat which can be dealt with fairly easily, especially when it is noted that these backlashers represent a minority of the larger blue-collar base of society. The current rage for austerity among lawmakers is the most recent face of neoliberalism, which entrenches finance capital, creates and disciplines an underclass of workers, subjects our universities to "ideological cleansing", and rejects any person bold enough to complain as a policy heretic (Mendoza 2014; Seymour 2014). Today in countries like Australia it has become self-evident to voters that policies which focus exclusively on unrestricted finance capitalism and promote unplanned economies do not work. In the 2017 UK elections, Jeremy Corbyn and his Labour party secured a huge swing from working-class and middle-class voters with an interventionist manifesto called *For the Many* (Sunkara 2017). Such a resurgent democratic socialism seriously challenges the view of political sociologists, that the left alternative to populist or conservative backlash politics is incapable of moving beyond "the logic of modernization" (Bluhdorn and Butzlaff 2018, p. 12), understood as neoliberalism and globalization.

In other words, blue-collar support for PHON would vanish if the center left of Australian politics (the ALP) partly abandoned neoliberal economic and social positions and returned to democratic socialism, as in the examples of Bernie Sanders in the US and Jeremy Corbyn in the UK. Such a return to some type of democratic socialism, with policies like planning, industry protection, public essential services, financial regulation, and full employment, offer a more credible cure than xenophobia. It is now incumbent on commentators and political scientists to admit that we were betrayed by supporters of neoliberalism. The defense of the political class which is currently upheld by influential political scientists should be challenged (Flinders 2012; Stoker 2017). By refusing to mend, all we are doing is adding fuel to the fire.

References

Bageant, J. (2007). *Deer hunting with Jesus: Dispatches from America's class war*. New York: Crown Publishers.

Becker, D. I. (1932). *Facing facts—The year of determination*. Sydney: One Mind Association.

Bluhdorn, I., & Butzlaff, F. (2018). Rethinking populism: Peak democracy, liquid identity and the performance of sovereignty. *European Journal of Social Theory*. https://doi.org/10.1177/13684 31017754057.

Blyth, M. (2013). *Austerity—The history of a dangerous idea*. Oxford: Oxford University Press.

Broinowski, A. (1996). *The yellow lady—Australian impressions of Asia*. Melbourne: Oxford University Press.

Cathcart, M. (1988). *Defending the national tuckshop—Australia's secret army intrigue of 1931*. Melbourne: McPhee Gribble.

Church, A. E. (1913). *Australian unity*. Sydney, the author.

Curtis, N. (2013). *Idiotism—Capitalism and the privatisation of life*. London: Pluto Press.

Davis, M. (2008). *The land of plenty—Australia in the 2000s*. Melbourne: Melbourne University Press.

Davis, A. H. (Steele Rudd) (1909). *Dad in politics and other stories*. Sydney: N.S.W. Bookstall.

Dean, M. (2014). Rethinking neoliberalism. *Journal of Sociology, 50*(2), 150–163.

Ellis, U. (1933). *New Australian states*. Sydney: The Endeavour Press.

Flinders, M. (2012). *Defending politics: Why democracy matters in the twenty-first century*. Oxford: Oxford University Press.

Frank, T. (2006). *What's the matter with America? The resistible rise of the American right*. London: Vintage. (i.e. *What's the Matter With Kansas?*).

Frank, T. (2012). *Pity the billionaire—The hard-times swindle and the unlikely comeback of the right*. London: Harvill Secker.

Frank, T. (2016). *Listen, Liberal: Or, what ever happened to the party of the people?*. Melbourne: Scribe Publications.

Gearon, P. J. (1946). *Communism—why not: A ruthless exposure*. Melbourne, the author.

Goodliffe, G. (2012). The price of disengagement: Radical populism in France and Germany. *Journal of Contemporary European Studies, 20*(2), 137–160.

Goot, M. (1998). Hanson's heartland: Who's for One Nation and why. In R. Manne, T. Abbott, J. Brett, R. Brunton, M. Frazer, et al. (Eds.), *Two Nations: The causes and effects of the rise of the One Nation Party in Australia* (pp. 51–74). Melbourne: Bookman Press.

Grant, B. (Ed.). (1997). *Pauline Hanson, One Nation and Australian politics*. Armidale: U.N.E. Press.

Holmes, E. L. (1932). *Australia's real wealth—And how to use it*. Sydney: Douglas Social Credit Association.

Hughes, C. A., & Graham, B. D. (1974). *Voting for the Australian house of representatives 1901–1964*. Canberra: A.N.U. Press.

Laqueur, W. (Ed.). (1979). *Fascism: A reader's guide*. Harmondsworth: Penguin Books.

Lynch, T., & Reavell, R. (1997). Through the looking glass: Howard, Hanson and the politics of "political correctness". In B. Grant (Ed.), *Pauline Hanson, One Nation and Australian politics* (pp. x–y). Armidale: U.N.E. Press.

Mackinolty, J. (Ed.). (1981). *The wasted years? Australia's great depression*. Sydney: George Allen and Unwin.

Marr, D. (2017). The white queen: One Nation and the politics of race. *Quarterly Essay, 65,* 1.

Marr, D., & Wilkinson, M. (2003). *Dark victory*. Sydney: Allen and Unwin.

McKnight, D. (2005). *Beyond right and left—New politics and the culture wars*. Sydney: Allen and Unwin.

McSwiney, J., & Cottle, D. (2017). Unintended consequences: One Nation and neoliberalism in contemporary Australia. *The Journal of Australian Political Economy, 79*, 87–106.

Mendoza, K.-A. (2014). *Austerity: The demolition of the welfare state and the rise of the zombie economy*. Oxford: New Internationalist.

Moore, A. (1995). *The right road—A history of right-wing politics in Australia*. Melbourne: Oxford University Press.

Moore, T. (1997). Economic rationalism and economic nationalism. In B. Grant (Ed.), *Pauline Hanson, One Nation and Australian politics* (pp. 50–62). Armidale: U.N.E. Press.

Moore, T. (2005). Unificationism in Australian political thought. In T. Battin (Ed.), *A passion for Politics—essays in honour of Graham Maddox* (pp. 75–85). Sydney: Pearson Education Australia.

Moore, T. (2017). The transformation of the Occusphere. *Social Identities: Journal for the Study of Race, Nation and Culture, 23*(6), 674–687.

Mudde, C. (2004). The populist zeitgeist. *Government and opposition, 39*(4), 541–563.

Page, E. (1917). *A plea for unification. The development of Australia*. Grafton: Daily Examiner.

Peck, J., Theodore, N., & Brenner, N. (2009). Postneoliberalism and its malcontents. *Antipode, 41*(1), 94–116.

PHON (Pauline Hanson One Nation). (2017). *What we stand for*. http://www.onenation.com.au/pr inciples Accessed November 6, 2017.

Representatives (1996). *Commonwealth of Australia Parliamentary Debates: House of representatives*. September 10: 3860–3863.

Senate (2016). *Commonwealth of Australia Parliamentary Debates: The Senate*. September 14: 78–82.

Seymour, R. (2014). *Against austerity—How can we fix the crisis, they made*. London: Pluto.

Seymour, R. (2016). *Corbyn—The strange rebirth of radical politics*. London: Verso.

Short, N. (2016). On the subject of far-right-wing politics. *Critical Sociology, 43*(4–5), 763–777.

Skitch, C. E. (1931). *The experts' plan—What it means to Australia*. Adelaide: The Financial Reform League of South Australia.

Soutphommasane, T. (2012). *Don't go back to where you came from: Why multiculturalism works*. Sydney: NewSouth Books.

Stephensen, P. R. (1986 [1936]). *The foundations of culture in Australia—An essay towards national self respect*. Sydney: Allen and Unwin.

Stoker, G. (2017). *Why politics matters* (2nd ed.). London: Palgrave Macmillan.

Sunkara, B. (2017). How Jeremy Corbyn pulled off one of the biggest upsets in modern political history *In These Times*. June 8. http://inthesetimes.com/article/20216/jeremy-corbyn-left-politic s-theresa-may Accessed June 9, 2017.

Tanner, L. (2011). *Sideshow: Dumbing down democracy*. Melbourne: Scribe.

Walter, J. (2010). *What were they thinking? The politics of ideas in Australia*. Sydney: UNSW Press.

Chapter 11
Shifting Repertoires of Populism and Neo-Nationalism: Austria and Brexit Britain

Alan Scott

Abstract This chapter seeks to contribute to an understanding of the Hanson phenomenon by locating it in a global context. More specifically, it focuses on developments in Europe which in many respects parallel those in Australia: the rise of populism and neo-nationalism. I take two examples from two distinct phases of the emergence of right-wing populist repertoires: Phase One (1980s/90s): the populist-neo-nationalist right in Austria; Phase Two (current): the UK and Brexit. The term 'repertoire' is borrowed from social movement analysis and has the advantage of highlighting the open-ended and shifting nature of populism. Repertoires shift and are open to innovation. The chapter examines the pioneering phase in which small or peripheral countries (e.g., Austria, The Netherlands, and Australia) had a disproportionate influence, and how the repertoire developed there is adopted and adapted in the course of—and after—the EU referendum in the UK. The chapter concludes by arguing that populism and neo-nationalism have become increasingly mainstream; common property across the political spectrum. The broader context here is one in which nation states narrow their *raison d'être*, and the source of their legitimacy, as they increasingly focus upon a single task: the defense of borders, above all against migrants.

Keywords Austrian politics · Brexit · Far-right populism · Neo-nationalism

11.1 Introduction

Most of the chapters in this volume focus on the specifically Australian context and features of the Hanson phenomenon. The aim of this chapter, as with the previous one (Chap. 10), is to introduce a comparative component. It is important to do so because Hanson and One Nation are part of the wider international development that the polit-

A. Scott (✉)
School of Humanities, Arts and Social Sciences, University of New England, Armidale, NSW 2351, Australia
e-mail: ascott39@une.edu.au

© Springer Nature Singapore Pte Ltd. 2019
B. Grant et al. (eds.), *The Rise of Right-Populism*,
https://doi.org/10.1007/978-981-13-2670-7_11

ical economist Mark Blyth (2016) has dubbed "global Trumpism". A European case study is germane here not least because, until the election of Donald Trump in November 2016, Europe had a good claim to be the key stronghold of right-populist[1] politics. The New York Times (2016) listed the following as the "most prominent" far-right parties in Europe: Alternative für Deutschland (AfD) (Germany), Front National (France), Party for Freedom (Partij voor de Vrijheid (PVV)) (The Netherlands), Golden Dawn (Greece), Jobbik (Hungary), Sweden Democrats (Sverigedemokraterna (SD)), the Austrian Freedom Party (Freiheitliche Partei Österreichs (FPÖ)), People's Party Our Slovakia (Ľudová strana—Naše Slovensko (ĽSNS)). The list is selective and somewhat arbitrary. It might equally have included the Finns Party (Perussuomalaiset (PS)), the Danish People's Party (Dansk Folkeparti (DF)), Lega (formally, Lega Nord) (Italy), or many other worthy candidates. Any such list could also include two parties currently in government in Europe: Fidesz—Hungarian Civic Alliance (Fidesz—Magyar Polgári Szövetség (MPSZ)) and Poland's Law and Justice Party (Prawo i Sprawiedliwość (PiS)). Also missing—presumably because by "Europe" *The New York Times* means continental Europe—is UKIP (the UK Independence Party). While not achieving the electoral success of some of its continental sister parties, UKIP was a major factor in what, up to now, has been the most dramatic and significant achievement of the populist right in Europe: Brexit.

Rather than give an overview of the situation in Europe—which has in any case been done well elsewhere (e.g., Kriesi and Pappas 2015)—here I want to discuss two examples: the FPÖ in Austria and Brexit in the UK. The former is chosen because the FPÖ has been among the most electorally successful of European far-right parties over an extended period and because Austria was the first EU member state to have a government including such a party as more-or-less equal coalition partner.[2] This means, first, that Austria is something of a laboratory for what happens when a populist opposition party becomes (part of) a government and, second, that the FPÖ has a good claim to be a leading pioneer of right-populism, giving it an influence well beyond the borders of this small central European country.[3] In addition to providing a sense of developments in Europe that in some ways parallel those in Australia, I want to return to some of the themes set out in Chap. 1 and examine the kinds of analysis social scientists have offered to account for the emergence and persistence of right-populism and neo-nationalism.

---

[1]I have used the term right-populism in line with the usage in this collection. Most of the parties covered here could also be characterized as far right or radical right.

[2]Silvio Berlusconi's first coalition had already briefly included Lega Nord in the Italian government in 1994. In the Austrian case, the FPÖ had won more votes and seats in the 1999 election than had the ÖVP, coming in second to the SPÖ. The Chancellor in the coalition (Wolfgang Schüssel) was nevertheless from the ÖVP. Unlike the earlier Italian case, the inclusion of the FPÖ in the Austrian government triggered a strong—but ultimately ineffectual—negative reaction from leading EU politicians (falsely characterized as 'EU sanctions' in parts of the Austrian media and political discourse).

[3]The international prominence of the Austrian case is illustrated, for example, by the publication of an extended analysis by Jan-Werner Müller in the *New York Review of Books* (25 July 2016).

The notion of "populism" is contentious. It has been argued that—in the case of the far right—ethnic nationalism better characterizes the commonalities among this family of parties (Rydgren 2017). There has also been the more fundamental objection that the term has been reduced to a derogatory label that seeks to tar left and right with the same brush and "defines those who use it rather than those who are branded with it: (D'Eramo 2013, p. 8) or is used within "liberal internationalism" as a "general polemical term" (Streeck 2017a, p. 11). Moreover, there is ambiguity about what populism is: Is it an ideology (and, if so, how thick/thin, how coherent?), a discursive formation (Laclau 2005), or simply a political style (Moffitt and Tormey 2013)? The closest populism has to a core theme (and what gives it its name) is an appeal to "the people"—and to the "will of the people"—against the elite. A definition based on these characteristics (Mudde 2007) is intentionally minimalist. On such a minimalist view, left and right forms of populism are distinguished, first, by how "the people" and the "elite" are understood (as demos, as ethnos, as a social class, etc. in the former case, or as cultural, as economic/political elite, as experts, etc. in the latter) (cf. Nash 2016) and, second, by how inclusive or exclusive the definition of "the people" is (Blokker 2018).

In light of these ambiguities, I need to justify my continued use of the term here. I will treat populism as a potpourri of all the above-mentioned elements: ideology, discourse, and political style, plus a set of typical political strategies. Here I am not concerned with questions of definition—we are dealing at best with sets of family resemblances—but with the practices of those parties usually taken to be far right and populist. While this, of course, sidesteps the key conceptual questions, it has the advantage of highlighting the open-ended and shifting nature of (that which is called) populism. To this end, I shall borrow a term from social movement literature: repertoire, or action repertoire (Tilly 1993). Repertoires shift and are open to innovation. They are not stable across localities or time. There are, however, recognizable influences which can be traced, borrowings, affinities, overlaps. A repertoire in this sense is a common resource available to anyone to adopt and adapt. Thus, contra D'Eramo, not only can we speak of a left populist repertoire (e.g., Podemos in Spain, Syriza in Greece), but also one of the center (indeed, Macron has recently demonstrated this). The repertoire cannot, however, be completely open ended, and one consistent feature is that populist parties take a subordinate theme of normal politics (a Schmittian 'friend-foe' logic) and transform it into a central theme and strategy.

The notion of a shifting repertoire implies that there is more than a contingent relationship, and more than an "elective affinity", between these cases. This in turn raises the question of how this repertoire gets transmitted across nations and over time. What links an example like Austria in the 1980s and '90s to Brexit Britain in 2016 and beyond? First, right-populist parties, within and beyond Europe, are networked, at least at the level of their leadership.[4] Ironically, given far-right Euroskepticism, in the European case this has been facilitated by EU institutions (notably the European

---

[4]For an informative media account of far-right networking in Europe, see Bernhard Odehnal's piece in the *Tages-Anzeiger,* 5 May 2016.

Parliament) and by a common platform: hostility to further EU integration, or to the EU itself. Second, there is a mimetic factor: the high profile of right-populist leaders, even those from small nations such as Austria and The Netherlands, in the international (Anglophone) media supplied a model which could be imitated. Third, new social media have both facilitated and accelerated the exchange of information, ideas, and strategies. Finally, the populist repertoire has its limits, and common themes may emerge in the absence of direct or indirect influence.[5]

In order to structure this discussion, I draw a distinction between the pioneering phase of the populist repertoire [from the 1980s up to the early 2000s; up to the FPÖ entering government in Austria (2000) and the assassination of Pim Fortuyn (2002)] and its current phase of refinement.[6] In the first phase small countries (e.g., Austria, The Netherlands) had a disproportionate influence. In the current phase, it is the UK, USA, Turkey, Poland, Hungary, and now (once more) Italy that appear to be making the running. Thus, my choice of Austria and Brexit also corresponds to examples taken respectively from Phase One and Phase Two.[7]

11.2 Phase One: Pioneering the Repertoire. The Populist Far Right in Austria: From Opposition to Incumbency, and Back

The first thing anyone unfamiliar with Austrian politics needs to know is that Austria has long been considered a paradigm example of "consociationalism" or "neo-corporatism"; that is to say, a consensus- or compromise-oriented political system in which the "social partners"—government and representatives of major social interests (notably, business and employees)—are formally incorporated into the (tripartite) negotiation of key aspects of social and economic policy, most importantly the annual setting of wage levels. The Austrian consociationalist regime has been associated with (i) high levels of party membership; (ii) strong associations representing collective interests, such as chamber of commerce, chamber of labor, employers' association (Industriellenvereinigung), farmers' association (Bauernbund), trade unions (coordinated by a powerful, centralized federation, the Österreichische Gewerkschaftsbund (ÖGB));[8] (iii) highly stable voting patterns and strong party identification, to the point where party allegiance signalled affiliation to either the social

---

[5]One example of a striking affinity across place and time that is certainly coincidental is that 'Österreich zuerst' (Austria first) was the name of a FPÖ-sponsored people's initiative (*Volksbegehren*) in 1992, nearly a quarter of a century before "America first" became a Trump slogan.

[6]Elements of right-populist repertoire are, of course, much older than my foreshortened historical framework implies—e.g., going back to *völkisch* movements of the 19th century. Here I am concerned only with the revival of rightwing populism in post-war Europe.

[7]Pauline Hanson is interesting in this context because she is the one actor who appears in both phases of my tentative periodization.

[8]Some of these collective interests have close links to the major parties or, as in the case of the Bauernbund and ÖVP, are formally affiliated to a party.

democratic ("red", SPÖ) or Christian democratic ("black", due to the clerical association of the Peoples' Party (ÖVP)) "camp"; and (v) coalition government. In the Austrian case, all this was reinforced through the *Proporzsystem*, the allocation of posts among state employees to members of the two major parties according to a principle of proportionality. The rise of right-populism in Austria is both a symptom of and force for the destabilization of these traditional political cleavages (see Aichholzer et al. 2014) and of the institutional arrangements that supported, and were supported by, them.

The political arrangements of the Austrian Second Republic avoided the political polarization (to the point of civil war) that had plagued the First Republic (1919–1934) and ensured (not least economic) stability. In this sense, they were highly successful. They enabled residual strong allegiances with forces that had historically been hostile to be tempered by political alliances between those very forces at the highest level. There had been a "grand coalition" between ÖVP and SPÖ for 30 of the years between 1949 and 2000. The other 21 years consisted of a short period in which the ÖVP governed alone (1966–1970), a longer period of SPÖ government (1970–1983), and a period of SPÖ-FPÖ coalition (1983–1987). Political systems that work along these consensual lines have been characterized in political science literature as "negotiated democracies", in which there is a high degree of agreement and close links between political parties.

It was in this peaceful, stable, prosperous, and consensus-oriented context that the FPÖ, under the leadership of Jörg Haider, was able to reposition itself as one of the most successful right-populist parties in Europe, if not the most successful. One plausible explanation of this seeming paradox has been offered by Yannis Papadopoulos (2005), who argues that negotiated democracy provides fertile grounds for the emergence of populist parties because, however successful it is in output terms, it comes to lack input legitimation. Political parties increasingly become "cartel parties" (Katz and Mair 2009) offering no genuine choice between distinct programs, and "real decisions" are taken at elite level within non-majoritarian institutions. Consociationalism and negotiated democracy are powerful mechanisms of depoliticization, but precisely this opens up a political "void" (Mair 2013, p. x) that can be filled from left or right, and encourages what has come to be called—even in the English-language literature—*Politikverdrossenheit*, discontent, or disillusion with politics as such. In this context "the vote in favour of populist parties should, above all, be interpreted as a vote of protest" (Papadopoulos 2005, p. 73). How was the FPÖ able to tap into this vein of frustration and discontent?

The FPÖ had been closely associated with German nationalism (*Deutschtümelei*),[9] but by the 1980s (and particularly during its coalition with the SPÖ, 1983–87) had been gradually moving towards the center, remodelling itself on the German FPD as a small center-right party available as a coalition partner. However, like many small parties in or potential partners for coalition, the FPÖ vote share suffered (falling to < 5% in 1983), and it was in this context that in late 1986

---

[9]The FPÖ was founded in the mid-1950s, largely by ex-Nazis, including its founder Anton Reinthaller, who had been a SS officer.

Haider ousted the party leader Norbert Steger. The right-populist course on which Haider was to take the party was incompatible with both Steger's more centrist, economically liberal course *and* with the party's previous right-authoritarianism; unlike their anti-democratic predecessors, right-populists play the democratic game (see Pelinka 2013).[10] The strategy between Haider's takeover and the FPÖ's entry into coalition with the ÖVP in 2000 was one of "populist vote-maximisation" (Luther 2008). Consociationalism offered an open flank for such a strategy. *Proporz* could be characterized as cronyism (*Freunderlwirtschaft*), state employees as 'privileged', and the political system as a whole as elitist, undemocratic, and ossified. The party could thus claim to speak for the guy in the street (*der kleiner Mann*) against elite privilege. *Der kleiner Mann* did not only have a gender, he also had an ethnic and class identity. The Austrian far right abandoned German in favor of Austrian nationalism: it emphasized the notion of the "homeland" (*Heimat*) and was fervently opposed to immigrants, to Islam, and to the EU. It also sought to compete directly with the SPÖ for urban blue-collar votes (cf. Oesch and Rennwald 2018), particularly those of younger workers who were less protected than their elders by strong trade unions and the class-compromise logic of consociationalism.

Rather than go into more detail concerning this period of right-populism in Austria, I want to sketch in an ideal-typical fashion the main features of the populist repertoire that was emerging in this period and which the Haider-FPÖ (along with Jean-Marie Le Pen in France and Pim Fortuyn in The Netherlands, and indeed Hanson Mark I in Australia) shaped and which the current generation of right-populists—from Farage to Trump—have both deployed and refined.

- *Personalization of politics and candidate-centered campaigning:* In Austria, "parties had been strong organisations and a far cry from functioning as vehicles for individual politicians" (Eder et al. 2015, p. 317). But even here "the relative decline of parties, changes in their competitive environment, and reform of the electoral system have provided candidates with a set of incentives to move in the *direction* of 'candidate-centred campaigns'" (ibid, p. 324). The far right was the first mover. One of the common features of right-populism is that the leader becomes more than simply a party leader, and sometimes seemingly more than the party. Populist leadership is "characterized by the direct allegiance and loyalty of followers to the person of the leader" (Pappas 2012, p. 14) rather than being part of a conventional party bureaucracy. That the subtitle of this volume refers to "Pauline Hanson's One Nation" is itself an echo of this, as is my use above of the term the "Haider-FPÖ" (once common in both the Austrian media and academic discourse).[11] The logical end point is the reduction of the party to a leader's list (e.g., Lijst Pim Fortuyn

---

[10] It should be noted, however, that German nationalist and authoritarian elements remain influential within the FPÖ; above all via (student and old-boy) fraternities (*Burschenschaften*) whose influence has, if anything, recently grown within the party.

[11] Thus two of the leading authorities on Austrian politics and rightwing discourse—Anton Pelinka and Ruth Wodak—could, with some justification, speak of "the Haider phenomenon" (Wodak and Pelinka 2002). This collection remains a useful source for a much fuller account of the developments sketched here.

(LPF)). There are two sides to this development: first, the party can become a "leader party" whose role is largely reduced to the acclamation of and support for the leader (see Pakulski and Higley 2008); second, the personality, values, and style of the leader increasingly becomes the party platform. The latter both reintroduces a charismatic element into politics and makes leader-style crucial. Haider, like his contemporary Pim Fortuyn in The Netherlands, was flamboyant and unpredictable (e.g., Haider, like Nigel Farage after him, was forever threatening to leave (or come back into) politics).

- *Provocation, scandal, and the permanent campaign*: Haider was also a master of the calculated use of provocation and scandal, most notoriously his praising of the Waffen-SS. As Ruth Wodak (2013) has argued, the use of scandal and provocation conforms to a pattern that unfolds in stages that might be described as follows: the statement (or stunt); finessing it in response to the backlash; the faux-apology for any offense that might have been taken (due to possible misinterpretation); claiming victimhood, that is, being misrepresented and/or the victim of biased reporting ("fake news"). This kind of pattern Wodak calls "calculated ambivalence" which can effectively send a "double message". The effect or aim is threefold: (i) to grab and hold media attention during the scandal's natural course; (ii) to move the leader (and party) into a space in which the boundaries of what can be said are pushed ever further back (ideally to a point where anything can be said and the leader is immune from normal expectations and sanction); and (iii) to leave the base with a clear sense of the message in its pre-retracted form, and thus with the impression that the leader is on their side. Provocation and scandal are also part of the oft-noted fact that populist parties are in a state of permanent campaigning, whether in opposition or government (see, for example, Luther 2007).
- *Stronghold and power-base outside the main metropolitan centres*: In the case of the FPÖ, this was the province of Carinthia (largest city, Klagenfurt, population < 100,000) in which Haider was Governor from 1999 until his death in an alcohol-fuelled car crash in 2008. Here there are clear parallels (even if the geographical scale is different) to the One Nation Party and Queensland. However, it should be noted that the FPÖ also has strong support in Vienna (the base of its current leader Heinz-Christian Strache) and in the deindustrializing parts of Styria. Furthermore, the similarity (e.g., in terms of class/occupation) between FPÖ and SPÖ voters means that target voters for both parties are likely to be urban based (Aichholzer et al. 2014, p. 130).
- *Plebiscite*: Plebiscites, along with petitions and referenda, tend to be the political devices of choice for right-populist parties. These instruments of "direct democracy" facilitate campaigning outside the electoral cycle, appealing to emotion, and setting the political agenda (not least in the media). Furthermore, as Claus Offe argued some time ago, the idea of popular will, which such instruments presuppose, is fictitious, fallible, and seducible: "the will of the people *does not exist* prior to these procedures and independent of them, but instead *arises* in them" (Offe 1996, p. 91). The binary yes/no response of plebiscitary instruments both suits populist parties' strategy of forming new majority coalitions via polarization and is open to interpretation and political capture after the event. An emphasis

upon the "authenticity" of the popular will as expressed via these devices is often contrasted with the inauthenticity of standard institutions of representative democracy, notably parliaments (once described by Haider as mere "theater"; or think of Farage's contempt for the European Parliament, from which he, as an MEP, still draws a salary). The emphasis upon the authenticity of the popular will in contrast to the corruption of the elite is part of a wider trope of "draining the swamp" (Innes 2017, p. x) that national (or EU) politics is said to have become. Although (as noted above) right-populists play the democratic (and electoral) game, there is here the explicit or implicit threat of going anti-constitutional. In the case of the FPÖ this threat largely remained at a rhetorical level. In the current context of Poland and Hungary, it maybe becoming a reality with populists in office eroding "*formal* democratic rules and liberal institutions" and undermining "*informal* democratic norms" such as respect for the opposition (Grzymala-Busse 2017, p. 6).

- *Neo-nationalism*: The term "neo-nationalism" was introduced into the literature on right-populism by social anthropologists (Gingrich and Banks 2006) and has been taken up by quantitative social researchers (Eger and Valdez 2014). Rather than focus on the most visible aspect of right-populist campaigning—its anti-immigrant/anti-refugee stance—neo-nationalism subsumes that theme into a broader trope that includes welfare chauvinism (welfare rights for citizens) and a general anti-globalization, anti-cosmopolitan, and (in the European context) anti-EU stance. Each of these subthemes work on a binary opposition between that which is solid, stable, rooted, and bounded and that which is in flux and rootless (Theresa May's "citizens of nowhere"). Eger and Valdez (2014) argue that neo-nationalism has allowed right-populist parties to move away from their free-market policies of the 1970s through to the 1990s and adopt more left-wing protectionist economic policies, to the point where they can no longer be considered "right wing". This analysis is supported by extensive data. However, there are some conceptual issues concerning the framing of their argument. First, the equation of "right wing" with free market economic policy is rather narrow, and possibly arbitrary. Second, and more importantly, in placing political parties along two axes (social (libertarian vs. authoritarian) and economic (left vs. right)). the approach ascribes too great a coherence and consistency to the position of right-populist parties. This misses the point of Wodak's "calculated ambivalence" and "double messages". If the aim is one of maximizing votes then inconsistency and the ability to send different messages to different audiences supplies a tactical advantage. For the same reason I am sceptical about Mark Blyth's assertion that "the era of neoliberalism is over" to be replaced by "the era of neo-nationalism" (Blyth 2016). The repertoire of right-populist parties is more flexible and opportunistic, and less consistent than either quantitative social research or diagnostic periodization tend to allow.

In the case of the FPÖ, the deployment of this repertoire paid dividends. From less than 5% of the vote at the start of the period of coalition with the SPÖ (in 1983), their vote share had risen to 26.9% by the election in 1999, which allowed them to enter coalition with the ÖVP in 2000.

This is where Phase One of my account ends. Thus, I shall not attempt an account of the period of incumbency and the return to populist voter-maximization that followed the split within the FPÖ and the formation of the (initially Haider-led) breakaway BZÖ (Bündnis Zukunft Österreich, Alliance for the Future of Austria) in 2005, and the final collapse of the ÖVP-FPÖ coalition in 2006 (see Luther 2011 for a full analysis). There are, however, two points that are relevant to the argument here and which should be noted briefly. First, incumbency marked the end of the innovative and pioneering phase of the Austrian populist far right. Haider's successor as leader of the FPÖ (Heinz-Christian Strache), while a perfectly good tub-thumper, lacks Haider's flair. The FPÖ remains a force to be reckoned with (it has clawed back its strong, sometimes leading, position in opinion polls and re-entered coalition government in December 2017), but its campaigning is largely a rehash of the best tunes from its pre-2000 phase. Second, the FPÖ's reputation has been tarnished in two ways: by the turbulence of its years of incumbency (Luther 2003, 2011), and the growing realization of the degree of incompetence and corruption of Haider's period as Governor of Carinthia, a period which saw the collapse of Hypo Alpe-Adria-Bank International AG (see Biegelbauer 2015), the source of the biggest financial problem Austria currently faces. Admittedly, these two elements have tarnished the FPÖ's reputation less than they might have, not least as an instrument for draining the political swamp. The party has also faced setbacks, notably the failure, at the second attempt, of its candidate (Norbert Hofer) to win the presidential election in 2016 when Austria, in the year of the Brexit referendum and Trump, became (temporarily) the country in which the seemingly unstoppable MARCH of right-populism faltered.

It is, however, now time to discuss one of the places to which the action has moved: the UK.

11.3 Phase Two: Refining the Repertoire. from Beer Tent to Pub: Sovereignty, Borders, Brexit

The problem with the European Union is not the free movement of labour, it's the free movement of people". Rt Hon Liam Fox MP, Secretary of State for International Trade at a fringe meeting of the Tory Party Conference, 2017.[12]

The closest the UK ever came to consociationalism was occasional "beer and sandwiches" with TUC leaders at No.10 (Downing Street) during post-war Labour governments, but even that under-institutionalized form was swept away in the Thatcher revolution. Nor can the Westminster model be described as negotiated democracy. It is adversarial, and the one-past-the-post electoral system has generally—until recently, at least—secured single-party government in which the ruling party has a working majority, or better. What then to make of Papadopolous's argument that there is a link between negotiated democracy and right-populism? One possibility would be to take

---

[12]This was part of a response to a question asked by the journalists John Harris, John Domokos, Adam Sich and Renasha Khan, *The Guardian* online, 2 October 2017.

the rise of UKIP in the UK as a falsifying instance: there is no such link. An alternative would be to argue that even traditionally adversarial party systems have converged on, or at least moved in the direction of, negotiated democracy. Much of the recent critical literature on 'governance' lends support to the second of these interpretations. Faced with declining legitimacy, governments have increasingly been forced to adopt 'partnership' or 'network' governance; partnerships with those forces in organized civil society that may be in a position to hinder the government's policy agenda (Offe and Preuss 2006) . This has coincided with the increasing convergence of party pro- grams (New Labour's "Third Way" being the obvious example) and the outsourcing of political decisions, regulation, and accreditation to non-majoritarian institutions. These institutional shifts are, as Papadopolous (2005, p. 80) indeed suggests, creat- ing conditions similar to those more usually associated with consociationalism and negotiated democracy. All this has been said to result in what Peter Mair (2013) has characterized as a double-disengagement: the electorates' withdrawal into the private sphere (*Politikverdrossenheit*) and the withdrawal of the political elite into governing institutions.

Perhaps the most significant manifestation of these shifts is the growing distance between social democratic or center-left parties, which have abandoned class politics and accepted the logic of TINA, and their traditional support-base. It is this, above all, that has been the focus of debate following the result of the EU Referendum of 23 June 2016 (as indeed it has in the US following the election of Trump). In both the media and in much academic literature in the UK, this has been framed in terms of "the left-behind".[13] The sociological story here is one of the shrinking of the working class (see Crouch 1999 for an early analysis) on the one hand and the, in part resultant, embourgeoisement of party politics, and of social democratic parties in particular, on the other. The term "left-behind" is somewhat patronizing—though less so than alternatives such as "globalization losers"—and can easily become pejorative. But in reporting the UK debate, I shall continue using the phrase, and without the scare quotes, because of its centrality.

What the academic literature describes can be summarized as growing socio- cultural divisions (and corresponding opening of political cleavages) along a number of interrelated and mutually reinforcing dimensions: class, education, generation, geographical/spatial. These might be set out schematically as follows:

- *Class*: Here the division is increasingly one between, on one side, those whom Adrian Favell (2008) has called "Eurostars"[14] (professionals who are cross-border movers within Europe) plus inhabitants of culturally-diverse metropolitan centers and, on the other side, the geographically and socially non-mobile, particularly in deindustrialized areas hardest hit by the post-GFC austerity measures.

---

[13]This is the dominant framing, but there is a dissenting view; namely, that a pro- or anti-EU stance has less to do with differences *between* groups than with differences of *personal* values that are unsystematically distributed socially and spatially. See Kaufmann (2016).

[14]The label is a pun. The Eurostar is the name for the trains that link London to Paris and Brussels via the Channel Tunnel.

- *Education levels*: Level of education has been identified as one of the key factors—or in one study (Zhang 2018) as *the* key factor—differentiating Remain
  and Leave voters, with what has been sardonically labelled "the exam-passing
  classes"[15] strongly tending towards Remain.
- *Generation*: Up to the age of 44, the majority of voters were Remainers (with
  18–24 being the strongest at 73% Remain). After 45, the majority voted Leave
  (with the 65 + group being the strongest with 60% Leave): "local jurisdictions
  with large numbers of pensioners and a history of voting UKIP ... recorded very
  high turnouts and 'Leave' shares" (Ford and Goodwin 2017, p. 25).
- *Geographical/spatial*: With the exception of Birmingham (the UK's "Second
  City") in which there was a narrow victory for Leave (50.42%), all the major
  metropolitan (one might say, cosmopolitan) areas, not just London, voted Remain.
  This was true even of Newcastle (50.7% Remain) in the otherwise heavily Leave
  North-East. A similar pattern is to be found in smaller university cities. Again,
  this is the case even for cities such as Cambridge and Norwich, two university
  towns in the Leave stronghold of East Anglia. This pattern was true of England
  and Wales, but not of Scotland and Northern Ireland, where Remain won, which
  opens up another spatial division, that between England and Wales and the two
  other parts of the United Kingdom. The spatial aspect has one further dimension:
  Ethnically diverse jurisdictions were more likely to vote Remain than those which
  were more ethnically homogenous.

This is the context in which the term the left-behind is used to identify both a cultural divide and the stakes that distinct groups within the population have in the EU
(and perhaps more broadly in freedom of trade and movement). The cultural divide
has been characterized as one between a "socially liberal outlook" which regards
diversity as a "core social strength" and "the more nationalistic communitarian, and
inward-looking outlook of the declining segments of the electorate: the older, white,
and working-class voters with few qualifications" (Ford and Goodwin 2017, p. 19).
With respect to the stakes, the EU—and particularly freedom of movement—offers
more obvious benefits to young, educated, urban professionals (actual or potential
Eurostars) than it does to those living in declining, deindustrialized cities and suffering, even more than elsewhere, from years of stagnant (or falling) wages and
dwindling social services: in other words, austerity.

Who were the left-behind left behind by? In two words, and at the risk of over-
simplification: New Labour. This was part of an international trend in the programs
of center-left parties: "by the end of the 1980s at the latest, neoliberalism had become
the *pensée unique* of both the centre left and centre right" (Streeck 2017a, p. 6). In
office, New Labour pursued social-democratic policies which benefited their traditional voter-base (e.g., increases in public expenditure) but in an attempt to demonstrate their economic competence (the Achilles Heel of Labour election campaigns)
they came to embrace the neoliberal and New Public Management agenda pioneered
by the right; and frequently (as in the case of public service performance targets) with

---

[15]The phrase has been used by Vernon Bogdanor, some of whose arguments are discussed below.

even greater enthusiasm than their predecessors (see Le Galès and Scott 2010) . The main markers of "progressive" politics were less-and-less expressed in economic terms (left-right), but in socio-cultural terms: 'Cool Britannia', multi-culturalism, equal marriage rights, a "socially liberal outlook", and openness towards a globalizing world. The last of these linked the cultural-political stance of New Labour to its economic stance: its commitment to globalization, and thus also to the EU's "four freedoms": free movement of goods, capital, services, and workers/citizens. Wolfgang Streeck (2017b) uses a classical Weberian distinction to characterize this shift: from *class* to *status*. In response to the shrinking of their class base, center-left parties have increasingly appealed to status groups (life-style communities) rather than to economic classes. At work here is also a self-reinforcing mechanism: the less people are appealed to as members of a social class, the less they will come to understand their social identities and their interests in class terms, and the less likely they will be to vote on the basis of class-party loyalty (Przeworski 1985). Those with weakening class identity are now free to see themselves as members of status groups (e.g., in terms of ethnicity or locality). They may also, and not without good reason, believe themselves to have been abandoned or betrayed, particularly by center-left parties which have increasingly become part of what Streeck (2017a, p. 14) sarcastically calls "the globally bourgeoisified left", metropolitan, cosmopolitan, and bourgeois.

In what is proving to be perhaps the most fateful expression of this disconnect between Labour and its working-class voter base, in 2004, when 10 countries (eight of which were Eastern European ex-communist states) joined the EU, the Labour Government decided to forgo transitional arrangements for temporarily controlling levels of immigration from new member states.[16] The government was both convinced of the benefits of immigration and grossly underestimated the numbers of potential immigrants. Instead of the Home Office's expected 5000–13,000 per year, in the years following the 2004 EU expansion net EU-immigration into the UK varied between c.50,000 and c.120,000 per year (ONS 2015). The scenario here is almost Durkheimian: rapid social change challenging societal capacities for adaptation. Add to this the effects of post-GFC austerity measures placing enormous pressure on the delivery of local and social services and you have created, whether by accident or design, the conditions in which those most affected by austerity come to view immigrants as competition for shrinking welfare and social services. In this sense, Labour's conversion and commitment to the EU was one aspect of its increasing disconnect from its traditional voter base: "Labour used to be a working-class party—and, when it was, it was Eurosceptic" (Bogdanor 2016, p. 8).

The left-behind—like the "disorganised working class" (Streeck 2017b) who voted for Trump—is not a sufficiently large part of the electorate to have, on its own, secured a Leave victory. But declining class identity and class-party loyalty opened up the possibility of narratives around sovereignty and the control of borders (and around "Englishness" or "Britishness") that facilitated voter coalitions with socially conservative status groups, such as older and comparatively well-off voters in the suburbs and shires of southern and middle England. As in the Austrian

---

[16]See Watt and Wintour's investigative piece in *The Guardian*, 25 March 2015.

case, populists, via a strategy of polarization, were able to harness popular resentment against the political "establishment" and take advantage of the new political cleavages opened up to create new majority coalitions (see Pappas 2012).

It is when we come to examine the Leave campaign that the similarities between the Austrian case and Brexit become clearer. The right-populist repertoire characterized in an ideal-typical fashion above now appears in modified and adapted form, but with the core themes largely intact: the personalization of politics, the use made of provocation, neo-nationalism (here in the guise of anti-immigration plus anti-EU). The three key figures in the Leave campaign, Nigel Farage (UKIP), Boris Johnson, and Michael Gove (Tory), were broadly seen as "larger-than-life" figures for whom even the low level of veracity expected of normal politicians could be placed on hold. We also had the spectacle of Johnson (Eton and Oxford), Farage (ex-stockbroker), and Gove (Robert Gordon's College (on a scholarship) and Oxford) running a populist anti-establishment and anti-elitist campaign whose most notorious expression was Gove's: "I think the people of this country have had enough of experts" (interview on Sky News, 3 June 2016). But more interesting are the ways in which the Leave, in contrast to Remain, campaign was able to take advantage of the social shifts sketched above to forge a referendum-winning voter coalition.

In focusing on rational self-interest, the Remain campaign, with its dire warnings of the economic consequences of leaving the EU, was simply talking past people who did not believe that they had a stake in, or benefit from, EU membership in the first place. By emphasizing getting "our country back" and "taking back control" (of borders and laws) the Leave campaign directly targeted the concerns of the left-behind; the restoration of what was once "ours" but has been lost or taken away. In terms of another key Weberian distinction, for the Remain campaign staying in the EU was a matter of instrumental rationality; for the Leave campaign, leaving it was a matter of value rationality. The latter is what Weber would have called *wirtschaftsfremd*, indifferent to economic (or other instrumental) considerations.[17] Whereas instrumental rationality is inherently directed to the future in its concern with means towards ends (i.e., is consequentialist), value rationality can accommodate the backward- and inward-looking in its orientation towards absolute values. The Remain campaign made little attempt to address value-rational considerations by offering positive reasons for EU membership. Indeed it would have been difficult to do so given (i) the general lack of enthusiasm for the EU within the UK (or at least within non-metropolitan England and Wales) (Curtice 2016); and (ii) the advantage British governments have consistently taken of the opportunities multi-level governance offers for shifting blame upwards, in this case towards the EU level, even for unpopular domestic policies. On 23 July 2016, the identity/control/value-rational side gained 52% of the vote; while the self-interest/economic/instrumentally rational side gained 48%. The politicians' (and indeed many social scientists') assumption

---

[17]This point has been underlined by a YouGov poll in which they identified what they, rather melodramatically, called "Brexit extremism": the stated willingness of many (mostly older) voters to accept "significant economic damage" as a price worth paying to Brexit (YouGov@YouGov 2017).

that in the solitude of the voting booth self-interest trumps values and identity was rudely refuted.

One frequently noted point about the Leave campaign was that it was built on lies, for example, the poster stating "Turkey (population 76 Million) is joining the EU". The most notorious of these "lies" was the slogan painted onto the side of the Leave battle bus: "We send the EU £350 million a week let's fund our NHS instead". This is taken to be a lie because there was never any chance of this happening, and indeed leading Brexit campaigners, including Farage, distanced themselves from this "promise" as soon as the referendum was over. Strictly speaking, the slogan does not actually make a promise. It is what linguists call a "hortative": a statement which urges action, in this case common action (a "cohortative"). It appeals to solidarity, collective identity, and community: *We* spend… *Let's*… *our* NHS. In conjuring up a joint collective project which "we" are all in together this is not so different from Obama's "Yes *we* can!" or Merkel's "*Wir* schaffen das!" (*We* can do this!) on her decision to open German borders to Syrian refugees in 2015, only the "we" implied in the UK case is less inclusive. In this sense, the slogan had its effect—of creating a we-identity—irrespective of whether or not one believes the (non-)promise.[18] The "other" posited by this we-identity is not simply an elite, but a foreign elite: the EU politicians, civil servants, and judges (of the European Court of Justice (ECJ) and the European Court of Human Rights (ECHR)), from whom control is to be taken back.

The referendum on EU membership looks like a paradigm case demonstrating Claus Offe's argument (discussed above) that plebiscitary instruments presuppose a "will of the people" that is fictitious, fallible, and seducible. Indeed, perhaps Offe's argument can be pushed a little further, in two directions. First, rather than the popular will emerging in the course of the plebiscite or referendum, it may be said to emerge post hoc: in the competing interpretations of the 'will of the people' that emerge as politicians seek to capture its meaning for their own self-serving ends. In the Brexit case, it was once more Michael Gove who gave the game away: "the day after we vote we hold all the cards and we can choose the path we want" (*Huffpost, UK*, 20 April). The first "we" refers the voters, the other three de facto to the political leaders who will, after the vote, shape Brexit. The referendum question was: "Should the United Kingdom remain a member of the European Union?" This, of course, says nothing about what the UK's relationship to the EU should look like after the UK has left it, nor what position should be adopted in the two-year period of negotiations following the triggering of Article 50. PM Teresa May's "Brexit means Brexit" was an attempt to capture and interpret the will of the people as a mandate for "hard Brexit", leaving the single market and the customs union. Second, in addition to Offe's list, the popular will is also fickle. It is a construct behind which lies not a single will, but two roughly equally sized and opposed camps of opinion. The snap

---

[18]The straightforward lie may be the £350 million. The figure ignores the UK's rebate and, depending on which Treasury figures one takes, may overestimate the weekly contribution by c. £100 million. The UK Statistics Authority (2017) has noted its "disappointment" at the use of the £350 million figure.

election May called for 8 June 2017 had one aim: to produce a Parliament more closely aligned with the "will of the people" and thereby supplement the "clear" mandate given by the referendum with a fitting parliamentary majority. The result has been called "the Remainers' revenge": the Tory Party lost its majority and the UK's already weak negotiating hand was weakened further. The attempt to capture the meaning of the referendum as support for a 'hard Brexit' had hit an obstacle: "the people" seem to have two wills rather than one.

11.4 The Aftermath

Where has the diverse experience of right-populism left our two case-study nations? In Austria the restoration of the grand coalition in 2007, after seven chaotic years of ÖVP-FPÖ government, looked like a return to normality. But, perhaps inevitably, in the course of a further ten years of grand coalition the relationship between the two coalition parties became increasingly fractious, and the government unloved. The rise of the FPÖ in its right-populist guise has left two quite distinct legacies: first, a string of long-running court cases against FPÖ politicians of the first coalition era and, as noted, the country's biggest financial headache; second, a repertoire which has altered the political mainstream. As an example of the latter, when Sebastian Kurz became leader of the ÖVP in 2017 (in his early 30s) he sought to free himself from the Party's hierarchical structure and the power of party grandees by insisting on a List-Kurz on the grounds that his name was the less toxic brand. This is an attempt to do the seemingly impossible: to turn the ÖVP into a leader party. How successful this will be in the short run will depend on his success as a vote-getter, the ultimate test of the populist even more than that of the normal party leader. Kurz has also been banging the border-protection drum as loudly as any FPÖ politician. The populist repertoire in Austria is not only common property, it has become increasingly mainstream. For the Kurz-ÖVP, as for the Haider-FPÖ in the 1980s and '90s, the strategy has worked. After a quick makeover (which included changing the party colors from black to turquoise) the ÖVP's vote share at the general election on 15 October 2017 rose by 7.5% (from the 2013 election) to 31.5% making it the largest party (SPÖ = 26.9%; FPÖ = 26%). The convergence of the ÖVP's program with that of the FPÖ on all matters except the EU (where the ÖVP remains pro-EU) has resulted in a further instalment of ÖVP-FPÖ coalition government, sworn in on 18 December 2017. The government program for the next legislature period includes a continuation of tough migration policies combined with tax cuts, which will disproportionally advantage corporations and the better off, and radical cuts in state expenditure (a "*Sparpaket*"): Austro-austerity, or at least austerity lite. The election also confirmed the shift of working-class support from the SPÖ to FPÖ.[19]

---

[19]The SORA/ISA (2017) voter transition analysis showed a flow of voters from the Greens to the SPÖ (the Green Party failed to clear the 4% hurdle for entry into parliament), but also a flow of (particularly blue-collar worker) votes from the SPÖ to the FPÖ. The FPÖ received 59%

The Austrian election, and the election in the Czech Republic that followed, open up the possibility of a new phase of right-populism and neo-nationalism in Europe: the emergence of a bloc of states in Eastern and Central Europe acting as a counterweight to the French-German axis within the EU and resisting the latter's project of further integration.[20]

In the UK the current situation is much more dramatic. The referendum result has turned an issue—Europe—that has long been capable of generating political crises into a source of weekly, or daily, political turbulence. It has created an impasse with no clear way forward and "the will of the people" blocking the retreat. In his 2017 Gresham Lecture, Vernon Bogdanor, the doyen of British constitutional analysis and Oxford tutor to several generations of British political leaders, carefully went through all the options for a "soft" Brexit (Brexit with access to the single market and/or something like membership of the customs union): Norwegian, Swiss, Canadian, Turkish, and—the fantasy version—"bespoke Brexit", and arrived at the view that it is "questionable whether there is any such animal as a so-called 'soft' Brexit. This form of Brexit seems to me to mimic EU membership, to give Britain many of the disadvantages of membership without the ability to influence EU legislation" (Bogdanor 2017). In contrast, the model of Britain beloved of Leave-supporting Tory libertarians—namely, a low-tax and low-regulation Britain "open for business" as a kind of North Sea Singapore—is, he argues, a more consistent position, *except* this was not what Leave voters voted for. They wanted more, not less, protection from the global economic system, economic nationalism, and a stronger, not weaker, welfare system: "they sought protection against the excesses of globalisation, against market forces which, so they believed, were costing them their jobs and holding down their wages" (ibid). On the other side of the divide, the young are faced with the prospect of incarceration in the social cage that post-Brexit Britain threatens to become.

The American political sociologist Richard Lachmann concluded his excellent book on the state (2010) with the observation that globalizing forces will not weaken or "hollow out" the nation state, but that the state's *raison d'être*, and the source of its legitimacy, will, in part as a result of public pressure and push-back against those very forces, become increasingly focused upon a single task: the defence of borders, above all against migrants. How right he was.

---

of blue-collar votes and the SPÖ 19%, only 4% more than the ÖVP. This scenario is similar to the "left-behind" issue in the UK with left-of-center parties becoming increasingly middle class in their support base as working-class voters look elsewhere. These trends support Oesch's and Rennwald's (2018) contention that left-of-center parties are able to hold on to, or increase, support from "sociocultural professionals" but continue to lose working-class votes to the far right. An important difference between the UK and Austrian cases is that the FPÖ voter-base has a very different demographic from the Brexit vote: 30% of FPÖ voters in 2017 were under 30 and only 19% over 60. In contrast, the SPÖ had a 17% share of the under 30 vote and 34% among the over 60s (see SORA/ISA 2017).

[20]The vote of the social and Christian parties collapsed in the Czech election, 20–21 October 2017. The ANO, under the leadership of billionaire Andrej Babiš, won the largest share of the vote (29.6%) on an anti-corruption and EU-sceptical ticket.

References

Aichholzer, J., Kritzinger, S., Wagner, M., & Zeglovits, E. (2014). How has radical right support transformed established political conflicts. The case of Austria. *West European Politics, 37*(1), 133–137.

Biegelbauer, P. (2015). Der Fall Hypo Alpe Adria: Wie können wir aus Fehlern lernen? *Austrian Journal of Political Science, 44*(2), 106–109.

Blokker, P. (2018). Populist constitutionalism. In C. de la Torre (Ed.), *Routledge Handbook of Global Populism.* (pp. 113–127)London: Routledge.

Blyth, M. (2016). Global Trumpism. Why Trump's victory was 30 years in the making and why it won't stop here. *Foreign Affairs*, November 15. https://www.foreignaffairs.com/articles/2016-1 1-15/global-trumpism. Accessed May 28, 2018.

Bogdanor, V. (2016). A new way back for social democracy? The EU referendum and its lessons for the left. *Juncture, 23*(1), 8–11.

Bogdanor, V. (2017). Britain and the EU: In or Out—One Year On. 2017 Gresham Lecture transcript. https://www.gresham.ac.uk/lectures-and-events/britain-and-the-eu-in-or-out-one-yea r-on. Accessed May 28, 2018.

Crouch, C. (1999). The parabola of working-class politics. *The Political Quarterly, 70*(1), 69–83.

Curtice, J. (2016). Brexit: behind the referendum. *Political Insight, 7*(2), 4–7.

D'Eramo, M. (2013). Populism and the new oligarchy. *New Left Review, 82,* 5–28.

Eder, N., Marchelo, J., & Müller, W. C. (2015). Winning over voters or fighting party comrades? Personalized constituency campaigning in Austria. *Electoral Studies, 39,* 316–328.

Eger, M. A., & Valdez, S. (2014). Neo-nationalism in Western Europe. *European Sociological Review, 31*(1), 115–130.

Favell, A. (2008). *Eurostars and eurocities: Free movement and mobility in an integrating Europe.* Oxford: Blackwell.

Ford, R., & Goodwin, M. (2017). Britain after Brexit. *Journal of Democracy, 28*(1), 17–30.

Gingrich, A., & Banks, M. (Eds.). (2006). *Neo-Nationalism in Europe and beyond: Perspectives from social anthropology.* Oxford: Berghahn Books.

Gove, M. (2016, April 19). The facts of life say leave: Why Britain and Europe will be better off after we vote leave. *Huffpost,* United Kingdom: The Blog. http://www.huffingtonpost.co.uk/mic hael-gove/michael-gove-vote-leave_b_9728548.html. Accessed May 28, 2018.

Grzymala-Busse, A. (2017). Global populisms and their impact. *Slavic Review, 71*(1), 3–8.

Harris, J., Domokos, J., Sich, A., & Khan, R. (2017, October 2). Anywhere but Westminster: return to Brexit Britain—video. *The Guardian* online. https://www.theguardian.com/commentisfree/ video/2017/oct/02/anywhere-but-westminster-return-to-brexit-britain-video. Accessed May 28, 2018.

Innes, A. (2017). Draining the swamp: Understanding the crisis of mainstream politics as a crisis of the state. *Slavic Review, 76*(1), 31–38.

Katz, R. S., & Mair, P. (2009). The cartel party thesis: A restatement. *Perspectives in Politics, 7*(4), 753–766.

Kaufmann, E. (2016). It's NOT the economy, stupid: Brexit as a story of personal values. blogs.ls e.ac.uk/politicsandpolicy/personal-values-brexit-vote/. Accessed May 28, 2018.

Kriesi, H., & Pappas, T. S. (Eds.). (2015). *European populism in the shadow of the Great Recession.* Colchester: ECPR Press.

Lachmann, R. (2010). *States and power.* Cambridge: Polity.

Laclau, E. (2005). *On populist reason.* London: Verso.

Le Galès, P., & Scott, A. (2010). A British bureaucratic revolution? Autonomy without control or "freer markets, more rules." *Revue Française de Sociologie*, 51, Supplement (Annual English Selection), 117–143.

Luther, K. R. (2003). The self-destruction of a rightwing populist party? The Austrian parliamentary election of 2002. *West European Politics, 26*(2), 136–152.

Luther, K. R. (2007). Wahlstrategien und Wahlergebnisse des österreichischen Rechtspopulismus, 1986–2006. In F. Plasser & P. A. Ulram (Eds.), *Wechselwahlen. Analysen zur Nationalratswahl* (pp. 231–282). Vienna: Facultas Verlag.

Luther, K. R. (2008). Electoral strategies and performance of Austrian rightwing populism 1986–2006. In G. Bischof & F. Plasser (Eds.), *The Changing Austrian Voter, Contemporary Austrian Studies* (Vol. 16, pp. 104–122). New Brunswick, NJ: Transaction Publishers.

Luther, K. R. (2011). Of goals and own goals: A case study of rightwing populist party strategy for and during incumbency. *Party Politics, 17*(4), 453–470.

Mair, P. (2013). *Ruling the void. The hollowing out of Western democracy*. London: Verso.

Moffitt, B., & Tormey, S. (2013). Rethinking populism: Politics, mediatisation and political style. *Political Studies, 62,* 381–397.

Mudde, C. (2007). *Populist radical right parties in Europe*. Cambridge: Cambridge University Press.

Müller, H-W. (2016, July 25). Austria: the lesson of the far right. *The New York Review of Books*. http://www.nybooks.com/daily/2016/07/25/austria-freedom-party-populism-lesson-far-right/. Accessed May 28, 2018.

Nash, K. (2016). Politicising human rights in Europe: Challenges to legal constitutionalism from Left and Right. *International Journal of Human Rights, 20*(8), 1295–1308.

New York Times (2016, December 4). Europe's rising far right: A guide to the most prominent parties. https://www.nytimes.com/interactive/2016/world/europe/europe-rightwing-political-parties-listy.html. Accessed May 28, 2018.

Odehnal, B. (2016, May 5). Europas Rechte vernetzt sich. *Tages-Anzeiger*. https://www.tagesanzeiger.ch/ausland/standard/europas-rechte-vernetzt-sich/story/19044780. Accessed May 28, 2018.

Oesch, D., & Rennwald, L. (2018). Electoral competition in Europe's new tripolar political space: Class voting for the left, centre-right and radical right. *Europrean Journal of Political Research*. doi/abs/. https://doi.org/10.1111/1475-6765.12259.

Offe, C. (1996). *Modernity and the State. East, West*. Cambridge, Mass: MIT Press.

Offe, C., & Preuss, U. K. (2006). The problem of legitimacy in the European polity. Is democratisation the answer? In C. Crouch & W. Streeck (Eds.), *The Diversity of Democracy. Corporatism, Social Order and Political Conflict* (pp. 175–204). Cheltenham: Edward Elgar Publishing.

ONS [Office for National Statistics]. (2015). *Migration Statistics Quarterly Report: August 2015*. London: ONS.

Pakulski, J., & Higley, J. (2008). Towards leader democracy. In P. t'Hart & J. Uhr (Eds.), *Public Leadership: Perspectives and Practices* (pp. 45–56). Canberra: ANU ePress.

Papadopoulos, Y. (2005). Populism as the other side of consociational multi-level democracies. In D. Caramani & Y. Mény (Eds.), *Challenges to consensual politics: Democracy, identity, and populist protest in the alpine region* (pp. 71–81). Bruxelles: Peter Lang.

Pappas, T. S. (2012). Populism emergent: A framework for analysing its context, mechanisms, and outcomes. *EUI Working Paper RSCAS 2012/01*. Friesole: European University Institute. http://cadmus.eui.eu/handle/1814/20114. Accessed May 28, 2018.

Pelinka, A. (2013). Rightwing populism: Concept and typology. In R. Wodak, N. Khosrivi, & B. Mral (Eds.), *Rightwing populism in Europe: Politics and discourse* (pp. 3–22). London: Bloomsbury Academic.

Przeworski, A. (1985). *Capitalism and social democracy*. Cambridge: Cambridge University Press.

Rydgren, J. (2017). Radical rightwing parties in Europe. What's populism got to do with it? *Journal of Language and Politics, 16*(4), 485–496.

SORA/ISA. (2017). *Wahlanalyse Nationalratswahl 2017. SORA/ISA im Auftrag des ORF*. http://www.sora.at/themen/wahlverhalten/wahlanalysen/nrw17.html. Accessed May 28, 2018.

Streeck, W. (2017a). The return of the repressed. *New Left Review, 104,* 5–18.

Streeck, W. (2017b). Trump and Trumpists. *Inference: International Review of Science 3*(1). http://inference-review.com/article/trump-and-the-trumpists. Accessed May 28, 2018.

Tilly, C. (1993). Contentions repertoires in Great Britain, 1758–1834. *Social Science History, 17*(2), 253–280.

UK Statistics Authority. (2017). UK Statistics Authority statement on the use of official statistics on contributions to the European Union. https://www.statisticsauthority.gov.uk/news/uk-statistics-authority-statement-on-the-use-of-official-statistics-on-contributions-to-the-european-union/. Accessed May 28, 2018.

Watt, N., & Wintour, P. (2015, March 25). How immigration came to haunt Labour: The inside story. *The Guardian*. https://www.theguardian.com/news/2015/mar/24/how-immigration-came-to-haunt-labour-inside-story. Accessed May 28, 2018.

Wodak, R. (2013). "Anything goes!"—the Haiderization of Europe. In R. Wodak, N. Khosrivi, & B. Mral (Eds.), *Rightwing populism in Europe: politics and discourse* (pp. 23–38). London: Bloomsbury Academic.

Wodak, R., & Pelinka, A. (Eds.). (2002). *The Haider phenomenon in Austria*. New Brunswick, NJ: Transaction Publishers.

YouGov@YouGov. (2017, August 1). "Brexit extremism" is rife in the UK. https://twitter.com/i/moments/892339625682927617. Accessed May 28, 2018.

Zhang, A. (2018). New findings on key factors influencing the UK's referendum on leaving the EU. *World Development, 102,* 304–314.

Index

© Springer Nature Singapore Pte Ltd. 2019
B. Grant et al. (eds.), *The Rise of Right-Populism*,
https://doi.org/10.1007/978-981-13-2670-7

MIX
Papier aus verantwortungsvollen Quellen
Paper from responsible sources
FSC® C105338

If you have any concerns about our products,
you can contact us on
ProductSafety@springernature.com

In case Publisher is established outside the EU,
the EU authorized representative is:
Springer Nature Customer Service Center GmbH
Europaplatz 3, 69115 Heidelberg, Germany

Printed by Libri Plureos GmbH
in Hamburg, Germany